THE PRACTICAL STEP-BY-STEP GUIDE TO

MARTIAL ARTS
T'AI CHI & AIKIDO

A STEP-BY-STEP TEACHING PLAN WITH OVER 1800 PHOTOGRAPHS AND ILLUSTRATIONS

A COMPLETE GUIDE TO THE MARTIAL ARTS OF TAE KWONDO, KARATE, JU-JITSU, JUDO, KUNG FU, KENDO, IAIDO AND SHINTO RYU WITH A SPECIAL FOCUS ON T'AI CHI AND AIKIDO

FAY GOODMAN, ANDREW POPOVIC & PETER BRADY

southwater

This edition is published by Southwater,
an imprint of Anness Publishing Ltd
Blaby Road, Wigston, Leicestershire LE18 4SE;
info@anness.com

www.southwaterbooks.com; www.annesspublishing.com

If you like the images in this book and would like to investigate
using them for publishing, promotions or advertising, please
visit our website www.practicalpictures.com
for more information.

Publisher: Joanna Lorenz
Project Editor: Daniel Hurst
Production Controller: Wendy Lawson
Photographers: Clare Park and Mike James
Jacket Design: Simon Daley

Previously published in two separate volumes, *The Ultimate
Book of Martial Arts* and *The Complete Illustrated Guide to
T'ai Chi and Aikido*

PUBLISHER'S NOTE
The author and publishers have made every effort to ensure
that all instructions contained within this book are accurate
and safe, and cannot accept liability for any resulting injury,
damage or loss to persons or property, however it may arise.
If you do have any special needs or problems, consult your
doctor or another health professional. This book cannot
replace medical consultation and should be used in conjunction with professional advice. You should not attempt martial
arts, T'ai chi and Aikido without training from a properly
qualified practitioner.

CONTENTS

Introduction

This book brings together a collection of some of the world's most widely practised martial arts, with a special focus on the disciplines of t'ai chi and aikido. The dedicated study of any martial arts form will help to improve tone and flexibility while simultaneously balancing your mind and emotions, and this book offers a showcase of disciplines for the martial arts enthusiast, or those just starting out, to choose from.

There are millions of martial arts practitioners all over the world. Through the disciplines these arts impose, men, women and children of all ages and abilities are actively involved in learning how to improve their awareness, health, fitness, confidence and their ability to protect themselves.

The popular perception – learned largely from movies and fictional television dramas – that martial arts are mainly concerned with violence and general mayhem, has done much harm by discouraging people from achieving a more in-depth understanding. Anyone who becomes involved with the martial arts soon learns that the aggressive, brutish perception people have of these disciplines could not be

Below Although the popular conception of many martial arts is one of physical aggression, this is far from the reality, which demands respect, courtesy and self-discipline.

further from the truth. Inherent in their teaching are the guiding principles of respect, courtesy and self-discipline – in fact, most skilled martial arts practitioners are less likely to initiate or become involved in physical aggression than non-practitioners, preferring instead to remove themselves from a potentially violent situation. Rather than fighting other people, the martial arts encourage us to fight the enemy within in an effort to become better people. Combine this attitude with the inner strength one gains from their training, and the rewards to be gleaned are peace of mind and a richer, more rounded quality of life.

While some arts may, superficially, appear to be aggressive, especially when weapons are used, this is far from their true meaning. The use of the sword, for example, in its philosophy and teachings, is concerned with developing your mind and body to work harmoniously together and, if you relate this to self-protection, it is about having the confidence and ability to be aware of a confrontation before it happens. This enables you, if you are threatened, to have the courage to walk or talk your way out of a difficult situation without resorting to physical confrontation. In nearly every situation, the price of violence is too high to pay. In the words of Musashi Miyamoto, one of Japan's most famous swordsmen (1584-1645): "We need to win the battle before we enter and in many ways we should never need to draw our sword."

About this book

The aim of this volume is to give you an insight into a selection of martial arts commonly practised throughout the world today. The first half of the book is a comprehensive directory of martial arts, featuring dedicated chapters on many of the world's most famous and widely-practised martial arts. While some of these chapters give step-by-step instruction on how to practise the basic moves of the chosen discipline, there can be no substitute for learning from a professionally recognized, experienced and highly skilled teacher, who will instruct and assist you in the development of your chosen art. It is important that you train in a safe environment, that you are aware of emergency procedures in case of accidents, and that you have proper insurance cover.

Above The study and philosophy of Shinto lies behind the majority of martial arts disciplines.

Within these opening chapters you will find a brief overview of each martial art's history and philosophy and the essential clothing and equipment you need in order to take part. Etiquette, warm-up exercises and basic techniques are also included, as well as an insight into some of the weaponry that is traditionally used. Some of the techniques are for demonstration purposes only, designed to give you an idea of what the chosen art has to offer in terms of stances, postures and the use of weapons, if any.

If you are a more experienced martial arts practitioner, this section of the book may introduce you to disciplines that you have not yet explored. It is very common for practitioners to study more than one art – the chief difficulty usually lies in deciding which others would be most beneficial. The wide-ranging view given here of the different philosophies and skills, and an appreciation of what each discipline has to offer, along with the benefits, will hopefully assist you in making the best decision.

Throughout this book, references will be made to the training area, which is known as the dojo. This term is very common in the martial arts and was first used in kenjutsu –

now more commonly known as kendo. There are a variety of spellings of some of the martial art disciplines featured in this book. Be aware that you may see the names spelt differently, where for example, ju-jitsu can also be spelt ju-jutsu or jiu-jitsu. The same can be said of tae kwondo which is also commonly referred to as tae-kwondo.

The second half of the book features specially designed, dedicated training programmes for two of the world's most widely practised martial arts: t'ai chi and aikido. At first approach, t'ai chi and aikido seem to be two completely different disciplines. T'ai chi, which originated 5,000 years ago in Taoist China, focuses upon emotional balance, slow, fluid movement and spiritual self-development. Aikido is a dynamic Japanese budo (meaning "martial way"), developed from the 9th-century Japanese martial form aikijujutsu. It is usually learned in a dojo (training hall), where movements are practised with an opponent and are based upon self-defence. But t'ai chi and aikido are both fully involving, offering practitioners a form of exercise that becomes part of life; so much more rewarding than forcing yourself to go to the gym. Although it can be daunting to a beginner to see the number of stances and movements that there are to learn in either discipline, it is important that you should approach both t'ai chi and aikido as activities to enjoy over a long

Above T'ai chi appeals to all ages. It is one of the most powerful longevity practices in existence.

period of time. There is no need to try to learn everything as quickly as possible – in fact, this would have no benefit. The key is to relax, work at your own pace and enjoy the feeling of well-being with which you will end each session.

This section is clearly split into focused t'ai chi and aikido chapters, so whether you choose one discipline or aim to practise both, you should find it easy to navigate through. In one sense these sections take a linear approach to learning t'ai chi and aikido. You can start at the beginning, passing through an overview of the art form and the tradition it stems from, then read the in-depth chapters on the different aspects of t'ai chi or aikido. After that, practical sections give you exercises to prepare you for learning the moves, and to help you relax and release tension in your body. However, you will find that learning to understand and practise these art forms is not really a linear process. As you progress, you will return to information and exercises that you read previously, relearning and reinterpreting them many times in the light of your developing understanding and ability. This is one of the reasons why both t'ai chi and aikido represent a life-long journey – if you persevere and practise you will never feel

bored or limited. Instead you will gain a deepening appreciation of the power in these disciplines, which can both take you on a rewarding journey into your own nature. The Taoists say that you need to learn something three times before you truly start to understand it. Try reading the t'ai chi section three times over before starting to practise. Absorb the information first, and you will progress faster. Once on your way, you will understand previously read material in a new light.

APPROACHING T'AI CHI

Learning t'ai chi can be both simple and complex. The essence of t'ai chi is simple; the methods used to get to an understanding of that essence can seem complicated. T'ai chi is about feeling rather than thinking. It is possible to collect a lot of intellectual knowledge about t'ai chi, without really penetrating the essence of what it is to practise t'ai chi. The real benefits of the art come from integrating its core principles within your being. In this sense, simplicity is best. This book contains fundamental information, t'ai chi principles and exercises that, if applied, can give you a taste of this extraordinary art. You will gain genuine understanding and experience of t'ai chi, and learn the entire Wu short form, without being overwhelmed by too much information all at once.

Taoist breathing skills and patient preparation are essential "first steps" for any student of t'ai chi. As you work through the preparation section, relax and enjoy these first movements. Even this early on in your t'ai chi practice, you will start to feel the benefits of release as you learn to relax your entire body. This state of body and mind is essential to you as you progress to learning your first form, the Wu style short form.

Once your understanding has developed, you may decide to move on to further t'ai chi training, or have reached a stage where t'ai chi fits into your lifestyle comfortably, and you are happy to practise and continue at your own pace. You'll find the "Taking it Further" section has more advanced information, and exercises for meditation to help you to develop and integrate your practice into your life.

In t'ai chi the real skill lies in learning to relax and control your movements. A key phrase traditionally used in learning the Taoist internal arts translates as "more or less". One more or less learns something and more or less does it correctly. With time and practice, and with a relaxed attitude to one's progress, it becomes more rather than less. You will never do t'ai chi perfectly, just "more" rather than "less".

Above Advanced throws and weapons are used after establishing the traditions and basic moves of aikido.

APPROACHING AIKIDO

You need to be patient with yourself when learning aikido, and realistic about the speed at which you can develop. In aikido it is difficult to detach yourself from the idea that you are competing to win or be dominant. But if you manage to do this, you will progress faster than if you place high demands and expectations on yourself.

Traditions and etiquette are a huge part of the practice of aikido. Once you have grasped the fundamental elements and basic practices you will be well on your way to approaching aikido with the right attitude, which is absolutely fundamental to executing the moves correctly, as well as gaining physical and spiritual benefits. The aikido section guides you through the history of aikido as well as giving a solid grounding in these codes of conduct, before introducing the most basic moves. As you embark on your physical practice, increasingly complex moves are shown. Try these as and when you feel ready to develop.

Of the hundreds of techniques that make up aikido, this book can show only a small number. But the techniques have been carefully selected to give you a good understanding of

aikido and a solid basis from which to begin your practice. Each technique is clearly pictured, with inset "close-ups" in many cases, which show the finer details of the movements.

It is extremely important to view aikido as a progression, in order to avoid hurting yourself or picking up bad habits that may affect your work with a partner. Start with the warm-ups, which promote strength and flexibility, before moving on to repeated practice of tandoku dosa, the solo exercises that involve the core movements of aikido. These will teach you how to move fluidly and evasively while maintaining the hamni stance. Perhaps by this stage you will have joined a dojo, where you can begin paired exercises, test your inner stability and learn how to stay centred or displace the centre of your partner. This guide to aikido acts as a back-up to any instruction or practice you get at a dojo by clearly showing you the correct stances and moves, and indicating the path of progression that you should travel.

As you progress and enjoy aikido, you will be able to refer back and improve your basic skills, as well as working through the book towards finessing techniques and building confidence.

It is hoped that this book will give you a sense of the wide scope of martial arts, and set you on the path to a life-long enjoyment of one or many of these extraordinary and enduring disciplines.

Part One

A DIRECTORY OF MARTIAL ARTS

This section of the book is a fascinating journey through the world of martial arts with useful information on the history and philosophy of each discipline, as well as practical step-by-step exercises and techniques.

This easy-to-use directory features dedicated sections on tae kwondo, ju-jitsu, judo, kung fu, t'ai chi, kendo, iaido and shinto ryu, making it the perfect resource for the martial arts enthusiast or those new to martial arts and trying to find the best discipline for their needs.

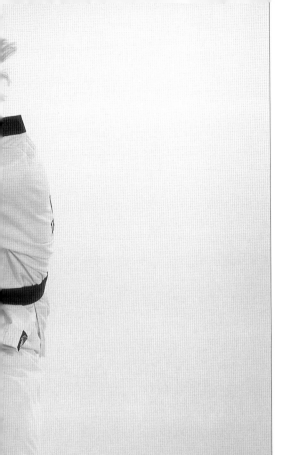

Tae kwondo

It is widely believed that a Buddhist monk named Won Qwang originated the five principles – etiquette, modesty, perseverance, self-control and indomitable (invincible) spirit – that today form the basis of tae kwondo. This art is renowned for its exceptional kicking and jumping techniques. It is viewed not only as an extremely effective self-defence system, but is also a very popular international sport. Early training involves simple punching and blocking techniques, which many may also relate to karate.

History and Philosophy

Korean in origin, tae kwondo is now one of the world's most widely practised martial arts, and has been an Olympic sport since the year 2000. Tae kwondo practitioners require strict dedication and focus to master this complex and impressive physical art form.

Tae kwondo is derived from several martial arts, with the main influence being tae-kyon – Korean kick fighting. *Tae* means "kick" or "smash with the feet"; *kwon* means "intercept" or "strike with the hands"; and *do* means "the way of the art". Thus, the foundation of the art is the use of the hands and feet to overcome an attacker swiftly.

Tae kwondo was originally developed in Korea in the 1950s, when a group of leading martial arts experts came together to unify their respective disciplines under a single fighting system. The inauguration took place in South Korea on 11 April, 1955, with Major-General Choi Hong Hi, a 9th-*dan* black belt, being credited as the founder. However, its roots stretch back nearly 2,000 years, when it was born from an art known as *hwarang do*, meaning "the way of the flowering manhood".

The *hwarang* were young noblemen, influenced by Confucian teachings, who formed a patriotic society during the unification of Korea, in the Silla dynasty, in about AD600. The Silla kingdom was the smallest of three within the Korean peninsula, and was constantly under attack from its stronger neighbours. It was these constant invasions that led the Silla nobility to develop a fighting system to protect their kingdom.

Below An instructor demonstrates the flexibility and balance that tae kwondo requires by performing a kick to the head.

Below Nepalese martial arts practitioners demonstrate one of tae kwondo's most difficult and instantly recognizable techniques.

Towards the end of the 10th century, following the unification of Korea, learning tae kwondo became compulsory for all young men. However, in about the 16th century the military traditions of the country fell out of general favour and the practice of tae kwondo was kept alive only by Buddhist monks. Following the Japanese occupation in 1909, the suppression of any form of martial art only served to further its decline. The few remaining dedicated practitioners emigrated to China and Japan and, thus, the art survived.

Following liberation in 1945, many Korean exiles returned to their homeland and reintroduced an improved version of tae kwondo. The Korean government, as part of its campaign to reassert national identity following years of Japanese occupation, supported the practice of tae kwondo by officially sponsoring it. This led to a more formal approach to the teaching and grading of the discipline.

Tae kwondo spread worldwide from Korea in the 1960s, and the first World Tae Kwondo Championship took place in Seoul, South Korea, in 1973. Since 1988, tae kwondo has been listed as an Olympic sport.

COMPETITION FIGHTING

Competition fighting in tae kwondo is purely optional. For those who participate, competitions are split into three sections: sparring, patterns and destruction.

Sparring involves two practitioners practising fighting techniques to develop their timing, focus and speed. It is performed in a controlled environment so that no unnecessary injuries occur. In competition, the aim is to score points through the delivery of correct techniques to target areas.

Patterns are a set series of combination techniques performed in a sequential order against an imaginary opponent. This is similar to karate, which refers to patterns as *kata*, or kung fu, which uses set movements called "forms". One of the first patterns a practitioner learns is *chon ji tul* (the heaven and earth pattern).

Destruction refers to "breaking techniques", in which practitioners learn to break, for example, a piece of wood. The aim is to ensure that the power and skill of the technique are truly effective. It is also designed to focus the mind.

Above Modern tae kwondo's biggest influence is Korean kick fighting. Here a practitioner demonstrates an impressive scissor kick used in tae kwondo.

Left Korea's Dongmin Cha celebrates after winning gold at the 2008 Beijing Olympic Games. Tae kwondo is one of only two martial arts competed at the games, the other being judo.

Benefits of tae kwondo

The benefits derived from learning tae kwondo affect many aspects of your everyday life. These include:

- Health and fitness
- Flexibility and stamina
- Confidence and well-being
- Self-awareness and assertiveness
- Comradeship
- Self-defence skills
- Stress reduction
- Positive attitude
- Strength of mind and character
- Discipline of mind and body

Clothing and Equipment

Tae kwondo techniques are performed using the hand or foot, so no specialist equipment is necessary to practise. Like all martial arts though there is a strict etiquette to adhere to, and it is essential to be wearing the correct attire.

Practitioners in tae kwondo require a plain white heavy weight cotton suit. This consists of a plain V-neck white jacket and trousers with elasticated waist. Instructors of 1st-*dan* and above wear a slightly different suit (*dobuk*) which has black edging around the neck. Higher grades, 4th-*dan* and above, wear a black stripe down the side of the trousers. It is important to ensure that the suit (*gi*) is the right size for a smart appearance and to feel comfortable when practising various techniques. Protective clothing is worn on occasions when this is deemed necessary by both men and women – and usually when free fighting (sparring) is taking place or a public demonstration. Clothing should always be kept clean and tidy.

white belt

yellow belt

green belt

blue belt

red belt

black belt

Belt gradings

10th-*kup*	White
9th-*kup*	White with yellow stripe
8th-*kup*	Yellow
7th-*kup*	Yellow with green stripe
6th-*kup*	Green
5th-*kup*	Green with blue stripe
4th-*kup*	Blue
3rd-*kup*	Blue with red stripe
2nd-*kup*	Red
1st-*kup*	Red with black stripe
1st-*dan* and upwards	Black

A gold tag denotes the level achieved for *dan* gradings.

Left Clothing needs to be clean, comfortable and durable for the many kicking techniques practised.

Etiquette

There is only one bow performed in tae kwondo. Practitioners perform a bow (*kyong ye*) upon entering the training area (*dojang*) as a sign of respect. This bow is also performed to the instructor and students prior to instruction or training.

1◁ Stand in a relaxed position, with your feet a shoulder-width apart, and your hands held behind your back.

2◁ Bring your open hands to the sides of your body and bring your feet together, with your heels touching and your toes slightly apart.

3▷ Bow, lowering your body approximately 30 degrees, with your eyes looking forwards.

Warm-up Exercises

Warm-up exercises stretch the muscles required before practice. Correct stretching of the whole body will minimize any risk of injury. The following depicts a selection of exercises to be found in tae kwondo, showing the flexibility which can be achieved.

Warm-up 1 – This exercise will stretch your legs, hamstrings and inner thighs.

◁ Lower your body into a squatting position and push your left leg out to the side so that it is flat to the floor and with your toes pointing upwards. Clasp your hands in front of your body and try to maintain an upright posture. Repeat this exercise on the opposite side. This is not an easy exercise to perform in the early stages, so do not worry if you are unable to lower your leg as depicted. As long as your leg is kept straight, regular practice will enable you to become very supple.

Warm-up 2 – This is a hip-joint exercise.

▷ While sitting on the floor, place your left leg across your right thigh. Place your right arm across your left knee and pull your left leg backwards. Ensure that your right heel is tucked well back towards your right thigh. Look in the opposite direction from your knee when levering your left leg backwards to cause a twisting action on your body. Repeat on the opposite side.

Warm-up 3 – This exercise is particularly beneficial for your lower back and the backs of your legs.

◁ Sit on the floor and pull your right heel into your groin area. Keep your left leg straight with your foot and toes pulled back. Lean forwards from the waist and grab your left foot with both hands. Try, if possible, to lower your head on to your knee, keeping your leg straight and flat to the floor. This may not be possible in the early stages but, with practice, you will eventually be able to achieve this position quite comfortably.

Warm-up 4 – This exercise is useful for stretching your hamstrings, and increasing mobility of the hips, calf muscles and knee joints. The degree of flexibility may vary depending upon experience.

1◁ Sit on the floor and push your legs apart as far as you comfortably can. Take hold of your left ankle with both hands and pull your body downwards towards your left knee. Try to touch your knee with your forehead. It takes time for your muscles to become sufficiently supple to allow you to perform this exercise to its full extent. Hold this position for a few seconds and repeat on the opposite side.

2◁ With your legs still apart, take hold of both ankles. Lower your body as far as you can, with the aim of trying to touch the floor with your forehead. Hold this position for a few seconds and do not worry if your head does not touch the floor – it is the lowering movement which stretches the muscles and this must be built up gradually. Be patient – it may take months before you can fully achieve this movement.

Warm-up 5 – An important part of the warm-up routine is preparation for kicking.

1◁ With your partner turned away from you, place both of your hands on his shoulders for support. Swing your right leg sideways and as high as you can and repeat the exercise several times to loosen your thighs. Repeat the exercise with your left leg. Try to keep your leg as straight as possible throughout the movement.

2▷ A similar exercise is to swing your leg, forwards and then to the rear, while resting the side of your face on the top of your partner's back. Repeat this exercise several times with your right leg and then your left.

Warm-up 6 – Advanced exercise utilizing a partner to assist in stretching the inner thighs.

Caution
This exercise must be performed only under professional supervision. Both partners must be well experienced and of similar weight and build.

◁ Sit on the floor and draw your feet in towards your groin. Your partner, from the rear, places both hands on your shoulders. He then carefully places his feet on your knees but does not bear down with all his weight. It is important that your partner maintains good balance and control as he pushes down on your knees. It is not the intention initially to bring your knees flat to the floor, as this could cause discomfort or even injury, but over a period of time you will come closer and closer to achieving this.

Techniques: Basic

There are a variety of basic techniques in tae kwondo, of which the following demonstrates two blocks and strikes. Beginners need to practise slowly in the early stages in order to progress. Speed will come in time, with practice.

Basic technique 1 – Lower parry block and spear hand strike to the chest.

1△ Face your partner in a formal stance with your right foot forward. Make sure that you have a good bend on your front knee and that your back leg is straight. Your partner adopts a left forwards stance, with his left leg forwards and right rear leg straight. Your partner then aims a punch at you with his left hand as he moves in towards you. Your response is a right-arm downwards palm block to prevent contact while you bring your left hand back, fingers straight and palm uppermost, in preparation to strike.

2△ Strike your partner with your spear hand, aiming for your partner's solar plexus. Your thumbs should be tucked in and your fingers straight and locked together. Ensure that your right hand is under your left elbow to give support to the striking technique.

Basic technique 2 – Middle body block and ridge hand strike to temple.

1△ Remaining in the same stance, aim a punch towards your partner's solar plexus with your right fist. Your partner brings his left hand around in a semi-circle to deflect your attack.

2△ Your partner then moves through to strike with the ridge of his right open hand to the side of your neck.

Techniques: Women's Self-defence

These techniques are useful skills for women, although they are also applicable to men and children. The key here is to develop confidence to handle an aggressive situation by practising a strong stance and effective delivery of a technique.

Self-defence technique 1 – Elbow defence.

△ Here you can see the elbow strike to the mandible. Note the scream (kiai) – an exhalation of air that tenses the body and enhances the delivery of the strike.

1△ Face your partner. As she strikes at your solar plexus with a left fist, step back with your left leg into a back stance, with about 70 per cent of your body weight on your rear leg, and deflect the attack with a circular open-hand knife-edge block. Ensure that your thumb is tucked in and your fingers firmly pushed together. Simultaneously, bring your left fist back to your hip in preparation to deflect or strike, whichever is required.

2△ Step through with your right leg and strike with your right elbow to your partner's mandible.

Caution
When training, never make contact. Only experienced practitioners have the ability to execute techniques that almost make contact.

Self-defence technique 2 – Knee defence.

1△ Your opponent attempts to apply a stranglehold. Step back with your left leg, keeping a bend on your front knee. Move both hands outwards in a double open-hand wedge block to deflect the strike.

2△ Take hold of the back of your partner's head with both of your hands and pull her face forwards and towards your left knee.

3△ The conclusion to this technique is a fully executed knee strike to your partner's head. Be careful when practising these exercises, aiming at least 10 cm (4 in) away from your partner's head.

Techniques: Advanced Leg Strike

The following are some of the leg-kicking techniques integral to tae kwondo.
They are designed to strike the opponent from a variety of angles and are difficult
to block. Tae kwondo uses a variety of kicks as legs are a powerful natural weapon.

Turning kick – Using the ball of the foot to strike with an outwards, inwards kicking motion.

1△ With your left foot firmly planted on the floor, lift your right knee as high as you can to the side. Place your fists in a front guard position. Look directly at your opponent.

2△ Bring your right leg around to the front in a circular movement as you fully extend it into a kick. The aim is to strike your opponent with the ball of the foot.

Twisting kick – Using the ball of the foot to strike with an inwards, outwards kicking motion.

◁ This is fundamentally a form of spinning kick designed to catch your opponent on the move. This is a technique that requires a lot of practice to perfect into a proficient leg-striking technique. Note the unusual angle of the kick and the alignment of the body.

Jumping side kick – Using the side of the foot when elevated in order to strike.

△ This is often viewed as one of the most spectacular of leg-striking techniques. Practitioners aim to reach great heights through constant training. A skilled practitioner, utilizing the jumping side kick, can easily strike the face of a tall opponent.

Downward kick, or axe kick – Using the heel to deliver a strong kick from a high raised position.

◁ The aim of the axe kick is to raise your leg as high as possible, and then bring the heel down hard enough to break an opponent's collar bone.

Techniques: Children's Leg Strike

These self-defence techniques are suitable for children to practise. In all cases the kick falls short of actual contact to maintain safety. It is important that children only practise techniques which will not hinder their physical development.

Front kick – *Ap chagi.*

△ Demonstrating the front kick, striking with the ball of the foot to an aggressor's solar plexus.

Side kick – *Yap chagi.*

△ A side kick to the solar plexus area is an effective deterrent, giving a child time to get to a place of safety.

Back heel kick – *Dwit chagi.*

△ Demonstrating an effective back heel strike aimed towards the solar plexus area.

Turning kick – *Dollya chagi.*

△ The speed of the side turn adds to the effectiveness of this leg-striking technique, which uses the ball of the foot to make contact.

Techniques: Women's Techniques

While the following techniques are demonstrated by women, they are also utilized by both men and children. Women, in particular, will find that these techniques can enhance their health, fitness, confidence and self-defence skills.

Jumping turning kick – Catching the opponent off guard by jumping and striking the face area.

◁ Demonstrating a jumping turning kick, aiming for an opponent's throat or face.

Back kick – Demonstrating flexibility of kicking techniques when striking to the rear.

△ A back kick to an opponent's solar plexus. This is known as a short range back kick where the leg is kept bent. There are similar techniques where the rear kick requires the leg to push back and become straight.

Side kick from the floor – An effective self-defence technique.

△ Here is a demonstration of self-defence from what seems to be a vulnerable position. The side kick from the floor aims for an opponent's solar plexus, but could be equally effective if delivered to the groin, knee or shin.

Techniques: Advanced Kicking and Breaking

The following demonstrates the skills that people, even those with major disabilities, can achieve. There are no barriers on the grounds of age, gender or ability, even though tae kwondo is viewed as a highly skilled leg-striking art.

Crescent kick

△ A very complicated move, involving a back twist, a spin and a jump kick. This movement is achieved by swinging the leg in a crescent motion towards the target area.

Side kick

△ This is a side kick to the head. Note the introduction of protective equipment. In tae kwondo practitioners are required to wear hand mitts, shin guards, feet protectors, gum shields (mouth guards), head guards and groin protection (athletic cup), along with any other necessary equipment, when performing sparring.

Back-hook technique

△ Note the good posture and balance involved in this back-hook technique. The practitioner receiving the strike has complete confidence that it will be well focused and that no contact will be made.

Turning kick

△ Demonstrating a turning kick to the back of an opponent's head. Again, note the good posture and body guard and how the top of the foot is being used to deliver the strike. In a street-defence situation the instep of the foot could be used to strike. The ball of the foot can also be implemented when performing breaking techniques.

Breaking technique

Caution
Do not practise this technique without strict professional supervision. Breaking techniques are solely for demonstration purposes and they show the powerful leg techniques of the art. They can take years to perfect.

△ The ball of the foot being used to perform a breaking technique.

Karate

Karate is a self-defence system that utilizes the whole of the human body and the ways in which it moves and twists. Techniques vary from punching and striking with the fist, hands and elbows, to kicks and strikes with the feet, shins and knees. As with many of the martial arts, karate is often seen by those who have no experience of it as a "killing art", but to true practitioners the opposite is, in fact, the case. Karate, whether practised as an art, a sport or as self-defence, carries the motto "never strike the first blow".

History and Philosophy

Though karate was developed in Japan, parts of its history can be traced back to ancient Indian and Chinese civilizations. Today it is one of the world's most popular and instantly recognizable martial arts and is revered as the ultimate combination of focus and agility.

Karate, or karate-do, loosely translated means "empty hand" (*kara* means "empty" and *te* means "hand"), and this art is indeed predominantly concerned with fighting with bare hands and feet. The basic principle is to turn the body into an effective weapon to defend and attack when and where it is appropriate.

Karate can be regarded as both a sport as well as a self-defence art depending on the emphasis of the club or association that is followed. Some instructors or coaches of karate place great emphasis on classical teachings, which incorporate traditional movements (such as *kata*) and philosophy, while others focus more on competition training. Some instructors, like Eugene Codrington, teach all aspects of the art. Karate is also an effective system of self-defence, which originally evolved on the Japanese island of Okinawa, where the carrying of weapons was forbidden, and so the inhabitants had to learn surreptitiously to protect themselves by other means.

Karate is one the most widely practised of the oriental martial arts. It evolved during one of the Japanese occupations of the island of Okinawa, part of the Ryukyu chain of islands, in the 15th century. Its roots, however, can be traced back

Below Competitive karate practitioners battle it out at the 2007 Pan Arab Games, in Cairo.

Below A figure from the Shaolin Temple illustrates the link between Okinawan karate, Japanese karate and weaponry.

much further than this – all the way back to ancient India and China. Many people hold the view that what we today regard as the oriental martial arts have their roots in India. Indeed, when we look at such disciplines as yoga and the breathing techniques that originated in India, there does seem to be a great similarity between those and many of the modern martial arts systems.

Above Synchronized karate performers put on an impressive show during the opening ceremony of the 2008 Beijing Olympic Games.

Below Concentration, focus and intensity are the essential qualities needed for success in competitive karate.

It is believed that Zen Buddhist monks took the Indian fighting techniques to China from as early as the 5th and 6th centuries BC. Bodidharmi, the most famous of these monks, travelled at the end of the 5th century AD from India to China, where he became an instructor at the Shaolin monastery. He taught a combination of empty-hand fighting systems and yoga, and this became the well-known Shaolin kung fu – the system on which many Chinese martial arts systems are based.

In 1470, the Japanese had occupied the island of Okinawa. The law of the land dictated that anybody found carrying weapons would be put to death. In order to protect themselves from local bandits, who largely ignored the prohibition on weapons, Zen Buddhist monks developed the empty-hand system known as *te* ("hand"), importing new techniques from China. Eventually the new art was translated as *t'ang* ("China hand"), but was familiarly known as *Okinawa-te* ("Okinawa hand"). It was not until the 20th century that t'ang became known as *karate-do* ("empty hand"). The suffix *do* was added by Gichin Funakoshi's son Yoshitaka Funakoshi, in friendly opposition to his father's *Okinawa-te* style. Practice and demonstrations until that time had been extremely violent. Punches were not pulled

and full contact was an integral part of the *Okinawa-te* style. Yoshitaka Funakoshi transformed the techniques of *Okinawa-te* into a gentler system, seeking not to deliver blows fully, but to "focus" strikes at skin level. The *do* suffix expressed the move away from the "aim of the warrior" and towards physical and spiritual development.

GICHIN FUNAKOSHI

Gichin Funakoshi (1868–1957) was a student of the Chinese classics and of the martial arts, and is credited with introducing karate to mainland Japan in the early part of the 20th century. Prior to this, in 1905, the occupying Japanese had authorized the inclusion of karate in the Okinawan physical education programme for middle school students. They appreciated the discipline inherent in karate and soon it became an integral part of the school educational system.

In 1917, at the request of the Japanese Ministry for Education, Funakoshi travelled from Okinawa to Kyoto in Japan and gave the first display of *t'ang*. In 1921, Funakoshi demonstrated his system for the Crown Prince of Japan at Shuri Castle. So impressive was this that Funakoshi was asked to appear at the first national athletic exhibition in Tokyo. Jiguro Kano, the founder of judo, among others, persuaded Funakoshi to stay on mainland Japan. In 1924, Funakoshi began teaching in several schools and dojo and founded the first University Karate Club at Keio University. Other styles started to develop, including *kyokushinkai*,

shukukai and wado ryu. By 1936, karate had started to spread and the first purpose-built karate dojo was built, called shotokan (the "hall of Shoto" – a pen name of Funakoshi). The same year he published his second book, *Karate do Kyokan*.

In 1955 the first dojo of the Japan Karate Association was opened. Two years later in Tokyo, on 26 April, 1957, Funakoshi died. By this time, karate was well established, and today it is enjoyed throughout the world.

Above Two senior karate sensei here illustrate attack and defence. Master Enoeda defends against Steve Arniel.

Left A senior student of Gichin Funakoshi – Hironori Ohtsuka – later devised his own "style" of karate: wado ryu.

Above Children showing a dedication to karate. Many adult karate practitioners have been training since a young age.

STYLES OF KARATE

There are numerous styles of karate practised, and its influence even spreads into many other martial arts, so a book such as this cannot explore them all. This chapter will focus on the forms of wado ryu and shotokan.

It is also important to realize that the various styles of karate are the results of the personal ideas of many individuals about how each basic technique should be carried out or applied. The different techniques within the styles of karate also dictate whether strength, speed, or hand or leg techniques are emphasized.

KARATE AS A SPORT

Karate has always been a self-defence system and a form of physical exercise. The competitive and sporting elements have a further part to play in the individual's enjoyment of this activity. It is because of the possibility of participation in competition that many people take up this art.

Competition comes in different forms, in which varying degrees of contact are allowed. In this book, we are concerned with traditional karate competition – sometimes termed sport karate. Certain dangerous techniques are omitted and strict rules are applied, making karate both safe and enjoyable for the competitor. One of the main purposes of karate competition is to show your skill at controlling the permitted techniques in a one-to-one combat situation.

The individuals are allowed to move freely in a given area, which is controlled by a referee and a judge, or judges. Kumite is the word used to describe this type of competition.

Another form of competition that is also featured here is kata. Kata is a series of karate techniques performed alone against imaginary opponents. A kata competition resembles gymnastics or figure skating, in which points are awarded for correct technique and good balance, timing, rhythm, attitude and other attributes.

Competition is not the only reason for engaging in this art. It is possible to learn karate without participating in competitions – but for some people, competition provides stimulation and motivation for training. The sense of achievement that comes from just taking part, whether in kata or kumite, can be carried over into everyday life.

Benefits of karate

The benefits derived from learning karate extend into many aspects of your everyday life. These include:

- Fitness, flexibility and mobility
- Well-being (through the balance of mind and body)
- Concentration and self-control
- Confidence
- Teamwork
- Honesty and integrity
- Stress reduction
- Sociability and courtesy

Wado Ryu Karate

The main focus of wado ryu karate lies in keeping both yourself and your opponent away from any harm. It is a hybrid martial art that is based on karate, but also contains core elements of ju-jitsu, which makes it a unique and technically advanced self-defence style.

Hironori Ohtsuka (1892–1982) was the founder of the wado ryu system of karate. He commenced training in *shindo yoshin ryu jujitsu* at the age of six, and at the age of 30 he began training under the supervision of Gichin Funakoshi (the founder of *karate-do*) before founding the wado ryu system in 1939. Wado ryu is one of the four main Japanese styles of karate that are taught around the world. In 1939, Ohtsuka organized the All Japan Karate Do Federation Wado Ki and the Worldwide Headquarters for the Wado Ryu System. In 1967 he was the first *karateka* to be awarded the 5th order of merit of the sacred treasure of the Emperor of Japan as an acknowledgement of his achievements.

Following his death in 1982, Hironori Ohtsuka's son, Jiro, became the chief instructor of the wado ryu system. Today, there are a number of senior, well-respected representatives of wado ryu in Japan, who are also leaders of their own federations or associations.

CHARACTERISTICS OF WADO RYU KARATE

To practitioners of wado ryu, the main philosophy is to better their attitude both within and outside the art. This is one of the main aims of *budo* (martial art), which emphasizes the

Above Although wado ryu is a form of karate it also contains key elements of ju-jitsu.

Below A wado ryu exhibition in honour of the Crown Prince of Japan in 1921 at Shuri Castle.

Left Karate contains a number of airborne techniques.

Above The dove symbolizes a gentle or innocent person, as a means of advocating negotiation rather than violence.

development of respect, discipline and understanding in a mental as well as physical capacity. This aim affects our attitude towards ourselves and others in our home life, work and social activities. To show aggression outwardly, even during training sessions, is greatly discouraged. The name wado ryu, approximately translated, means "the peaceful way".

Another characteristic of wado ryu is that large movements are kept to a minimum. Importance is placed on the speed and efficiency of movement with which each technique is performed, rather than the strength or physical effort outwardly shown. Exponents of wado ryu place great emphasis on the coordination of body movement with each particular technique. This principle is found in many other martial arts, such as ju-jitsu, aikido and kendo. This coordination is stressed at all stages of learning, from the execution of basic techniques to the application of advanced, free-fighting combinations.

Left As with many martial arts, respect and discipline are central to wado ryu. A bow (rei) is performed before undertaking any training.

Benefits of wado ryu

There are numerous benefits derived from learning wado ryu, which will extend into many aspects of everyday life. These include:

- Fitness
- Physical strength
- Mental Strength
- Confidence
- Self discipline
- Self-control

- Sense of well-being
- Teamwork
- Concentration
- Integrity
- Sociability
- Courtesy

Clothing and Equipment

Like many forms of martial art, the grade (or *kyu*) that a wado ryu practitioner has attained is clearly visible from the colour of the belt that is worn around their waist. There are strict requirements for every grade, and a black-belted martial artist is highly respected.

white belt   white/yellow belt   yellow belt   orange belt

Karate practitioners wear a light, medium or heavy weight white cotton suit. The club badge or a combination is usually worn on the left side of the jacket. The white trousers have a drawstring waist and it is important to ensure you have the right size for comfort, practicality and safety. Protective equipment is used in karate by both men and women, especially in sparring (controlled fighting practice) and competition. Practitioners must be clean and tidy at all times, as a sign of respect to the art, teacher and fellow practitioner.

green belt   blue belt

Belt gradings

Beginners	White
10th-kyu	White
9th-kyu	White with yellow stripe
8th-kyu	Yellow
7th-kyu	Orange
6th-kyu	Green
5th-kyu	Blue
4th-kyu	Purple
3rd-kyu	Brown
2nd-kyu	Brown
1st-kyu	Brown
1st-dan	Black
and upwards	

purple belt   brown belt

black belt

Protective Equipment

Extra protection in the form of groin protection (athletic cup) for men and breast protection for women are recommended for use at all times.

groin protection (athletic cup)

Bust protector

karate top

karate trousers

Above A smartly dressed karate instructor.

Etiquette

Etiquette is a key part of training and enables individuals to work safely together. Any distractions in a class could result in injury, and helping others to develop their abilities is an intrinsic part of being a good *karateka* (karate practitioner).

Pre-training discipline

The instructor is always addressed by students as *sensei* (teacher or instructor). It is not quite accurate to translate *sensei* in this way; it actually means "he who has gone before", which indicates that whatever it is the student is about to do or perform, the teacher will have done before, and understands its relevance.

There is nothing to distinguish one student (*karateka*) from another, other than the belt that is worn (*obi*), which is an acknowledgement of that person's experience. All *karateka* are equal as people, as indicated by a plain white cotton suit (*karate gi*). All must remove their footwear by the doorway and pause to bow (*rei*) before entering the training hall (*dojo*).

Helpful hints

- Training must be technically and physically demanding.
- Be sure to warm up before training and take time cooling down afterwards.
- Constantly check and adjust the actions of individual techniques.
- Check the coordination of your movements for each technique.
- Practise all techniques using both sides of your body equally, switching between alternate legs and arms.
- Use a mirror to monitor your movements during training.
- Use punch bags or pads as aids for correcting specific actions.

1△ Stand upright and relaxed, hands in front of your thighs and with your fingers together and straight, thumbs tucked in. Place your heels together with your feet angled outwards, forming a V shape.

2△ Perform a bow (*rei*) by lowering the top part of your body 45 degrees. Keep your back straight and bend from the hips. Keep your eyes looking forwards. Bring your body back to the upright position.

3△ Turn slightly to the left and lower your body down into a squatting position. Place your hands on top of your knees, which should naturally splay apart. Keep looking forwards while you maintain your balance.

4△ Complete the kneeling position by placing your right knee, then your left knee, on the floor with your knees approximately one fist-width apart. Your feet must not be crossed while in this position and the tops of your insteps should be flat on the floor.

5 ◁ To perform the bow (*rei*) bring both hands around your knees and place them on the floor in front of your body. Your forefingers and thumbs should be touching in the shape of a V. Lower your upper body to perform the bow, stopping when your face is, depending on your size, about 10 in (25 cm) from the floor – it is not correct for your head to touch your hands. The object is to maintain a level posture, with your head and back in a straight line.

△ Seen from the rear, your big toes are touching and your insteps are flat to the floor.

The bow

Usually, the bow is performed several times before practice begins. The order of the bows is fixed: the first bow is to *Shomen* (the Founder); the second is to the teacher (who is usually positioned towards the east); and the third bow is to each other.

6 △ Straighten your back and sit back upright in the kneeling position, in preparation to stand.

7 △ Start to return to the standing position by stepping forward with your left foot. Note the position of the rear right foot.

8 △ Once you are on your feet and standing in the original relaxed start position, perform a final bow.

Meditation

This is the meditation (*mokuso*) position, which you use to clear your mind and prepare yourself for the practice to come. Keep your back straight and your shoulders relaxed.

There are two possible hand positions during meditation. The first is to place your hands open on top of your knees. The other is to turn your palms upwards into a cupped position with the tips of the thumbs touching. Close your eyes and try to clear your mind. Keep your breathing slow and controlled.

Hold this position for a minimum of 60 seconds. If you are not used to sitting like this, build the exercise up gradually. Never hold a position if you feel pain.

Warm-up Exercises

The following are some of the exercises used in the warm-up and cooling-down sessions. To reduce the risk of injuries, advice should be sought before starting any exercise programme. The following exercises should be held for 3–10 seconds.

Warm-up 1 – This series of movements is a very gentle exercise designed to loosen up the neck and so minimize the risk of any injury during the practice session. It helps to stretch the muscles at the back of your neck as well as helping to relieve tension.

1△ Stand in a relaxed position with your head upright.

2△ Carefully lower your chin downwards towards your chest. Keep relaxed and gently push down as if nodding to say "yes". Hold for 6–10 seconds and then return your head to the upright position.

3△ Continue the exercise with a side-neck stretch. Keep your head lowered and slowly move it towards your left shoulder.

4▽ Keeping your head facing forward, slowly lower your head towards the top of your left shoulder to stretch the muscles in the right side of the neck for 3–4 seconds. Repeat this exercise, lowering your head towards the right shoulder to stretch the left neck muscles.

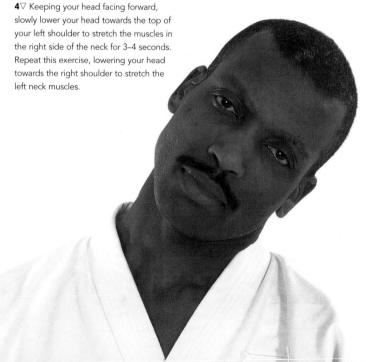

5△ With the head in the upright position, turn your head so that you are looking over your right shoulder for 3 or 4 seconds. Repeat the exercise towards your left shoulder.

Warm-up 2 – This series of exercises loosens and warms the body.

1△ Keeping your arms bent from the elbows, rotate your arms in a full circular motion approximately 5–6 times, first clockwise, then anticlockwise (counterclockwise). This helps to stretch your shoulder muscles. Repeat 3–4 times in each direction.

2△ Stand in a relaxed position, feet apart. Push your left hand up and back five or six times. Reverse your arm positions and repeat the exercise. This stretches your chest and shoulder muscles. Push back and release 2–4 times on each side.

3△ Use a twisting motion to the right, bringing your arms in a circular action across your body and towards the rear. Repeat the exercise by turning towards the rear again. Hold for a few seconds then repeat the exercise to the left side.

4△ Stand in a relaxed position with your hands on your hips and feet apart. Lean slowly as far as possible to your right and extend your left arm as far as possible over your head. Hold for 3–10 seconds. Repeat the exercise to the opposite side. Repeat this 2 or 3 times.

5△ Go into a squatting position and tuck your bottom in. Extend both arms forwards as far as possible at shoulder height. Hold this position for 3–10 seconds.

6△ With your legs spread apart, bend your right knee to lower your body. Hold at your lowest point for 3–10 seconds. Repeat this exercise to the other side.

7△ Stand upright and turn your body to the right. Come up on to the ball of your left foot and bend your right knee to lower yourself. Hold the position for 3–10 seconds.

8◁ From an upright position, move your right foot slightly in front of your left. Slowly lower your body, as if bowing, with your arms hanging forwards. Hold at your lowest point for 3–10 seconds. Bend both knees before returning to the upright position. Repeat, starting with the left foot forward, and alternate 2 or 3 times.

9▷ From a squatting position, move forwards on to your hands with your body raised – like a sprinter's starting position. Slowly press one heel down and backwards towards the floor. Hold for 3–10 seconds. Repeat the exercise with your other foot flat to the floor and alternate 4 or 5 times. This stretches your calf muscles.

Techniques: *Kata – Pinan Nidan*

The *kata – pinan nidan –* shown below is one of the first introduced to low grade students. *Kata* are a compilation of individual techniques put into various sequences, in which a practitioner encounters one or more imaginary opponent(s).

1◁ Stand with your shoulders relaxed and make sure that your hands are open and lightly touching your thighs. Note: a *kata* is designed to enable the practitioner to respond, defend and counter from a number of different angles and attackers. Emphasis is placed on good posture, coordination, timing and understanding basic technique and its application.

2◁ Perform the bow (*rei*). Bow from the waist, but avoid bending too far forward. Keep your eyes alert and looking ahead.

◁ This is a side angle view of the bow performed in step 2. Here you can see the optimum angle of the body, and the straightness of the back following on from the bend at the waist.

3◁ To remain in a central position, and prepare for the natural standing position, *shizentai*, first move your left leg away from your right, followed by moving your right leg slightly away from your left leg. You should then be in a balanced position, with your feet shoulder-width apart, still splayed at approximately 20 degrees.

4△ Move your left leg towards the left, dropping your body weight by bending your knees. At the same time take your left arm in a circular motion (as the arrow suggests) to your left side to perform the defence (*tetsui otoshi uke*). The bottom of the left fist is used to strike while the right fist is pulled back to your side. Keep your elbows tucked in.

5△ Step through with your right leg, striking at the aggressor's solar plexus (*junzuki chudan*) with the right fist. For the next move, you will step to the rear, turning your body 180 degrees, following the direction of the arrows.

6△ When you turn, perform a lower defence action (*gedan barai*) in a clockwise direction. This technique will stop a kick or punch aimed at your lower body.

7△ Pull the right front leg backwards as you perform the hammer fist (*tetsui otoshi uke*) downward circular defence. The fist depicts a "hammer", hence the term, and can be used as both a defence and strike to an opponent.

8◁ Step through with your left leg and strike with your left fist to the opponent's solar plexus. Prepare to turn to the left, as the arrow shows, for the next move.

9▷ Turn and perform the lower sweeping defence (*gedan barai*). Keep your body upright, shoulders relaxed, and legs well braced. The key points of this stance are: feet a shoulder-width apart, back straight, eyes forward, back leg straight and a good bend on the front leg with your knee in line with your toes.

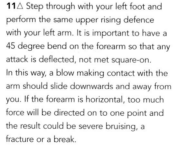

10△ Step forwards with your right foot and perform an upper rising defence with your right arm to protect your head. Take care not to obscure your own vision by, for example, allowing your arm to cover your eyes. Bring your right arm up across your body, ensuring you completely cover the torso as you raise your arm, as if aiming for your left shoulder. Push your arm upwards and slightly backwards to ensure your defence fully covers your head.

11△ Step through with your left foot and perform the same upper rising defence with your left arm. It is important to have a 45 degree bend on the forearm so that any attack is deflected, not met square-on. In this way, a blow making contact with the arm should slide downwards and away from you. If the forearm is horizontal, too much force will be directed on to one point and the result could be severe bruising, a fracture or a break.

12▷ Step through for a third time, performing the same upper rising defence with your right arm and using *kiai*. This is where you exhale with a short, sharp sound to emphasize your focus. The shout, or scream as it is sometimes called, can cause fear or distract your opponent. In the next move, your left leg will follow the direction of the arrow to the left, to initiate a turn.

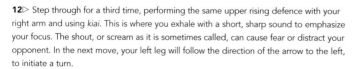

13△ Leading with your left leg, turn anticlockwise (counterclockwise) and utilize the lower sweeping defence.

14△ Step through, right leg forward, and punch at your opponent's solar plexus with your right fist (*junzuki chudan*).

15△ Move across to the right side, again performing the lower sweeping defence.

16△ Step through with your left leg and punch with your left fist at your opponent's solar plexus (*junzuki chudan*).

17△ Move 45 degrees in an anticlockwise (counterclockwise) direction and perform the lower sweeping defence.

18△ Step through, right leg forward, and punch at your opponent's solar plexus with your right fist (*junzuki chudan*).

19△ Step through again for a second *junzuki chudan* strike with your left leg and left fist forward.

20△ Step through for a third time, with your right foot and right fist forward. Perform the *junzuki chudan* strike, using your shout (*kiai*).

21△ Bring your left leg behind and across the rear of your body, turning in an anticlockwise (counterclockwise) direction into a cat stance, *neko ashi dachi*. 70 per cent of your weight should be on your right leg.

22△ As you move through from one stance to another, try to maintain the same height i.e. do not push the body upwards or lower the body as you move forwards to each stance. By doing this, you make it more difficult for the aggressor to detect your intended movements.

23△ Step through with your right leg, still maintaining the same body height, and keep your left arm extended.

24△ Strike at your imaginary opponent with your open right hand, aiming at the lower abdomen (*yoko nukite*).

25△ Take your right leg through 90 degrees into the cat stance (*neko ashi dachi*), with your right hand, palm uppermost, above the left, in preparation to strike. Reach forwards with your right leg in preparation for the next move.

26△ Twist your body into a low stance (*shiko ashi dachi*) to perform the lower open-hand strike with your right hand. In the next move, you will step through with your left leg, in the direction of the arrow.

27△ Step through with your left leg in preparation for making the final strike.

28△ Twist your body and strike the lower body with your left hand. In the next move, your left leg will move in the direction of the arrow.

29△ Now bring your left leg back to resume the upright standing position (*shizentai*).

30△ Bring the left foot in, followed by the right, with the back of your heels together and feet splayed.

31△ Bow from the waist to complete the sequence. Maintain a calm manner and keep alert until you have left the practice area.

Techniques: *Kumite* Technique for Two People

Developing techniques in wado ryu is achieved through practising with a partner.
The following demonstrates the initial etiquette in preparation for the two-person practice
(*kumite*) and some basic defence and striking actions.

1△ Stand opposite your partner in the ready position at approximately one metre's distance (minimum arm and a half distance).

2△ Perform the etiquette bow (*rei*), keeping your eyes on your partner all the time.

3△ Move into the *hidari shizentai* position, ready to perform the techniques. In this position, the left foot is slightly forward in preparation to defend or attack.

4△ You are grabbed at the front by your partner's left hand.

5△ Perform a circular action with your left arm to break the grip, stepping through with your left leg in preparation for the arm lock.

6△ Once you have completed the circular movement, your partner's grip will be broken and they will be in a vulnerable position.

7◁ Move through with your right leg and apply pressure to his left arm by maintaining the arm lock and strong upright posture.

8▷ Step through with your right leg and move your body into a deep (low) stance. Your partner's arm should now be fully trapped by the application of pressure on his upper arm from your right elbow. From this position you can continue to maintain the restraint on your partner or progress onwards to apply another wado ryu technique.

Techniques: Blocking

Blocking is the term used to describe the method of arresting an attack. Various parts of the body are used in different ways to defend against an on-coming attack. This is complemented by the correct body movement for the nature of the attack.

1△ Step to the side and deflect your partner's kick by using a left lower forearm defence. The hand is made into a fist and a short circular action is used to deflect the kick.

2△ Pull your deflecting left arm around in a circular motion, bringing it down across your partner's neck and face. This action will push your partner backwards and off balance.

3△ A possible follow-on from this technique is to pull around behind your partner and apply a neck lock.

△ Here you can see a more detailed side view of the neck lock described in step 3.

Techniques: Defence

There are a variety of defensive moves in wado ryu which can be applied in a self-defence situation. The following technique demonstrates a combination of blocks and strikes, utilizing both hands and feet for different parts of the body.

1△ Your partner moves through with his right leg and right fist, aiming a punch at your face.

2◁ Defend by stepping back and angling yourself slightly to the right. Use your left hand to deflect the blow downwards and, simultaneously, counter-strike with the palm of your right hand, aiming for the side of his jaw (mandible) – or deliver a front strike to his chin. Timing is important and the area to aim at depends on which is more accessible.

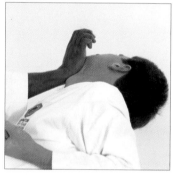

△ This angle of the action in step 2 shows how you deliver the palm blow.

3◁ Pivot on your left leg and lift your right knee in preparation to strike with the top part of your foot to your partner's groin area.

△ In this close-up of step 3, you can see that the strike has been focused on the inner top part of the thigh. This is essential when practising to avoid injuring your partner. It is also advisable to wear groin protection when practising this technique.

Techniques: *Taisabaki*

The main principle of *taisabaki* (evasive) techniques is to avoid contact if possible.
Taisabaki practice increases the ability of the practitioner to move quickly in a variety of
directions and be at an advantage to counter-strike.

1◁ As your partner moves in towards you with his left leg forward and right fist aimed towards your head, you should lean backwards to avoid contact.

2△ As your partner steps through with *mai te zuki* (front punch delivered with the same arm and leg forward), drop and twist towards the right, taking your left shoulder down towards the floor.

3△ An effective defensive manoeuvre when faced with a *maigeri* (front kick) from your partner is achieved by twisting and side-stepping to avoid the kick.

Shotokan Karate

Shotokan is a form of karate that was developed in Okinawa, Japan. The basic moves of shotokan focus on demonstrations of strength and power, its more fluid transitionary movements are not learned until these essential foundations are mastered by the student.

Shotokan karate is both a young and an ancient martial art. It is ancient because its roots are deeply entrenched in the past, and young because, as it is expressed today, it is an art that is less than a hundred years old. Shotokan is characterized by its long, low stances, its powerful techniques and its dynamic forms.

The "founder" of shotokan, Gichin Funakoshi, was an Okinawan. He trained in the oldest of the Okinawan *te* ("hand") systems as a young man and in the early 20th century brought what he had learned in the island of Okinawa to mainland Japan, where he demonstrated his art before the Emperor. He originally intended to return to Okinawa but was persuaded to remain and continue teaching in Japan. Funakoshi's pen name was Shoto (which means "waving pines"), and *kan* means "hall", so shotokan karate can be translated to mean, "Shoto's hall of the way of the empty hand".

While Funakoshi was the originator of shotokan, it was his son, Yoshitaka Funakoshi, who developed it into the form we know today. It rapidly grew in popularity, supported, encouraged and regulated by the Japan Karate Association, and before long was to be found all over the world.

Below Harada Sensei, a direct student of Gichin Funakoshi, defends against a double-wrist grab.

Below Early days of shotokan karate in a dojo in Tokyo. Notice the traditional tatami mat flooring.

Shotokan has produced some of the world's greatest karate exponents, including Hirokazu Kanazawa. It is believed by many *karateka* (karate practitioners) that Hirokazu has come closest to possessing the most perfect technique. He studied karate at Takushoku University and won all the Japan Championships in 1962, with a broken hand after his mother had persuaded him to fight. Shotokan continues to be practised by thousands of people, adults and children, throughout the world.

TRIADS

Shotokan karate is built on what are known as "triads", which are both real organizations and metaphors for something much deeper within the human psyche. There exists the physical triad of *kihon* (basics), *kumite* (sparring) and *kata* (forms), which require dedicated training and the constant perfecting of technique. This is followed by the moral triad of justice, mercy and compassion and finally by the ethical triad of duty, honour and loyalty.

Right Gichin Funakoshi, the founder of shotokan, is largely accredited for the popularization of karate through public demonstrations of the discipline, such as the one seen here.

If you put all of the nine triad principles together (nine symbolizes perfection) you achieve the whole, rounded person. When these principles are practised in a martial art, they illustrate one of the fundamental concepts of shotokan karate, as advocated by the founder, Gichin Funakoshi. His aim was to focus on the development of the human character as a whole being, rather than on winning and losing.

Quite apart from the normal reasons why somebody would take up a martial art, such as self-defence, there are other reasons that, while they may not be clear at the time, emerge during the course of training. Shotokan not only provides the means to defend yourself against an aggressor, it also gives you a sense of self-confidence. Self-confidence stimulates a sense of well-being and a greater sense of awareness when in difficult situations. It also heightens your consciousness of the environment and the very nature of unjust aggression. In this context, the *karateka* (students of karate) can make a mature and reasoned judgement as to what response, if any, to make – provided, of course, that the response conforms to the rules laid down by law, governing the use of reasonable force.

Below Taiji Kase, a senior member of the shotokan fraternity, illustrates the Chinese influence upon modern-day karate.

In this sense, shotokan (and the pursuit of excellence) brings with it grave responsibilities that must be exercised with compassion and mercy. The physical development and improvement of technique and ability is useless without this other dimension. Ultimately, karate exists to perfect the individual, to produce men and women who are just, compassionate and honourable members of society, people who recognize injustice and, through their own behaviour, challenge it.

While shotokan is a wonderful form of relaxation or sport for many people, for those who practise it seriously it has a much wider and deeper significance. But this deeper realization can come only after years of dedicated practice. While this is a dimension of the art that emerges only slowly, karate can still be enjoyed at all levels by hundreds of thousands of people throughout the world.

Benefits of learning shotokan

Learning shotokan can have benefits in many different aspects of your everyday life. These include:

- Fitness, flexibility and mobility
- Well-being (through the balance of mind and body)
- Concentration and self-control
- Confidence and assertiveness
- Teamwork
- Honesty, integrity and humility
- Appreciation of justice and fair play
- Stress reduction
- Sociability and courtesy

Clothing and Equipment

Shotokan practitioners wear a white suit similar to that worn for most similar martial arts disciplines, but the coloured belt grading system used in shotokan is unique. A black belt is still a sign of great accomplishment, but a true shotokan master wears red and white.

Shotokan practitioners wear a white cotton top and draw-string trousers. Most schools follow the belt grading system below, with beginners usually wearing a white or blue belt. At 3rd-*dan* a *karateka* may be addressed as "*sensei*". At 4th-*dan* it is assumed that the *karateka* is well acquainted with the style and has a deep knowledge of the technical syllabus. A 5th-*dan* can be awarded after the writing of a technical thesis on karate. All *dan* grade awards after this are for progress within shotokan, with emphasis on style, devotion, dedication and commitment to the art. With the award of 6th-*dan* can come the title "*shihan*" which freely translated means "master" or literally "a teacher of teachers". At this stage the *karateka* is regarded as a master of his/her style and is given the right to wear the red and white belt or may continue to wear the black belt. Although it may take 30 years of hard, disciplined training and study to achieve 6th-*dan*, the pursuit of excellence should never cease.

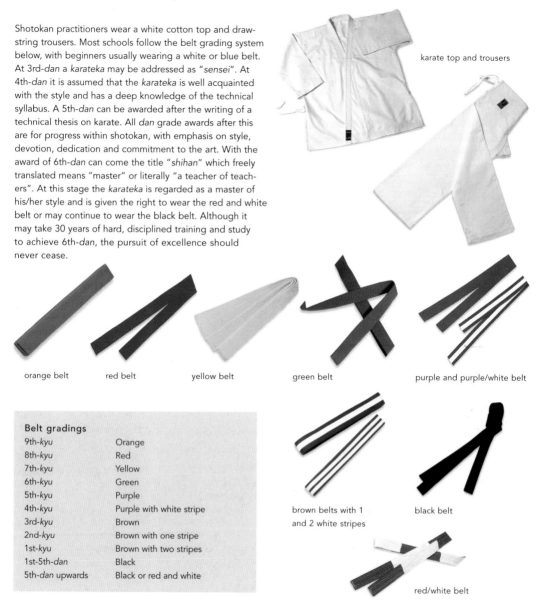

karate top and trousers

orange belt   red belt   yellow belt   green belt   purple and purple/white belt

brown belts with 1 and 2 white stripes

black belt

red/white belt

Belt gradings

9th-*kyu*	Orange
8th-*kyu*	Red
7th-*kyu*	Yellow
6th-*kyu*	Green
5th-*kyu*	Purple
4th-*kyu*	Purple with white stripe
3rd-*kyu*	Brown
2nd-*kyu*	Brown with one stripe
1st-*kyu*	Brown with two stripes
1st-5th-*dan*	Black
5th-*dan* upwards	Black or red and white

Etiquette

In shotokan there are three types of bow (*rei*): *shomen ni rei*, showing respect to the training area; *otagani rei* (shown below), performed to the great masters of the past and present; and *shihan rei*, which is used by both teachers and students.

1△ Stand in a natural position (*hachichi dachi*), with your feet splayed slightly outwards and with your hands hanging relaxed at the sides of your body. Keep looking forwards.

2△ Move your right leg in towards your left so that your heels are touching.

3△ Turn your left shoulder forwards.

4△ Lower your body towards the floor, placing your left knee on the floor, and make sure that you keep looking forwards.

5△ Place your right knee on the floor, aligning it with your left, and place your hands on top of your thighs.

6△ Leaning slightly forwards from the kneeling position (*seiza*), place your left hand in front of your body.

7△ Follow through with your right hand so that your forefingers and thumbs make a triangular shape. Make sure that you keep your gaze directed forwards.

8△ Bend forwards from the waist, keeping your fingers in the same position and your gaze forwards. Reverse the process back into kneeling and stand upright.

Warm-up Exercises

The warm-up exercises below are a sample of the exercises performed prior to a shotokan karate training session. Make sure that you approach every exercise gently, building up your pace to an acceptable and comfortable level.

Warm-up 1 – This exercise is designed to stretch your triceps, back and chest area.

△ Bring your left arm across the back of your head and place your right hand on your left elbow. Pull your elbow in a downwards motion towards your right side. Repeat 2 to 3 times each side.

△ This is a rear view of the position. It shows the correct arm and hand positions, with your right hand on the left shoulder blade and your left hand gripping your right elbow.

Warm-up 2 – The following movement exercises the fingers and assists in making the wrists more supple.

1△ Push your hand downwards and outwards, keeping your fingers open and splayed.

2△ Push your fingers well back, with your palm facing upwards, using a downwards rocking motion. Hold this position for several seconds and perform the same exercise on the opposite side.

Warm-up 3 – This exercise is useful for stretching your hamstrings, and increasing mobility of the hips, calf muscles and knee joints. The degree of flexibility may vary depending upon experience.

▷ Sit on the floor and cross your right leg over your left, keeping your right knee bent. Look to the rear so that you stretch the upper part of your body as well as the lower back, hip and upper thighs. Make sure that your right hand is placed well behind you so that you feel securely balanced. Place your left arm across the outside of your right knee and twist your body backwards. Hold this position for approximately 20 seconds, then reverse leg and hand positions and repeat 2 or 3 times each side.

Warm-up 4 – This exercise stretches your inner thighs and leg muscles and promotes good body balance.

△ Place your right leg to the side to adopt a wide stance. Carefully lower your body so that your left knee is well bent and your right leg is straight, toes pointing forwards. Keep your hands stretched out in front of you, palms facing forwards, your right hand gripping your left. If you have not done this before, it may take a lot of practice to maintain your balance. Hold this position for 20 seconds, then reverse leg positions and repeat 3 times for each side.

Warm-up 5 – This exercise will stretch the back of your thighs and calf muscles.

△ Place your left foot in front of your right, with your heel down and toes facing up. Place both hands on your left thigh, pushing your hips back and leaning forwards with the top part of your body. Hold for several seconds and reverse the leg position. Repeat 2 to 3 times.

Techniques: Basic

Learning a series of basic techniques is important to all martial art traditions. In this way, you build a foundation of moves that can be safely executed. Some of these moves will be common to several martial arts, while others may be unique.

Zenkutsu dachi – Shotokan is well known for its use of a very low stance called *zenkutsu dachi*, or front stance. This is used in the majority of the basic moves.

△ From the natural position, with your feet shoulder-width apart, step forwards into a low stance with your left leg. Keep your back leg straight with the heel flat on the floor. Make sure the knee of your leading leg is bent to an angle of approximately 90 degrees.

Kokutsu dachi – An effective defensive move.

△ Step forwards with your left leg, keeping most of your body weight on the rear leg. Hold your hands in a protective open hand position, with the right hand covering the solar plexus and the left hand in the guard position ready to defend or strike.

Judachi – This stance is a shorter version of the front stance and is more suitable for close-quarter combat, competition and basic self-defence moves.

△ Note that your legs should not be positioned as low as in the classic front stance. Keep both hands in a protective position in front of your body. Practise this stance, moving forwards and backwards with both your right and left legs.

Kiba dachi – This position is known as the horse stance.

△ Move your right leg to the side into a low posture as if riding a horse. The knees must be bent forwards, with heels parallel to each other and feet facing forwards. Keep your back straight and your hands in a closed hand (fist) guard position.

Neko ashi dachi – The feeling of feline lightness and poise gives this position its name of "cat stance".

Sanshin dachi – This gives the figure a pinched-looking middle, so it is named the "hour-glass stance".

△ Move forwards with your left leg, with most of your weight on the back leg. Practise this, moving forwards and backwards with both your right and left legs. Ensure that your knees are bent and your right hand is placed on your right hip ready to execute a technique, while your left hand is in the lower guard position.

△ With your feet a shoulder-width apart and your right foot slightly in front, turn your feet inwards and bend your knees. Keep your back upright, chin straight and eyes forward. Put the left hand at shoulder level and right hand on the waist. Use the palm heels to strike the face and groin simultaneously. Repeat on the other side.

Fuda dachi (sochin) – Because of the very low, strong body position, this is known as "the rooted stance".

▷ Move forwards with your leading leg, ensuring that most of your weight is on the back leg. Practise this stance, moving forwards and backwards with both your right and left legs. This posture is excellent for developing strong calves and thighs. The clenched fists are positioned to protect the face and body prior to striking.

Guard position

It is important to protect your body when being confronted. The stance you adopt dictates the most appropriate hand guard position. This can vary from having both hands in front of the torso, with one hand just above the other, to having one hand in front of the face and the other in the lower body region. This position ensures the body is effectively covered and ready either to defend or to strike.

Techniques: Blocking

Shotokan embodies a variety of blocking techniques. *Kata* (set forms where the practitioner strikes an imaginary opponent) also differ in application and shotokan has its own unique *kata*. The following are two of the blocking techniques used.

Soto uke (body block – This is a defensive move against an attack to the chest (middle body) area.

1◁ Stand with feet together and bring your right arm in line with the back of your head. Simultaneously bring your left arm in front of your upper chest. As you start to move forwards with your right leg, into a low stance, bring your right fist through in a circular motion. At the same time, pull your left hand back on to your left hip. *Note: Imagine you have a piece of string attached to both hands, and as the left hand pulls back, so it brings the right arm into position.*

2▷ Keep looking towards your opponent and maintain a strong posture as you deliver this technique. Keep your left fist well back on your left hip and right arm in a bowed position. Aim to use the inside of your forearm, near the elbow, when delivering the block against the opponent's strike.

Gedan barai (lower body block).

◁ From the natural position (*hachichi dachi*), make a fist with both hands and bring your left fist across your chest, in line with your right collar bone. Step forwards with your left foot into *zenkutsu dachi* stance. At the same time, bring the left arm across your body in a downwards motion to finish with the left fist approximately 4–5 inches (10–13 cm) above the left knee. This blocking action is very effective against lower body strikes, especially kicking techniques.

Techniques: Kicking

Shotokan uses a selection of kicking techniques, which have two applications.
The first is *keage* (shown here), which means to strike in a "snapping action".
The second variation is *kekome*, which emphasizes thrusting and using the heel.

1△ Move into the low horse stance (*kiba dachi*). Make sure that your hands are in the guard position.

2△ Bring your left leg across your right, so that your knees are in a "scissor" position.

3▷ With your guard still in position, bring your right leg up to the side of your body and push outwards, striking towards one of your imaginary opponent's vulnerable areas, such as the face, solar plexus, rib or groin. This is known as *yoko geri*. Twist your foot to the side so that the "knife edge" of the foot will be tense – this is the part that delivers the technique. To assist in this action, push your toes inwards and downwards while keeping your foot horizontal.

4△ Bring your kicking foot back in a snapping action, in line with your left knee. It is important to bring your foot back before going down into a fighting posture, to avoid having your leg swept away from under you.

5△ Go back down into the *kiba dachi* posture, still in fighting stance, keeping your eyes on your opponent.

Techniques: *Soto Uke* Blocking Technique

It is important to practise basic techniques, such as this exercise, working from both right and left positions. If you are right-handed, work twice as hard with the left side so that you can balance the strength of your skill.

1△ Bow to show respect to your partner. Remember the "respect but no trust" principle, which is why it is important to look at your partner, not down towards the floor.

2△ Your partner steps back with his right foot, preparing to strike your solar plexus region. Note the low front posture (*zenkutsu dachi*).

3◁ You step back with your right leg into the formal *zenkutsu dachi* stance and defend with the middle body block (*chudan soto uke*). This is a block from outside inwards. Apply this defence by starting with your left fist in line with your left ear and, using a circular motion, bring your arm forwards, around and across your body. Make sure you turn your forearm inwards so that it is the muscle part of the arm that makes contact with the incoming blow. At the same time, pull your left shoulder back so that your body turns to the side, thus becoming a smaller target.

4▷ Whether you block with your left or right arm dictates where you punch your opponent. In this case, when you have executed your block, use a downwards motion to push the attacking arm away. A circular action draws the opponent or partner off-centre and exposes his chest area in preparation for your counter-attack, a front-lunge punch (*oi-tsuki*).

5▽ Deliver a strike to your opponent's solar plexus region with your right fist. Remember to maintain a low, strong posture (*zenkutsu dachi*).

Techniques: Elbow Strike and Wrist Take-down

The following is a sequence of moves utilizing *soto uke* block, elbow strike (*empi*) and wrist locks (*kokuto*) to restrain an opponent. It is important to utilize your strengths against the opponent's weakness.

1△ Step back and perform *soto uke* block to the right fist attack from your opponent.

2△ Immediately follow through with an elbow *empi* strike to the hinge of your opponent's jaw.

△ This close-up shows in detail the position of your hands and fingers on your opponent's hand.

3△ Bring your right hand back to your opponent's right wrist in preparation to apply a wrist turn and lock.

4△ Rotate your opponent's wrist by turning the hand outwards so that the palm faces upwards. Secure your thumbs on the back of his hand, with your fingers wrapped around his wrist.

5△ Maintain the lock and keep the momentum going as you start to push the hand downwards, forcing your opponent to submit.

6△ Continue to push downwards so that your partner will be restrained on the floor.

7△ As your opponent reaches the floor, bring your left leg forwards and over his right arm. Aim to turn your body 180 degrees and apply pressure on his elbow joint as your body moves over his right arm.

8△ The follow-on advanced technique is an arm lock. Bring your right leg over and across your opponent's arm and turn around so that you are facing in the opposite direction. Slowly lower your body so as to apply pressure on his elbow joint and form an arm lock. This advanced technique should be practised with qualified supervision, slowly and with caution.

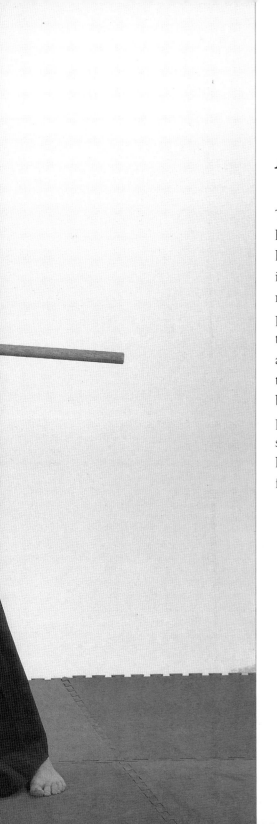

Aikido

The art of aikido teaches one to
harmonize completely with any attack,
leading an aggressor to a point of
imbalance, and then applying a
neutralizing technique. Some
practitioners believe that it is possible
to study aikido as a spiritual discipline
alone, whereby students learn to unite
their spiritual energy with the universe to
become "one with nature". It is equally
possible to study aikido as a dynamic
system of combat. For most individuals,
however, the reality of aikido training
falls between these two positions.

History and Philosophy

Aikido focuses on absorbing and redirecting the force of an attack, rather than opposing it head on. The movements use little physical energy but require great skill and foresight, and when performed successfully they protect both the victim and the attacker.

Aikido in its present form is a relatively recent innovation within the martial arts tradition, and was developed in Japan in the early 20th century by Morihei Ueshiba (1883–1969), who was introduced to the classical martial arts as a boy by his father, Yoroku. He is known to have studied some martial arts, such as various styles of ju-jitsu as well as kenjutsu and the art of the spear. In 1912 Morihei moved to Hokkaido, where a chance meeting with a man called Sokaku Takeda changed his life.

Below In aikido the force of an attack is redirected with the intent of causing as little physical harm as possible.

Takeda was a master of *daito ryu-aiki ju-jutsu*, a martial art that had originated in the 6th century AD and had been passed down through the military hierarchy and formalized by members of the Aizu clan, becoming known as the *Oshikiuchi*, or "striking arts". The young Ueshiba quickly became drawn to the fierce demeanour of this little man, and studied under Takeda until 1919. On returning to his native Tanabe on the death of his father, Morihei met Onisaburo Deguchi – the charismatic founder of an esoteric religion called *Omoto-Kyo* – and spent the next six years as his disciple, travelling throughout Asia.

In 1927, Morihei set up the Kobukan dojo in Tokyo and began teaching an amalgam of the martial traditions he had learned from Takeda, together with the spiritual beliefs he had gleaned from Deguchi. This new discipline he called *Ueshiba aiko-budo*. Morihei finally settled on the name of aikido. This word is a combination of three concepts: *ai* meaning "harmony"; *ki* meaning "spirit"; and *do* meaning "way". In the spiritual sense, this means harmonizing your individual spirit, or ki, with the spirit of Nature itself. In the dojo, this means that you harmonize with an attack, lead it to a point of exhaustion and then neutralize it with a throw, a joint lock, or an immobilization.

As with many other martial arts, aikido is seen not only as a system of self-defence, but also as a means of self-cultivation and improvement. Today there are various systems of aikido, but traditional aikido has no tournaments, competitions or contests. Physical strength is not a prerequisite, so age is no impediment. According to Morihei Ueshiba, the goal of aikido is not the defeat of others, but the defeat of the negative characteristics that inhabit one's own mind and inhibit its effective functioning.

WHAT IS AIKIDO?

If you look at the classic Chinese *yin* and *yang* icon, you see a symbol explaining that all phenomena are governed by antagonistic, yet complementary opposites, forming the two halves of the whole. You will also observe that the two halves are not entirely opposite, however, since they have elements of each other within them – the black dot in the white half and white dot in the black half – and this esoteric symbolism is designed to suggest that all of life and nature is in a perpetual state of flux.

Above The antagonistic yet complementary opposites of the Chinese *yin* and *yang* icon underly the philosophy behind aikido.

If you are attacked by a force (*yang*) and you apply force yourself (*yang*), a collision of energies ensues which results in disharmony, and accordingly the strongest force wins. If, however, you meet that force with an absorbing movement (*yin*) and then exhaust it to the point of imbalance before applying a force of your own (the aikido way), you are, in effect, restoring harmony or redressing an imbalance. This is the basic logic and underlying philosophy of aikido.

Aikido is a discipline that seeks not to meet violence with violence, but instead looks towards harmonizing with and restraining an opponent. Aikido is, in many ways, unique among the martial arts, in that the majority of techniques are based on the aggressor making the first move. Therefore, aikido techniques are usually aimed at joint immobilization, and throws which utilize an opponent's energy, momentum and aggression. Many body movements have been taken from Japanese sword and spear fighting arts, and the use of the *bokken* (a replica sword) and *jo* (a stick) is intended to develop the practitioner's understanding and skill.

Aikido teaches one-on-one and multiple-attack defence. It incorporates knife-taking, sword- and stick-taking, and even defence from a kneeling position. Differences in size, weight, strength or age are negated, as you learn to use your inner *ki* (flow of energy). Weapon training with a *bokken* and *jo* indicates the ancestry of the discipline as well as helping to improve your body movements. Most of these techniques are covered in this book.

It should be emphasized that aikido is a *budo* – literally a "martial way". You practise each technique with total commitment, as if your life depended on its success, for only in this way is it possible to bring about the true spirit of *budo*. This is not to say that training has to be hard or violent: it is possible to be physically soft and still generate the power to control a confrontational encounter.

TRAINING

By training cooperatively with a partner, you can practise even potentially lethal techniques without risk, but professional supervision and safe practice are always required for students to avoid injury. Mutual respect and the careful consideration of what you are learning, together with its consequences,

must always be your main concern. There are no shortcuts or easy paths to ability in aikido. Attaining proficiency is simply a matter of sustained and dedicated training, just as it is in many of the martial arts disciplines. Nobody becomes an expert in a few months.

While there are different styles of aikido – such as *tomiki*, or sport aikido, in which rubber knives are used and practitioners compete to score points – the founder, Morihei Ueshiba, was firmly opposed to competition in any form.

STYLES OF AIKIDO

In reality, there are several major styles of aikido today. As Ueshiba was continually refining and modifying the art he had created, some of his students at various stages left to pursue their own ideals. Thus, Master Gozo Shioda created the *yoshinkan* style, characterized by short, sharp movements and powerful joint applications; Kenji Tomiki created sport aikido, as it is widely known, characterized by competitions in which rubber knives are used; Minoru Mochizuki successfully amalgamated aikido with other martial arts within the International Martial Arts Federation; and Koichi Tohei created *shin-shin toitsu* aikido, which concentrates on the *ki* aspect of aikido. All of these men trained with and listened to Ueshiba and yet each came away with a different idea of the discipline.

Left Students demonstrate one of aikido's flowing movements and the flexibility of its practitioners.

Above Demonstrating the dynamics of aikido in action, showing *gyaku* (reverse) *kotegaeshi* (outward wrist twist).

THE GRADING SYSTEM

The grading in aikido consists of *kyu* (student) grades, 6th to 1st, after which students become eligible for a 1st-*dan* (1st-degree black belt), and then 2nd-*dan*, 3rd-*dan* and so on. These gradings are based on a national grading syllabus and are spaced apart according to the dictate of the clubs' governing association.

There are no coloured belts in traditional aikido, except for children. This is in accordance with directives from the *hombu* (headquarters) in Japan. Because there are no weight or strength divisions, it is possible for men, women and children to train together, although certain techniques are eliminated from children's practice for safety reasons.

As a first step, students learn how to fall properly and how to absorb the effects of the various techniques, so that they can be performed with total commitment. Next come the freestanding solo body movements, where students learn about shifting weight, balance and similar aspects of the discipline. Finally, the techniques themselves are taught, and the degree of difficulty is dependent on each individual's own progress.

THE PURPOSE OF AIKIDO

People learn aikido for a variety of reasons: as a way of becoming physically fit, as self-defence, or to understand something of Japanese culture. It is up to each individual to

decide upon which facet of the discipline to concentrate. In addition to the development of strength, stamina and suppleness, students learn to tap their internal powers to generate an energy that is far greater than muscular power alone, and to use it at will. Students may also find mental stimulation in knowing that they are practising movements dating back to Japan's feudal past.

Breathing techniques are learned to promote mind and body coordination. Students also come into contact with other Japanese practices, such as shiatsu (finger therapy), a form of total body massage, and iaido (Japanese sword drawing). Both of these disciplines are complementary to the study of aikido and are occasionally taught in tandem.

Benefits of aikido

Aikido offers many benefits to enhance health and well-being including:

- Enhances strength, stamina and suppleness
- Promotes a good mental attitude and discipline
- Promotes defensive moves as opposed to aggression
- Increases your awareness of danger
- Increases body reflexes
- Promotes a calmness of mind
- Develops internal energy and power

Clothing and Equipment

Unlike many other martial arts, students of aikido do not wear coloured belts to signify their rank, unless they are children. Instead a black pleated skirt (*hakama*) is worn by practitioners who have attained their 1st-dan, the equivalent of a black belt examination.

In accordance with directives from *hombu* (headquarters) in Japan, adult students do not wear coloured belts, although the *kyu* (student) grading system still applies. It is acceptable for children to wear coloured belts and the student system starts at 6th-*kyu*, which requires the wearing of a white belt with one red stripe. Children then progress through a number of coloured stripes and belts until they reach 1st-*kyu*, which is the final *kyu* grade before they are ready to take their black belt (lst-*dan*).

When students pass the examination for their 1st-dan (shodan), they are entitled to wear a *hakama* (a divided/pleated skirt). This is considered an honour and the grade is recorded at *hombu*. Students also receive a membership card, an international *yudansha* (*dan*-grade) record book and a certificate signed by the founder's son, Doshu (Kisshomaru Ueshiba).

Students who set an example or who work exceptionally hard for the benefit of the club i.e. administration, may be awarded permission to wear a hakama before they attain dan grade, subject to the senior instructor's discretion.

black *hakama*

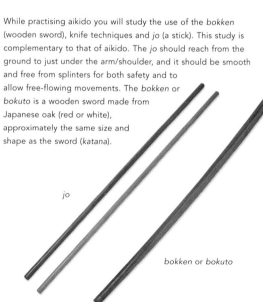

While practising aikido you will study the use of the *bokken* (wooden sword), knife techniques and *jo* (a stick). This study is complementary to that of aikido. The *jo* should reach from the ground to just under the arm/shoulder, and it should be smooth and free from splinters for both safety and to allow free-flowing movements. The *bokken* or *bokuto* is a wooden sword made from Japanese oak (red or white), approximately the same size and shape as the sword (*katana*).

jo

bokken or *bokuto*

Left An aikido student smartly dressed with *hakama* tied correctly, prior to commencement of training.

Aikido has strict codes of discipline and etiquette. These are necessary to ensure that the original spirit and attitude towards the art are maintained, with respect for the dojo and each other being observed at all times.

Respecting the founder – In most traditional aikido dojos, it is very important to have a picture of the founder, Morihei Ueshiba. This may be positioned on the dojo floor, or on a table or wall, but it should be positioned centrally at the front of the dojo, or *kamiza* (meaning "seat of the Gods").

1△ Kneel facing the picture of Morihei Ueshiba. Make sure your back is straight, feet are together and you are sitting on your heels. Place the big toe of your right foot over the big toe of your left. Stay relaxed.

2△ Place your left hand in front of your body, with your fingers pushed together and your thumb forward, so that when the right hand meets the left they form a triangle.

3△ Bow deeply towards the *kamiza*. Make sure that your back is straight, and do not let your head touch the floor.

Bowing to a partner – Demonstrating respect prior to practising with a partner.

1△ When practising with a partner, the same form is followed. Sit opposite your partner, ensuring that there is a reasonable distance between you (usually an arm and a half). The bow (*rei*) is performed again, to show respect towards your partner. This seated bow is called *zarei*.

2△ Using the same hand and body positions as those in the bow (*rei*) to the *kamiza*, perform the bow towards your partner. Both partners bow simultaneously to show mutual respect.

The bow

Why, when and how to bow are natural questions raised by anyone taking up aikido. Most practitioners very quickly come to understand and enjoy the ritualized etiquette as an important part of their training process.

Correct etiquette is an expression of respect and courtesy to those with whom you are training. On entering the *dojo* (training room), perform a standing *rei* (bow) to the *kamiza*

(designated area of respect). Once you have asked, and been given permission to enter on to the *tatami* (mat) by the highest grade holder, perform a further standing *rei*. Practitioners then line up in a kneeling position, facing the *kamiza* in grade order: *kohei* (beginners) to the left of *sempai* (seniors), with the most senior on the right side of the dojo. You then wait until the class instructor comes on to the mat.

Warm-up Exercises: General

Aikido uses certain exercises to prepare the body for training and to ensure that muscles and tendons are warmed to avoid injury during practice. The following are a selection that relate specifically to aikido.

Warm-up 1 – This exercise is performed to make the body more supple and relaxed. This is achieved by gently tapping against the skin, which relaxes muscles and encourages blood to come to the surface.

Warm-up 2 – After relaxing the body as in warm-up 1, you are ready to engage in stretching exercises. The following exercises continue to enhance blood circulation, while stretching the upper body.

△ Place your right arm across your upper chest area and your left hand on your right elbow. Push your right arm as far around your body as you comfortably can, and half close your right fist. Starting at the back of the neck area, tap your body, working your way across the shoulder and down the arm.

△ With feet astride, drop the top half of your body forwards and swing your arms to either side. Keep your arms straight and look towards the arm that is moving in an upwards direction. This ensures that you fully stretch your body, in particular the waist, hips and arms.

Warm-up 3 – Inner thigh and hip exercise.

△ With your feet shoulder-width apart, lower your body, spreading your feet so that they face outwards. Place your elbows inside your knees with hands open and palms facing outwards. Gently push outwards to stretch your inner thighs. Repeat several times, trying to push a little further each time.

2△ Push your hands forwards and open them in preparation to bringing them around in a circular motion.

Warm-up 4 – Yoga type stretch and *tanden* exercise.

1△ With your legs astride, as far apart as you can comfortably manage, lower your body, elbows together and fists clenched, cushioning your forehead. It is very important to ensure that you have your elbows together, since this helps to stretch your upper body.

3△ As you push your hands forwards, have a feeling of using your stomach area (centre of gravity). Bring your hands back into the centre position. Repeat this entire sequence 3 to 4 times.

Warm-up Exercises: Neck Loosening

Everyday stresses can cause tension in the back of the neck. Tension can be relieved through the application of appropriate exercises. The following technique to enhances blood flow and stimulates muscles and tendons in the back of the neck.

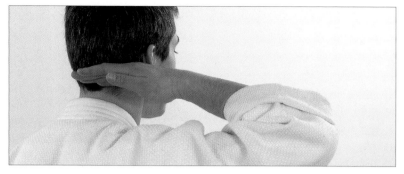

◁ Place your right hand at the back of your neck, palm downwards and fingers pushed together. With the knife edge side of your hand, use a gentle "chopping" action, then gradually work up from the lower neck to the base of the skull, and then back down to the base. Repeat this exercise with your left hand on the opposite side of your neck.

Warm-up Exercises: Kneeling Practice

Kneeling techniques (*suwariwaza*) date back to the days of the samurai. Their purpose is to teach economy of movement and to make you aware of your *tanden* (centre) and hips. The techniques promote flexibility in the lower limbs.

1△ Go down into a kneeling position with your left knee raised and your right knee lowered towards the floor. You should be on the balls of your feet with your heels close together. Keep your body upright with your hands forward as a defensive guard. Make sure you are looking forwards, not at the floor or around the dojo.

2△ Move forwards by placing the left knee down on to the floor and swivelling on it as you bring your right knee forwards. Swivel your knee and hips together to move forwards. This exercise is useful as a means of helping to develop the lower part of your body and is known as "walking on your knees" (*shikko*).

Warm-up Exercises: Wrist Flexibility

Many aikido techniques apply pressure to the wrist, elbow and shoulder joints, and wrist exercises play an important part in the warm-up. The exercises follow a prescribed technique, each one preparing the practitioner for the relevant method.

Exercise 1 – This exercise, known as *kote gaeshi* ("wrist-out turn"), enhances the flexibility of your hands and wrists.

Exercise 2 – Preparation for *sankyo* wrist techniques. *Sankyo* is a painful, but very effective wrist restraint.

△ Take hold of your left hand with your right hand. Push downwards and inwards in a twisting motion, pulling inwards towards your sternum. Ensure that your forearms are horizontal. Repeat this exercise 2 or 3 times.

1△ Turn your left hand slightly inwards with your fingertips pointing towards your abdomen. Prepare for the grip, using your right hand to turn your left hand inwards so that your knuckles are facing towards your chest.

2△ Twist and turn your wrist to the left side to rotate the lower arm and wrist. Release and repeat the exercise with the right hand. Your hand needs to be well drawn in and move in an inward, circular motion, to apply pressure on the ligaments in your forearm.

Exercise 3 – This exercise is used in preparation for the technique called *shiho nage* or four-direction throw.

Exercise 4 – A preparation for the *nikkyo* or "wrist-in turn" technique.

1△ Take hold of your left hand at the centre of your body, with the palm of your right hand on top of the back of your left, fingers facing upwards. Keep your hands close to your chest and your elbows down with your arms tucked in close to your body. The elbow forms the fulcrum of this exercise.

2△ Using a rotating action towards the outer part of your body, start to turn your fingertips in a downwards, circular motion. Then rotate your wrist about your elbow. Apply gentle pressure on the left hand to stretch the forearms, elbows and wrists. Repeat this exercise 2 to 3 times each side.

3△ Cover the back of your left hand with your right hand. Pull in towards the solar plexus area. This exercise assists in loosening and strengthening the wrist area.

Warm-up Exercises: Spiritual Development

Aikido develops your spiritual side in order to promote inner calm. The following exercises seek to bring together the qualities of correct breathing, known as *kokkyo* (breath power), as part of the spiritual development of aikido.

Rowing exercise – *torifune* – Think of this rowing exercise as a way of "rowing" from this world to the next. The exercise starts slowly but, towards the end of the session, the tempo is increased. It is used as a centring technique to instill good body posture and to increase the awareness of your own centre of gravity.

1△ Stand in the upright posture known as *migi hanmi* – right foot forward. *Migi* is Japanese for "right" and *hanmi* means "posture". Lean forwards and feel a sense of pressure from the hips. Fully extend your hands and start a rowing action, as if in a boat with oars.

2△ Pull back your fists to your hips, with your elbows tucked in, and most of your weight on your rear leg. Repeat several times and then change leg positions. Breathing is important in this exercise – exhale on the forward movement using the sound of "*hei*", and as you move back, inhale, then exhale, using a low "*ho*" sound.

Calming exercise – *furitama* – This exercise is designed to bring an overall feeling of calmness to the body.

1△ Stand in a relaxed position with your feet a shoulder-width apart. Extend your arms at the sides, palms upwards, fingers open. Keep your eyes closed to maintain a feeling of calm.

2△ Bring your hands together, palms touching, above your head, with your fingers pointing upwards.

3△ Bring your hands down in front of your lower abdomen. Clasp your hands together, using a shaking motion, as if vibrating a heavy ball. This helps to disperse the energy you have throughout your body.

Warm-up Exercises: Breathing

Correct breathing oxygenates the blood and also stimulates internal organs.
In order to generate *kokkyo* (breath power), it is necessary to breathe deeply,
with the emphasis on abdominal expansion and contraction.

2△ As you slowly bend at the waist to lower your body, with your arms still stretched, begin to gently exhale.

1△ Stretch your body, arms above your head, with your palms facing upwards. As you perform this exercise, breathe in through your nose, imagining the breath going up to the top of your head, down the spine and into the centre of your abdomen.

3△ Try to touch your knees with your forehead by clasping the back of your ankles to pull your body inwards. At the same time, exhale fully. As you return to the original standing position, inhale then exhale as you remain standing. Repeat this exercise several times.

Warm-up Exercises: Back-stretching

Traditional aikido places great emphasis on having a supple spine. The following exercises focus primarily on back-stretching and have benefits for the whole body in terms of flexibility and fitness.

Exercise 1 – *Sotai-dosa* (paired practice) back-stretching exercise.

Caution
These techniques require close supervision by a qualified instructor. It is best to practise with a partner of similar build, since you should be able to lift safely a person of around your own weight without risking injury.

1△ With feet shoulder-width apart, step forward into a natural right foot posture. As your partner takes hold of your wrists, extend your fingers and imagine you have a sword in your hands.

2△ Using a circular motion, bring your right foot forwards and upwards, approximately 45 degrees in front of your partner. Twist your body 180 degrees with the feeling that you are now cutting with the sword as you turn to the rear. You will then be back-to-back with your partner.

3△ Keep turning your body as if you are cutting with your sword across your partner's throat. Hold your partner in this position for 5–6 seconds and then change roles, before repeating the exercise to the opposite side.

△ Your partner at this point should have a very arched back and be gripping hold of your arm for support, as you can see above, in this alternative view of the position that is described in step 3.

Exercise 2 – *Ganseki otoshi* (head over heels throw). An effective defence used as a back-stretching exercise.

1△ Your partner moves in with an overhead strike to the top of your head. Come in to meet the strike with your right forearm. In this exercise, this is purely a defensive move, although the defender treats the strike as a committed attack.

2△ With your right foot forward, bring your left foot around and pivot on the ball of your right foot so that you are behind your partner. Maintain arm contact as you prepare for the next stage.

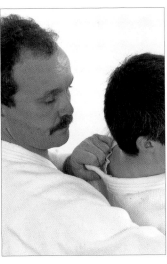

3△ Take hold of your partner's collar at the back of the neck with your left hand, while pushing your right arm and elbow into the centre of your partner's back in preparation for the lift.

4△ Once you feel secure, with your arm well positioned in the small of your partner's back, drop into a very low posture, keeping your knees well bent. *Note: while this is only an exercise, it must be performed with care and caution at all stages.*

5△ Lift your partner up so that their body is arched and relaxed. The purpose of this exercise is to offer your partner support by using your body to lift and gently bounce as your partner relaxes. Hold for 15–20 seconds, then change sides and repeat once only.

Exercise 3 – *Ushiro ryote* (rear attack, both wrists held). Here, defence techniques are used as a back-stretch.

1△ Your partner approaches from the rear and grabs hold of both of your wrists.

2△ Start to move by bringing your right arm directly above your head to pull your partner off balance.

3△ Turn completely around, moving towards your partner at the same time. You should now be facing your partner, who must still hold on to your wrists in preparation for the back-stretching exercise. It is important to work cooperatively to ensure the success of this exercise.

4△ Your partner's back will now be fully arched. Their body must stay relaxed. You must maintain a good, strong, upright posture in order to support your partner. Note: *maintain this position for no more than 10 seconds, especially when first learning this exercise. Gently allow your partner to move back to an upright position.*

Exercise 4 – Another defence technique that can be used as a warm-up stretch for your partner.

85

AIKIDO: WARM-UP EXERCISES

1◁ Your partner takes hold of both your wrists.

2▷ Start to move in with your right foot, pulling your left foot inwards. At the same time, bring your right arm across your partner's chest, keeping your left arm fully extended and forward.

3◁△ Slowly push your arm downwards and across the area of your partner's neck, as shown in the close-up image above. With the twist of your hips, by following this movement through, you can throw your partner. *Note: do not apply any pressure to the neck. This is an exercise purely to promote suppleness. Hold position for 5–10 seconds and repeat.*

Techniques: Basic Stance and Posture

Aikido adopts the back triangle stance (*ura-sankaku*). This is the only posture from which the *tanden* (centre) can be held effectively when executing a technique, and from where rapid movement in any direction is possible.

1◁ Align the heels of both feet, with your front foot facing forwards and slightly outwards, and your rear foot at an angle of 60 degrees. Bend your knees slightly and place about 60 per cent of your weight on your front leg. Keep your hands in the guard position to protect your body. This stance is known as *hanmi* (half stance).

△ Ideally the heel of your front foot must be in line with the heel of your rear foot, in a triangular shape, like being on a tightrope.

2△ In this overview, the 180 degree turn (*tenkan*) is being demonstrated. This is a continual turning movement to assist in the flowing techniques used in aikido. With your left foot forwards, turn on the ball of the foot and bring the left foot around circularly.

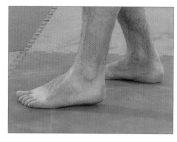

△ Use a pivoting action to bring your left leg around in a circular motion towards the rear. This detailed close-up shows the correct feet position in preparation for the turn.

3◁ After pivoting, you will have turned around 180 degrees and will be facing in the opposite direction, with your right foot forward. Qualified supervision is required to practise.

Learning to defend from a variety of different angles is important. The following demonstrates the use of the wrist technique *sankyo*, during an attack called *yoko menuchi* – a roundhouse strike to the side of the head.

1△ Your partner comes in with a *yoko menuchi* technique, which is similar to a bottle being swung around to the side of the head. You defend yourself against the attack by coming in to meet the technique and deflect it with your left hand, while placing your right hand in front of your partner's face as a distraction.

2△ Using a large circular motion, step through with your left foot as if walking through your partner. Keep the upward circular motion going, and then pull your partner's right hand back with your right hand, ensuring that their palm is facing outwards, while applying pressure on their elbow joint with your left hand.

3◁ Step through with your left leg, into a deep stance. Change the grip by moving your left hand down to take a secure hold of your partner's right hand. Keep your body in close and lean forwards to ensure that your left shoulder is well in to the side of your partner. From here there are a variety of final techniques that can be applied to fully restrain your opponent.

Techniques: *Ikkyo – Suwari-waza*

Ikkyo is the first principle in arm pinning techniques and mastery of it is required to understand subsequent methods and skills. It can be practised from any attack, whether kneeling (*suwari-waza*), as shown here, or standing (*tachi-waza*).

1△ Your partner comes at you with an overhead strike to the top of your head. This is known as *shomen uchi* and can be executed with the open hand or with the use of a weapon such as a knife. Defend by using both hands in an upwards motion to meet the attacking arm. *Note: use minimal aggression – a flowing motion and circular action have more impact than a static movement.*

2△ The twisting and turning action of the movement will help to bring your partner to the floor. This demonstrates the force that can be successfully applied. *Note: it is important that your partner is well experienced in break-falling techniques, to perform the technique as depicted. If not, you must gently position your partner in preparation for the final restraining technique.*

3◁ The final pin is made effective by holding above the elbow and wrist, making sure the arm is slightly higher than the shoulder. Push from the centre of gravity with a twisting action.

Caution

In any technique when your partner is face down on the floor, you must ensure that they always have at least one arm free to tap on the ground if they feel any discomfort, and release them immediately if they do. Otherwise there can be a serious risk of asphyxiation. It is important that your partner only feels enough pressure to restrain them gently but firmly – anything more is dangerous.

Techniques: *Kotegaeshi*

Kotegaeshi (wrist-out turn) is a technique whereby the defender places his hand on the back of the attacker's hand and applies pressure – inwards to break the power in attacking wrist and arm, and outwards to cause the attacker to fall on to their back.

1◁ As your partner moves in with the overhead attack, move in and underneath to meet the attack with your right forearm. Your left arm is to the side and ready to go over your partner's right arm. Start to draw your hands downwards towards your partner's wrist, simultaneously keeping the momentum of the circle going towards you, and prepare to swing your body round to the left side.

2△ Take hold of your partner's right wrist to bring their arm down towards your thighs. This is important, since this is part of a flowing, continuous movement that uses your partner's energy as well as your own.

3◁ Continue the circular movement in the opposite direction. The complete motion is almost like a figure eight, with your partner's fingers being bent back to face downwards.

4◁ Move through with your left knee, keeping a grip on your partner's wrist, while securing pressure on their elbow. As they are about to hit the floor, bring your left knee around and both hands downwards in the same direction, forcing your partner to roll on to their back.

△ A locking technique showing how to immobilize your partner.

Techniques: *Kata Dori*

Kata dori is a self-defence move against an attacker grabbing a shoulder, or clothing, in one hand and striking with the other or kicking. The grasping arm is stretched sideways to take the attacker's balance prior.

1△ Your partner moves in and grabs you by the sleeve.

2△ Bring your right hand across your partner's attacking right arm. Start to move your body forwards with your left foot so that you can start to pull your partner off balance.

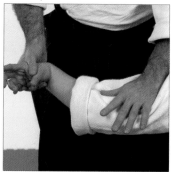

△ To move into step 3, bring your left hand under your partner's right elbow, with your palm open and fingers upright. Bring your right hand under their wrist to apply a large circular forwards and downwards motion so that their right arm is in front of you.

△ To apply this alternative arm lock, place your left hand on your partner's elbow and your right hand on her wrist. Next, with your right hand, twist your partner's right hand so the fingers point away from you. Maintain pressure on the elbow joint.

△ A wrist technique such as *sankyo* can also be applied as an alternative manoeuvre. Pull your partner's left arm backwards and inward. This will cause the ligaments and nerves to twist.

3△ Continue to step forwards to completely take your partner off balance and slide your left arm down towards her right thumb. This is in preparation to secure a wrist lock.

4△ Apply a wrist lock by placing your left hand on the elbow joint to secure the restraint.

5△ Maintain the wrist lock by taking hold of your partner's hand. Make sure their fingers are facing upwards.

6△ Using a circular motion, bring your partner's right hand upwards, with her fingers pointing towards your face. This technique will cause discomfort and she may well come up on to her toes to release the pressure. This demonstrates that the technique has been correctly applied. Do not continue to apply pressure and release the hold as soon as possible.

Techniques: Rear Defence

Aikido incorporates defence from any attack. Attacks from the rear are called *ushiro waza* (rear techniques). The following is an example of *ushiro katate dori kubeshime* (rear strangle with one hand held).

2△ Step back with your left leg, going underneath the attack. Project your energy forwards to take your attacker off balance. From this position a variety of techniques can be applied, as in step 3 below.

1△ You are grabbed from behind, around the throat, by your partner's right arm, and your left wrist is held by their left hand.

3△ In this case, apply a wrist lock to restrain your partner. Place your left hand on top of her left hand and your right hand on her wrist. Pull her hand to your chest and twist her fingers outwards, towards your right side. This will cause the ligaments and nerves to twist.

Techniques: Front Defence

The following demonstrates a defence against a two-handed strangle known as *udehishige* (arm smashing). This technique is one of the few transmitted from *daito-ryu-ju-jutsu* that has not been changed from its original form.

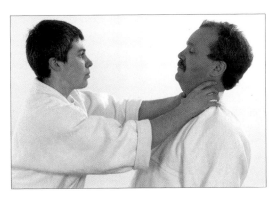

1△ You are grabbed by your partner around the throat from the front. Ideally, you need to start your defensive action before they get a good hold, but if this is not possible there are various techniques taught in aikido to defeat the attack.

2▷ Practise this technique with the aim of taking hold of your partner's right wrist before contact is made or contact is still loose.

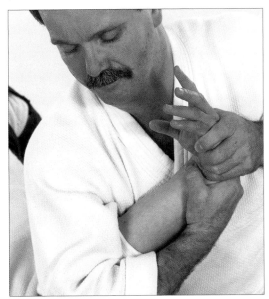

3△ Once you have grabbed your partner, bring your right arm over her arm, at the same time grabbing her right hand with your left hand and, simultaneously, twisting your body forwards to execute a lock on her arm, wrist and hand. The tips of your partner's fingers need to be pointing backwards.

4△ Twist your body around as far as you can away from your partner. Keep the lock close to your body, however. This will ensure an effective restraint or, alternatively, you can release your partner, projecting her forwards as part of a take down technique. Once the armlock is in place, apply pressure by twisting your hips to the right.

Techniques: Women's Self-defence

While this is referred to as "women's self-defence", the same techniques are also used by men and children. These techniques mean that regardless of the size of the aggressor, your body weight can be used to maximize your advantage.

Shiho nage – Four-direction throw – once the elbow is controlled it is possible to throw an attacker forwards, backwards or to either side.

1△ The attacker pins the arms to the sides from behind, affecting a hug. Step forwards and extend your arms outwards in order to avoid encirclement.

2△ Extend your arms outwards with your right arm moving upwards and left arm moving downwards. With your left hand take hold of your partner's left wrist.

3△ Maintain the circular momentum as you step back and throw your partner forwards. Keep your body calm and extend your energy as you move through and throw.

Irimi nage – This technique means "entering body throw".

1△ An aggressor tries to deliver a punch to your chest or stomach. Side-step to your left with your left foot to avoid it and deflect the aggressor's right-handed punch. Once you have avoided the attack, bring your right hand up and across in a large circular action as you step through with your right foot. Simultaneously, bring your right arm under the aggressor's jaw line in preparation for a throw.

2△ Moving through, well into the aggressor's space, and breaking his posture, will cause him to lose balance and succumb to your technique. This requires minimal force but needs calmness, a flowing action, good timing and continuous movement.

The category for knife defences is known as *tanto* or *tanken dori*. The aikido principle
is to evade the attack and use the aggressor's force against them. The knife is kept at
a distance and the aggressor's energy used to work in your favour.

Caution

When learning defences against a
weapon attack it is vital to have
qualified supervision and to practise
in a safe environment. Never practise
with a real weapon when you are
learning, especially in the early
stages. Wooden or plastic knives are
ideal, but you still need to treat them
with respect – any item can be
dangerous if it is used incorrectly.

1▷ As the aggressor comes in with a right-
handed knife attack to your stomach, move
to your left and block the strike with the
outside edge of your hand (if the attacker is
left-handed, it would be better to move to
your right). Bring your left foot forwards
into *irimi tenkan*, which is a 180-degree
turn, where you move in towards your
opponent, turning your body. The circular
action and the physical movement will
bring your opponent with you. You are
turning outside your opponent's attacking
energy, which is the principle of *tenkan*.

2△ Seize the attacker's wrist with your left hand and take hold of
his sleeve with your right hand. Move forwards with your left foot,
pivoting on its ball, turn, and bring your right foot around in a half-
circle movement. Bring your left foot across, into an L-shaped
position, and then step through with your right foot. This move can
vary, depending on where you wish to manoeuvre your opponent.

3△ Twist underneath the attacking arm and into a large circular
movement, using your hands to take the aggressor off balance.
As the aggressor enters into your movement, he is spun around –
an action used for many of the dynamic throws employed in aikido.
The force of the fall should ensure that he drops the knife. If the
attacker still has the knife, apply further restraint to remove it.

Techniques: *Nage Waga* – Throwing Technique

The following shows one of the throwing techniques found in aikido, called *kaiten-nage*. The defender is learning the mechanics of the movement, as the partner also learns to use their agility to roll out of the throwing technique.

1△ An aggressor comes in with a punch to your solar plexus. You side-step and block with your right arm, bringing your left hand across to the back of the aggressor's neck. This technique is called *kaiten-nage*, which means "spin throw".

2△ Next, pull the aggressor's head down towards the floor with your left hand, while simultaneously pushing the aggressor's left arm upwards with your right hand. *Note: keep an upright, well-centred posture.*

Caution
As with all advanced techniques, especially throwing, it is important for both partners to be experienced in break-falling before attempting any of these techniques.

3◁ Finally, apply a throwing technique by pushing the aggressor's left arm forwards.

Techniques: Advanced Weapon Techniques

The following are some of the moves and techniques practised when using weapons. Various *kata* (sequences) are taught to develop skills in the use of weapons, and also to give an understanding of posture and timing.

1△ As the attacker thrusts with a *bokken*, the defender comes up underneath with their *bokken* to block the oncoming attack, prior to cutting the aggressor.

2△ The defender brings the *bokken* around his head and strikes the aggressor on the side of the neck.

3◁ Demostrating using the *jo*, a technique called *otoshi tsuki* (meaning "drop thrust").

Cool-down Exercises

Aikido practitioners believe it is important to cool down at the end of a session. One partner takes the other on to their back and gently extends upwards and outwards – the idea being to relax worked muscles and stretch the spine.

Cool-down 1 – *Haishin undo* **(back stretching).**

1△ Your partner takes hold of both your wrists.

2△ Turn underneath and completely around, while your partner maintains a hold on your wrists, so that you are now back to back.

3◁ Drop your body down and place your buttocks well under your partner's buttocks in preparation for the lift. Lift your partner up and across your back, stretching your arms forwards. It is important that your partner totally relaxes while you gently stretch forward to loosen their spine.

Caution

This exercise puts pressure on the back and must not be performed if either practitioner has any history of back problems. If in doubt, be sure to consult a doctor before commencing the exercise.

Cool-down 2 – A technique unique to aikido is to use the *bokken* in cool-down exercises.

1△ A similar cool-down technique uses the *bokken*. Stand facing each other in the standard *hanmi* posture. Your partner takes hold of your right wrist with both hands.

2△ Turn to the side with your right foot and pivot completely around on your left foot in an anticlockwise (counterclockwise) direction by bringing your right leg to the rear. At the same time, raise the *bokken* as if to start to cut.

3◁ Continue the turn so that you are now facing the opposite direction and bring the *bokken* above your head as you turn. This will lift your partner and bring her across your back. Hold for 15 to 20 seconds and change sides. Perform this exercise slowly and carefully.

Ju-jitsu

Ju-jitsu is an effective self-defence system used extensively by the military and police forces around the world. Special features of the art include defences against knife attacks and immobilizing techniques. Another unique skill taught to highly qualified practitioners is the art of resuscitation. This technique, known as *kuatsu*, was developed on the battlefield where, following the delivery of a non-fatal ju-jitsu technique, rather than deliver a final killing blow, a Japanese samurai would revive the injured enemy for questioning.

History and Philosophy

Ju-jitsu practitioners follow strict moral and dietary regimes, in an attempt to attain a state as close to physical and mental perfection as possible. Their aim is to overcome the opponent by using minimal physical force, but ju-jitsu is still a very dynamic art.

The art of ju-jitsu is interpreted as being the "science of softness". Translated literally, *ju* means "gentle" or "soft" and *jitsu* means "art". While referred to as "a gentle art" some of the techniques are, nevertheless, extremely dynamic in their delivery and would appear to be anything but soft.

There are many stories regarding the origins of ju-jitsu, dating as far back as the 8th century, with historical lines indicating roots even before the time of Christ. While some people claim that ju-jitsu originated in China, the ancient chronicles of Japan

Below A few practitioners of ju-jitsu choose to keep alive the warrior spirit of the fighting techniques.

Above Despite its ethos of minimal force, some forms of ju-jitsu can be extremely dynamic.

describe how, in AD712, Tatemi Kazuchi threw Tatemi Nokami, like "throwing a leaf". Reference is also made in the Nihon Sho-ki chronicles to the Emperor Shuinjin holding a martial arts tournament to celebrate the seventh year of his reign in 23BC. One of the bouts resulted in the death of a participant, a sumo wrestler, who was thrown to the ground and kicked by Nomino Sukume. These accounts provide evidence of early "empty-hand" techniques in Japan. There is also reference to ju-jitsu developing as an art from the work of a Buddhist monk, dating back to the 13th century. These ancient techniques were known as *kumi-tachi* (or *yawara*), which is described in the *Konjaku-monogatari*, a Buddhist work dating back to that time.

Above The samurai (also known as *bushi*), wearing colourful and elaborate armour.

Another reference to a form of combat that shows some similarity to ju-jitsu is found in the 15th-century martial arts tradition known as the *katori-shinto ryu*. It is widely believed, however, that true ju-jitsu was brought to Japan by a Chinese monk called Chen Yuanein (1587–1671). So, although ju-jitsu is commonly viewed today as a Japanese martial art, there is strong evidence pointing to Chinese origins.

While ju-jitsu was first practised in Japan by the samurai, followed by the ninja, it inevitably spread further afield and was, sadly, embraced by many of the bandits of the time. Through this dubious association, ju-jitsu earned a poor reputation. It was during this time that Jiguro Kano developed the art of judo, meaning "the gentle way", from a combination of ju-jitsu techniques. His aim was to correct the reputation ju-jitsu had acquired as a deadly art through its connections with banditry.

Above Ju-jitsu followers conform to a strict discipline – both mentally and physically.

Right The essence of ju-jitsu is the power of resistance and effective timing.

WHAT IS JU-JITSU?

The central philosophy behind ju-jitsu is to conquer an opponent by any and all means – as long as minimal force only is used. Consequently, this precept demands from its followers a strict conformity to various disciplines – both mental and physical.

Physical fitness has always been a fundamental prerequisite for practitioners of ju-jitsu. A characteristic of this art is that it involves strict moral and dietary regimes, which are seen as being necessary if one is to reach the highest level of perfection. It is therefore not surprising that, historically, many ju-jitsu masters withdrew to religious institutions, such as Buddhist or Shinto shrines.

Although the fundamental principle behind modern ju-jitsu as a self-defence art is to conquer an opponent using minimal force, the older art of ju-jitsu focused on literally annihilating the enemy, which led to the development of many dangerous and fatal techniques.

WARRIOR TRADITIONS

The samurai followed a strict code of discipline called the *bushido* – the "way of the warrior". This code included such concepts as loyalty, duty, obedience, honour and respect. The code influenced not just their behaviour in battle, but extended to every element of the way they lived their lives. This absolute conviction and belief in the importance of your

actions would become the basis of the Zen Buddhist philosophy – reaching for salvation within, rather than turning to a monument or god. The samurai believed that man could influence his own destiny, especially when faced with warfare and possible death – a concept which certainly appealed to them. The samurai's path was not completely preordained, but paved by the samuarai himself, his actions affected his destiny.

The traditional art of ju-jitsu is still carried on today by a minority of practitioners, who wish to keep alive the warrior spirit of the deadly fighting techniques of the art. They do not enter competitions and their only goal is to ensure the continuation of the mental, spiritual and physical purity of the art of ju-jitsu.

Benefits of ju-jitsu

The principal benefits that derive from studying the art of ju-jitsu include:

- Enhanced fitness and flexibility
- Increased confidence and well-being
- Self-defence skills
- Greater assertiveness and awareness
- Stress reduction
- Comradeship with fellow practitioners
- Self-discipline and a positive attitude

Like students of many martial arts, those starting out in ju-jitsu wear a white suit with a coloured belt to signify their grading. More advanced practitioners wear black to signify their seniority and will be adept at using the many defensive weapons of the art.

In ju-jitsu students generally wear a white suit (*gi*) and a red belt. This depicts their beginner status. They will then follow the grade system, changing belt colours as they achieve each grade detailed below. When students attain their first black belt grade (1st-*dan* – *shodan*) their clothing is changed to a black jacket and white trousers, which can become a blue jacket from 4th-*dan*. It is always important to ensure that the suit fits comfortably for safety and practicality. It is also necessary that students and instructors keep their suits in good repair and are always smart in appearance. Personal hygiene is very important, particularly when practising in close proximity with another partner. Practitioners must ensure that their nails are clean and short, that jewellery is removed and hair is tied back where appropriate. This is important, as there are many close proximity techniques in ju-jitsu, and this will avoid unnecessary injury. It is compulsory in this style of ju-jitsu for both men and women to wear groin protection (athletic cup) from the day they begin their training.

zori

gi top

groin protection
(athletic cup)

trousers

red belt

white belt

yellow belt

orange belt

green belt

blue belt

purple belt

brown belt

black/brown belt

black belt

red/white belt

Belt gradings

7th-*kyu*	White (red stripe)
6th-*kyu*	Yellow
5th-*kyu*	Orange
4th-*kyu*	Green
3rd-*kyu*	Blue
2nd-*kyu*	Purple
1st-*kyu*	Brown
Shodan-ho	Black and brown (provisional black)
1st-5th-*dan*	Black
6th-*dan* upwards	Red and white

Equipment

The *hojo jutsu* rope is unique to the art of ju-jitsu. It was originally used by the samurai to detain prisoners of war as part of their duty when they served as feudal police. Today, around the world, the *hojo jutsu* rope is still used by many police and special security forces to detain criminals, prisoners and terrorists. Below is a selection of the weapons used in ju-jitsu. There are many other weapons, such as the *hoko* and *yari* (spears), *naginata* (wooden staff) and *nunchaku* (small rice flail).

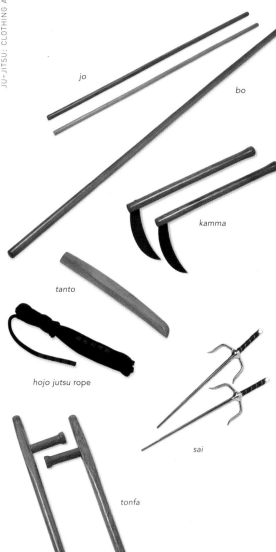

jo

bo

kamma

tanto

hojo jutsu rope

sai

tonfa

Above A *hakama* is also worn in ju-jitsu usually for the specific practice of certain techniques and for demonstrations.

Below With a slipknot and loop, the *hojo jutsu* rope is used mainly as a method of restraint.

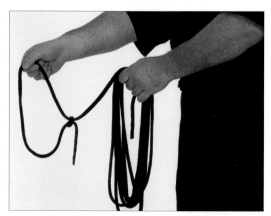

Etiquette

Etiquette is important as a sign of respect to the spirit of the art (*shomen*), instructors, students and to the training environment (*dojo*). The following demonstrates the kneeling bow (*rei*), and the standing bow.

Kneeling *rei* (bow).

1△ Slowly lower yourself down on to your left knee whilst moving both of your hands over towards the left hip. This is designed to represent the holding of a sword as in the day of the traditional Japanese samurai.

2△ Take hold of your trousers with your right hand on your right knee. (This represents the samurai wearing the *hakama*, pleated trousers/skirt.) Bring your right foot back so as not to compromise your stance in the event of an attack.

3△ Bring your right leg back so that you can lower your body to sit on both heels with your feet flat. Position your hands at the top of your thighs and keep your arms and shoulders relaxed. Make sure your knees are no more than two fists apart. Place your hands on the tops of your thighs with your fingers pushed together. Continue to look forwards with your back and shoulders in an upright position, whilst keeping your body relaxed.

Standing *rei* (bow)

▷ Following the kneeling bow, come back into the kneeling position and stand up, stepping forwards with your right foot, then the left. With your heels together and feet at a 45 degree angle, keep your hands flat to your sides in line with the seams of your trousers. From this position, lower the top part of your body from the waist, approximately 30 degrees, and then move back into the starting position. You are now ready to commence your ju-jitsu practice.

4△ Prior to performing the *rei*, there is a more assertive posture in the form of a slight "snap" action. As you start to bow, place your left hand to the front of your body. This depicts protecting the sword, which would be carried on the left side of the body.

5△ Follow through with your right hand, making sure that your fingers and thumb touch to make a diamond shape – this is known as the *kongo zen* diamond. This side view of the bow shows the correct angle of the head, hands and feet.

Warm-up Exercises

It is important to carry out warm-up exercises before ju-jitsu practice.
These usually consist of running around the dojo to loosen up your body and
increase your heart rate, often incorporating other physical moves.

Warm-up 1 – This exercise will loosen your shoulder muscles and joints.

1△ With feet a shoulder-width apart, rotate both your arms in a forwards, circular motion.

2△ Continue the circular action to the rear and then return to the start position. Use a large, circular action at a medium pace only. Repeat this exercise several times and then reverse the action.

3△ With your feet a shoulder-width apart, cross your arms in front of your body by bringing your left arm on top of your right arm.

4△ Push your right arm upwards, as if to touch your left shoulder. This will apply gentle pressure to your elbow joint and increase suppleness. Repeat this movement with your left arm 2 or 3 times.

1△ Stretch out your right hand in front of your body with your palm facing outwards. Keep your fingers tightly closed together and your thumb tucked in.

2△ With your left hand, take hold of the back of your right hand. Ensure your left thumb is placed on top of your right hand. Again, your fingers need to be pushed together.

3△ Pull your right hand in towards your nose or chin area. Maintain pressure with a slight twisting action. Relax and repeat 3 or 4 times. Repeat with the left hand.

Warm-up 3 – A series of exercises designed to loosen up your hips and knees and to stretch your leg muscles.

1△ Standing with your feet a shoulder-width apart, place your hands on your hips and start to rotate them in a clockwise direction. Make sure you keep your feet firmly flat on the ground and that you are working the middle part of your body. This is particularly good for the base of the spine and pelvis.

2△ With your feet together, bend your knees. Put the palms of your hands on top of your knees and push in a circular clockwise motion. Do this several times. Repeat in an anticlockwise (counterclockwise) direction. Perform this movement slowly and gently to increase the suppleness of your knees without causing cartilage problems.

3△ Stretch your left leg out to the side, heel on the floor and with your toes raised, and lower your body towards the right by bending your right knee about 90 degrees. Keep your left leg straight. You will feel a stretching sensation on the hamstrings of your left leg. Repeat this exercise on the opposite side, once only.

4△ Start with feet shoulder-width apart and step forwards. Place your hands on your hips, turn to your right and push forwards with your right knee. Keep your left leg straight with your heel firmly on the floor. Push forwards with your hips to stretch the left leg. Repeat this exercise to the left side once only.

Warm-up 4 – The following exercise will strengthen and condition the feet, making them more supple.

1△ Stand with your feet a shoulder-width apart and turn them outwards, as if rocking on the outside edges of your feet.

2△ Pull your knees inwards and transfer your weight on to the inside edges of your feet in a rolling action.

3△ Straighten your legs and roll your weight forwards, so that you are balancing on the balls of your feet.

4△ Roll your weight backwards so you are balancing on your heels. Keep your arms forward for balance. Repeat 3 or 4 times each side.

Techniques: Blocking

There are various defensive techniques in ju-jitsu that involve blocking, covering the head, upper body and lower body. There are comparable techniques in other martial arts such as karate and tae kwondo.

S block – Swan neck block.

1△ Face your partner with your left hand forward, assuming a guard position.

2△ As your partner moves towards you with a right hook to the head, turn to the left and bring your left arm forwards through the centre of your body the left palm downwards and fingers together. Repeat, reversing roles with your partner.

3△ As you move through with the S block, prepare your right hand, ready to strike your partner.

▷ This close-up of the technique described in step 3 clearly demonstrates the effectiveness of the S block. *Note: blocking will incur contact with your partner, but be sensible with the delivery of your techniques.*

4△ With your right hand palm heel, aim towards your partner's chin, focusing your strike at least 3–5 in (7.5–13 cm) away from the target.

Cross block – Defending the middle to upper part of the body.

113

1△ Move into a formal posture (left-hand fighting stance) with about three-quarters of your weight on your back leg. This enables you to perform a rapid kicking or other defensive technique, if necessary.

2△ As your partner moves towards you with a right-fist strike at your head, step across and block with both of your hands. Ensure that your left hand is in the "open-hand" position.

3△ Grab your partner's right wrist and prepare to inflict a strike. It is important to adopt a strong posture, while you bring your fist across your body, before delivering the strike.

4△ Strike your partner in the floating rib with the side of your right fist (hammer fist). Your fingers should be tightly clenched with your thumb locked over the top of your fingers.

5△ You can now apply an arm lock. Use your right arm to clasp your partner's right arm just above the elbow joint, while using your left hand to secure his wrist.

Techniques: Advanced Shoulder Lock

The following demonstrates a combination of blocking, striking and locking techniques that can be used to restrain an aggressor. This sequence of moves is typical of ju-jitsu, which combines the hard and soft concept.

1◁ Stand opposite your partner in the formal stance position with your fists raised.

2▷ Move into the back stance, with about 75 per cent of your weight on your rear leg, and prepare to block, using a downward circular motion, with the palm of your hand. Your fingers should be straight and locked together, with your thumb bent and locked inside the hand. Your left hand blocks your partner's right arm, striking his inner forearm. Have your right fist ready to make a counter-strike.

3△ Strike at your partner's floating rib with your right fist. Use hip momentum when delivering the strike.

4△ Raise your right arm in a large circular motion to chop into your partner's neck, thus enabling you to eventually roll him down and apply a shoulder lock.

7△ Bring your right arm up in front of your forehead, almost as if you are saluting.

8△ Take hold of your partner's right wrist with your right hand and push his fingers outwards.

5△ To develop this technique to a more advanced stage, apply a restraining technique by moving your left arm under your partner's right arm. Note the posture and bent knees.

6△ Go with the restraint until you lock your partner well into your body. His right arm is now secured against the left side of your neck and both your hands are clasped above his right shoulder. Keep a low posture (horse stance) and keep your partner well secured and close to your body.

9△ Continue to push his fingers and arm away from you. From this particular position you could then keep the momentum going and throw your partner, creating distance and giving you time to escape.

10△ Alternatively, to restrain your partner, bring his right arm across his back in a figure-four arm lock.

Techniques: Advanced Passive Defensive Stance

The purpose of the passive defensive stance is to lull an attacker into a false sense of security. This is an advanced technique requiring qualified supervision. The following is intended as a guide only.

1△ Step back with your left leg into the passive defensive stance. Most of your weight should be on this leg. Bring your hands up level with your partner's eyes, palms facing forwards and fingers splayed. This depicts the body language of a submissive, calming nature. You are trying to communicate "I don't want any trouble".

2△ As your partner moves in and grabs your clothing, take hold of his right wrist with your left hand. Secure your partner's right hand with your left hand. Maintain a good, strong stance.

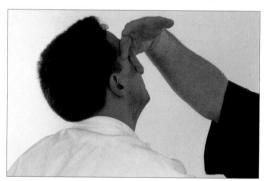

3△ Using your right hand, flick at your partner's eyes to distract him. *Note: this sequence is intended as a guide only, and should only be performed by experienced practitioners.*

◁ This close-up shows the correct position, necessary for the securing hand grip as described in step 4.

4△ Bring your right arm up and over your partner's right arm. Keep his right wrist firmly secured with your left hand.

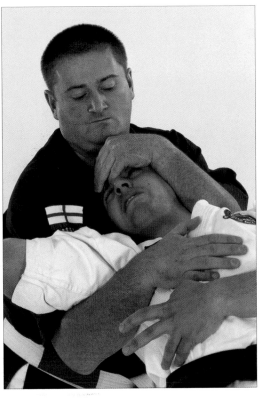

5△ Push through with your right arm under your partner's right elbow, in order to trap his arm.

6△ Place your right hand on your partner's chest, still maintaining the arm lock.

7△ Bring your partner down by twisting his body towards your chest. Keep your right arm on his chest, with the left hand holding his forehead. Keep your partner close to your body in order to maintain control.

8△ In a self-defence situation you may feel it necessary to strike in order to incapacitate an aggressor. One option is to strike with the knife edge of your hand into the groin area.

9△ Alternatively, if you are an experienced practitioner and there is no danger from other quarters, you may wish to restrain an aggressor until assistance arrives.

Techniques: Wrist Defence

This is a defence against a wrist attack, with the aim of countering the aggressor's attack and turning it to your advantage. The combination of hard and soft is shown by the use of wrist control (soft) and striking techniques (hard).

1△ Your partner moves in and grabs your wrists. Maintain your distance and move into a formal posture in preparation to defend yourself.

2△ With an open hand, push downwards and forwards.

3△ Turn your wrist like a corkscrew against your partner's thumb, pushing your right hand straight down. Make sure to keep a deep, low stance for stability.

4△ Bring your hand right back, ready to strike with the back of your hand to the area of your partner's groin.

5△ Strike at your partner's groin area with the back of your right hand.

6△ Take hold of your partner's elbow with your right hand.

7△ Your left hand begins to roll outwards from your partner's grip.

8△ Twist your left hand in an inwards and outwards circular action so that it rotates your wrist and is freed from the grip.

9△ Hold your partner's right arm with your right hand at the elbow. Release your left hand in preparation for a left-hand palm heel strike.

10△ Strike your partner in the face with the heel of your open left hand.

11△ Dependent on the force and angle of the strike, your partner would either fall to the floor or stagger backwards.

Techniques: Elbow Restraint

The following defence could be used against a variety of attacks, such as a push or a grab to the chest. As with all self-defence techniques, you should practise it with your left and right hands.

1△ Your partner moves in to push you in the chest by placing his right hand on the region above your solar plexus. This could also be a grab at your clothing.

2△ Immediately place your right hand across your partner's right hand, pinning it against your body.

3△ Place your hand firmly across your partner's hand to restrain him from grabbing you while you begin to apply the elbow restraint.

4△ Place your left hand behind your partner's elbow while maintaining your grip on his hand. Push in from his elbow towards the centre of your body to apply a wrist lock.

5△ Continue pushing inwards and upwards. This will cause an aggressor extreme pain, as well as lifting him on to his toes and unbalancing him.

Techniques: Defence from Rear Stranglehold

This is one technique which can be applied against a rear stranglehold.
The intention could be to pull you back, so the following demonstrates the use of
the body position to minimize the attack in preparation to strike.

1△ Your partner grabs you around the throat, either to pull you back or to try to strangle you.

2△ Turn into a low horse stance position by jumping half a turn to your right. With your left hand open, defend your head area with a palm heel facing towards your partner. Close the fingers of your right hand to make a fist, in preparation to strike your partner.

3◁ Strike your partner with a hammer fist to his floating rib.

Techniques: Advanced Tactical Search

The following restraint technique is used when you attempt to apprehend an aggressor who is attacking another individual. In view of its complexity, this technique requires qualified supervision and tuition.

1△ As you come up behind the aggressor, grab the back of his clothing at the base of his neck, with your left hand. Keep your distance to avoid being kicked.

2△ You then bring your right hand across the aggressor's throat in order to prevent any further assault.

3△ Place your left hand on the aggressor's forehead to secure a headlock. Note that the aggressor is being pulled backwards in order to upset his balance.

4△ Step back and go down on your left knee, ensuring the head lock is still in place. Jut your right leg out with a 90-degree bend on your knee.

5△ Bring your right leg around the aggressor's right arm and pull it back to secure a further restraint lock.

6△ Kneel to secure the arm lock. Ensure that your body weight is leaning over the opponent for maximum control. Make the arm lock close to the body ensuring that the aggressor cannot manoeuvre his way out of the technique.

7△ Roll the aggressor around on to his front, keeping the head lock as secure as possible. Release your right hand and take hold of the aggressor's left wrist, with your left hand securely on top of his head in the ear and temple region. Lean across the back of the aggressor so that your body weight makes an effective restraint.

8△ Maintain a secure arm lock and place your right hand across the back of the aggressor's neck. Start to manoeuvre your body upwards in preparation for the next part of the restraint.

9△ Bring your left knee across the upper part of the aggressor's body, maintaining the shoulder lock, and push his arm up his back, keeping your body weight slightly forward.

10△ Lift the aggressor's arm up his back to secure the restraint.

11△ Bring the aggressor's left arm across the front of your body, and to your right side, to effect a locking action.

12△ At this point the aggressor is fully restrained and can be searched. A search could be carried out if, for example, you were the armed forces, police or security. Start in the area of his neck, working down his spine and into the rear of his waistband. Then search the inside and outside of his legs and groin and other areas of his body.

Techniques: Knife Defence

There are a variety of knife techniques practised in ju-jitsu. Unless extremely experienced and highly qualified, a dummy knife is always used for safety. Using a dummy knife can enhance the reflexes in the event of a real threat.

Attack to the stomach – Learning to develop body evasion skills against a weapon.

1△ An attacker draws his knife and threatens your stomach.

2△ Breathe in and turn to your side, clasping the aggressor's knife hand close to the flat of your stomach.

3△ Draw your elbow back in to pull the aggressor off balance and to keep him close in to you.

4△ Strike to the aggressor's face, or any other part of his body that is accessible and vulnerable. This will disorientate the aggressor.

5△ Now take a firm double-handed grip on the aggressor's knife hand and prepare to sweep through with your left leg.

6△ As you sweep your left leg around, moving in towards the aggressor, keep the knife well away from your body. This is a flowing movement which prepares you to takedown and restrain the aggressor.

7△ After the aggressor is on the floor, make sure that the knife is still well away from your body.

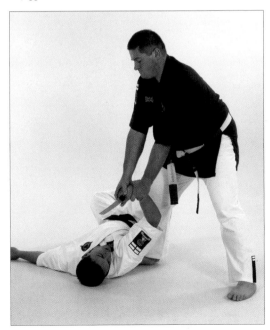

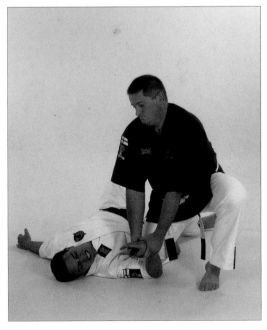

△ This is the position described in step 7 when viewed from a different angle.

8△ Apply a knee lock to the aggressor's elbow, maintaining the restraint until assistance arrives.

Face slash – Close range evasive tactics.

1△ An aggressor moves in with a knife attack to your face. Step back and prepare to use a double-handed knife-edge block to the aggressor's right arm.

2△ A double block requires both hands simultaneously striking the aggressor's attacking arm, to ensure the knife does not make contact. The use of both hands reinforces the ability to defend more effectively.

Caution
Never practise with a real weapon. Wooden or plastic knives are ideal for training, but you still need to treat them with respect.

3△ Keeping the knife attack away from your body, move in sideways and strike with your elbow to the aggressor's floating rib or solar plexus, depending on which is more accessible.

4△ Feed your right hand through in a snake-like movement, bringing your hand over the aggressor's right wrist to create an arm lock (key lock).

5△ Continue the momentum, keeping the knife well away from your body, and take the aggressor down to the floor. Apply a finishing strike, if necessary.

1△ An attacker moves in and grabs you in an arm lock from behind.

2△ Step forwards and simultaneously grab the aggressor's wrist to pull him off balance.

3△ Strike with the knife edge of your left hand to the area of the aggressor's groin.

4△ Following the groin strike, move under the aggressor's right arm in preparation to apply an arm lock. Keep both hands on the aggressor's right wrist to secure the restraint.

5△ Final technique demonstrating the application of a knee strike. In all cases, it is better to remain with a restraint, in view of the injuries which could be inflicted by using a "hard" strike.

Techniques: Advanced Weapon Techniques

The following will give an insight into some of the weapons (*kobojutsu*) used in
ju-jitsu. Qualified supervision must be sought when learning to use any weapons,
and the following is for demonstration purposes only.

Kamma – a type of sickle used to cut moss, hay and corn. It was developed on the Japanese island of Okinawa.

1△ This demonstrates the position in which
to hold the *kamma*. Your body should be
upright, your feet a shoulder-width apart
and a *kamma* in each hand, in a crossed
position, with the right hand uppermost.

2△ Move into a ready position by moving
your right foot back into a long stance.
Draw the right *kamma* above your head,
ready for a downwards strike, and hold the
left *kamma* as a defensive guard.

3△ From this position, step forwards with
your right foot, bringing your right hand
down in a striking movement. Draw the
left-hand *kamma* back ready for a follow-up
strike if necessary.

△ Here, each *kamma* is being held in a blocking and striking
position. The wooden part of the *kamma* could be used to deflect
a strike, while being in the ready position for a follow-up strike.

△ The *kamma* was traditionally used by peasants against
aggressors. This stance would be used to assist the cutting-up
motion of the *kamma* towards an opponent's groin or lower body.

Sai – A defensive weapon traditionally used against a sword, staff, stick or empty hand.

1△ Stand upright, feet a shoulder-width apart, with the *sai* resting invisibly against the inside of your forearm. When holding a *sai*, place your forefinger down its handle, with your other fingers wrapped around the outside, and your thumb tucked securely in on the inside.

2△ Seen from the rear, the *sai* resting against the forearms and body are clearly visible.

3△ The *sai* being flicked inwards and outwards in a guard position, ready to guard and/or strike.

4△ The left-hand *sai* being used in a blocking position, while the one in the right hand is ready to strike.

Tonfa – A baton-like implement, adapted from an agricultural tool used for grinding coal, maize and corn.

1△ In the starting position, stand upright with your feet a shoulder-width apart, and with the *tonfa* held hidden behind your forearms.

2△ Note how the fingers and thumb are securely wrapped along the top part of the *tonfa*, so that it can be used as a blocking device, as well as pivoting through the hand as a striking weapon.

3△ This illustrates one of the positions adopted when up against an armed opponent. The left-hand *tonfa* is aligned against the edge of the forearm, where it can block any incoming blow.

4△ The right-hand *tonfa* is held flexibly, so that it can be twirled in a circular action to strike an opponent across the head.

Bo – A 6ft (2m) pole made of red or white oak. The *bo* developed from the staff used by Buddhist priests.

1△ This is the basic stance when using a *bo*, which should be held at the side of the body behind the right arm.

2△ Before striking with the *bo*, the practitioner steps back in a large circular motion.

Tanto-jutsu – traditionally used to attack at close quarters the weak points of an opponent's armour.

△ This classic guard stance is used to deliver an attack with this short-range weapon.

Jo – Similar to the *bo*, but much shorter. It is also lighter and usually smaller in diameter.

△ The *jo* practitioner is seen here having delivered a strike to an opponent's throat or solar plexus.

Hojo jutsu – The traditional art of binding and restraining an aggressor on the battlefield. It is probably most commonly used today in security situations by the armed forces. The purpose of the *hojo jutsu* techniques is to immobilize an opponent or aggressor until assistance arrives.

1△ This picture portrays one of the *hojo jutsu* techniques to restrain an opponent. This is a specialized technique requiring considerable skill and special training.

2△ Here you can see that no knots are used – restraint is based on a series of loops and half hitches.

3△ This shows the correct method of keeping hold of the *hojo* rope. The remaining rope is kept hidden within the *gi* top to conceal its true length.

Judo

Judo, meaning "the gentle way", is regarded as a modern sport, deriving from ju-jitsu. The essence of judo is the skilful application of a combination of techniques, such as the power of resistance and effective timing. The main focus of judo, however, is the utilization of your opponent's body weight and strength against him or herself. There is some similarity in principle between judo and sumo wrestling, in that a small person can overcome a much larger opponent using skill, strategy and technique.

History and Philosophy

Judo is one of the world's best-known martial arts, and one of only a handful featured at the Olympic Games. Practised as a sport a well as a martial art, judo incorporates principles from several disciplines of ju-jitsu, taking the best elements of each.

Professor Jiguro Kano, the founder of judo, graduated from the Imperial University of Tokyo, Japan, in 1881. He attended several ju-jitsu schools, seeking to develop a system of physical exercise. He adopted the best principles of each ju-jitsu system and called it judo, which, literally translated, means "gentle way". Kano's interpretation, however, was "maximum efficiency". He came to Europe in 1889 to spread the practice and philosophy of judo.

Below Dismissing early doubts, judo was being taught to women by 1935.

Above Close quarter gripping in preparation to throw or defend.

Kano envisaged judo as the development of a lifetime art, as opposed to a sport. Unusual for his time, he spoke perfect English and, breaking with Japanese tradition, his great respect for women prompted him to take on a female martial arts student, Sueko Ashiya. Criticisms were made that teaching women martial arts could lead to health problems because they had certain physical and other limitations that made them unsatisfactory students. Concerned with these comments, Kano undertook research into the impact that judo had on women, utilizing the knowledge of some of the leading medical experts of his day.

The research refuted his critics' claims concerning the negative impact of judo on women, and it was at about this time that Kano set up a dojo (training hall) for women in Koubun school, Tokyo. By 1935 judo was being successfully taught to women, especially in high school.

The first international judo tournament took place between Great Britain and France in 1947. Britain took the title but, in 1951, the first European Championship was won by a French team. By 1956, judo was being taught in many

Above An impressive demonstration of one of the many throws used by the judo practitioner.

Japanese schools. Unfortunately, Kano was not to witness any of this, since he died in 1938, while at sea, returning from the Cairo International Olympic Conference. Some people claim that he was assassinated because of his actions and manifest sympathies towards the West.

It is worth bearing in mind that Kano did not create judo to be a public competition sport, and he felt strongly that it was a personal art to train the mind and body.

He insisted that its mastery required an appreciation of the inherent philosophy that supports all aspects of judo. With this in mind, it is interesting to read the oath that all judo students at the Kodukan dojo (the name given by Kano to his dojo) must make on admission: "Once I have entered the Kodukan, I will not end my study without reasonable cause; I will not dishonour the dojo; unless I am given permission, I will not disclose the secrets that I have been taught; unless I am given permission, I will not teach judo; pupil first, teacher second, I will always follow the rules of the dojo."

COMPETITION

Judo today is one of the most widespread martial arts in the world, with reputedly more than 8 million students. Practitioners are referred to as *judoka* and competitions (*shiai*) are conducted under the supervision of a referee and judge. Contests and training take place in the *judojo* (hall). Free-style combat in judo is known as *randori*; the submitting opponent is known as the *uke*; and the winning partner is referred to as the *tori* in judo.

"Judo is the means of understanding the way to make the most effective use of both physical and spiritual power and strength. By devoted practice and rigid discipline, in an effort to obtain perfection in attacking and defending, it refines the body and soul and helps instil the spiritual essence in judo into every part of one's very being. In this way, it is possible to perfect oneself and contribute something worthwhile to the world." JIGURO KANO

MORE THAN JUST SPORT

Judo is not purely about physical skill. Its aim is to teach good attitude and behaviour and to instil a sense of decorum in its *judoka*, best summed up in two terms used to describe the mental attitude expected from a *judoka*: *hontai*, demonstrating the state of permanent alertness, and *bonno*, demonstrating a disciplined mind, serene and calm, controlling the body and being able to react positively to any situation.

Below Judo is suitable for people of all ages and abilities and is one of the most popular martial arts.

Benefits of judo

The benefits derived from judo affect many aspects of your everyday life. These include:

- Health, fitness and stamina
- Confidence and well-being
- Self-defence skills
- Comradeship
- Flexibility and awareness
- Awareness and assertiveness
- Strengthened limbs

Above Demonstrating the skill of break-falling.

Left It is important that the training area is always kept clean. The floor is swept before practice and usually the first student to arrive will undertake this responsibility. Any holes or chips in the floor area must be noted and avoided. All practitioners must be aware of emergency exits and emergency procedures e.g. local emergency numbers and escape route. The first aid kit must always be available in the dojo.

Clothing and Equipment

Unlike other forms of ju-jitsu, no weapons are used to practise judo. A practitioner will wear a white suit (*judogi*) and a coloured belt to indicate their rank. The belt grading system differs in some countries, but the order shown below is the most widely recognized.

A judo practitioner, a *judoka*, wears a *judogi*. This consists of a heavy cotton jacket and trousers made of strong material so that it can withstand the many grabs and tugs delivered in the judo "way of gentleness" (Jiguro Kano 1860–1938). The word judo is based on jikishin-ryu of ju-jitsu. Jiguro Kano wanted to turn ju-jitsu into a "martial sport" to train and educate young people. Kano said, "the aim of Judo is to understand and demonstrate the living laws of movement."

The techniques which upset an opponent's balance and/or immobilize him or her is known as *kuzushi*. The main aim of judo is to neutralize an opponent as opposed to injure or kill. It is very much viewed as a self-defence system.

Judoka train with bare feet on the matted (*tatami*) area.

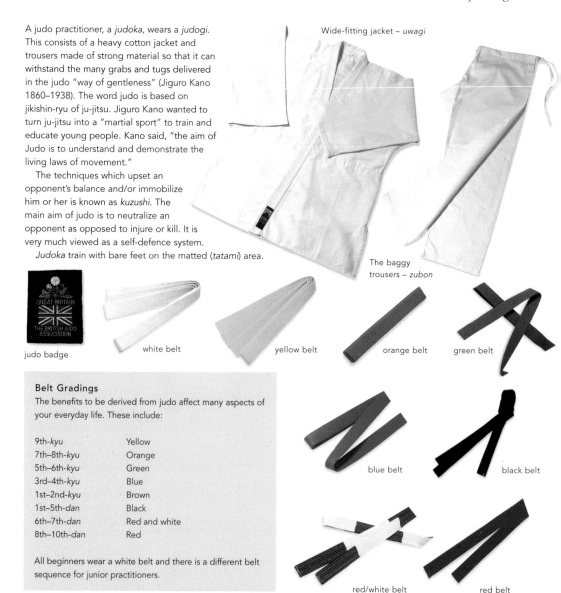

Wide-fitting jacket – *uwagi*

The baggy trousers – *zubon*

judo badge

white belt

yellow belt

orange belt

green belt

blue belt

black belt

red/white belt

red belt

Belt Gradings
The benefits to be derived from judo affect many aspects of your everyday life. These include:

9th-*kyu*	Yellow
7th–8th-*kyu*	Orange
5th–6th-*kyu*	Green
3rd–4th-*kyu*	Blue
1st–2nd-*kyu*	Brown
1st–5th-*dan*	Black
6th–7th-*dan*	Red and white
8th–10th-*dan*	Red

All beginners wear a white belt and there is a different belt sequence for junior practitioners.

Etiquette

Etiquette and discipline are of the utmost importance in judo, to show respect and courtesy for the art and also to ensure safety. All practitioners must look after their personal appearance – especially their nails, which can scratch if they are too long.

1△ Stand upright and relaxed, with your eyes looking forwards and your feet a shoulder-width apart.

2△ Perform the bow by inclining your body by about 30 degrees. Let your eyes follow the bow to the floor, since this is given as a sign of respect to the art, the training environment and your fellow practitioners.

3◁ When practising or in competition with a partner, the same bow is performed. It is important to allow adequate space between yourself and your partner to avoid bumping heads! Ideally, you need to be at approximately one and a half arms' distance, as this maintains a safe personal boundary. In competition, you take one step back and then bow to your partner.

Warm-up Exercises

This routine loosens your body, making it as flexible as possible. What is unique to judo is the emphasis on preparing the body for grappling and throwing moves. A warm-up must be carried out in preparation for the techniques.

Warm-up 1 – Sit-ups develop stomach muscles and stamina. Be careful to build up gradually to avoid injury.

◁ Lie flat on the floor. Bend your knees at approximately 90 degrees, with your partner holding your ankles. Place your hands at the sides of your head. The tips of your fingers should be in the region of your temples. Keep your elbows tucked in and raise your body about 45 degrees from the floor as you exhale. Then lower yourself down as you inhale. Repeat this exercise several times over.

Warm-up 2 – The star jump assists in the overall body warm-up process and builds stamina.

1△ For the star jump, stand in a relaxed, natural position, feet a shoulder-width apart, and hands at your sides.

2△ Jump into an X position – legs spread and arms raised – and then back into the standing position. Repeat this about ten times.

Warm-up 3 – Press-ups (push-ups) develop the upper part of the body. Build up gradually and carefully.

◁ Lie face down, with your legs slightly apart. Make sure you are on the balls of your feet and place your hands in line with your shoulders. Slowly inhale as you raise your body upwards. Keep your body level and arms straight. Gently lower yourself, just touching the floor, but do not take the weight off your arms. Build up to sets of 10 if possible.

Warm-up 4 – This inner-thigh stretch is an important part of your preparation for judo practice.

◁ Sit with legs spread as far as possible. Lower your upper body as far as you can towards your left knee. Keep your leg straight and aim to go a little further down each time you practise. Don't worry if you cannot manage this in the early stages: it takes time. Repeat 10 times to the left side and then the right side, holding for approximately 10 seconds.

Warm-up 5 (*uchi-kome*) – An important part of the warm-up routine is preparation for throwing.

1△ Face your partner and take hold of his right sleeve with your left hand. Your partner takes hold of your left lapel with his right hand. *Note: this technique is also performed to the opposite side.*

2△ As you move, step through with your right foot and bring your right arm under your partner's left arm.

3△ Rotate until your back touches your partner's front and your feet are between your partner's, with your legs bent. Push your right hip towards your partner and pull him forwards over your right shoulder.

Techniques: Basic Throws

Throwing techniques form the basis of judo and do not rely on strength, but on skill and good timing. Professional supervision is important when practising all throws. The following techniques are a guide to some of those used.

Body drop (*tia-otoshi*) – Disrupting the partner's point of balance in preparation to throw.

1△ Stand facing your partner. Grab your partner's lapel with your right hand and her sleeve with your left hand. Your partner also takes hold of your lapel with her right hand and your right arm with her left hand.

2△ Step forwards with your right leg, turning your right shoulder in towards your partner. Keep an upright posture and maintain a secure grip of your partner's clothing in preparation for the throwing technique.

3△ Lower your stance to maintain good posture and balance, and use your body momentum to throw your partner.

Hooking technique (*ko-uchi gari*) – Overcoming a larger person.

Sweeping technique (*ashi waza*).

1△ Your left arm is grabbed, above the elbow, by your partner. Move in close.

2△ Hook the inside of his right leg while holding the outside of his thigh with your right hand.

3◁ Project your body forwards using your momentum to throw your partner backwards and downwards.

△ A popular technique in judo is the "sweep". The aim is to catch your partner's lower leg/foot with a scooping action as they move forwards, using the inside of your foot in an outwards and inwards motion. At the same time, grab your partner's clothing. Both partners must be well versed in break-falling and beginners must have supervision.

Following a take down to the floor, a variety of restraints can be applied.
When correctly performed, a partner can be kept restrained for some time.
In competition, the partner has to be held for 25 seconds to qualify for any points.

△ After throwing your partner, pin her down by lying across her chest. Position your right arm around her right leg and your left arm around the back of her neck. Take hold of your partner's clothing where it is accessible. Spread your legs to give balance and to increase the pressure on your partner.

1▷ If you are attacked while sitting on the floor, control your partner with your legs and secure her head with your arms. Turn her on her back. Move through with your left arm in preparation for securing your partner and turning her towards the floor.

2◁ Once you have turned your partner towards the floor, secure her by applying an upper body hold.

Caution

It is important to ensure that your partner's windpipe is not smothered by your restraint, so that they can breathe freely and advise you of any possible discomfort. This is particularly important in training where a technique is being demonstrated by an adult against a junior. Some techniques are not allowed to be practised on young people under the age of 16, particularly choking techniques.

Techniques: Self-defence

There are a variety of self-defence moves in judo which equip a student to deal with attacks from different angles. The following demonstrates a defensive move from a rear attack, using the opponent's body weight to their disadvantage.

Self-defence 1.

1△ An aggressor grabs you around the neck from the rear, with his right arm placed across your throat.

2△ Take hold of the aggressor's right sleeve and push your hips back into his body. At the same time, pull his right arm over your shoulder in a forward and downward action. Bend your legs and rotate your body so that you can throw the aggressor.

△ In this side view of step 2 you can see how projecting your hips backwards unbalances the aggressor. This demonstrates how to move into the aggressor's centre of gravity to break their balance.

3△ Keep the momentum going so that your opponent is thrown over your shoulder and on to the floor. The force of the throw should incapacitate him, giving you time to get to a safe place.

1△ An aggressor stands in front and grabs the clothing on either side of your neck.

2△ Put your hand on his jaw and take a step forwards.

3△ Sweep away his legs while maintaining the pressure on his jaw.

4△ Keep the momentum going and throw the aggressor down on to the floor.

△ This side view shows the hand grip, used to throw the aggressor in step 4, in more detail.

Techniques: Advanced Choke and Strangle Holds

This section demonstrates a variety of choke and strangle techniques. When a choking technique is employed the aim is to diminish the air supply, while a strangle technique cuts off the blood supply.

Hadaka-jime.

◁ The *hadaka-jime* is a choke technique in which the forearm is locked against the windpipe. It is important to keep your body close with feet astride to maintain control.

▽ Place your forearm against your partner's windpipe and pull him towards you, forcing the head forward. Keep your hands well clasped together and secure your head close to your partner's. Any gaps will allow your partner to escape.

Okuri-eri-jime.

◁ In this basic strangle technique (*okuri-eri-jime*), pressure is applied to the side of the neck, cutting the blood supply, as opposed to the air supply.

Caution
These techniques are advanced moves that have been specially developed for the purpose of restraining in a self-defence situation. They are very specialized and must always be practised under strict supervision by a trained instructor. Young people under 16 years old, in particular, must not practise certain moves, or have such techniques applied to them.

Here *juji-gatame* (straight-arm lock) and *ude-garame* (bent-arm lock) are shown.
Juji-garame involves using both your arms and legs. The pressure that is applied
by this technique restricts your opponent's ability to break free.

Juji-gatame.
▷ By pinning your opponent in this position, her body is immobilized by the straight-arm lock. Pull the arm across your body and lift your hips in order to apply pressure to the extended straight arm.

Ude-garame.
▽ Take a figure 4 position with your arms and bend your opponent's arm upwards by pressing downwards on his wrist.

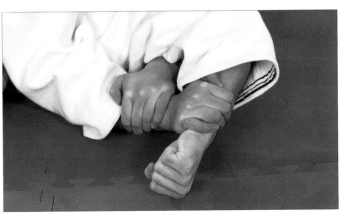

◁ There are several variations of this technique, namely a straight-arm lock (*juji-gatame*) and a bent-arm lock (*ude-garame*). Ude-garame is shown demonstrating the bent-arm lock as part of a floor restraining technique. *Note: you should be lying across your opponent with your legs splayed, to maintain body pressure.*

Kung fu

Kung fu, meaning "sustained effort or skill", incorporates hundreds of styles such as wing chun and tai chi. However, there are common traits which complement the overall picture within kung fu. All disciplines start with basic stances and motions which act as a platform from which a student may learn and study different styles and forms. As skill levels rise, these forms progress into higher levels of difficulty, allowing the student to gain fluidity and dexterity before competitive training.

Wing Chun Kung Fu

Wing chun is a form of kung fu that focuses on close range combat and soft movements. Its effectiveness as a defence technique is reliant on a combination of good posture and balance. The wing chun practitioner should be rooted yet flexible, like a bamboo plant.

Wing chun kuen kung fu is just one of many styles of martial arts, whose origins are to be found in southern China, and compared with other martial arts, it is a relative newcomer. The term wing chun is attributed to a woman called Yim Wing Chun, who was the protégé of a Buddhist nun called Ng Mui. Wing chun is known as a "soft" style, but is in fact a blend of both "hard" and "soft" techniques. With reference to the hard concept, in simple terms this means meeting force with force, whereas the soft term refers to more evasive manoeuvres and techniques.

Below The late Grand Master of wing chun kung fu Yip Mun uses the wooden dummy apparatus (*mook yan jong*), in order to condition both body and mind, while also improving his kung fu techniques.

Above The wing chun practitioner must maintain excellent posture and balance to suceed in the art.

Roughly translated, wing chun means "beautiful spring-time" and kuen means "fist" or "fist fighting style". However, many people refer to the style as being "wing chun". This blending of hard and soft is due to the fact that it was developed by a woman and refined mainly by men. It is also said that Ng Mui once observed a battle between a snake and a crane. From her observations sprang ideas on how to develop this art. Mimicking animal movements is particularly common in Chinese martial arts.

There are many varied accounts of the history of wing chun in relation to names, dates and places. The following attempts to give one account of the history of its origin. During the reign of Emperor K'anghsi of the Ching Dynasty (1662–1722), the Shaolin monastery Siu Lam of Mt Sung, in the Honan province, had become very powerful

Above Shaolin monks demonstrate breaking techniques.

Below A stretching exercise typical of southern Chinese martial arts.

through kung fu training. The Manchurian government, fearing an uprising, sent troops to destroy Siu Lam. However, the fate of the monastery was settled internally, with traitorous monks setting it alight. Only a handful of monks and disciples managed to escape the onslaught of the Manchurian army. Among these were Abbot Chi Shin, Abbot Pak Mei, Master Fung To Tak, Master Miu Him and Abbess Ng Mui. Ng Mui was a master of Siu Lam kung fu and and became the creator of the wing chun system.

Ng Mui's ideas of close-quarter combat were totally different from the Siu Lam system of that time. She discarded many of the old traditions, which often required years of dedicated practice at each stage, and started to develop a system based on the principle of winning at all costs, by using speed and subtlety to overcome an opponent's natural advantages. Her system, as yet unnamed, therefore had less stress on muscular strength (*lik*), bone conditioning or muscular flexibility. The emphasis lay in sudden contraction and relaxation (*ging*) causing the practitioner to explode into action, using natural weapons such as finger jabs to the eyes, elbow strikes to the face and the powerful use of knees and feet to an opponent's lower body.

Ng Mui later met and befriended a young, intelligent and beautiful woman named Yim Wing Chun, who was just fifteen years of age. Little is known of Yim's childhood, other than that her mother died when she was in her teens and her father, Yim Yee, was falsely accused of a crime. To avoid possible imprisonment, father and daughter moved to Mt Tai Leung, along the border of Hunan and Szechuan provinces.

Left The Zen-like appearance of the Shaolin temple evoked by nature – *Shaolin* means small forest.

Here Yim soon attracted the attentions of a local landowner, Wong. He attempted to bully her into marriage and even tried to rape her. It was at the Temple on Mount Tai Leung, where Ng Mui had taken refuge, that the two women met and befriended each other.

To help protect Yim Wing Chun, Ng Mui took her into the mountains and taught her the techniques of her new fighting system, in an effort to teach her how to protect herself. Under Ng Mui's direction, Yim studied kung fu religiously, and mastered the style. Naturally, Yim Wing Chun subsequently returned to her village and defeated the bully Wong, and it is believed that Ng Mui named her new style wing chun kuen, after her protégée.

Bong sau

One of the important techniques taught in wing chun is *bong sau* (meaning "wing arm"). It is taught to beginners as a basic cover against an attack, and is particularly useful to their understanding of the style. The technique is designed to protect a wide area of your body, to yield under extreme pressure yet never allowing your arm to become trapped. It can change easily into a palm-up block and allow you to slip your hand free. The rear protective guard hand (*wu sau*) can grab and deflect the incoming strike and allow the bong to become an effective throat-cutting technique.

This *bong sau* movement demonstrates just how flexible wing chun can be. It also illustrates that if a single technique can be used in many situations, why then learn several different moves for several different situations? This reinforces the simplicity of the system.

Wing chun is centred on the Taoist principle of "take the middle road". In essence, this says that you should not go to extremes, and that success is based on balance. If you are on the middle road you can see both the left and right paths, but if you venture too far to one side you may lose sight of the other. This can also be interpreted as the concept of the hard and soft principles – or *yin* and *yang*. *Yin* (the feminine side) focuses on diverting the flow of energy; *yang* (the masculine side) seeks to resist any opposing energy flow.

Subsequent generations of wing chun practitioners have refined the system further, but always keeping to the simple principles of the art: the centre-line theory (protecting and striking at the major pressure points); economy of motion (keeping every movement as simple as possible); and the self-explanatory principle of combined or simultaneous defence and attack.

Below The *bong sau* or "wing arm" technique allows practitioners to defend themselves against attack.

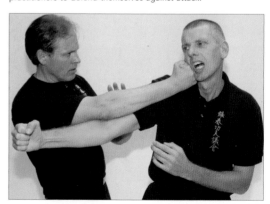

Above A Shaolin monk demonstrates the flexibility that can be achieved from practising this art.

The centre-line theory is viewed as being the most definitive part of the wing chun system, since there are many attacking strikes that seek to obscure the vision of an aggressor. The centre-line is also defensive, since your own vulnerable points are protected by the counter-attacks. The practitioner is not regarded as an aggressor in a martial arts situation, because wing chun is an art of self-defence. However, if you are fighting multiple assailants, the situation may dictate the need to attack aggressively. In this type of situation, wing chun practitioners find the use of finger strikes, elbows and knee kicks to be of great value. Even the most skilled wing chun practitioner can fight only one person at a time, so the need to strike and escape is the main objective.

"STICKY HANDS"

One of the most important techniques in wing chun is "sticky hands" (*chi sau*). Since wing chun is a close-quarter system, it is potentially dangerous for the practitioners themselves, who are at risk of being hit, grabbed or kicked. This realization has led to a particular training method called *sheung chi sau* ("double sticky hands").

To the uninitiated, this technique is best described as a hurt boxer trying to "spoil" his opponent's moves by clinging to his arms. The aim is to prevent an opponent striking freely, giving the wing chun practitioner the opportunity to control, trap and break free to strike. The real skill lies in both parties wanting to achieve the same goal, and this has led to exceptional techniques, in which either one or both parties can train blindfolded. A skilful practitioner can eventually predict and nullify the danger.

The main areas that "sticky hands" seeks to develop fall into the categories of sensitivity, power and general fitness. Sensitivity covers such aspects as the centre-line concept, reaction to direction change, striking when the hand is freed, going with the power and not resisting force, continuous techniques (fluidity), and balance in the vertical and horizontal planes. Power involves guiding power, aggressive and explosive power, and power control and balancing-power techniques.

Benefits of wing chun kung fu

The benefits derived from learning wing chun affect many aspects of your everyday life. These include:

- Physical and emotional control
- Confidence and well-being
- Assertiveness and reflexes
- Health improvement through physical exercise, breathing and body movement
- Comradeship
- Stress reduction
- Good posture and stability
- Mobility and flexibility

Clothing and Equipment

Although wing chun is highly skilled and requires strict discipline, it has no official grading system, so coloured belts are not worn by practitioners to indicate rank. Training is often solitary, using devices such as wooden dummies (*mook yan jong*) to develop techniques.

Practitioners of wing chun usually wear casual, clean clothing consisting of a comfortable top and trousers. Soft footwear such as slippers are worn on the feet, along with protective equipment when it is necessary, such as gum shields. There is no official grading system in wing chun, although different organizations have now developed their own systems. The sash is an integral part of clothing yet does not depict any grade. A variety of weapons is used such as butterfly knives and the 6½ point pole. The wooden dummy (*mook yan jong*) is one of the main pieces of equipment used for training in wing chun.

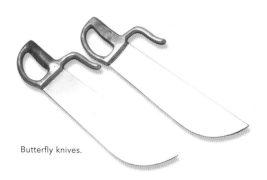

Butterfly knives.

Below A smartly dressed wing chun practitioner.

Above The wooden dummy (*mook yan jong*) is an impressive piece of equipment and is unique to wing chun. It is designed as a replica of the human body, in terms of the position of the torso, hands and legs, and practitioners use it to develop their blocking and striking techniques.

Etiquette

Etiquette is used as a sign of respect to the art, instructor, fellow practitioners and training area. It is also used as a form of welcoming. The practitioner can smile when performing this ritual, as a friendly greeting, with no aggression intended.

Salutation 1.

1◁ Stand in a relaxed position with your feet together and hands at the sides of your body. This is a formal manner of displaying etiquette in wing chun.

2▷ Make a fist with your right hand and nestle it into the palm of your left hand in front of your face, approximately at chin level. Keep the fingers of your left hand pointing upwards. This shows a more informal gesture.

The etiquette demonstrated here is similar to the traditional greeting that is used at the time of Chinese New Year, which commences each February, and is part of a long tradition. As a part of this tradition the fist would be fully covered to convey sentiments of friendship and peace to the person being bowed to.

▽ Side view of the etiquette. Make sure that you can still see above your hands, which should be about 10–12 in (25–30 cm) from your chin.

Salutation 2 - There is an alternative formality, which is characterized by a particularly friendly facial expression.

◁ Stand as you would for the formal *rei* above, but note that the fingers of your left hand curl over the fist, partially hiding it from view. Your facial expression should be receptive and pleasant – almost like saying "hello".

Warm-up Exercises

This is a selection of warm-up exercises found in wing chun. In view of the close-range techniques and circular action required in certain moves, emphasis is placed on forearm power to improve strength.

Warm-up 1 – This exercise is designed to make your wrists supple and increase their flexibility.

1◁ Kneel on the floor, facing forwards. Place both hands on the floor in front of you with the fingers facing backwards, towards your knees. Your back should be slightly arched. Keep looking forwards. *Note: it is the body weight on your wrists that enhances the effect of this exercise, but be careful to increase pressure gently, with practice, over a period of time.*

2◁ Remain in the kneeling position and turn your right hand inwards, palm uppermost, and fingers facing towards your left arm. Gently apply pressure on the wrist, increasing the weight with practice, over a period of time. Hold for approximately 30 seconds and repeat the exercise with your left hand. Repeat 2 or 3 times.

Warm-up 2 – The following is a series of actions extracted from the wing chun first form *sui nim tao* designed to increase flexibility of the wrists. Perform all movements with the right hand first. This *heun sau* sequence translates as "circling hand" and is of fundamental importance to wing chun.

1◁ Start with your feet a shoulder-width apart. Keep your left arm withdrawn at chest level and place your right hand, palm up, in front of you. Slightly bend your right elbow and position it about 5 in (13 cm) from your chest. Position your left fist just above your left hip. Rotate your outstretched hand in an inwards, circular motion, starting and finishing with the palm in the upwards position. Repeat 3 or 4 times and change to the left hand.

2◁ Twist your outstretched hand inwards, with your fingers facing back towards your body. Make sure your thumb is well tucked in. Your fingers need to be close together to maximize the benefit of this exercise. Hold for 10–20 seconds.

3△ Twist your hand with an inward-turning circular action. This technique is called *fook sau* (bridge on arm). Hold for 10–20 seconds.

4△ Continue the *fook sau* by pushing the tips of your fingers downwards, forming part of the circular action.

5△ Complete the circle so the hand finishes, fingers facing upwards, with the wrist pushing in a short and powerful descent. Bring the palm back closer to the body and repeat steps 3, 4 and 5 again.

Techniques: *Kau Sau*

Kau sau (circling hand or arm movement) is a popular exercise in wing chun. It requires the assistance of a partner and seeks to develop the practitioner's evasive and striking skills.

1△ The partners stand opposite each other in the ready position – both adopt frontal guard positions. Only the left practitioner is demonstrating wing chun.

2△ Your partner strikes at your face with his right fist. Step back and block with your right inner arm. This technique is called *gaan sau* or "splitting block".

3△ Circle your partner's right wrist with your defending hand and counter-attack by stepping through and striking with your left fist to your partner's short ribs.

4△ Bring the low punch up and support the elbow. Use both arms to pull your partner on to a low front kick. In this sequence the opponent's forwards momentum is used to your advantage.

Chi sau ("sticky hands") is one of wing chun's most famous techniques. The term "sticky hands" describes the continuous contact between two practitioners. To master this technique you need to attend regular classes.

1△ Stand in a relaxed fashion, opposite your partner, with your feet a shoulder-width apart and your arms in contact with your partner's forearms. Look forwards. Gently rotate your arms.

2△ Keep rotating your arms upwards and downwards, maintaining contact with your partner's forearms and wrists. You should sense a flow of energy throughout this contact.

3△ The left-hand practitioner senses an overlap in the arms and moves from the left of his partner, to the right. He pushes through and pulls the head forwards from the back of the neck.

4△ The practitioner then follows up with an elbow strike to the face (*cup jarn*). Note that the opponent's arms are temporarily trapped during this exercise.

Techniques: Children's Practice

When children practise any of the martial arts, it is very important that they receive strict and professional supervision. All exercise and practice must be appropriate to the age of the child and their stage of physical and mental development.

1△ When children are practising, they should stand far enough apart so that any strikes miss by between 5–8 in (13–20 cm). This is especially important when striking towards the face area.

2△ Your partner uses a left fist strike towards your face. Notice that the strike finishes well short of the face.

3△ Defend against the attack by bringing your right arm upwards in a circular motion. Turning the body helps to avoid and redirect force, making wing chun ideal for young people, as there is less contact.

4△ Finish with a right-hand strike to your partner's nose. Hold their left wrist with your left hand. The image above is for demonstration only, when practising you should avoid contact.

Taan sau is a blocking move and is practised by all ages. It develops the ability to place a cover in the way and attempt to turn. Blocking in wing chun is often termed "bridging arms".

1△ Face your partner, feet a shoulder-width apart and both fists against your chest. Bend your knees slightly. This closes the inner area of the legs and protects the groin and knees when turning.

2△ Your partner uses a right fist strike towards your face, ensuring a safe distance to avoid physical contact. Maintain your posture and focus as you prepare to defend.

3△ Deflect by using a forward and upward open-hand block with your left hand. Keep your right hand ready to either push your partner away, block or strike. Deflect the punch as soon as possible.

4△ Counter-attack with a right-hand fist strike to the solar plexus. Focus your technique carefully to avoid any injury to your partner. When using speed and force, it is important to maintain your focus.

Techniques: *Lok Sau* – Rolling Arm Technique

The fact that the founder of wing chun was a woman is significant, since the techniques used do not necessarily require strength or force. What is required is skill, timing and anticipation to know when a vulnerable area is available to strike.

2△ Place your right hand on your partner's right arm ready to twist and turn (*laap sau* means deflecting arm).

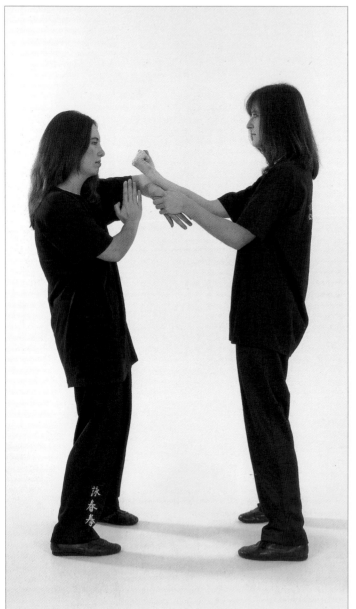

3△ Maintain a rolling action that delivers a certain amount of pressure on your partner.

1△ Face your partner with your feet a shoulder-width apart, keep your back straight and look forwards. Your hands should be forward and forearms in contact with your partner. This is the ready position for *lok sau* practice.

4▽ The technique has now completely reversed from the original starting point.

5△ As in step 2, move on to perform the same technique, taking you back to step 1. You will find the technique alternating between you and your partner.

6△ You now change sides to perform an alternative to continuing to roll back and forth with your arms. As you feel your partners desire to deflect your arm, take hold of their arm and deliver a right punch. Your partner, feeling the grab, responds by blocking the incoming strike through performing a left *bong sau*.

7▷ The sequence follows through as in steps 1–4. Whenever there is an attempt to deflect the strike, the other side has a chance to grab and change sides. This sequence develops good reactions to grabs, punches and changes of direction. This technique can be developed to an extremely high speed with the correct supervision and plenty of practice.

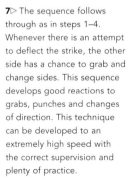
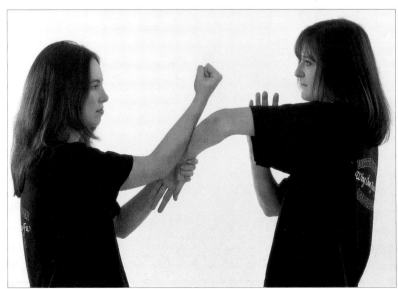

Techniques: *Mook Yan Jong*

Wooden dummy practice (*mook yan jong*) is used to develop blocks and strikes.
The dummy is a unique piece of equipment found only in the art of wing chun and
it plays an integral part in a practitioner's development of the techniques.

△ Demonstrates a low kick used to break an opponent's stance.

△ Demonstrates a sweep kick and counter-strike.

△ Demonstrates a double-palm push known as *po pai jeung*.

△ A complex movement called *gaan sau*, meaning "splitting block".

Many of the weapons in wing chun have developed from everyday tools used in farming and boating, such as staffs which were used to carry water to and from wells. Thus techniques for self-defence developed from familiar objects to hand.

△ The *luk dim boon kwun* is an 8 ft (2.5 m) length of sturdy, tapering wood. There are six main movements where the pole is used to block and strike, as well as small half movements. It is tapered at one end to prevent it becoming heavy and allow the tip to be moved faster.

△ Butterfly knives being used for "trapping the spear".

△ A deflective movement known as *laap do*.

△ Using the hilt of a butterfly knife to trap and control a spear or pole attack.

Mok-gar Kung Fu

Mok-gar kung fu, first studied by Shaolin monks, is a Chinese martial arts system centred around a combination of shorthand fighting techniques and powerful kicks. Students of mok-gar must develop great stamina and flexibility before they can begin to master the art.

Below Developed and practised by Shaolin monks, mok-gar's impressive kicking techniques are instantly recognizable.

Below The spirit of kung fu is often reflected within the face and poise of Asian temple guardians.

Shaolin mok-gar kuen is one of the original family disciplines of kung fu, from southern China, and is well known for its kicking techniques. Practitioners are not restricted just to kicking, however, since the use of a full range of weapons is also part of the system. The resulting flexibility of attack and defence epitomizes the original concept of Chinese martial arts: to express yourself fully in the attempt to triumph in combat. When engaging in combat, the objective is to win, so practitioners believe that to place any restrictions on one particular movement would be to put themselves at a disadvantage.

Shaolin mok-gar kuen, so legend has it, was originally developed by a monk called Mok-Da-Si, in the Shaolin monastery in southern China. He taught this style, known then as shaolin chuen, to his family in the Tong-Kwun district of Kwong-Tong province, and the name was retained until the third generation, when it was renamed mok-gar (after Mok's family).

The style has passed virtually unchanged through many generations, and is still faithfully taught today, according to its original concept. Indeed, it shares the same good reputation with four other contemporary southern Chinese

Above The elegant roof of a traditional Shaolin temple with ornate wood carvings.

Right The training stumps upon which Shaolin monks would stand to improve their skills of balance and one-on-one harmony.

family styles: *hung-gar*, *choi-gar*, *lee-gar* and *lau-gar*. Each family became well known for its specific strength within the style. The Chinese have a traditional saying, which when translated, calls to mind the strong points of these styles: "Hung's fists, mok's kicks and lee's staff."

Mok-gar kuen practice traditionally involves the use of two wooden dummies. One is called *mook-yan-jong*, with projections which resemble arms, and is used for blocking and countering. The other is called *darn gee* and is particular to mok-gar. The *darn gee* consists of a hollow bamboo post 13 ft (4 m) high and 4 in (10 cm) in diameter, which is set into the ground by about 3 ft (1 m). It is filled with washers (originally coins) and is used to practise all of the attacks necessary for a student to learn. This training is excellent for building physical power and developing effective punches and kicks. This is important in mok-gar, since every student has to pass through a stage where he or she develops a considerable amount of power before progressing.

One of the unique training drills found in mok-gar kuen is that of the *darn gee* kicking technique. In kung fu, each school has its own method of teaching the kicks using various mechanical facilities. Irrespective of the method, the aim is the same: to increase the freedom of leg movements, enhance speed, improve accuracy, and to develop and harden the soles of the feet.

During the course of training, the *darn gee* helps practitioners to improve their stamina, hardness, speed, accuracy and strength in kicking techniques. This unique training drill is a stage that all mok-gar practitioners must experience if they wish to develop a high standard within this style. The 108 movements that are the basis of the mok-gar style can be used in many ways, from just a single punch, which may be all that is needed to win a fight, to multiple jumping kicks.

Above Well known for its kicking techniques, mok-gar kuen kung fu also teaches how to withstand being kicked. Here a Shaolin monk is totally open to a vicious groin kick.

When experienced, students progress to learning a soft form of kung fu, called tai chi. Sifu Chan, who came to England to develop the system which incorporated the use of weapons, teaches the wu style tai chi, based on the Taoist symbol of *yin* and *yang* (soft and hard). Tai chi teaches you to be aware of, and to react to, any form of attack, and to be ever-changing and formless. To learn and combine these two systems of kung fu is not an easy task, but once acquired, the knowledge and experience can prove invaluable.

MADAME MOK KWEI LAN

Madame Mok Kwei Lan, known as the Tigress, was only a teenager when she started giving kung fu instruction some sixty years ago. Madame Mok was a native of Kao Yao, a small town near Canton. As a child, she was taught the family art of mok-gar kung fu – known as "Snapping the Iris" – by her uncle. In the face of strong disapproval – women were not encouraged to learn martial arts – she continued to study secretly with her uncle, by whom she was eventually adopted, with her parents' approval. She eventually married her uncle's friend, Wong Fei Hung, whom she assisted by

looking after his gymnasium, giving kung fu instruction and practising as a trained osteopath.

There are many stories regarding Madame Mok, as the Tigress, being challenged to fight. Once, when buying food in the marketplace, Madame Mok saw four men bullying a fishmonger. As she intervened to help him, the four men turned on her and attacked her with poles. She then proceeded to take away all of the men's weapons and knocked the aggressors down one by one. The four attackers ran away in great pain, as the onlookers clapped with delight. Stories regarding this incident spread far and wide, enhancing her already formidable reputation.

Benefits of mok-gar kuen
The benefits derived from learning mok-gar kuen affect many aspects of your everyday life. These include:

- Flexibility and durability
- Confidence and assertiveness
- Assertiveness and reflexes
- Stamina and fitness
- Health and well-being
- Comradeship
- Stress reduction

Left The ability to defend oneself against an armed attacker is the mark of a competent and assured mok-gar kuen practitioner.

Left Demonstrating a technique to a group of students.

Clothing and Equipment

Rather than belts, mok-gar practitioners wear coloured sashes around their waists, ranging in colour from yellow to black. These sashes denote a practitioner's rank, and once a black sash has been achieved it is adorned with red bands to indicate greater accomplishment.

In general, practitioners of mok-gar wear a white T-shirt, which may or may not depict black writing showing the name of the art and training area, together with black trousers. Instructors may wear red trousers. It is also permissible for instructors to wear a white mandarin jacket. Trainers (sneakers) or bare feet are permissible during the practice of mok-gar. Weapons in mok-gar include the three-section staff, spear, staff, split staff, *siu so gee*, *tee-chec*, *dip do* (butterfly knives), *guay*, pegs, broad sword, tai chi sword, three-section steel whip and nine-section steel whip.

white mandarin top

slippers

trousers

Sash grading
Mok-gar kung fu instructors wear a black sash and practitioners wear the following:

Novices

Yellow sash	1st grade
Orange sash	2nd grade
Green sash	3rd grade
Blue sash	4th grade
Brown sash	5th grade
Black sash	1st degree

Once a practitioner has achieved the first degree thay can wear a black sash, they progress in degrees, with one red band per degree. After achieving 10th degree they can wear a red sash.

sashes

black sash

dip do knives

4 red-banded sash

red sash

3-section staff

siu so gee

broad sword

Etiquette

Respect in mok-gar is manifested as a "salute" by practitioners. It is performed at the beginning and end of every session to demonstrate that the practitioner is following the true Shaolin way (showing respect towards the art and its beliefs).

1◁ Stand in a relaxed position with your hands behind your back. There are no specific rules about which hand should be over which – it is just a natural posture with feet facing forwards, a shoulder-width apart, back straight, shoulders relaxed and eyes looking forwards.

▽ Rear view of hand positions.

2△ Make a fist with your right hand and keep your left hand open with your thumb relaxed. Place your fist into the centre of the palm of your left hand and prepare to move forwards.

3△ Step forwards with your left foot into the cat stance. At the same time, bring your hands round to the centre of your upper body.

4△ Side view of the salute position. Following the etiquette, practitioners stand in a relaxed position with their hands behind their back, as in step 1. *Note: this salute is also used before sparring.*

Warm-up Exercises

Mok-gar uses a variety of warm-up routines which are designed to prevent injuries during practice. Since this discipline is primarily centred around leg techniques, leg stretching exercises are particularly important.

Warm-up 1 – Stretching the leg tendons and hamstring muscles is a vital part of the warm-up.

1△ Raise your leg as high as is comfortable. Gradually build up the tempo and height of the kick. Perform ten kicks while counting from one to ten in Cantonese. Then change to the other leg.

△ A variation of the front-kick stretching exercise is to kick your leg forwards and outwards in a circular motion. Try to keep the heel of your stationary leg firmly planted on the ground while kicking.

Warm-up 2 – This exercise stretches the inner thighs and develops good body posture.

Warm-up 3 – The following exercise demonstrates dynamic tension, which is a body tensing exercise.

△ Take hold of your left foot with your left hand and bring it in towards your body and then out towards your left side. This is not an easy exercise for beginners. Only go as high as is comfortable.

△ Lower your body, knees bent, feet forwards. Breathe in through your nose, hold this for a few seconds, then breathe out through your mouth. While breathing, move both hands in a circular action, forwards, then back towards you, finally pushing out to the sides.

Warm-up 4 – When exercising with a partner, take care not to stretch him too far. Apply the exercise gently, pushing the leg a little further each time you practise.

Warm-up 5 – This series of moves is designed to develop your arms.

△ Lie down on the floor and allow your partner to secure your right knee and raise your left leg. Keep your leg straight. Your partner then pushes your left leg upwards. Change to the opposite leg and repeat the exercise 3 or 4 times each side.

1△ Gently make contact with your partner's forearms in a rotating action, first left, then right.

2△ Bend your arms so that you are now making contact with your partner's upturned fists in line with your chin. As you perform this exercise, try to use hip rotation to enhance the technique.

3△ Lower your arms so that you are making contact with the lower part of your partner's forearms. This looks very similar to the first position.

Techniques: One-man Blocking

This technique develops basic blocking forms. Each movement is a block towards an on-coming attack. The second stage involves the two-man blocking form to develop awareness, timing, distancing and body movement.

2△ Keeping your toes together, move your heels outwards.

1△ Stand in a natural position with your feet together and both fists at your side.

3△ Twist on the balls of your feet and then twist your heels as you move into a wider stance. Straighten your toes as you then move outwards.

4△ Continue to pivot on your heels and toes into a low horse stance. Keep both knees bent while pushing them outwards.

5△ Raise your right hand into an upper block position. Keep your left fist and elbow tucked into your side. Look straight ahead and repeat this exercise with the left arm.

6△ Push your right arm forwards with your right palm moving forwards and upwards. Keep your left fist on your left hip in preparation to move forwards.

7△ Repeat the exercise with your left arm and follow through with your right. It is important to keep your back straight and maintain the same posture.

8△ With an open right palm, prepare to block across your body.

9△ Follow through with a downwards, circular block to your right side. Repeat these moves, reversing hand and arm positions.

10△ Push both hands forwards, palms upwards and thumbs tucked in.

11△ Rotate your hands in a circular motion towards your face, keeping your little fingers together to start the rotation movement.

△ The rolling-finger technique seen from the side view.

12△ Continue to rotate the hands so that they move into the tiger-claw position.

13△ Defend with your left hand crossing your body. Keep your right hand on your hip and maintain the low horse stance.

14△ Move into the butterfly position by crossing your right palm over your left.

15△ Push your hand down, keeping your right hand on top.

16△ Both hands need to be flat as they push down in a circular action. Note the low body position. Ensure your right hand is on top of your left hand, with fingers straight. Draw your left leg up to your right leg and bring your fists back to your waist to finish – this is similar to the starting position.

Techniques: Two-man Blocking Form

The two-man defence develops blocking and striking techniques. Using a partner promotes awareness of movement, timing and delivery of the block. Practice sharpens the ability to focus on a moving target and develops a "feel" for when and how to defend and strike.

1△ Lower your posture and transfer 70 per cent of your weight on to your back leg. Slightly bend your front knee and keep your toes turned slightly inwards. Place your hands in the guard position with your right hand open. *Note: you can use either hand, depending on the fighting posture adopted.*

2△ Your opponent delivers a strike to your face. Deflect the attack using an upper-arm block with your left arm. The front arm must always be in a fist position with the rear in an open hand guard.

3△ Bring your arm back in to your body and bring your left leg up in preparation to strike your opponent in the floating rib.

4△ Deliver a kick to the floating rib. Ensure that it is the heel of your foot that makes contact, otherwise your kick will be weak and you could hurt your toes. Maintain a good posture and keep looking at your opponent.

Techniques: Drilling Stance

The drilling stance is designed to improve general fitness, flexibility, balance and strength. Regular practice enhances leg mobility, coordination of movement and breathing in preparation to perform many of the skills utilized in mok-gar.

1△ Lower your body into the horse stance and place both fists on your hips. Maintain a low posture and keep looking forwards.

2△ Turn to the left and move into the bow stance – so called because it echoes the shape of a bow and arrow. Place the fists out forwards (natural, relaxed breathing ensures that the practitioner exhales on the strike). Return to the horse stance and repeat the exercise to the opposite side. Repeat 2 or 3 times each side.

3△ Move through with your right leg into a forward cat position. Keep your knees well bent with about 70 per cent of your weight on your rear leg. Your hands should be in the claw style – known as the tiger-claw movement. Repeat, moving to your right side.

Techniques: Self-defence

Mok-gar utilizes many of the basic techniques and forms into effective
self-defence applications. The following demonstrates one such application,
showing the use of body blocks, hand strikes and leg techniques.

1△ Use a lower-forearm block as your opponent moves in with his
right hand to strike at your upper body.

2△ Take hold of your opponent's right wrist with your right hand.

3△ Bring your left hand up in a circular inwards and outwards
motion, aiming to strike the aggressor's nose with the back of your
knuckles. At this point the aggressor should be disorientated,
enabling you to either escape or to further restrain him.

△ An alternative defensive strike would be to utilize your legs,
making contact with the knife edge of your foot. Mok-gar is
well known for its front kicking strikes (sickle kicks).

Techniques: Advanced Weapons

Mok-gar utilizes a variety of weapons, many of which are unique to the art and were adapted from agricultural tools. Today, these weapons are used to maintain the tradition of mok-gar, and they are seen as an extension of the hand.

Tee chec – metal sai.

△ This is a classical pose using the *tee chec*. Here, a block and striking action, taken from a mok-gar form (a set of pre-designed moves), is being illustrated.

Pegs – two rounded pieces of wood.

△ This weapon gets its name of "the peg" because of its similarity to a wooden dowel. The pegs are principally used to strike at an aggressor's vulnerable spots, such as the mandible, limbs and pressure points.

Dip do – butterfly knives.

△ Illustrating the *dip do* (butterfly knives).

Siu so gee – two pieces of wood joined together by a metal chain.

△ The *siu so gee* was reputedly conceived when an instructor broke a favourite fighting stick. The *siu so gee* is sometimes referred to as the "little sweeper".

△ Demonstrating the *siu so gee* as an effective blocking weapon.

Three-section staff.

△ This staff is effective in both close and long-range combat. When extended it has a 9 ft (2.75 m) range. At close quarters, it can be used for choking and striking.

Kick Boxing

Characterised by high kicks and graceful poise, kick boxing is practised as much for general fitness as for self-defence. It is a highly popular and challenging modern martial art that has evolved from a combination of other disciplines.

Kick boxing is a relatively modern martial arts system, whose syllabus was derived by combining several fighting techniques from a variety of the more traditional disciplines, including kung fu, *kyokushinkai* karate, Thai boxing, *kyokky shinkai* and tae kwondo.

Martial arts boomed during the early 1970s and interest was greatly increased by their emphasis on competition fighting. Chinese styles of fighting began to take on a more Westernized form in the UK, and even more so in the United States, where the first real freestyle systems were beginning to be developed. Indeed, many people claim that kick boxing originated in the US during the 1970s. This, they say, was due to various American karate practitioners becoming frustrated with the limitations of tournament competitive scoring. While karate and the other disciplines were viewed as being entrenched with theories and set *kata*, and were performed in a controlled environment, practitioners wanted to see how effective their moves would be in a more realistic environment.

Great emphasis began to be placed on specialized techniques, such as kicks and punches, being delivered with full force. Although full-contact karate was already established, concerns were expressed for the safety of competitors. The first tournament stars of kick boxing were Bill "Superfoot" Wallis, Demetrius Havanas, Joe Lewis, Jeff Smith and Benny Urquidez.

Initially, some people felt that kick boxing looked amateurish, and questioned its validity as a traditional martial art. It is viewed by many as a sport that is a relatively new discipline and has yet to establish long-term traditions and history.

The World Kick Boxing Association (known as the WKA) apparently came into being in the early 1970s following a tournament with Benny Urquidez, who was sent to Japan to represent America in a kick boxing championship. He won his first world title in 1974. Although many other

Below Training with hand-held equipment and protective gear is essential if practitioners plan to take their skill into the ring.

Above Demonstrating superb leg control and posture when undertaking a strike to the head.

kick boxing representatives were defeated, Urquidez was able to hold his own, and he was successful to some extent because of his research into Eastern training methods and

his well-developed boxing and judo skills. One memorable bout was against the renowned Fujiwara, who was skilled in both karate and Thai boxing.

There is a close affinity between kick boxing and Thai boxing. While it is believed that the Americans had created this concept in their attempt to find a sport that could refine

Above As with conventional boxing, full contact kick boxing tournaments are conducted in a boxing ring environment.

as a ring matchmaker, staging a variety of successful events with such stars as Bill "Superfoot" Wallis.

New rules evolved and were introduced into kick boxing, most notably weight divisions – from fly weight to heavy weight – similar to those in orthodox boxing.

A down-side to the discipline in those early days was criticism of a high risk of injury. This led to improvement in the safety rules, such as contestants wearing protective clothing to cushion the impact of blows. When wearing protective clothing, there are two main fighting distinctions: semi-contact and full contact.

Semi-contact is where two fighters are allowed "reasonable", light contact in an attempt to score points off each other, in the same way as fencing. Full contact is usually fought under the same conditions as a standard boxing match, in which a knock-out is the ultimate aim. Individual clubs compete at inter-club competitions or in open, national and international, martial arts tournaments. Women do not generally compete against men, but women's kick boxing competitions are becoming more common.

Rules vary, but more recently tournament organizers have insisted on competitors wearing full protective clothing, for even in "semi-contact with control" bouts, injuries can still occur. Men are expected to wear a head guard, gum shield, groin guard, shin, hand and foot pads. Women are expected

full-contact competition, it is believed that the development of kick boxing was borne out of the WKA finding common ground between Eastern and Western fighting culture.

It is also believed that Joe Cawley and Don and Judy Quinn, along with Howard Hansen, a *shorin ryu* karate black belt, were the initial promoters of kick boxing and worked together for improved recognition. Hansen took kick boxing a stage further, by introducing fights in a boxing ring, rather than the usual karate tournament bouts. He became known

Below Protective clothing or not, care and caution are always of paramount importance.

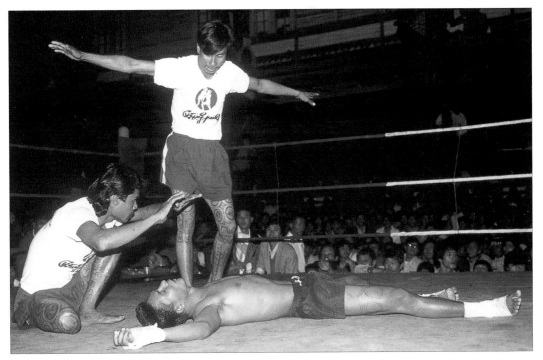

Above In Thailand many fights end this way!

to wear the same, except that the groin guard is swapped for a chest guard. These rules apply to children.

The order of belts (representing degrees of proficiency) are: white, yellow, orange, blue, green, purple, brown and black. Once the black-belt level has been achieved, progression to a higher grade is through degrees of *dan*, signified by a stripe in the belt – for example, a 1st-*dan* practitioner is entitled to wear a black belt containing one stripe.

Below Although competitive kick boxing is a full contact sport, etiquette forbids opponents from striking each other once one party has hit the ground.

Although traditional moves are not really taught, there are set moves that practitioners need to acquire in order to attain each belt. These include hand and kick blocks, shadow boxing, sparring, kicks, punches and wood breaking.

Caution: any breaking techniques must be supervised by an instructor. Never try to perform breaking techniques without professional guidance, as serious injury may result. Injuries may be immediate or take years to become apparent, but the risk is very real. It is an aggressive sport, but as with most other martial arts disciplines, the true kick boxer is less likely to initiate or be involved in violence, preferring to walk away from a difficult situation.

Benefits of kick boxing

There are numerous benefits derived from learning kick boxing, which extend into many aspects of everyday life. These include:

- Appeals to both men and women, irrespective of occupation or level of fitness
- Develops strength and flexibility
- Improves mental agility and stamina
- Powerful and skilful sport
- Increases confidence
- Promotes fitness and well-being
- Reduces stress
- Promotes comradeship
- Assists with self-defence skills

Clothing and Equipment

In competitive kick boxing men are bare-chested, and both sexes wear shorts and protective guards. General practitioners will often wear a loose top and trousers for comfort, and occasionally padded footwear to protect themselves and their partner.

The clothing of kick boxing practitioners can vary from club to club. Designs are similar and usually consist of a comfortable top and elasticated trousers. Any colour is acceptable. In view of the emphasis on controlled fighting (sparring), it is very important to wear protective clothing and equipment. Protective equipment must be checked regularly to prevent any unnecessary injury to either the practitioner or their partner.

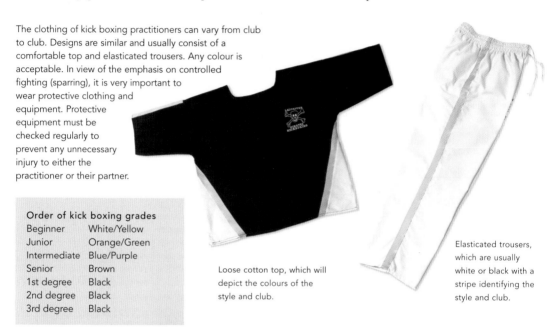

Order of kick boxing grades

Beginner	White/Yellow
Junior	Orange/Green
Intermediate	Blue/Purple
Senior	Brown
1st degree	Black
2nd degree	Black
3rd degree	Black

Loose cotton top, which will depict the colours of the style and club.

Elasticated trousers, which are usually white or black with a stripe identifying the style and club.

△ Protective head-guard and gloves for full contact sparring. The head-guard must fit securely.

△ Padded footwear to protect both the practitioner and his/her partner during kicking strikes.

Etiquette

Etiquette in kick boxing is used at the beginning of a practice session and when competing in a tournament. As with other disciplines, etiquette is used as a sign of respect towards your partner or opponent. There is only one bow, as shown.

Ready position.

1◁ Stand with an upright posture – back straight and eyes looking forward. Ensure your shoulders are relaxed and stomach muscles firm. Turn your hands into fists by curling the fingers (starting with the little finger). Place your thumb securely on top of your fingers and position both hands in front of your body. Make sure your elbows are tucked in and feet comfortably astride. Bend both knees slightly and keep your elbows close in to your waist, to ensure there are no vulnerable areas where an opponent could strike. Maintain an inner calm while adopting an assertive, well-focused attitude towards your training partner.

2▷ Lower your body, keeping your elbows well tucked in. Perform a bow at about 30 degrees without taking your eyes off your partner.

Fighting stance.

◁ Move forwards from the ready position, using your preferred leg and with your fists raised. Keep your elbows close to your body and your fists clenched. Keep your guard up in front of your body as a protective measure, to deflect or strike, as required. In this side view you can see the correct upright posture and the angle of the fists. Fists that are too high increase the vulnerability of your lower body; if they are too low, your face is at risk. The centre-body position offers the best overall protection.

Warm-up Exercises

Exercises in kick boxing improve stamina and enhance flexibility. Below is a selection of the more important exercises used in warm-up sessions, prior to basic practice. There is particular emphasis on leg stretching and stamina building.

Warm-up 1 – This exercise is excellent for stretching the spine and increasing general flexibility.

1△ Lie down on a flat, comfortable surface and slightly raise your knees off the floor. Place your hands at the side of your head.

2△ Keeping your hands lightly at the side of your head, raise your torso while pulling your knees up and into your chest. Lie back down without letting your feet or head touch the ground and repeat 4 or 5 times.

Warm-up 2 – This exercise is called the horse-riding stance. It is intended to strengthen buttocks, inner thighs, triceps and biceps.

Warm-up 3 – This exercise needs to be performed slowly and gently, to allow yourself to become supple naturally. It stretches and strengthens the hamstrings and needs to be practised regularly.

△ With your legs stretched fairly wide, bend your knees while keeping your back straight. Thrust your left fist out in front of your body in a striking position and place your right fist on your hip, touching your waistline. Hold this position for about 60–90 seconds. Alternate with your opposite fist and repeat 4 or 5 times.

△ Let your partner take hold of your leg at the ankle and gently raise it, stopping periodically to ensure you are comfortable. Keep a straight back leg and upright posture. Hold for 20–30 seconds and repeat 3 to 4 times each side.

Warm-up 4 – It is important to perform this exercise sensibly, with both partners working together. You will cause unnecessary pain if you push down too heavily.

Warm-up 5 – This strengthens the stomach muscles and the lower back of both partners. Cooperation is important to ensure maximum benefit and safety.

△ Lie on your back and place your hands either at the sides of your body or lightly on your stomach and your legs raised straight up. Let your legs fall apart and keep your breathing slow and calm. Your partner then gently pushes down on your inner thighs, stretching your legs apart, for approximately 60 seconds.

△ Lie on your back and bring your knees into your chest. Place your hands, palms down, on the floor at your sides. Allow your standing partner to lean forwards at 45 degrees, resting her stomach on the soles of your feet with hands clasped behind her back. Both partners need to keep the stomach muscles tense. Hold for 20–30 seconds and swap positions.

Warm-up 6 – This exercise strengthens the upper body muscles through the application of mild resistance against your partner's applied reasonable pressure.

Warm-up 7 – This wheelbarrow press-up is an advanced exercise for experienced practitioners. It develops the triceps, biceps and abdomen.

△ Lie face down on the floor in a press-up position with feet together, hands flat and back straight. With your partner's hands on your shoulder applying gentle downward pressure, push your body up by straightening your elbows. Relax for a few seconds after each press-up. Repeat the exercise no more than 5 times in a session. Change roles and repeat.

△ Go into the press-up position and then let your partner take hold of and raise your ankles to waist level. Push down to perform the press-ups, ensuring maximum pressure on the upper part of your body, while your partner continues to hold your legs by the ankles. Then lower your body towards the floor and do not let your face make contact with the ground. Push down as near to the floor as you can. Finally, push your body up from the floor as high as you can and then clap your hands before going back down. Perform this exercise fairly slowly and no more than 10 times.

Techniques: Fighting Stance

The fighting stance is used when practising techniques with a partner and in preparation for sparring. If your partner is not wearing correct body and head protection it is important to make sure you do not make actual contact.

1◁ With your feet shoulder-width apart, step back into the ready position and assume the guard position. With your preferred leg forwards place your feet firmly on the floor with your front foot facing forwards and the rear foot at an angle of about 45 degrees. Keep your eyes forward and fixed on your partner.

2▷ As your partner moves in to strike your face with a left punch, maintain your body position and perform an upward rising block (known as an upper block) with your left arm. Keep your right fist at your hip, ready to perform a counter-strike. Maintain a good posture and keep your eyes on your partner.

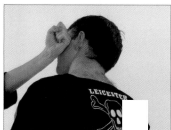

△ Alternative counter-strikes can be seen in close-up. First, a back fist strike to the temple. Make sure your fist is tightly closed with the thumb locked on top.

△ A ridge hand blow to the temple. Tuck the thumb into the centre of your palm and keep your fingers straight. Deliver this blow by making a large circular action from the centre of your body to enhance the power of the strike.

3△ As the left arm block exposes your partner's body perform a right-hand punch to the solar plexus. Make sure your blocking arm is pulled back as this will add extra power to the blow.

Side kicks are difficult to block and are very effective in sparring. The body is turned to the side, having the advantage of making the practitioner a smaller target. The knife edge of the foot is the striking area which makes contact.

1◁ Lift your knee high, as close to your chest as you can. Point your toes downwards and keep your hand guard in the front position. Your back foot must be firmly placed flat on the floor – avoid lifting the heel since this will take you off balance.

2△ Perform a side kick by extending your raised leg, turning the toes inwards so that the side of the foot (the knife edge) makes contact. Try to keep a good, upright posture to assist your balance. Keep your guard hands up and maintain focus on your partner.

3△Complete the practice by bringing your kicking foot back again. Maintain the hand guard position. This requires strength and control and it minimizes the risk of your leg being grabbed when extended and in a self-defence situation. Bring the kicking foot back down to the floor in preparation to begin again.

Techniques: Self-defence

Kick boxing utilizes various self-defence moves, and the following technique is just one example of the many strategies available when seeking to learn self-protection. Physical defence is used only as a last resort, when all else has failed.

1△ Stand in the ready position with your fists at waist level. Your opponent adopts a fighting posture.

2△ Your opponent moves in with a side-kicking attack.

3△ You move 45 degrees to the right (away from the kicking leg) and then move back in with a hooking block. This is immediately followed by a punch to either the upper body or head region.

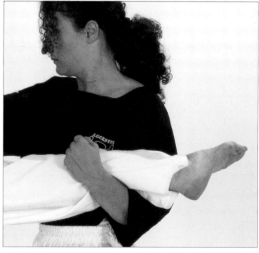

△ The close-up view shows how the hooking block works. This is achieved by using a scooping motion to sweep the attacking leg, and then control the opponent's body, by immediately securing the leg in towards your body. This puts the opponent in a very vulnerable position, where it is difficult for him to maintain balance with only one foot in the air.

4△ You can now perform a leg sweep to unbalance your opponent by bringing your right leg around his leg. *Note: it is important to continue securing the opponent's right leg to maintain control of the technique. This technique is only used in self-defence practice.*

△ This close-up shows your hand position on your opponent's shoulder, ready to push him forwards and downwards on to the floor. It is important to hold on to your opponent when practising this technique, by taking hold of his clothing on the right or left shoulder.

5△ Once your opponent is on the floor, start to move your head and body to the side and out of reach, so that you cannot be grabbed and pulled to the floor. Maintain a good stance and posture to help you avoid losing your balance and falling down with your opponent.

6△ A variety of finishing techniques can be applied, ranging from punching to kicking. Ideally a kicking technique is useful, as it enables you to maintain a safer distance.

Techniques: Contact Sparring

Contact sparring is a fundamental element of kick boxing. It is commonplace for men and women to practise with each other, although in the competition environment sexes are usually demarcated. The following demonstrates one basic routine.

Competition techniques
It is important that you use the correct protective equipment – head padding, body armour, shin, hand and foot protection – in competition. Both partners will wear gum shields, and men must wear groin guards and women chest guards. It is very important that you show respect towards your partner. Sparring should not be seen as an opportunity to hurt somebody.

1◁ Stand opposite your partner, making sure you maintain focus. Keep your guard up and your feet a shoulder-width apart. An inner sense of assertion and control is vital. Stand about one and a half arm's length away from your partner, in readiness to commence sparring. If you are too close you increase your vulnerability to being punched or kicked.

2△ Perform a bow by lowering the top part of your body by about 30 degrees. Maintain your guard by keeping your eyes fixed on your partner.

3△ Move into fighting posture by touching gloves. This is a sign of respect, indicating that although you intend to go into a fighting situation, you are still showing sportsmanship and friendship.

4△ The object of the sparring is to increase speed and agility. As one partner may try to score a point with a kick, the other must try to block. Note the good upright posture when kicking and the guard being kept in place in preparation for a counter-attack.

5△ If you manage to block a kick or punch, try to score a point by punching the body or head region.

Techniques: Close Punching

The following examples demonstrate a variety of close punching techniques. It is important to practise these techniques under proper supervision from a qualified instructor, and while wearing the correct protective clothing.

1◁ A round-house hook to the side of the head. This technique demonstrates an effective strike to a vulnerable area of the head, e.g. hinge of jaw (mandible), and therefore warrants points.

2▷ An uppercut to the chin. This strike has to be delivered at close range and could follow a number of other striking techniques. As with all striking techniques which make contact, an opening has been created, either by your partner letting his guard down, or their position inviting an opportunity to strike at a vulnerable area.

3▽ A straight punch to the body. As your partner's guard has moved, a vulnerable area has been exposed, which creates an opportunity to strike the solar plexus or stomach region, for example.

Caution

Although partners wear protective equipment, a degree of caution is still exercised through the sensible application of punching techniques. Remember: when sparring, partners are moving around, which requires skills in distancing and focusing. It is easy to hit an accessible partner, and therefore the skill lies in effective control and discipline of movement.

Techniques: Competition Blocking

The following demonstrates a variety of blocking techniques which may be employed against different attacks. Leg movements feature predominantly in kick boxing and are difficult to block, as the legs are the most powerful striking tool.

△ A defence against a head attack, using an upper block.

△ A double-handed block to defend against a kick to the body.

△ An open-handed block to defend against a circular leg strike.

△ An outward-hooking block to a leg attack.

Techniques: Advanced Kicking

The following demonstrates some of the advanced kicking techniques used in kick boxing. The top two pictures display kicks used in competition fighting, and the bottom pictures show more advanced techniques not found in competition sparring.

△ A head kick being counter-attacked by an upper-head block.

△ A spinning back kick into the solar plexus region.

△ A flying side kick, known as a "jump or flying technique", achieved by jumping, turning and kicking your partner while in mid air. A jump kick is to the body whereas a flying kick is to the head.

△ A flying front kick.

Scores

In competition, points are awarded for particular techniques, with extra points being scored for more complicated and difficult manoeuvres such as combination techniques.

Points can vary, but the standard scoring system is usually:
- One point for a hand technique to the body or head
- Two points for a leg technique to the body
- Three points for a leg technique to the head

T'ai chi chuan

T'ai chi chuan combines the *yin* and *yang* approach of serene movements for health and wellbeing with a strong fighting system of self-defence. It is an excellent discipline for people of all ages and abilities, including children as young as five years of age. Older people also benefit from t'ai chi chuan, such as the 81-year-old Chinese Grand Master Jiang Hao Quan, who is convinced that his youthful appearance and healthy mind and body are all due to his t'ai chi chuan training.

History and Philosophy

Associated with good health and longevity, t'ai chi is often practised as a means of attaining serenity and peace of mind. Its simple, fluid movements require a focus and calmness of mind that practitioners believe can influence many aspects of everyday life.

The initial aim of t'ai chi chuan is to teach the practitioner to relax. "Relax" in this sense does not mean to flop loosely around, but rather to use the body as efficiently as possible, with no muscular tension. The foremost requirement is good posture with relaxed shoulders, an upright back and firmly rooted stance. T'ai chi chuan incorporates chi kung exercises, which encourage deep breathing, improved blood circulation and greater efficiency of the body's systems. On a mental level, the quiet concentration required for t'ai chi chuan brings a serene state of mind, in which the everyday stresses of life can be placed in their proper perspective. This leads to a more tolerant, even state of mind, and a calm mind is able to respond more quickly and effectively to challenges in any situation.

At this level, the art is accessible to anyone – age, health or infirmity are not barriers to reaping some of the rewards that t'ai

Below T'ai chi is suitable for people of all ages and abilities and is often practised in public places.

chi chuan has to offer. However, to reach the higher levels it is necessary to study the art in its wider context. Practising the martial aspects of t'ai chi chuan involves more complex forms of chi kung, body strengthening, two-person practice and various supplementary exercises. Such training is more demanding than basic-form practice, but it does bring greater benefits in terms of mental and physical health, as well as providing an excellent self-defence method. At the higher stages the theoretical aspects of the art also become more apparent.

As a martial art, t'ai chi chuan works on a number of levels, but the principal aim is to teach practitioners to relax and become fluid in their movements. This allows for smoother actions and quicker response times. The objective is for self-defence to become a reflexive action rather than a repetition of technique. There is a variety of sensitivity exercises which allow the practitioner to adapt instantly to an opponent and to react in the most appropriate manner. Incoming force will, typically, be diverted, however slightly, and the corresponding opening in the opponent's defence exploited. The level of response can range from applying locks and holds, to immobilizing an opponent, through to highly damaging strikes against nerve centres and acupuncture points (*dim mak*).

THE ORIGINS

T'ai chi chuan is usually translated into English as "the supreme ultimate fist". The term t'ai chi refers to the *yin-yang* symbol prevalent in Chinese culture, more commonly known as the "hard" and "soft" sign – the two opposites coming together. The term chuan refers to a boxing method – boxing in this context means a method of empty-hand combat, rather than a sporting contest. Thus, as the name suggests, t'ai chi chuan is a self-defence method, one that is based on the Chinese Taoist philosophy of life.

T'ai chi chuan is also referred to as internal kung fu. The reference to "internal" here refers to the general rule that t'ai chi emphasizes the development of the internal aspects of the body – breathing, flexibility and the mind – as opposed to external tension or muscular strength.

The roots of t'ai chi chuan are enshrouded in myth, and all but lost in legend, but one of the most popular theories refers to the art being originated by Chang San Feng, who was born in 1247. Chang studied at the famous Shaolin temple and mastered its system of martial arts. He then travelled to Wutang Mountain, a

region populated by Taoist hermits where, as the legend goes, Chang watched as a stork and a snake fought. Fascinated by the fluidity of their movements and their ability both to evade and attack simultaneously, Chang adapted his system to incorporate the movements he had witnessed. It is also said that Chang had developed a high degree of skill in striking the body's acupuncture points, which he also incorporated into his art, though heavily disguised.

This art was passed down in great secrecy for many generations, eventually reaching the Wang family. The Wang family passed it on to the Chen family, who absorbed it into their own system, known as *pao chuan* (meaning "cannon fist"). The art at this stage was not called t'ai chi chuan: that name came to be applied only many years later. The Chens were held in high regard for their martial arts prowess and this attracted Yang Lu Chan (1799–1872) to the Chen village. The art was still being taught in great secrecy, but through his dedication and commitment Yang was able to ingratiate himself and learn from

Above The tranquility of early morning practice.

Left Chang San Feng, the legendary founder of t'ai chi chuan.

the head of the style, Chen Chan Hsing. Then, after a short period of studying with the Wang family, Yang travelled to the imperial capital of Peking.

Once in Peking, Yang met many challengers from other styles of martial art, but remained undefeated, earning the nickname "Invincible Yang". Due to his reputation, Yang was ordered to

Left Yang Lu Chan (1799–1872), the undefeated founder of the Yang family t'ai chi chuan.

Below Flowing and serene movements in group practice.

teach the imperial family and the Manchu imperial bodyguard. It was impossible to ignore such a decree, yet Yang taught just a part of the art to the unpopular Manchu, retaining the knowledge of the complete system only for close family and trusted students.

T'ai chi chuan's popularity began to spread among the nobility of the day and Yang's sons, both of whom were formidable fighters, continued this process, although the art was to some extent modified to suit the less rigorous lifestyles of the rich.

TRANSITIONARY PROCESS

It was during the 1920s that t'ai chi chuan really began to spread to different parts of the country. China at that time was in turmoil, with the population sick and ailing. The health benefits of the art became recognized and the once-secret art of the Chen family became a national exercise. You should note, however, that the art in its more popular form contains only part of the training of the traditional family styles, which, even today, are taught only to close students in order to maintain their secrecy and discretion. The main family styles – Chen, Yang, Hao and Wu – form the basis for many variations of style and form. Since the 1960s the art, in many guises, has spread to the West, making it a truly global phenomenon and the most widely practised martial art in the world.

Above Yang Lu group broad sword practice.

Right Group t'ai chi practice.

CONCLUSION

Power training consists of *chi kung* to develop internal strength, as well as methods to strengthen the tendons and ligaments. The ability to issue power (*fa jing*) from close range is a primary feature of t'ai chi chuan. This involves incorporating the whole body into one unit behind an attack. T'ai chi chuan includes punches, kicks, locks, open-hand techniques and throws in its repertoire, as well as traditional Chinese weapons: sword, broadsword, staff and spear.

Today, while traditional practitioners of t'ai chi chuan are still in evidence, the majority practise the art in order both to maintain and improve their health and to provide an increasingly necessary antidote to the stresses and strains of modern-day life.

Benefits of t'ai chi chuan

- Enhances the ability of the practitioner to maintain an inner calm
- Enhances motivation and performance in all areas of life, such as work, social and home life
- Increases flexibility of muscles and movement of the body
- Increases quality of life through the "inner-calmness" approach to difficult situations
- Improves the sense of humour

- Works towards a healthy mind and body, which can slow down the ageing process
- Reduces stress through increased awareness of relaxation skills
- Reduces tension through the development of inner energy and calmness of mind
- Reduces the need for other stimulants, such as alcohol and drugs
- Develops deep concentration and mental focus

Clothing and Equipment

Although it is traditional to wear a black suit, many t'ai chi practitioners choose to practise dressed in loose, comfortable clothing that is conducive to the free, graceful movements of the art. Weapons, such as swords, are used to demonstrate the skill and elegance of the techniques.

The traditional clothing and equipment for t'ai chi chuan is much the same as that for other Chinese martial arts: a black mandarin suit, flat-bottomed shoes and the traditional weapons – staff, sword, broad sword and spear. Generally speaking, class students wear any suitable loose clothing. Traditional uniforms are usually reserved for special occasions and public demonstrations.

Other than this, there are also various types of equipment available, such as focus pads and kick bags used in self-defence training, or for various supplementary exercises, such as grip training and body conditioning. Protective clothing may be worn in some instances, such as for students who are just beginning to spar.

Right Standard clothing required for t'ai chi chuan.

black mandarin jacket

black trousers

gim

broad sword

Etiquette

Etiquette is important within most martial arts disciplines and is carried out as a sign of respect. The following moves are performed at the beginning and the end of the training session, and before practising with a partner.

1△ Stand in a relaxed position with your feet together and hands at your sides. Keep your back straight and shoulders relaxed. Clear your mind and try to induce a feeling of inner calm.

2△ Bring both hands up in front of your chest, making your right hand into a fist and keeping the left hand open, fingers together. Place your right hand in the palm of the left and keep your eyes looking forwards.

3△ Make a 30-degree bow forwards, keeping your hands together and eyes looking forwards. This is done to show respect to the art and to your training partner during practice.

△ This profile view of the bow shows that the position of your arms is slightly extended forward. Move back into the upright position, ready to commence practice.

Warm-up Exercises

The following demonstrates two warm-up exercises that are usually performed before practising the basic techniques. The purpose of the exercises is to promote suppleness and flexibility within the body.

Warm-up 1 – This exercise helps make the waist, hips and the lower-back region more supple.

1△ Stand upright with both hands cupped together and your thumbs touching. Bend your knees slightly to lower your posture. Both feet should be facing forwards. Place your left thumb on top of your right.

2△ Pull your left hand around the side of your body, with the right hand following in a flowing action. Make sure you keep your feet facing forwards as your hands move around your body in a circular motion.

3△ Draw your hands backwards in a circular motion, ensuring that your palms are always facing upwards, almost as if you are holding a small bowl, and then start to move your hands in front of your body.

4△ Continuing the flowing movement, bring your hands slowly and gently in front of the body. Breathe naturally throughout the exercise.

5△ Continue the flowing action, with your left hand moving across the body towards your head.

6△ Lean backwards from the waist, flexing your stomach muscles to strengthen and increase flexibility. From this position rotate the upper part of the body and then resume the original starting position.

Warm-up 2 – This exercise strengthens the arms and requires the controlled breathing described below.

205

1△ Stand in the ready position with your feet a shoulder-width apart. Make both hands into fists by your hips, palms upwards. Make sure your posture is upright, knees are slightly bent and your feet are facing forwards.

2△ Slowly push your right fist forwards while exhaling. As you bring your fist back to the hip, inhale slowly. Perform this action slowly and with focus.

3△ Repeat the previous action, this time using your left fist, remembering to maintain the correct breathing pattern.

△ This side view shows the slightly bent knees and correct, upright posture that is required for this exercise.

4△ After performing this exercise several times, return both fists to your hips and bring your feet together.

Techniques: Hook Technique

A popular technique in t'ai chi is known as *tan pien*, or the "hook" position.
This technique has various applications, namely a strike using the back of the hand,
wrist strike, striking with the fingers, or blocking or breaking a gripping technique.

1◁ Adopt a forwards stance with your left palm pushing forwards at chest height and your right arm extended to the rear with the hand in the hook position. Ensure that 70 per cent of your weight is on your front leg in preparation to move backwards.

▽ Note the angle of the hand and the fingertips touching in this detail of the hook position.

2△ The rear foot turns outwards and the weight begins to move on to the back leg. This is a smooth and continuous motion. The left hand begins to drop as if blocking a striking technique.

3△ Lower your posture by bending your back (right) leg so that your upper and lower leg form a 90-degree angle. Transfer 70 per cent of your body weight on to your right leg. Keeping your back straight and eyes fixed on your imaginary opponent, slide your left arm down your left leg, palm uppermost and fingers outstretched.

Techniques: Striking

In this exercise you need the assistance of a partner, who assumes the role of an aggressor. Here, t'ai chi employs techniques in a continuous flow to defend against an aggressive strike. The following demonstrates the method of moving in from medium distance to close range.

1△ While it could be argued that in a street situation an aggressor might not approach you in quite this fashion, it is important when learning and practising techniques that safety and basic movements are applied to learn distancing and timing.

2△ In this situation the aggressor has thrown a punch. Note how the defender adopts the hooking technique, described earlier in this chapter, and applies it as self-defence in a circular blocking and striking action. Fluidity and timing are very important for this technique to be applied successfully.

3△ The defender aims to strike the temple. Note how the fingers are pushed together, with the thumb locked, while the back of the hand makes contact on the temple region.

4△ The defender moves through, with his left leg across the back of the aggressor's right leg, and applies his right hand around the throat, while the left hand is placed on the side of the aggressor's body.

5△ Another way to finish is to move in as in step 4, but to place the right hand on the back of the aggressor's neck, aiming for the pressure point that will render the aggressor unconscious. Energy is directed downwards to take the aggressor to the floor.

△ Demonstrating the correct hand position for accuracy on the pressure point.

Techniques: Locking and Striking

Set techniques have been developed to enhance body distance and mental awareness when practising with a partner. This technique enhances the skill of developing fluidity of movement from striking to grappling with an aggressor.

1△ As the defender in this exercise, you should adopt a more relaxed stance and alert demeanour than that shown by the aggressor, who has both fists forwards. Transfer about 70 per cent of your weight on to the back leg. Keep your left hand in the open position, palm forwards, in front of your chest. Your right hand covers the lower part of your body, ready to deflect a blow.

2△ Using a circular action with your arms, turn your hips forwards, towards the aggressor, to support a blocking action. Block the punch with the outside of your right forearm. This is known as the "ward-off", or *p'eng*. Your left hand is positioned either to apply another defensive move or a strike.

△ Showing the correct hand position to maintain close contact.

3△ Strike with the heel of your left palm into the pressure point on the side of the aggressor's right ribs.

4△ Pull your right hand up and over the aggressor's striking fist. At the same time, bring your left hand along to the aggressor's elbow position. Then push down on the aggressor's pressure point at the elbow, while simultaneously pushing the aggressor's arm forwards and away from his face. This locks the wrist in position and restrains the aggressor. At this point, bring your right leg completely around the aggressor's right leg, in preparation to apply a throwing technique.

Techniques: Rear Defence Escape

Many people fear being grabbed from the rear, especially around the throat.
The following movement describes one of the many defences that can be applied
to release such an attack, followed by an effective restraint.

△ Make sure that you take a firm grip of the aggressor's hand as you start to pull the hand and arm away from your throat. Step backwards also, to prepare for the full disengagement.

1△ In this scenario, an attacker has grabbed you around the throat with his left arm, taking hold of your right wrist with his right hand.

2△ Bring your free left hand up and take hold of the aggressor's left hand at your throat, aiming for the pressure point that is situated between the thumb and the forefinger. At the same time, step back with your right foot and bend forwards to start to unbalance the aggressor.

3△ Pull your body forwards in a downwards motion, at the same time pulling your left hand down and your right arm across your body. This pulls the opponent further off balance. Note that your rear leg is straight and your front leg is bent at 90 degrees.

4△ Use your elbow to aim a blow at the aggressor's solar plexus. Bring your right leg behind his left leg to prepare for an arm restrain. Push his left arm over your head into a locking position, maintain a low posture with a good bend on your left leg and your back leg straight.

5△ Push the aggressor's left arm down, making sure that the arm is straight by securely holding the wrist with your left hand and placing your right hand in an upwards fist position, against the aggressor's arm.

6△ Continue to apply pressure as you push the aggressor to the floor.

Techniques: Pushing Hands

The following is just one example of a basic technique of the pushing hands (*toi sau*)
method for which t'ai chi chuan is famous. *Toi sau* develops the practitioner's
awareness, sensitivity, skills and anticipation of an opponent's movement.

1△ As you can see, the age, height and gender of the partners in this exercise are irrelevant. Here, the woman (partner 1) places her right hand, palm inwards, in the defensive "ward-off" position against the man's (partner 2) open-hand, forwards position.

2△ Using a circular action with your arms, turn your hips forwards, towards the aggressor, to support a blocking action. Block the punch with the outside of your right forearm. This is known as the "ward-off", or "*p'eng*". Your left hand is positioned either to apply another defensive move or a strike.

3△ Partner 1 continues the circular action in a flowing motion, pushing forwards. It is very much like a circular, flowing action, twisting the side of the hand and the palm around. Partner 1 is now pushing towards partner 2's chest in a reversal of the original stance.

4△ Partner 2 now allows the circular action to go across his partner's body and towards his right side, preparing to push back into the centre as a prelude to repeating the whole exercise.

Techniques: Advanced Weapon Techniques

T'ai chi chuan utilizes a variety of weapons, including straight sword, staff and broad sword/sabre. Below are some of the moves taken from various *kata*, or sequences, demonstrating the use of weapons in both defensive and striking actions.

△ "Drift with the current." This is a slicing action to the lower leg.

△ This technique is known as the "big dipper" and is used when the practitioner is blocking with the straight sword and preparing to strike with the left leg.

△ The broad sword is kept out of view in preparation to strike. This technique is known as "conceal the sabre to kick".

△ This balanced stance is known as "lifting the leg to pierce" and it is used in a stabbing action.

△ "Turning the sword/sabre to pierce."

Kendo

On first impressions, kendo appears to be very physical and aggressive, with the dynamics of a fast-striking action and high-pitched screams. Yet it is an art that places great emphasis on the development of a high level of skill in concentration, timing, awareness, physical agility, footwork, body movement and inherent respect. Kendo was derived from the ancient art of Japanese samurai swordsmanship. Armour is worn for protection, and a sword made of four sections of bamboo is bound together to make what is known as a *shinai*.

History and Philosophy

The kendo practitioner seeks to discipline their character through the application of the principles of the *katana* (single-edged sword). It is based on ancient Japanese rituals of swordmanship, and is both a physically and mentally demanding martial art.

Kenjutsu is the earliest martial art, dating back to before 1590, followed by kendo, which had more intellectual and philosophical characteristics. Kenjutsu became modern kendo, which has developed a sport-orientated nature that still embodies many of the traditional values.

It is believed that the origins of kenjutsu are located in the classical Chinese era, which dates back more than 2,000 years. However, while kendo is very much a modern art that has been influenced by kenjutsu, its roots can be traced back as far back as AD789, through the history of the art of the sword which is linked inextricably to the history of ancient Japan. It was at this time that *Komutachi*, the sword exercise, was introduced as an instruction for the sons of the kuge (noblemen) in the city of Nara, then the capital of Japan.

Today's kendo very much relates to the changes in swordsmanship that came about in the early Tokugawa period of around 1600–1750. At this time, Japan embarked on a period of increasing stability, and the change from kenjutsu to kendo took place. It was not until the end of the 18th

Right Two kendo practitoners with *shinais* (wooden swords) locked in combat.

Below Kendo should not be treated simply as a sport but as a lifetime's study.

century, however, that the *shinai* (bamboo stick) became commonly used in basic practice. *Kendoka* (kendo students) would also work with the *bokken* (a wooden replica of a sword) and the *katana* (a practice sword).

It is interesting to note that, for the greatest part of Japanese history, kendo and/or kenjutsu were practised almost exclusively by the *bushi*, known more commonly today as the samurai. Today, people of all walks of life, gender, abilities and cultures can be found practising the art of kendo. No longer is it just confined to the boundary of Japan, as it opens its doors to many other countries

Above Kendo was derived from the ancient art of Japanese samurai swordsmanship.

worldwide. It can also be said that kendo, like other martial arts, is a unifying activity, creating a sense of harmony through its competitive element. This was witnessed in March 1997 when the Heian shrine in Kyoto opened its doors to representatives from around the world to demonstrate the art of iaido, another martial art. At the same time, teams from many different countries took part in the tenth World Kendo Competition.

As with iaido, the philosophy of kendo is challenging. In many ways, it is viewed as contradictory by those who do not appreciate the importance of abandoning their own desires. This is not easy in a competitive world, with its increasingly materialist attitude, but as Musashi Miyamoto, one of Japan's most famous swordsmen (1584–1645), once said: "to win the battle is to be prepared to die."

The concept of kendo

The following, extracted from the All Japan Kendo Federation's set of principles, highlights the true concept of kendo and the purpose of practising this art:

- To mould the mind and body
- To cultivate a vigorous spirit

Through correct and rigid training:
- To strive for improvement in the art of kendo
- To hold in esteem human courtesy and honour
- To associate with others with sincerity
- To pursue for ever the cultivation of oneself

Thus you will be able:
- To love your country and society
- To contribute to the development of culture
- To promote peace and prosperity among all peoples

This is very much the philosophy of the *kendoka*. Practitioners who enter into a fight, primarily concerned with not being hit, will find that their adversaries will more easily score points or win the battle. In kendo, the strike is viewed as a by-product of what has come before and what is about to follow, and there is a strong emphasis placed on initiative and taking control. This plays an important part in kendo development, along with a constant sense of alertness.

The aim of kendo is for *kendoka* to react intuitively, with fluency and elegance. Speed and body movement are of the utmost importance in the delivery of a skilful technique. Yet the aim is not to be the first one to score a point or to win in the kendo practice, but to work together, striving towards good technique, giving and taking along the way. Only in competition should this philosophical aim be different.

On first learning kendo, or any other martial art, it is very important to tread slowly. It is very easy when people wear armour to suddenly feel they can dive in regardless, without appreciating the need for continual practice to develop the skills to a standard acceptable in the art. It is important not only to demonstrate proficiency in the art but to ensure safe practice, both for yourself and your partner.

Kendo places great emphasis on moral values, discipline and self-control. Try to think of kendo not as a sport that you might participate in for a few years, but as a lifetime's study. Mental and physical control are of the utmost importance, since the balance of the two leads to harmony, not only in the art itself, but in your general well-being. It is for this reason that there are four deep-rooted mental hurdles that *kendoka* must overcome: fear, doubt, surprise and confusion. Collectively, these are known as "the four poisons of kendo".

COMPETITION (*SHIAI*)

When experienced practitioners come together, especially in competition (*shiai*), the atmosphere can be very exciting. Competition is a vital part of kendo, since it provides an opportunity for practitioners to try out, under conditions of pressure and stress, the various techniques. The judges look for good posture, composure and the ability to deliver a strike effectively with all the skill and mental confidence that is required to show a good *kendoka*.

In an effort to avoid kendo competition becoming a violent, attacking activity (sometimes referred to as "bash and dash") based solely on winning, it is important that *kendoka*, especially beginners, develop the mental confidence to remain calm (*shiai geiko*). Kendoka strive to remain calm, alert and decisive, and to accept defeat as a guide to developing their technique and skill for the future. A kendo *shiai* usually lasts for five minutes, and the winner is the first to score two points, or a single point if the time limit elapses first. There are three court referees and a senior referee off court. There is also a timekeeper to ensure that the competitors are within the allocated match period. The rules of the competition are always strictly adhered to.

Below More then 5,000 Japanese children during the All Japan Children's Military Arts Summer Training Meeting held in Tokyo.

Above Students of kendo (*kendoka*) demonstrating the dynamics of the fast cutting action and fighting spirit that are intrinsic to the art.

SCORING IN KENDO

During the *shiai* there are many opportunities for *kendoka* to learn and refine their skills. For example, there are differences between *shiai* (contests) and dojo *jigeiko* (free practice). This is perhaps best demonstrated in the example of opponents fighting within the parameters of the rules set by the leading organizations. This will result in a winner and a loser and, in comparison to Olympic fencing, where a point is scored simply by making contact with the target, in kendo several elements are required in order for the essential winning point to be scored. These include:

- Creating an opportunity to attack a vulnerable point on the body.
- The accuracy and skill of the strike itself, which must be delivered with the correct spirit – sword and body working together as one.

A very important part of kendo training is *zanshin*, which translates as "good awareness" – that is, of the opponent and the continuing element of battle. It is the ability to take in the environment, being sensitive to any threat or other factors that could lead to injury, even death. *Zanshin* enables *kendoka* to attain a heightened ability and awareness, and thus to react instantaneously to minimize risk.

Benefits of kendo

The benefits derived from learning kendo affect many aspects of your everyday life. These include:

- Speed and agility
- General fitness
- Self-discipline and positive attitude
- Precision and timing
- Self-confidence
- Self-control and well-being
- Comradeship
- Inner peace and calm

Clothing and Equipment

Kendo practitioners (*kendoka*) wear distinctive clothing, resembling armour, to protect themselves against the full-contact nature of this martial art. The donning of this clothing is a ceremony in itself and it is a source of great pride to students of kendo.

Kendo developed and evolved from actual battlefield conditions and therefore the utilization of armour became essential and intrinsic to the practitioners of this art. As a full-contact art, the relevant parts of the body must be well protected. For example, the head guard (*men*) is of extremely durable quality and can withstand the constant strikes made with the *shinai*. There is a set procedure for putting the armour on and great pride is taken to ensure that this is well-maintained, clean and correctly laid out before every training session. Practitioners practise sword exercises prior to any kendo training session, to maintain not only the tradition, but also agility and stamina.

Above Practitioner (*kendoka*) sitting (*seiza*) in preparation to place the head armour (*men*), gloves (*kote*) and *shinai* in the correct position, before commencement of practice.

Above The *kendoka* prepared, fully armoured, bowing (*rei*) to either the dojo, instructor or opponent. Note the *shinai* is in a lowered and relaxed position.

do (body protection for chest and side)

men (helmet to protect the head, face and neck)

kote (gloves for wrist and hand protection)

kote

tare (lower-body protection)

tenugui (head cloth worn under the *men*)

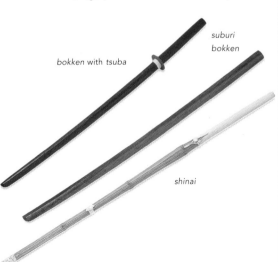

suburi bokken

bokken with *tsuba*

shinai

Safe practice and dojo etiquette

- It is important that you do not touch a practitioner's armour or *shinai* (bamboo sword), *bokken* (wooden sword) or sword without that person's permission. It is very important that you not only respect your own clothing and equipment, but also that of fellow practitioners.
- Always treat your *shinai* with respect. Never lean on it when being given instruction or discard it in the dojo without respect. Treat your *shinai* as a sword, since this is what it truly represents.
- Never step over a fellow practitioner's *shinai* or armour when it is laid out, whether it is in the dojo ready for practice or at the side of the dojo in preparation.
- If your armour or clothing comes loose, move to the side of the dojo opposite the *kamiza* (known as the *shimoza*). Go into a kneeling posture (*seiza*) and readjust your attire. Never adjust, retie or reposition your armour or clothing while standing as this is viewed as disrespectful and puts you at risk of attack in a real battle situation.

Etiquette

Etiquette is aimed at teaching *kendoka* (practitioners) respect for the dojo (training environment), their opponents and themselves. While dojo etiquette may vary slightly around the world, the following is considered as standard.

Safety in the dojo

- As you enter the dojo perform a bow (*rei*) to the *kamiza* – the area designated as the shrine or that is considered to be the point at which respect is given.
- You should always acknowledge the instructor (*sensei*) with a bow, or some other form that is considered appropriate, as he or she enters the dojo or gives you instruction or advice.
- Always be punctual and try to arrive early for training. This demonstrates discipline, respect and dedication.
- Make sure to remove your shoes when entering the dojo. Not only does this show respect for your training area, it is also more hygienic. The Japanese don't usually wear any outdoor footwear inside.
- Never drink, smoke or eat in the dojo.
- Ensure you are smartly dressed and that your clothing (*keikogi* and *hakama*) are well-pressed and clean. This demonstrates self-discipline and respect for the art.
- As a sign of respect and politeness, always pass behind any practitioner wearing armour. This shows respect and ensures safety in the dojo. If, however, you have to pass in front of an armoured practitioner who is seated, pause, make a slight *rei*, and extend your hand as you pass.
- If "*yame*" is called, you must immediately halt whatever you are doing. *Yame* is Japanese for "stop" and this rule applies to general practice, basics and competition.
- During all training, great emphasis is placed on manners (*reigi*) and respect. As with any sport or discipline, there is always a potential for injury, and so it is very important that you maintain self-control and a respectful attitude towards everybody within the dojo.

The Bow

1◁ Kneel down with your hands on your thighs, your back straight and looking forward. Place your armour at your right side with the guard (*tsuba*) on the sword handle level with your left knee. You should keep a relaxed yet assertive posture.

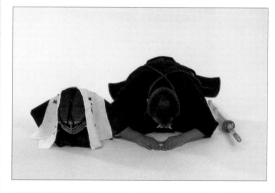

2◁ Lower your body forwards, placing your left hand, then right hand, flat on the floor, making a diamond shape with your forefingers and thumbs. Keep your elbows tucked in. This bow is a sign of respect to the dojo and instructor.

Meditation (*mokuso*)

This is a period of concentration, performed while kneeling. It is important to rid yourself of any worries, and it is considered helpful to think of running water. The nature of water represents tranquillity – one drop may be meaningless in the context of thousands, yet each drop is part of an important element of nature.

◁ Put your hands in a cupped position. Close your eyes and breathe slowly, in through your nose, out through your mouth. The length of this exercise varies, depending on your experience and your teacher's instruction.

Warm-up Exercises

Practitioners perform a variety of warm-up exercises before putting on their armour. At the start of training, practitioners practise what is known as *keiko* (free practice). Further warm-up is performed, when wearing armour, before training begins.

Warm-up 1 – Loosening your leg muscles and feet.

△ Step forwards with your right leg and place your hands on your hips. Keep your rear leg straight and apply a forwards and downwards pushing pressure. Change to your left leg forwards and repeat the exercise 2 to 3 times each side.

Warm-up 2 – Stretching your body for flexibility.

△ Bring your right arm up and over your head and place your left hand on your hip. Keep your feet facing forwards as you stretch your arm over your head, as if trying to touch the floor with your fingers. Keep your body relaxed for maximum benefit. Change to your left arm and repeat the exercise 2 to 3 times each side.

Warm-up 3 – Stretching of legs, hips and upper body.

△ Stand with your legs fairly wide apart and drop your hands so that your fingertips touch the floor. Repeat 3 to 4 times.

Warm-up 4 – To stretch your body, with particular emphasis on leg muscles and controlled breathing.

△ Keeping the same stance as in the previous exercise, take your right hand across to touch your left foot. Repeat on the opposite side, using your left hand to touch your right foot. Repeat the exercise 3 to 4 times each side.

Warm-up Exercises: Using the Shinai

The *shinai* is made of four pieces of bamboo, which are bound together for lightness and strength. The following shows the preparation needed prior to starting the basic cutting exercises and techniques.

Suburi

Basic cutting exercises, known as *suburi*, are performed by the practitioner as part of basic practice, both prior to wearing armour and with full armour. The practice can be performed individually, in a group session or with a partner. The purpose of the exercises is to develop technique, and to build strength, speed and stamina, with the benefit of developing focus, concentration and correct breathing. A loud shout, known as *kiai*, is made on the completion of each strike. The *kiai* helps to time breathing correctly.

Preparation

1△ Stand in a formal position, feet facing forwards, back straight and chin up. Hold the *shinai* in a relaxed position in your left hand.

2△ Lower your body 30 degrees to perform a bow (*rei*). This is performed to your instructor and partner before practice.

3△ Bring the *shinai* up to your left hip in preparation to move three paces forwards.

4△ Draw your *shinai*, step forwards and move into a squat (*sonkyo*). Keep your heels together with your feet at a 45-degree angle. The practitioner on the left demonstrates the angle of the draw, while the one on the right is in the *sonkyo* position.

5△ This is the standing position (*kamae*). The *kendoka* on the left is demonstrating the angle of the *shinai* in the forwards position. The *kendoka* on the right demonstrates the side view.

Exercise – Following the preparation, various exercises can be performed using the *shinai*.

1◁ Place the *shinai* in the small of your back, just behind your hips, and rotate your hips and the *shinai* in a circular motion towards the right.

2▷ Rotate the *shinai* in a circular motion towards your left side. Repeat this action several times.

Warm-up Exercises: Donning the Armour

Before wearing the head guard (*men*), you must first put on a cotton cloth called a *tenugui*. This cloth serves three purposes: it soaks up perspiration; it keeps your hair out of your face and eyes; and it acts as a cushion under the head guard.

Fitting the head guard (*men*).

1△ Lay the *men* (head guard) to your right side on top of the *kote* (hand guard), making sure the *tenugui* is placed on top of your *men*. The *shinai* must be placed to your left side with the *tsuba* in line with your left knee.

2△ Lift the *tenugui* and stretch it out in front of your body.

3△ Wrap the *tenugui* around your head. The *kendoka* on the left is showing the position of the *tenugui* and ties, while the one on the right is demonstrating how to tie the *tenugui* above the forehead.

4◁ The *tenugui* is now correctly tied in preparation for the *men*.

5▷ Secure the *men* by taking the cords or strings (*himo*) and wrapping them around your head. The *kendoka* on the left is showing the *himo* being pulled and wrapped around the *men*. The *kendoka* on the right, in profile, is showing the finishing position of the *himo*, neatly in place.

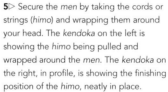

6△ Next, the hand guards (*kote*) are put on – first the left and then the right hand. The *kendokas* are now ready to commence their practice.

7▷ A standing bow (*rei*) is performed as a sign of respect to your training partner.

8△ Move into a squat (*sonkyo*), balancing on the balls of your feet (heels touching), knees at 45 degrees. This is the start position of all practice in kendo. Hold the *shinai* out from the centre of your body, your right hand gripping the handle (*tsuka*), above the left hand.

Techniques: Basic Competition Technique (*Shiai*)

△ A standing bow (*rei*) is performed as a sign of respect to your partner.

At the beginning of each basic competition (*shiai*) session, two contestants step into the contest area (*shiajo*) and bow to each other as a sign of respect. They then advance to the centre of the court, before drawing their *shinai* and sinking down into the squatting position (*sonkyo*). The main referee will shout "*hajime*" ("begin"), at which point the contestants stand and usually let out a shout, known as *kiai*, before initiating an attack. It is often thought that this relates to the philosophy of shouting as a way of generating fear within the opponent. Shouting is also thought to produce extra strength for the attack. The two contestants then try to score points by striking specific parts of the body: the head (*men*), the throat (*tsuki*), the sides of the body (*do*) or the wrist (*kote*). Even where a point is scored, contestants continue to maintain fighting spirit until the senior court judge yells "*yame*" (stop).

The contestants then reposition themselves at the centre of the court and the contest continues, until either one has scored the match point to win the *shiai*. At the end, both contestants lower themselves into the *sonkyo* position. As there is no *saya* (scabbard that protects the sword), the *shinai* is not sheathed but is placed in a natural position to the left side of the body (similar to wearing a sword). This is performed prior to and at the end of the competition. The contestants then walk away backwards, bow to each other, turn and exit.

Good Posture

A vital part of being skilled in kendo is maintaining a well-balanced and upright posture. Whether you are moving forwards or backwards, correct body posture is an important part of delivering a strike that has the correct force and energy. Leaning to the side usually results in an ineffective strike leaving you vulnerable to attack.

Stance

Your stance is an extremely important part of kendo practice. When standing normally, your feet should be a shoulder-width apart. Move forwards with your right foot, so that the heel is in line with the toes of your left foot. The heel of your left foot should be slightly raised – but no more than 1 in (2.5 cm), allowing you to move with agility and speed.

Hand position

Your left hand should be as near to the base of the hilt of the handle of the *shinai* (bamboo sword) as possible, with your right hand just below the *tsuba* (the guard that divides the handle from the "blade"). A firm yet relaxed grip on the *shinai* is required – it is the third and fourth fingers of your hands that actually grasp the sword, while the rest of your hands, wrists, forearms and shoulders should be relaxed. Holding the *shinai* in a hard and aggressive way burns up unnecessary energy, leading to fatigue and an ineffective style. This hand position does not change throughout the practice, whether you are holding the *shinai* with or without gloves (*kote*). Once you have the correct grip, make sure that the hilt of the *shinai* is approximately one to two hand grips away from your lower abdomen. Don't rest the *shinai* against your body, since this is considered disrespectful.

Techniques: Basic Strikes

Striking techniques in kendo are mainly aimed at three areas of the body, namely the head (*men*), body (*do*) and wrist (*kote*), with thrust or lunge (*tsuki*). These areas are well protected with armour, but were vulnerable in the days of the samurai.

Shomen uchi – **men strike.**

△ *Shomen uchi* is a cut executed towards the top of the head (*men*).

△ Aim to strike the centre of the head with the end of the *shinai*.

△ Evading a *shomen uchi* strike to the top of the head and preparing to counter-attack.

△ Counter-attack with *do waza* (body out). The aim is to cut the side of the body as the aggressor moves through to strike, presenting a vulnerable position. This requires precise timing and accuracy.

Kote

△ This strike is known as cutting the wrist (*kote*), in which the *shinai* makes contact with the forearm anywhere between the wrist and about half way to the elbow. It is a strike coming from above, and cuts are permitted to the front of the arm if your opponent's *shinai* is in a low position, and to the left arm when it is raised, depending on whether your opponent is moving forwards or backwards.

Chudan Tsuki

△ A thrusting action to your opponent's throat. This is performed, especially in competition, to try and score a point. The partner is well protected by a firm padded guard which covers the throat area.

Do

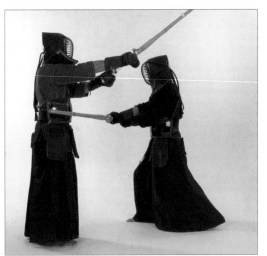

△ This is a cut to the side of the body between the armpit and the hip bone. It can be performed from either side and is a diagonal cut from above.

△ Upon making contact with the armour, the practitioner making the strike will shout "*do*", as this is the part of the body that they are striking.

Katata (thrust)

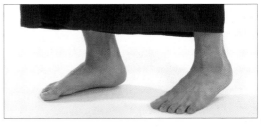

△ In this close-up of the correct footwork, note the short stance, with the feet a shoulder-width apart, the weight on the balls of your feet and the rear heel slightly raised. This is the main stance adopted by all practitioners.

Jigeiko

When practitioners have been through the various exercises, they get the opportunity to put their training into practice against each other, in what is known as *jigeiko*. This is not a free-for-all session, but a time to develop their skill, timing and precision, and to fine-tune their techniques. This is a form of practice in kendo and is not specific to competition or grading.

△ A single-handed thrust to your opponent's throat is known as *katata tsuki*. *Caution: this technique can be very dangerous, which is why kendo armour has protective padding, extending from the face grid to the breast bone. Take great care that your armour is of good quality and is correctly fitted.*

Tsuba zeriai

△ *Tsuba zeriai* is the name given to this position, in which you and your opponent are very close together, with both *shinai* pushing against each other, looking for an opening from which to strike.

Men uchi

△ The movement through to strike the head (*men*) is used in various exercises. For example, *keiko* (free practice), which is divided into various areas including *uchikomi keiko* and *keri kaishi*, during which students rapidly attack exposed target areas of their opponent with power and full concentration.

Iaido

Iaido is the art of drawing your sword and striking an armed opponent at lightning speed. It is the art of strategy, achieving precision in all aspects of mental and physical ability, including accurate footwork, balanced posture and critical timing. "Live" blades are razor-sharp, and experienced practitioners are the only ones permitted to use them. The risk involved is thought worthwhile, because this is the only way to achieve the ultimate in awareness and concentration, and to bring mind and body together in total harmony.

History and Philosophy

The traditions of iaido are descended directly from those of the samurai warrior (or *bushi*), and are steeped in ancient codes of honour and etiquette. The dynamic, sweeping swordsmanship of the art takes years of dedicated training to master.

Iaido derives from the ancient way of the samurai warrior (*bushi*), and the forerunner of the art we know today, *iai-jutsu*, was used in earnest on the battlefield, whereas iaido was designed to practise "the way of the sword".

Evidence suggests that the *bokken* used today in iaido has been used as a weapon since about AD400. The *bokken* is a solid wooden stick with the same shape, weight and approximate length as a sword, and is usually made of red or white oak. *Bokken* technique was followed by the art of *tachikaki* (drawing the sword from its scabbard). The blade (*tachi* or *katana*), was long and straight and the Japanese warrior would carry it on his left side. A shorter blade was used for quick-draw techniques, known as *batto*.

The curved swords seen today are not the original Japanese swords. Indeed, they were flat, straight swords of primitive construction, used for simple strikes and thrusts. It was around AD940, the middle of the Heian period, that the single-edged, slightly curved sword appeared, and the superb skill of the Japanese warrior developed. Until that

Right Haruna Matsuo Sensei – 7th-*dan* iaido.

Below Iaido practitioners display their swordsmanship at a martial arts demonstration in Japan.

time, single-handed swords were used in battle by mounted warriors. They were protected by heavy armour, using the right hand to draw and cut the enemy.

Some time during the mid-16th century, battle strategy changed and mounted warriors replaced foot warriors who wore lighter armour and used techniques requiring both hands on the sword hilt.

DOMINANCE OF THE *BUSHI*

In 1189, the samurai *bushi* of the Minamoto clan finally gained complete military and political dominance in Japan, a position that they maintained for nearly 700 years, until 1868. In the early part of the 14th century, however, there was a decline in the military skills of the *bushi*, but this was rectified during the third Ashikaga Shogun Yoshimitsu period (1358–1508), when great encouragement was given to proper training in such skills as archery, swordsmanship and the use of *naginata*, a curved blade spear.

Above Practitioners from all over the world practising iaido at the Heian Shrine, Japan.

The ability to draw the blade in a bold, fast and dynamic upward, sweeping movement, was intrinsic to the *bushi*. Nevertheless, this was not a standardized style of fighting, and it was during the early Heian period that much of Japanese culture was imported from China. It was not only the Chinese martial arts that captured the imagination and interest of the Japanese, it was also the study of Chinese philosophy, painting and poetry.

WHAT IS IAIDO?

Although iaido may be classed as a separate martial art, it is closely related and complementary to kendo. Kendo practice requires two people fencing each other armed with *shinai* (bamboo swords) and wearing armour, whereas iaido is practised on an individual basis wearing a *gi*, *juban*, *hakama* and *obi*. Practitioners use a real or an imitation sword, called an *iaito*. The aim of the exercise is to perform a set series of movements (*kata*), in which the sword is drawn, an imaginary opponent is cut, and then the sword is resheathed. The ultimate purpose of iaido, however, is to master the ability to overcome your enemy without the sword being drawn in the first place – in other words, to conquer your opponent "spiritually", with the sword still in the sheath, and so resolve problems without even having to resort to violence. There is one quote that explains this way of thinking: "Your mind is not disturbed by you being beaten up, but by you beating up others."

It has been said that many iaido moves passed down over the centuries were secret techniques related to Zen practice and enlightenment, as well as the secret physical techniques (*waza*). In the 15th century, a Zen master,

Right The true spirit of martial arts is founded upon detail and correctness. Note the positioning of the feet, whereby further movement is easily effected.

Takuan, discussed with Yagyu Munenori, a sword master, the concept of the "unfettered mind". This was defined as a person who could remain calm in the face of adversity. They agreed on the word *fudoshin* to encapsulate this concept. The term came to describe any person who demonstrates clarity of mind and purpose, even in the most difficult situations.

There are various traditional styles of iaido still practised in Japan today, although many have been lost over the centuries. Those that have survived have been passed down from generation to generation. These include *muso*

jikiden ryu, *muso shinden ryu* and *katori shinto ryu*. These styles of iaido are based on the more traditional schools of swordsmanship, employing fast-drawing techniques.

It is widely believed that Hayashizaki Jinnosuke Shigenobu founded the school of *iai-jutsu* (the precursor of iaido) in 1560. His sword techniques were perfected by Eishin in the 18th century, since which time the *muso jikiden ryu* style has developed, as well as the *eishin ryu* forms. In 1968–69, a system known as *seitei gata* iaido was developed, in order to provide a basic system around which all the varied styles of iaido could be unified.

Left Assisting practitioners to develop their skills in iaido.

Above Two Japanese swordsmen illustrate the concept of *zanshin* – total mental alertness and awareness.

Left The meeting of blades.

Benefits of iaido

The benefits derived from learning iaido affect many aspects of your everyday life. These include:

- Speed and agility
- Fitness
- Self-discipline and positive attitude
- Precision and timing
- Self-confidence
- Self-control and well-being
- Comradeship
- Inner peace and calm
- Harmony of mind and body

COMPETITION (*TAIKAI*)

Seitei gata iaido forms an important basis for gradings in iaido, no matter how senior or junior the grade. Many practitioners take part in competitions (*taikai*) throughout the year, and while there is an element of practitioners being able to demonstrate their own style, it is vitally important that they demonstrate the basic *seitei gata* iaido, so that the judges can truly evaluate their skills and techniques.

Taikai, in iaido, is performed by two practitioners running through their routines at the same time. Individual performance is judged by three referees who are looking and judging on a wide variety of technical, physical and mental attributes.

Many of the basic rules for the art of kendo also apply to iaido competition, with the addition of *kokorogamae*, which means "mental posture". *Kokorogamae* includes calmness, vision (*metsuke*), spirit, concentration, distance (between individuals) and timing. The Japanese expression of *shin gi tai-no-ichi* (meaning "heart, technique and body as one") sums up perfectly the aims and philosophy at the heart of *kokorogamae*.

Clothing and Equipment

An iaido practitioner's *shinken* (sword) is a source of great pride, and maintaining and caring for the weapon is a ritual in itself. Original Japanese blades are very expensive so training is often undertaken with a replica sword, known as an *iaito*.

The colour of the *hakama* in iaido can range from white, black and blue, to pin stripe grey or other similar colours. The materials of the clothing also vary from the less expensive polyester and cotton fabric to silk. Practitioners usually wear a *zekken*, which is a chest patch embroidered with their name, dojo and nationality. Great pride is taken in appearance, ensuring that all clothing fits correctly. *Bokken* and swords should be well cared for, being cleaned and maintained regularly, after every practice. It is equally important to check *bokken* and swords prior to the commencement of practice, to ensure safety in the dojo environment.

Jacket Jackets are available in a variety of colours and materials, with black, white and blue being the most common colours that are worn.

Obi The long, wide, band that is wrapped around the body underneath the hakama.

Zori The sandals that are used mainly outside the dojo. They are designed to be slipped on to either bare feet or over the *tabi*. Never wear *zori* inside the dojo or when training, as this is seen as both disrespectful and dangerous.

Tabi These are the formal footwear that are allowed in the dojo. They are usually of cotton material with a non-slip base.

Hakama A folded skirt, similar to culottes. There are five pleats at the front and one at the rear. Wearing a good-quality *hakama* is recommended, since it is extremely durable and will maintain its shape throughout practice.

Shinken The *shinken* is a "live" blade – razor-sharp and made in the traditional Japanese way, by folding the metal many times to obtain a blade that is light, yet incredibly strong. *Shinken* is expensive to buy, whether you purchase an original or a new blade.

Sageo The cord that is secured to the scabbard. The small wooden piece through which the *sageo* is fed is known as the *kurigata*.

Iaito The *iaito* is another type of practice sword used in iaido, which has a stainless-steel replica of a live blade (*shinken*).

Tsuba The *tsuba* is the circular fitting which is placed between the handle (*tsuka*) and sword. On a *bokken* it is usually made of plastic and on a live blade it can be a decorative piece of craftsmanship.

Bokken Most people start iaido practice using either a *bokken* or an *iaito*. A *bokken* is a wooden replica sword, usually made of white or red oak, with the same shape (curvature) as a real sword and a plastic guard (*tsuba*). The disadvantage of using a *bokken* is that there is no *saya* (the sheath, or scabbard, that covers the blade). This means that the practitioner will not benefit from *saya* practice with the left hand, which is equally as important as the right hand in the art of iaido.

Cleaning kit This includes *uchiko* powder, which is used to remove acidity and grime from the blade, caused through contact with the hand during practice. The powder ball is gently tapped on both sides of the blade, from base to tip, to cover it with powder.

Caution

Live blades should never be used by beginners or inexperienced practitioners. Take the advice of your professional instructor about when the time is right for you to use a *shinken*. The use of a *shinken* is not required until you have attained the level of 6th-*dan* (*rokudan*). However, it is preferable to start using a *shinken* at 4th-*dan* (*yondan*) and above. It gives real meaning to the feel of iaido when a live blade is drawn.

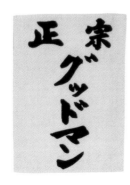

Zekken The embroidered patch with the practitioner's name, dojo and nationality written in Japanese.

Etiquette

Dojo etiquette is very important in iaido, as a sign of respect to the art and also to ensure everybody's safety. Etiquette follows Japanese tradition in placing great emphasis on small details. Using any weapon is dangerous if not handled with respect.

1△ Before walking on to the training area, hold your sword in your left hand with the blade (*hi*) facing upwards. When you arrive at your position for training, raise the sword to just below your waist (*taito*).

2△ At this point, your sword hand is resting just above your left hip bone, with the sword angled slightly inwards at about 45 degrees.

△ Side view showing correct posture and angle of the sword.

3△ Turn towards the *kamiza*, the area designated as the place of respect. This is usually towards the east of the dojo. You now pass the sword to your right hand.

4△ Turn the sword as you pass it from your left to your right hand, so that the edge of the blade is facing down towards the floor.

5△ Bring the sword down and hold it at a 30-degree angle on the right of your body, with the edge of the blade facing downwards.

6△ Bow to *kamiza*, ensuring minimum sword movement. This is a small bow only, so lower your upper body by no more than 15 degrees. Lower your eyes naturally as you bow.

7△ Return to the upright position. Pass the sword back to your left hand. Make sure the cord (*sageo*) is looped around your thumb.

8△ Position the sword back on your left hip.

9△ Kneel, keeping your eyes on your opponent. Perform a V-shaped cutting action with the edge of your right hand to prevent the *hakama* becoming entangled with your legs.

10△ Place your left knee down on the floor first, followed by your right knee.

11△ Lower yourself to settle on your heels. Rest the sword on your left thigh and your right hand on your right thigh.

12△ Pass the sword from your left hand to your right.

13△ Hold the *sageo* with your left fingers and slide that hand down the sword, stopping 4 in (10 cm) from the end.

14△ Hold the sword in front of your body as you pass the *sageo* underneath the sword with the fingers of your left hand.

15△ Place the sword neatly on the floor, directly in front of you. Avoid making any unnecessary movements.

16△ Next, place your left hand, then your right, on to your upper thighs.

17△ Lower your body, placing your left hand on the floor, followed by your right, with thumbs and forefingers forming a diamond shape. With elbows tucked in, keep the back of your head in line with your spine as you perform the bow (*rei*).

18△ Kneel upright, take the sword in both hands, the palm of your right hand upwards and the left downwards. Bringing the sword towards you, place your left thumb down the centre of your *hakama* to make an opening for the sword. Push the end of the scabbard (*saya*) through the ties of the *hakama* and *obi*, towards your left side, so that the sword sits ready to practice.

19△ Bring the *sageo* over the back of the *saya*, underneath and to the front. Tie the *sageo* through the *hakama* ties (*himo*). The tie is either a single loop pushed up between the ties, or a double loop (which is one loop inside another).

Warm-up Exercises

Here the emphasis is on the sword warm-up moves, to work the relevant parts of the body prior to technical practice, and using either a *bokken* (wooden replica) or *shinken* (live blade), depending upon level of qualification.

Warm-up 1 – This vertical cutting technique is known as *kirioroshi*.

1△ Draw your sword into the centre ready position (*chudan kamae*). Keep an upright posture with shoulders relaxed, back straight and the heel of your rear foot slightly raised. Your right hand is near the sword's guard (*tsuba*) and your left hand is towards the end of the handle (*kashira*). Make sure the V shape of your hand is uppermost on the *kashira*, with your thumb and forefinger on either side.

2△ Ensuring your grip is secure yet relaxed, raise the sword above your head (*jodan kamae*), ensuring that the tip of the blade remains horizontal. When cutting, avoid a hard grip, since this burns up unnecessary energy, which thus restricts your technique.

3△ Step forwards as you start to extend your arms fully in a "reaching" action, and commence a large, circular cut. The technique finishes with the sword at your waistline. Make sure you are looking straight ahead, maintaining the same body posture.

4△ Once the sword has completed its cutting action, the tip of the blade (*kissaki*) should be in line with the *habaki* – the metal fixture about 1 in (2.5 cm) long seated on the blade next to the *tsuba* between the handle (*tsuka*) and sword.

Warm-up 2 – The horizontal cutting technique is called *nukitsuke*.

1△ Hold the sword in your right hand, held across your body, the blade level with your upper left arm and the tip pointing backwards. Using a circular action across your body, swing the sword back towards your right shoulder.

2△ Cut in a circular action. Make sure the left hand pulls the *saya* round the small of the back in a horizontal action; this is simultaneous with the drawing action. The tip of the blade is level with the right side of the chest, at about nipple height.

Techniques: First Level

The following is a selection of techniques taken from particular styles known as *muso jikiden ryu*, *eishin ryu* and *oku-iai*. Once familiar and competent with *seitei gata* iaido, practitioners move on to practise the other *kata* within their chosen style.

Tsuki kage

△ *Tsuki kage* is a *kata* designed to enable the practitioner to draw and cut from a side attack. The aim is to draw the sword from a low posture, moving underneath the opponent's arms as the opponent attempts a cut to the head. This is an upward cut to both wrists. A variation is to cut just the right or left wrist.

Yae gaki

△ The first technique is taken out of a form (*kata*) called *yae gaki*. You perform this technique towards the end of the *kata*, when your opponent is on the floor and is making a final cutting action at the lower part of your leg. To prevent the cut, use the side of your sword (*shinogi*) in a blocking technique, before preparing to make the final cut.

Tsuke komi

△ This move is taken from the last part of the kata known as *tsuke komi*. It demonstrates the "blood wipe" action following the final cut, which is one way of cleaning the blade before sheathing (*noto*).

Oroshi

△ *Oroshi* is a cut made to the side of your opponent's neck.

Setei gata iaido

Today, many practitioners of iaido practise *seitei gata* iaido. This comprises a set of basic forms (*katas*) used in most styles of iaido to encourage uniformity in practice, so that people can be graded to a common standard. This, however, does not exclude the classical styles that are a part of iaido.

Forms (kata)

Number	Name	Meaning
Performed from a sitting (*seiza*) position:		
Ippon me (1)	Mae	Front
Nihon me (2)	Ushiro	Rear
Sanbon me (3)	Uke nagashi	Catch and slide off
Yonhon me (4)	Tsuka ate	Strike with *tsuka* (handle)
Performed from a standing posture:		
Gohon Me (5)	Kesa giri	Cross cut
Roppon me (6)	Morote tsuki	Thrust with both hands
Nanahon me (7)	Sanpo giri	Cut in three directions
Hachihon me (8)	Gan men ate	Strike to centre of face
Kyubon me (9)	Soe te tsuki	Thrust with supporting hand
Juppon me (10)	Shiho giri	Four-direction cut

Techniques: Advanced Level

The following shows a selection of techniques taken from a *kata* performed in the *muso jikiden eishin ryu* style. Included is a sequence demonstrating one of the cuts in *iwanami*, followed by a sequence taken from *taki otoshi* against a rear attack.

Tate hiza – Start position.

△ This position is called *tate hiza*, meaning "standing knee". It involves sitting with your left leg tucked under your body and your right leg slightly forwards and bent at the knee. This is a difficult posture for many Westerners to adopt, especially those with long legs. The Japanese are usually smaller in stature and are more easily able to sit in this position.

Finishing kneeling position.

△ This is the finishing posture at the end of some of the techniques performed in *eishin ryu* and *oku den*. After the cut, place the sword back in the scabbard (*saya*) – this is known as the *noto* movement. Next, bring your right foot back towards the left, maintaining a stable posture.

Iwanami

1△ This is part of the *iwanami kata* where you have turned and drawn your sword to your right side, taking hold of the blade with your left hand.

2△ Following the preparation to strike, you thrust the sword upwards and forwards into the stomach region. There are several other moves before this *kata* is complete.

3△ Using the *bokken*, we can practise the striking part of this technique to develop the take down which forms part of this *kata*.

4△ This demonstrates the *hiki taoshi* movement, in which the opponent is pushed down on to the floor by placing the blade of your sword (*bokken*) on their right shoulder.

1△ This is the first part of *taki otoshi*, where the opponent tries to grip the scabbard of your sword. As you feel the grip, the intention is to go with the grab in a sequence of moves, to eventually disengage the opponent.

2△ Pushing the sword in a downwards motion weakens the opponent's grip of the sheath (*saya*).

Sodome

Ryozume – Restrictive movement against obstacle or wall.

3△ Keep the momentum going in an upwards direction to fully disengage the opponent's grip.

△ Applying a stalking strategy, the intention is to cut three hidden opponents to the side of the neck, as you move forwards.

△ In view of the restriction, the sword is drawn very tightly in a forwards motion. This is followed by a lunge into the opponent.

Techniques: *Uke Nagashi*

The following pictures and captions are not fully instructional and are intended to show you an outline only of one of the *seitei gata iaido kata*. This *kata* is number three (*sanbon me*) and known as *uke nagashi* (catch and slide off).

1△ Turn to your right side and kneel down. Take both hands off your sword and place them on your thighs.

2△ Look towards your imaginary opponent, who is about 6 ft (2m) away. Your opponent has drawn his sword, which he has positioned at the right side of his head (the technique of the sword being prepared at the right side of the head is known as *hasso kamae*). As he moves forwards, start to draw your sword and bring your left foot forwards, so that it is just in front of your right knee. Raise your sword upwards to deflect the opponent's downwards cut.

3△ As you stand, parry the cut by bringing your right foot to your left, as if standing "pigeon-toed". Your toes are not touching. This position ensures you are moving to the side of your opponent, to evade the cut and prepare the counter-attack.

4△ Pull your left foot back at about 18 degrees and cut down at a slight angle. Bring your left hand on to your sword as you turn towards your opponent, and cut downwards at a diagonal angle, right to left (from your opponent's left shoulder to right hip).

5△ The cut will finish at a horizontal position and it is important still to maintain *metsuke* (direction of gaze – looking at your opponent and the wider environment) and *zanshin* (awareness), keeping alert in the event of any further danger.

6◁ Change your hand grip on the sword so that the blade is resting on your right knee.

▽ This detail shows the correct hand grip once you have reversed the sword in preparation for returning it to its scabbard (*saya*).

7◁ Sheath the sword by bringing it from the right knee, around the front of your body, so that it is at the mouth of the scabbard (*saya*).

▽ This is the hand and sword position at the beginning of the *noto*, before sheathing.

8△ Lower your body, aiming to fully sheath the sword as your keft knee touches the ground. Keep looking (*metsuke*) to where your opponent has fallen, and be alert (*zanshin*) in case there are other opponents. Return to the standing position.

9▷ You can practise this particular *uke nagashi kata* with a real opponent, both of you armed with a wooden sword (*bokken*), but careful timing is needed to prevent injury. Working with a partner is useful, because it gives you a real feel for the blocking action, so that your opponent's blade slides off yours when it makes contact.

Shinto ryu

Shinto ryu is a street defence strategy encompassing the "hard" (forceful self-defence) and "soft" (acceptance and deflection) elements of various martial arts styles. It has developed into a unique self-defence system suitable for all, irrespective of age, fitness or gender. Shinto ryu teaches practitioners skills they can adapt to any situation: hard techniques might be required in response to aggression or physical violence, yet shinto ryu's softer techniques might be more appropriate in an unsolicited or threatening situation.

History and Philosophy

Shinto ryu focuses on giving practitioners the ability to defend themselves in potentially dangerous situations. It is often used to help the vulnerable, especially children, to gain the skills they need to deal with potential threats confidently and effectively.

The martial arts that are popular today originated and evolved, sometimes over many hundreds of years, from the concepts and ideas of visionary individuals whose belief systems and cultures moulded and shaped their skills and techniques. Today, new systems and styles continue to develop throughout the world.

Shinto ryu is one of the disciplines practised under the umbrella organization of the European Martial Arts Academy, and its name means "nature's way" or "spirit of nature" – shinto meaning "nature" or "shrine" and ryu meaning "the way". It is by understanding its name that we gain an insight into how the system works, by developing self-defence skills in a "natural way".

The Junior Defence Line specializes in developing the well-being of children and young people, and works within the European Martial Arts Academy. It offers a basic street defence system for children and young people, to help them feel more confident and capable of protecting themselves in the street and at school. Bullying is a major problem within many societies and most bullies are usually cowards. Yet their victims can be traumatized and scarred for life. The key principles of shinto ryu spill into this very important area of developing good attitude, discipline and respect.

UNDERLYING PRINCIPLES

The philosophy of this discipline never manifests itself in seeking harm. Instead, it strives to equip practitioners with techniques that allow them to walk away from difficult situations.

Above Children learn how to defend against an attack.

Left Shinto ryu offers children a confidence boost and a chance to learn basic self-defence skills.

Defusing techniques are of paramount importance, but we need confidence to use these skills effectively.

Having knowledge of the physical skills we can put into practice at times of threat and danger can increase our confidence to handle a particular situation. Our body language gives away a great deal about us – research has identified that many victims of street crimes looked like victims before any aggression occurred, and it is possible to minimize risk by looking more confident. We only have to look at the posture used in many of the martial arts. The upright

Above Emphasis is placed on restraining techniques. Street clothing and footwear are encouraged in some training sessions, to give a feeling of reality.

relaxed posture, with shoulders back and looking forwards, projects a perception of awareness, confidence and strength. As Musashi Miyamoto, one of Japan's most famous swordsmen (1584–1645), said: "Perception is strong and sight is weak!"

Part of shinto ryu is learning once more to trust our intuition, an attribute that we have become complacent about in today's technological and materialistic society. How many times have you felt uncomfortable about a person you have been introduced to, and some time later this person does something to harm you in some way? Recalling your initial feelings, you say to yourself, "I knew I could not trust that person," and yet you still allowed that situation to develop, not having the confidence to listen to your gift of intuition.

SHINTO RYU IN PRACTICE

Shinto ryu is a modern discipline. Practical techniques are taught based on a "star" movement, which allows you to defend yourself from any conceivable angle – whether standing or seated. Reality is the key to this system of self-defence. Practitioners are taught how to respond to different real-world situations, such as being threatened on

public transport, while driving in cars, at work and in many other environments. Shinto ryu also teaches you how to improvise with objects you are likely to have at hand, such as using a chair or small table as a barrier, as part of a self-defence strategy. The use of a *shinai* (bamboo stick) has also been incorporated, but not in the same way as in the art of kendo. It is used to replicate a potential weapon such as a piece of wood, iron bar or pole that may be at hand, so that the practitioner can learn to strike and defend effectively.

Benefits of shinto ryu

The benefits derived from learning shinto ryu affect many aspects of your everyday life. These include:

- Speed and agility
- Fitness and stamina
- Awareness and intuition
- Self-confidence, self-control and well-being
- Precision and timing
- Respect and self-discipline
- Comradeship
- Inner peace and calm
- Stress reduction
- Character development

Warm-up Exercises

The following is a sample of some of the exercises performed in shinto ryu prior to training. The following is performed by an experienced young man. Remember it is important to build up exercises slowly for maximum benefit.

Warm-up 1 – Leg stretch to strengthen inner thighs.

△ From a standing position, bend your front (left) leg at an angle of about 90 degrees, while keeping your rear (right) leg straight. Push forwards to stretch your inner thigh. Repeat this exercise with your right leg forwards. Hold the tension for 5–10 seconds, change to your left leg and repeat the exercise 3–4 times.

Warm-up 2 – The splits stretch your inner thighs.

1△ With legs astride, gently lower your body as far as you can. It may take some months before you can fully reach the floor. Only go as wide as you comfortably can and practice on a regular basis to improve your suppleness in this exercise.

2△ The ultimate aim of this exercise is to be able to lower your head down to touch the floor. This increases the pressure on the inner thighs. Lean forwards, pushing your head down as far as you comfortably can.

Warm-up 3 – Press-ups develop the upper body.

△ With the palms of your hands down, feet together and body straight, gently lower your body to the floor. Do not touch the floor but keep your body elevated about 1–2 in (2.5–5 cm). Push back up to the starting position and repeat. Breathe out as you lower your body, and in as you push back up. *Caution: only perform this exercise 2–3 times and build up gradually. Children under 11 should not perform this exercise, except for a modified version, on knees, and under qualified supervision.*

Warm-up 4 – Back and leg stretch for suppleness.

△ Lower your body so that you can place your right leg to the side and your left knee facing forward at a 90 degree angle. Take hold of your right ankle with your right hand and lower your head towards your right knee. Keep your leg straight for maximum stretch. Do not be concerned if you cannot touch your knee in the early stages, as this will come with practice. Only lower yourself to a position that feels comfortable, pushing a little further each time. Change to the left leg and repeat the exercise 3 times each side.

Techniques: Children's Self-defence

Shinto ryu arms us to deal with any difficult situation wisely and safely. While it may be perceived that only the fit and young can practise a martial art, rudimentary skills can be applied to a defence situation by those of all ages, genders and abilities.

Defence 1 – Children can apply the power of the circle very effectively to disengage an attack.

1△ The attacker makes a double-handed grab, pulling you off the ground.

2△ Take hold of the aggressor's thumbs with both hands.

3△ Using an outwards circular motion, pull the aggressor's thumbs down. This should make him let go and allow you to escape.

Defence 2 – This demonstrates how children can use their strengths against an aggressor's weaknesses.

1△ The aggressor moves in with a single-handed grab to your body.

2△ Step back and bring the edge of your right hand up in a circular motion to deflect the grab. Slide your hand down and take hold of the aggressor's wrist. Keep this action continuous to enhance the technique.

△ Even though you may have a small hand, taking hold of the aggressor's little fingers and using the power of the circle can assist in breaking a grip.

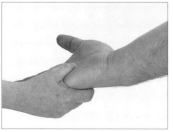

3△ Continue the circular action with your right hand. Bring your left hand up under the aggressor's right elbow to assist the action.

△ As the circular action continues, the aggressor's palm should turn upwards so that pressure can be applied to the elbow.

4△ Maintain pressure by rotating the hold, which will help to push the aggressor to the floor. Call for assistance or leave the area.

Defence 3 – Disengaging safely against a hair grab.

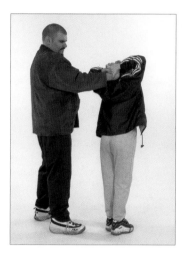

1△ An aggressor moves in and grabs your hair with the intention of pulling you back and off balance.

2△ Bring both your hands up above your head. Remain upright or slightly lower your position, depending upon the size of the aggressor. Either way, it is important not to lean back.

3△ Place both hands on top of your head and lock your fingers together. Push down firmly to apply a locking technique on the aggressor's hand. As you turn, you may find your hands starting to grip the wrist. This is acceptable if it assists in maintaining control by turning the aggressor's arm.

4△ Continue to turn your body in towards the aggressor, maintaining a firm grip.

5△ As you almost complete your turn you will feel his grip start to loosen. Be aware of his other arm and legs at all times, in the event he may try to strike. *Note: the faster you apply this turn, the easier it is to encourage him to let go, through the pain inflicted on his joints, tendons and muscles.*

6△ At the end of the turn, the aggressor should have released your hair. To maintain control bring your thumbs around on to the top of the aggressor's hand. Apply pressure with the thumbs in a forwards and downwards motion. Then, either push the aggressor away or apply a "hard" technique, such as a kick to the solar plexus or face.

Handling more than one aggressor at the same time may be viewed as an impossible task, but it is important to apply a strategy that utilizes your strength against an aggressor's weaknesses, so that you can escape from difficult situations.

Caution
As an initial strategy, it is always best to avoid conflict by applying such skills as verbally defusing the situation, body language and similar strategies. If this does not work, only then, as a last resort, apply physical self-defence, using "reasonable force" to protect yourself (or others). Even if you successfully defend yourself, an aggressor may have the right to sue you. The law varies from country to country and you may be called on to prove that only reasonable force was used. It is, therefore, preferable to use restraining techniques, depending upon the seriousness of the situation.

1△ One of the aggressors grabs your wrist with his right hand. If you have an item such as an umbrella, make use of this in your defence. Apply a circular action with your wrist (the same technique used with or without an umbrella) to disengage the grab.

2△ If you have an umbrella to aid your defence, twist to position it over the aggressor's wrist. Bring your left hand underneath and take hold of the umbrella to lock the aggressor's wrist. Push down to apply pressure and take him to the floor.

3△ Usually, if you successfully disengage the first aggressor, other aggressors can be dissuaded from continuing with the assault. Where this is not the case, apply the power of the circle to disengage the grab and strike to a weak point, such as the face or throat. *Caution: this is the last-resort application, when you believe your life is in imminent danger. When practising with a partner, focus (aim) your technique – do not make contact.*

4△ Strike to the vulnerable area, such as the throat. *Caution: this is an extremely dangerous area to strike and should only be used as a last resort in a serious situation.*

Techniques: Disengagement

Ideally, always try to talk your way out of a threatening situation and keep a safe distance between you and the aggressor. However, if an aggressor moves in to grab you, it is important to try to disengage the grip before you are physically struck.

Body grab – Defence against a body grab.

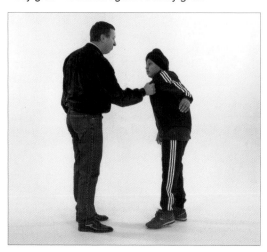

1△ An aggressor makes a grab with his right hand to your left lapel.

2△ Place your left hand over the aggressor's right hand, aiming to lock his thumb and fingers. Keep close to your chest for maximum control and pull outwards to cause the aggressor to release his grip. At the same time strike to the nose, this will cause the eyes to water and give you a chance to escape.

3△ Following the strike, bring your right hand under the aggressor's right arm and take hold of his right hand. You are now preparing to throw the aggressor to the floor.

4△ Continue the momentum of the arm movement forward, while at the same time stepping through. You need to ensure you are very close to the aggressor to break his posture and balance. Remember that these techniques are successful only when applied with correct timing, skill and body movement.

1△ As the aggressor grabs you with his right arm around your throat from the rear, immediately try to drop your chin downwards, to alleviate any pressure against your throat. At the same time, turn your body inwards towards the aggressor and aim to take hold of thumb and fingers.

2△ Pull the aggressor's arm forwards, locking his elbow on top of your right shoulder. Ensure that you push the aggressor's palm outwards, with his fingers pointing downwards for maximum effect. Keep your body upright to maintain pressure on his elbow joint.

3△ Using a circular motion, bring the aggressor's arm around your right side, preparing to throw him. Although a smaller child may find this throw awkward to execute, it should present little difficulty for a teenager or adult.

4△ The aggressor will be winded and disorientated as he hits the floor. This will allow you time to escape. If there is any chance that the attacker could still be a threat, strike with a leg technique of your choice. *Note: remember the law and the use of "reasonable force". It is always best to incapacitate the aggressor with minimum force.*

5△ Continue to maintain an assertive attitude because, in spite of being floored, the aggressor could try to retaliate (or there may be other assailants close by). You may have been successful in your defensive manoeuvre, but don't be overconfident. Keep alert until you are safely out of the situation.

Techniques: Knife Defence

While a knife attack is unlikely, being prepared builds self-confidence. Shinto ryu encourages students to practise defence moves against weapons to ensure that people have the ability to defend and disarm should the need arise.

Caution
When training with a partner, use a plastic knife unless you are very experienced. If you use a real knife (only if under professional supervision), control the technique so that the knife does not fall indiscriminately. When practising, it is very important to respect any weapon and to be aware of the potential dangers.

Defence 1 – Demonstrating how to counter a knife face slash.

1△ A slashing knife attack is very frightening, but as the aggressor comes in, duck down to avoid the knife.

2△ As the knife swings back round, bring your body up and block the aggressor's right arm with the edge of your right hand or forearm. Ensure you turn your body away from the knife attack as you block.

3△ Twist completely around inwards, towards the aggressor, leading with your left foot. Spin your body clockwise so that you are facing the same way as the aggressor. Keep the knife away from you by bringing your left arm over the attacker's right arm, ideally aiming for just above the elbow joint, and then under it to take hold of your own right wrist. Apply pressure by locking your arms. Keep your body close to the side of the aggressor for maximum control.

4△ Pivot on both feet, turning in an anti-clockwise (counterclockwise) direction to face the aggressor. At the same time, apply a circular action to the aggressor's wrist, bending his elbow so that the knife ends up behind the aggressor. This continuous, flowing movement will cause pain, and should encourage the aggressor to drop the knife.

5△ Keep the momentum going and take the aggressor to the floor. Ideally, pick up the knife, to prevent any further assault, before seeking assistance.

Defence 2 – Demonstrating how to defend against a knife body lunge.

1△ An aggressor moves in with a right-hand knife attack to the stomach. Side step the attack and block with your left arm, taking hold of his right wrist with your right hand to stop the knife attack. This technique is one of many knife defences used in shinto ryu.

2△ Bring your left arm over the aggressor's right arm and under his elbow joint, keeping hold of his right wrist with your right hand, to apply an elbow lock to release the knife.

3◁ If the aggressor has not already dropped the knife, this is the time to apply further pressure to release the weapon. Pin the aggressor's arm against your chest to apply pressure against the elbow joint, keeping the knife away from your body. Simultaneously move in and strike the hinge of his mandible (jaw bone close to the lower ear) with your left elbow. Remember, if the aggressor came in with a left-hand knife attack, you would apply the above from the opposite side.

Part Two

TRAINING PROGRAMMES:

T'ai Chi and Aikido

This second section of the book features two specially designed training programmes, one following t'ai chi, and the other aikido. These programmes build on the basic skills learnt in the first half of this book to give the reader a greater understanding of the physical and mental challenges and benefits that these two special martial arts pose.

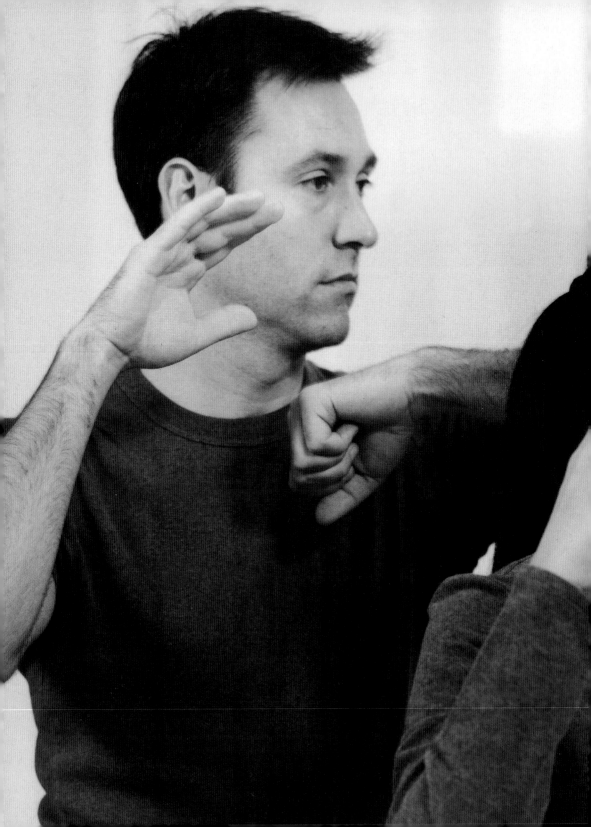

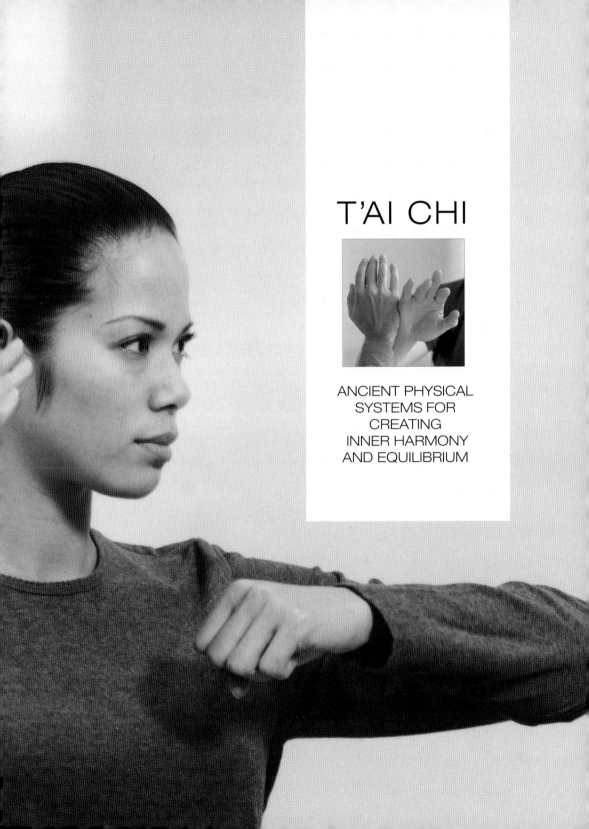

T'AI CHI

ANCIENT PHYSICAL SYSTEMS FOR CREATING INNER HARMONY AND EQUILIBRIUM

An Introduction to T'ai Chi

T'ai chi is an art of balance: physical, energetic, mental and emotional balance. T'ai chi began in ancient China, and is known as an internal art – meaning an art of self-development. From a t'ai chi perspective, self-development means gaining robust health, a balanced emotional life and clarity of mind, and evolving spiritually.

The practice of t'ai chi consists of a set of smoothly flowing movements called the "form". The form is normally performed at a relatively slow pace, allowing for the gradual release of tension in your body and mind; the healing of physical injuries and imbalances; and the opening and energizing of the energetic channels and centres of the body. The movements of the t'ai chi form are designed to enhance the energetic flows within your body – and they also happen to be very beautiful and graceful. Although as a beginning t'ai chi student one's main focus is on learning the external movements, or "form", as one progresses it is possible to focus more on the internal aspects of t'ai chi, including the use of one's mind to move and transform one's chi energy. This is where many of the deeper benefits of t'ai chi are found. In fact, t'ai chi can be a very powerful form of moving meditation, as well as an ideal health practice.

Below The practice of t'ai chi simultaneously balances the physical, energetic, mental and emotional aspects of your being.

T'ai chi has its roots in the Taoist tradition, whose origins date back 5,000 years. Later in the book we will look more fully at the origins and theories that underlie t'ai chi. Fundamentally, t'ai chi is concerned with the principle of balancing yin and yang – the mutually complementary aspects of existence that can be applied to all concepts, such as night and day, female and male, etc. The diagram Taoists use to illustrate this theory is known as the t'ai chi symbol. It shows yin changing into yang, and vice versa, in a never-ending cycle, and the totality of the two, and therefore the totality of existence, is represented by the entire symbol – hence t'ai chi or "Great Ultimate". The full name of this art is in fact t'ai chi chuan. The word chuan means "fist" – and this hints at its martial origins.

T'ai chi is most commonly practised purely for its health and self-development benefits, but it is also a martial art, and a highly effective one. Ancient China was a dangerous place, and self-defence was an essential skill, not a sport or pastime. Inseparable from the martial nature of t'ai chi are its self-development aspects. In fact, t'ai chi simply does not work as a high-level martial art without at least some of the self-development aspects being accomplished. However, you can use t'ai chi effectively as a self-development tool without ever engaging in martial practice. For the vast majority of people who practise t'ai chi today, this is the case. Becoming relaxed, healthy and balanced is a more important survival skill for most people in the modern world than becoming a proficient fighter. You are much more likely to die from a stress-related disease than be killed by a criminal. In this sense t'ai chi is a truly modern self-defence art – defence against the very real enemy of stress-related illness.

WHY LEARN T'AI CHI?

T'ai chi operates on several levels simultaneously: the physical, the energetic and the mental/emotional. Most people in the modern world (and probably in any culture) suffer from some form of physical imbalance or injury – for instance, back and neck pain, which is almost epidemic in developed societies, where many people lead sedentary, desk-bound lives. T'ai chi allows for the release and healing of physical tensions and injuries – over time it has the potential to completely eliminate back, neck and joint problems. This in itself is a compelling reason to learn the art of t'ai chi, but another, perhaps even more compelling, reason to practise t'ai chi is stress. Levels of stress have become almost intolerable for many people around the world. The only effective antidote to stress is to learn to relax, but this is often easier said than done. T'ai chi offers an enjoyable and engaging way to relax both your body and your mind – without giving up your existing life. With some initial effort to learn t'ai chi, and as little as 15 minutes' practice a day, you can greatly reduce the levels of stress you experience. More practice brings even greater calmness and balance in the midst of an often chaotic world. With no special equipment or space needed, most people could easily perform a t'ai chi form in their living room.

For those who have a deeper interest in meditation and spiritual practice, t'ai chi offers a solid foundation for these practices, as it allows for the release of emotional tensions, and develops stillness of mind within the practitioner – essential prerequisites for deeper meditation practices. Above all, t'ai chi works at the level of your energy – what the Chinese call "chi". Chi is the living energy that circulates through your body, and it is what makes you alive – a dead body has no chi circulating through it. The Chinese medical art of acupuncture works directly with your chi to release blockage and balance the flow of this energy through specific pathways in the body in order to cure the imbalances that lead to illness. By a combination of specific movements and mental intention in t'ai chi, you can move chi around your own body, in the process clearing blockages in, and balancing, your energy, as well as increasing your energetic reserves (relating to your energetic centre known as the lower tantien). This will in turn affect your physical body, allowing it to relax and heal itself – and it will affect your mind, because when your energy is balanced and relaxed, so is your mind.

Sometimes t'ai chi is referred to as a mind–body art, and this is a very appropriate term, because ideally there is no separation between the two when practising (in fact, the term could be mind–energy–body, as t'ai chi works on all these levels at the same time). With its emphasis on finding stillness in the midst of movement – both your own movement and that of the world around you – t'ai chi offers a practical way to improve your day-to-day experience of living in this often turbulent world, while also helping you evolve as a person and find greater happiness and peace within yourself.

To start learning t'ai chi, spend as much time as possible running through the exercises in the "Preparation" chapter. The sections titled "T'ai Chi Principles" and "Relaxing and

Above T'ai chi originated in ancient China and has since spread throughout the world due to its ability to benefit all types of people, in any walk of life.

Releasing" contain the essential information you will need to start moving in a "t'ai chi" manner. The section on "Taoist Breathing" contains exercises to help still your mind and relax your entire body – an essential t'ai chi skill. The section on "Cloud Hands" contains a complete chi gung exercise that embodies the essence of t'ai chi. This will help you develop your t'ai chi skills before, during and after learning the form.

In "The Wu Style Short Form" a complete t'ai chi short form is set out, clearly illustrated and described in order to guide you through the sequence of postures. These movements use principles that you will have already learned from the previous chapter. In keeping with the circular nature of this learning process, you will find it useful to refer back to "Preparation" as you progress through learning the form.

"Taking it Further" contains more advanced information, including push hands techniques, pulsing joints, and exercises for meditation to help you to develop your practice and integrate t'ai chi into your personal lifestyle.

T'ai Chi
in Context

This chapter looks at the origins and place of t'ai chi in relation to the other Taoist arts of China. Understanding how t'ai chi developed and evolved and how it relates to the other Taoist arts can lead to a much deeper understanding of what it is you are seeking to learn and practise. T'ai chi does not stand alone; it embodies aspects of, and is intrinsically linked to, all the Taoist arts and sciences, such as other Taoist internal martial arts, chi kung (energy work), meditation, feng shui (geomancy), Chinese astrology and Chinese medicine. The common thread running through all these arts is an understanding of energy, called chi. This energy underlies all manifestation in the universe – solid matter merely being a very condensed form of chi energy. By understanding chi we can begin fully to understand ourselves.

The Taoist Tradition

A Taoist (pronounced "Daoist") is a person who "follows the Tao". Tao means "way" or "path" in Chinese, and in this context it means the way of the universe and all existence. Following the Tao means living in total harmony with the universe and understanding the nature of reality. True Taoism is a spiritual tradition, the origins of which date back at least 5,000 years in China. Never an organized religion, it is rather a personal spiritual path.

The Taoists were never great in number, yet they had an enormous influence on Chinese thought, art and science: much of the cultural heritage that we would identify as being characteristically Chinese is of Taoist origin. The Taoists were the originators of Chinese medicine, calligraphy and art, feng shui, chi kung and the internal arts, astrology and cosmology, as well as traditional music and theatre. Taoist sages usually avoided entanglement in politics and government, but they were often the guiding light behind the wiser Chinese rulers. The most prosperous and peaceful periods of Chinese history have generally coincided with a strong Taoist influence.

Although Taoism had existed in some form for several thousand years before his birth, the concept is commonly attributed to the sage Lao-tzu (570–490 BC). He held the very important post of Imperial Librarian and was known during his lifetime as a great Taoist master. As an old man, he withdrew from worldly affairs, renounced his position and

Below Lao-tzu, the founder of Taoism, seen here seated on his buffalo, and followed by a disciple.

set off for Tibet riding a water buffalo. A border guard, himself a Taoist, insisted that Lao-tzu leave behind a manuscript of the most essential Taoist teachings before he disappeared from the world. Lao-tzu agreed to this and wrote what is known as the Tao Te Ching or the "Book of the Way and its Virtue".

The Tao Te Ching was the first book to be written on Taoism, which until then had been a purely oral tradition, hence Lao-tzu's reputation as its "originator". This short book, consisting of 81 verses, contains the essence of the ancient Taoist "water method" tradition (the metaphor of water is repeatedly used in the text). This emphasizes the dissolving of all tension in one's being, in contrast to the "fire method", which advocates making things happen.

TAOIST BELIEFS

Taoists hold that the source of all existence is emptiness. From this, two opposite and complementary aspects of energy arise: yin and yang. These two principles cannot exist independently of one another, just as you cannot define darkness (yin) without the concept of light (yang), or female (yin) without male (yang). Just as they are mutually dependent, yin and yang contain the essence of one another within themselves, shown in the t'ai chi symbol by the small dot of the opposite colour within each half. They constantly change into one another, as night changes into day and back again in an endless cycle, and this is also shown in the symbol: as one decreases the other increases, and as each reaches its maximum it starts to change into its opposite. For example, after midday, which is considered fully yang, there is a change to yin as the sun starts to descend. Midnight is fully yin: after that point yang energy increases.

The t'ai chi symbol (shown right) is perhaps the most famous symbol in the world and is an elegant way of describing the nature of the universe. "T'ai chi" is really another way of saying "Tao" – the totality of existence.

Right An elderly t'ai chi practitioner cultivating "stillness within movement, and movement within stillness". The deeper aspects of t'ai chi embody the principles of Taoist spiritual practice.

> Mysteriously formed,
> Born before heaven and earth.
> In the silence and the void,
> Standing alone and unchanging,
> Ever present and in motion;
> It is the mother of the ten thousand things.
> It has no name. Call it the Way [Tao].
>
> Lao-tzu, Tao Te Ching

THE FIVE ELEMENTS

Following the division of yin and yang energy out of emptiness, five distinct phases of energy – known as the Five Elements – are formed. These are Metal, Water, Wood, Fire and Earth. Just as everything can be described in terms of yin and yang, it can also be described in terms of the Five Elements. In the cycle of the seasons, for instance, midsummer has the quality of Fire, late summer of Earth, autumn of Metal, winter of Water and spring of Wood. Each element (and each season in this case) generates the next, in what is known as the Generation Cycle. The names of the elements are essentially ways of describing a particular type of energy: Wood, for example, has the quality of expanding energy, or growth. Five Element theory is fundamental to Chinese medicine. Each of the body's organs embodies a characteristic element – for instance, the heart is Fire, and the kidneys are Water – and people exhibit more or less of each element in their behaviour and physical make-up.

From the Five Elements are formed the Ten Thousand Things (symbolizing the multitude of objects found in the universe). This concept forms a complete description of how the universe unfolds out of nothingness – a description that has been supported in modern times by quantum physics.

THE I CHING

Another very famous Taoist book, the I Ching or "Book of Changes", further describes the universe in terms of patterns of yin and yang, represented by solid or broken lines. These are put together in groups of three to make eight symbols called trigrams. Together these are known as the ba gua, and they are often shown grouped around a t'ai chi symbol, further describing the process of change from yin to yang and back again. The eight trigrams are then combined in pairs to make 64 hexagrams, which represent all possible changes of energy in the universe.

Taoists say that if one understands the I Ching, then one truly understands the nature of existence. It can be used on many levels: for help in forecasting future events, for advice on how to deal with our current situation and as a key to understanding the universe and our place in it.

The essence of Taoism lies in its understanding of the nature of existence or, as Taoists would say, reality. Yin/yang theory, the ba gua, the I Ching and the Five Elements are all ways of describing this reality. Its source is the mysterious, unknowable Tao, the non-dual state of being beyond even the concept of yin and yang. During the Chinese Cultural Revolution in the 1960s, many Taoists went into hiding or were killed. Taoism was one of the "Olds", the traditional Chinese cultural values that Mao Tse-tung wanted to wipe out. Despite this, Taoism survives as a living tradition.

OTHER CHINESE TRADITIONS

There have of course been other spiritual and philosophical traditions in China, most notably Confucianism and Buddhism. Confucianism – named after Confucius, the Latinized name of the scholar Kung Fu-tzu (551–479 BC) – was very concerned with the role of society and man's place in it (women's roles were strictly defined and limited, whereas the Taoists considered women entirely equal to men). Many Taoist sages, including Lao-tzu himself and another famous master, Chuang-tzu, were openly critical of Confucianism. They felt that Confucianism's obsession with the structure and rules of society took humanity further away from a state of natural harmony and simplicity. Nevertheless, Chinese society to this day is largely Confucian in its attitudes; perhaps this is simply a reflection of the overall Chinese character.

Arriving in China from India in 520 AD, Buddhism was so strongly influenced by the non-gradual Taoist approach to enlightenment that it became a distinct form known as Chan Buddhism. This form later reached Japan, where "Chan" was translated as "Zen".

Another tradition worth mentioning is Neo-Taoism, which arose around the 3rd century AD. Its philosophy was similar to ancient Taoism, but it was much more concerned with sorcery, ritual and religious structure. The practices of this tradition are generally more of the "Fire" nature than those used by the ancient Taoists in the "Water" tradition.

Taoist Self-development

The Taoist world view, while fascinating as a philosophy, is not simply a body of intellectual knowledge. It provides the basis for a complete system of self-development that has been tried and tested over millennia. Human nature is no different now from the way it was in ancient China. The Taoist system of self-development views all human beings as essentially the same, subject to the same physical and mental constraints.

Becoming free of the constraints that limit human potential is the very essence of Taoist practice. It is not too bold to say that Taoist self-development is about personal evolution. How far you choose to travel along that path is your own, personal decision: you may be interested in developing balanced and robust health, or wish to become free of disturbing emotions or to move into the realm of spiritual practice. Taoists maintain that these choices are up to the individual and that no other person has a right to impose them – in other words, everyone has the right to determine the course of their own life.

THE MIND OF TAO

Taoism sees humankind as an integral part of the universe, in a harmonious relationship with heaven and earth – yin and yang. Human beings come from the joining of yin and yang. On a physical level we can see this is true: we are the result of the union of male and female potential. However, most human beings rarely experience a state of total integration and harmony. From the earliest times, Taoists sought to transcend the physical, energetic and spiritual separation of human beings from the rest of the universe, and reintegrate with all existence.

Taoism sees the problems we suffer as the result of a loss of this integration. Instead of doing what is natural and appropriate, and therefore beneficial to ourselves, we act in ways that unsettle the body, energy and mind. This causes problems ranging from physical ailments to mental and emotional turmoil, and takes us further away from understanding our true nature and our part in the universe. The Taoists contrast the human mind with the "mind of Tao", which in this context is wisdom, and the human mind represents confusion, or lack of wisdom and clarity. Since everything is Tao, we naturally possess the mind of Tao, but we are preoccupied with the human mind. Taoist practice is about opening ourselves up to, and developing, this potential until we are living with the mind of Tao. This is the state of enlightenment. Along the path to this state, we can learn to live more freely, more healthily, more joyfully.

Ancient Taoist tradition considers that since we are essentially "natural" it is only tensions that stop us enjoying this state. These tensions can exist on many levels, and the tradition talks specifically about eight distinct levels, or "bodies". They range from the physical body through progressively more subtle levels of energy (chi, emotional, mental, psychic, causal, the ego) to the "body of the Tao". These are all aspects of our intrinsic make-up. The tensions that may exist in all these bodies limit our potential and our enjoyment of life. The most obvious example would be a stiff

Left Cranes and pine trees are popular Taoist symbols of the long life and spiritual development they believe is to be gained by sexual and meditative practices, including the practice of t'ai chi.

neck or back – tension in the physical body – while we may all experience tension in the emotional body as anger, frustration or depression, or in the mental body as worry.

BECOMING SOONG

In order to overcome such problems we have to release these tensions and become "soong". This Chinese word has no exact translation, but loosely means "unbound". The analogy used is of slitting open a bag of coins and allowing the coins to tumble out freely. It conveys a sense of effortlessly relaxing and letting go. When we do this, our tensions dissolve, and this is what Taoist self-development is about: becoming free of tensions and constraints in the physical body, the mind and emotions. The metaphor of dissolving tension and blockage is at the heart of the water tradition in Taoism.

Since the physical body is the easiest to become aware of and to work with, Taoist self-development practice always starts here. However, the chi body is very closely associated with it. In order to effect change in the physical body, we need to work simultaneously with chi, hence the practices known as chi kung, or "energy work". These release tensions in the physical and chi bodies through physical positions, movements, breathing and mental intent. The benefits are robust health, ample energy and a calm, clear mind. By definition, t'ai chi is a chi kung practice.

Above This chi kung standing practice, known as zhan zhuang, or "standing like a tree", is a powerful method of developing energy.

As your practice develops, you will increasingly access the more subtle levels of your being, such as the emotional and mental bodies, and release tensions at those levels. This feeds back to the chi and physical bodies and you become more relaxed and comfortable. Conversely, mental and emotional tension invariably cause physical tension. You may find it useful to practise meditation, which continues the process of releasing tension, but at the more subtle levels. Its potential benefits are very great, including becoming free of mental and emotional tensions that may have existed for many years.

Taoism has developed many techniques, but all are aimed at achieving this natural state of being soong. The Taoists often refer to babies and very small children as a perfect example of this state: their bodies are relaxed and full of energy, their minds are clear and unconditioned, their emotions relate only to present events, not to past issues or future worries. Regaining the naturalness of a baby while retaining the developed mind of an adult is seen as the ideal. It is the mental and emotional conditioning and physical tension accumulated from early childhood that Taoists seek to become free of, allowing their true nature and potential to blossom.

The Taoist Internal Arts

The techniques of Taoist self-development are collectively known as the internal arts. They are considered arts because, although a precise theory underlies them, their actual practice is a creative process: since each person's condition is unique, their path is also unique. They are considered internal because they relate to your own being – both physically and at the level of your mind and emotions.

The techniques involve working with the internal processes and structures of the body and mind. This differentiates them from external practices such as physical exercise and gymnastics, which work only with the external physical structures of the body. The Chinese term for the internal arts is nei jia. Nei, meaning internal, leads to another term, nei gung, which means "internal work" and represents the methods that underlie all the internal arts. It is a more

Below A Taoist engaged in internal self-development practice. These arts lead the practitioner into an ever-deepening journey into their own nature, with complete freedom as the goal.

precise term than chi kung, as it specifically refers to the deeper Taoist self-development practices. The internal arts can be focused purely on upgrading health, or may include emotional, mental and spiritual development.

The Taoists found that the internal techniques could also be applied to the martial arts, which in ancient China were not sports or pastimes, but arose from a real need for self-defence in lawless and dangerous times. The nei gung techniques that give greater health, relaxation, clarity of mind and energy can also be used to generate incredible power. Accomplished practitioners of the "internal martial arts" are able to move and react in a way that could easily overcome most attackers, especially those using "external" techniques. Apart from their superiority as martial arts, what makes these practices so beneficial is that they inherently involve self-development practice. In fact, this is why they work so well as martial arts.

WU WEI

The highest level of these arts is the state of wu wei, which can be translated as "non-doing" or "empty action". Wu wei is a key principle in Taoism, as it implies a state of oneness with the Tao, "going with the flow" of the universe with no sense of imposing your own concepts or wishes on what is happening. In this state you act with total appropriateness to every situation, whether you are defending your life or making a cup of tea. There is no need for analytical thought: you respond naturally and effortlessly. In small ways we all experience this. For instance, if you accidentally touch something hot you pull your hand away without a moment's thought or hesitation. In that instant, you are in a state of wu wei. Athletes call this being "in the zone", where everything is perfect and effortless – like a surfer yielding to the flow of a wave. Applying the principle to all life's complex activities is the true challenge. Paradoxically, it is through deliberate training methods and long practice that you aim to transcend those very methods and truly enter wu wei.

A phrase in the t'ai chi classics, "Forget yourself and follow the Other", is a statement of the principle of wu wei. The "Other" is the Tao, the natural flow of events within

Below A posture from the single palm change of ba gua zhang. Studying the other two Taoist internal martial arts of ba gua and hsing-i can shed new light on one's experience of t'ai chi.

Below "Gods playing in the clouds" is a chi kung system containing all the Taoist nei gung principles. As these skills develop, they are incorporated into one's t'ai chi practice.

Above The various postures of the Wu style t'ai chi long form open different parts of the body and promote specific energy flows. Every posture is also a martial technique.

which you find yourself. Letting go of your ideas about what should happen, or what you would like to happen, and going with the flow, implies that you are not bound by your own ideas and concepts – in other words you are soong.

INTERNAL MARTIAL ARTS

There are three Taoist internal martial arts, all sharing the same Taoist nei gung foundations, but differing in the way they utilize these principles and methods. The most widely known, especially in the West, is t'ai chi chuan ("supreme ultimate fist"). Less well known are the arts of hsing-i chuan ("mind-form fist") and ba gua zhang ("eight trigram palm"). T'ai chi chuan is the easiest of the three to learn – typically it is said that everybody can learn t'ai chi but fewer can learn hsing-i and fewer still ba gua.

T'ai chi is based on and embodies yin/yang theory – it is primarily concerned with an unceasing flow from yin to yang and back again, both physically and in the energy and mind. It is essentially yin in nature (especially the Wu style, which is featured in this book) and is a superb method of relaxation and stress relief. This may account for its current popularity in the West. The stressed-out, yang nature of modern life requires a yin antidote, and t'ai chi is perfect. It is also an excellent method of healing the body, particularly for

correcting back, neck and joint problems – common results of stressful office work and sedentary lifestyles.

Hsing-i is based on Five Element theory, both the Generating (sheng) Cycle and the Controlling (ko) Cycle, in which each element or phase of energy has its antagonistic element: for example, Wood is "cut" by Metal. Hsing-i is strongly yang in nature, and its martial nature is very visible. It is externally simpler than t'ai chi, but as advanced internally, and is a useful art for those who are excessively yin or lack self-esteem, as it develops and sharpens the will and the ego. It is not ideal for those who are excessively yang; such people need a more yin practice such as t'ai chi.

Ba gua is based on the I Ching, and is the only purely Taoist internal art, as it has no elements of external martial forms within it. It is based on the very ancient Taoist circle walking meditation, and it embodies change – the constant flux of energies in the universe – as its core principle. As such it has a continuously moving, flowing and changing quality. It is generally considered to be the most sophisticated of the Taoist internal arts, and consequently the most difficult to master.

All these arts involve the cultivation of the energy centre in the abdomen known as the lower tantien ("elixir field") – pronounced "dandien". The lower tantien, usually referred to simply as the tantien, is the central point of all the body's chi energy, and therefore its cultivation is immensely beneficial for increasing martial power, attaining robust health, longevity and the energy needed to be fully active.

Chinese Medicine

Perhaps the most widely known of all the Taoist arts and sciences is Chinese medicine. Chinese medicine takes a typically Taoist view: that to achieve health and heal illness a holistic view of the patient is needed. This means taking not only their physical state and circumstances into account, but also their mental and emotional state: the idea that the two cannot really be separated is central to Chinese medicine.

A person's lifestyle choices and physical health are a reflection of their mental and emotional state, and vice versa; illness is seen as a result of imbalance in chi energy, with different types of imbalance resulting in different illnesses. Even infectious diseases are deemed to be a result of the body's lack of protective energy, or wei chi, which has allowed "invasion" by a pathogen. In a healthy, energetically balanced individual, the wei chi is strong and prevents pathogens from entering and causing illness.

Chinese doctors were traditionally paid a regular fee to maintain the health of their patients; if a patient fell ill the doctor would not be paid until they had restored the patient's health. So the paradigm of focusing on health rather than sickness was taken very literally indeed.

THE THREE TREASURES

Chinese medical theory is based on the concept of the three treasures, jing, chi and shen. Jing can be translated as "essence", chi as "energy" and shen as "spirit". Jing represents core energy – both the essential energy you were born with and that needed to maintain life. "Pre-birth" jing is

Below Chinese herbalists measure out the components of a formula. Certain combinations of herbs will benefit specific health conditions. Herbs are good for nourishing chi and blood.

your genetic inheritance, and determines your overall constitution and lifespan. As you age, it is slowly used up, and this is seen as the cause of ageing. When your pre-birth jing is exhausted, so is your life. In general, the amount of pre-birth jing is fixed at birth and cannot be added to (although there are advanced Taoist longevity practices that can enhance it). "Post-birth" jing is created from the food you eat and the air you breathe, as well as energy absorbed from your surroundings, such as sunlight, the cosmos or trees. If your post-birth jing is strong you feel that your core energy is good; if not, you feel drained. When you expend too much energy you temporarily exhaust your post-birth jing; if you do not rest and restore it, you start tapping into your irreplaceable pre-birth jing. This can cause premature ageing and permanent "burn-out". Practising t'ai chi can, over time, increase your store of post-birth jing, thus boosting your core energy reserves.

Chi is the active energy flowing through the body, and can be said to be produced from jing. If jing is the water, chi is the steam. It flows through specific channels in your body, sometimes called meridians, and takes many forms. It can be seen as your available energy, both for internal processes such as digestion and for external activity. The flow of chi varies according to the time, the seasons and even the movement of the stars and planets. Ill health occurs when the flow is disrupted by being blocked, scattered or even reversed. Since the physical body relies on healthy chi flow to sustain its structures and processes, ill health will result when imbalance occurs. The physical structures of the body are seen both as the result of, and the conduit for, chi flows. Physical injury can block the flow of chi, and vice versa: blocked or abnormal chi flow can result in physical abnormalities, such as skin disorders.

The third treasure, and the most subtle, is shen. This refers to mental/emotional aspects, as well as even more subtle "spiritual" levels. The state of a person's shen is said to be visible in their eyes, just as in the Western saying, "The eyes are the windows of the soul." A weak shen may result in depression, timidity or fearfulness. A disturbed shen would manifest as neurosis, or perhaps even mania and psychosis.

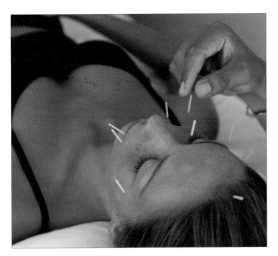

Left Acupuncture can be used to treat a variety of conditions, ranging from minor to life-threatening illnesses, and also for cosmetic rejuvenation treatments, such as the facial acupuncture session shown here.

While its exact nature is complex, it can be said to relate above all to the heart. If the shen is disturbed it will affect the state of a person's chi, while an imbalance of chi will eventually affect the shen, so they are mutually dependent. Since jing and chi are also mutually dependent, Chinese medicine always takes all three treasures into account when diagnosing and treating illness.

DIAGNOSIS

Practitioners diagnose a patient on the basis of many observations. One primary method is the taking of pulses on each wrist, with specific positions relating to specific organs of the body. The pulses are assessed on the basis of their speed and regularity and their quality: terms such as "empty", "choppy", "wiry" and "slippery" are used to denote its energetic quality. Taking the pulses can be an extremely powerful diagnostic tool, and is an art in itself. Observation of the patient's tongue will also yield key information about the state of the internal organs, with specific areas of the tongue relating to certain organs and functions of the body. In many ways, tongue diagnosis is less subjective. The results of the two are compared to form a fuller picture.

Observation of the patient's physical state and the way they move, talk and behave are also key diagnostic tools, with specific signs and attributes providing clues to underlying conditions. The practitioner will then ask a series of questions – some very similar to those a Western physician would ask, others very different, such as what kind of emotions the patient feels. A picture is thus built up of the physical, energetic and mental/emotional state of the patient in terms of Chinese medical theory (which uses several paradigms to categorize symptoms), and like a detective assembling seemingly separate pieces of evidence, the practitioner can then form a diagnosis and treatment plan.

The internal organs of the body play a major part in treatment, and the main channels or meridians each relate to an organ. The organs are divided into yin or zang organs, and yang or fu organs. Zang and fu are then paired according to the elements they represent and embody. The zang organs are seen to be of primary importance, and are also associated with certain emotions, as well as sounds, tastes, colours, smells and so on.

TREATMENT

Some treatments intervene with the patient's chi from the outside. Acupuncture uses very fine needles to access and correct the flow of chi within the channels at specific points, known as "cavities". A powerful herb – moxa, or mugwort – is sometimes burned above or on an acupuncture point, or even on the end of a needle, to move and tonify the chi: this is called "moxibustion". Another method of treatment is "cupping", where glass or bamboo jars are briefly heated and then placed on the body, creating a vacuum as the air within them cools. Chinese herbal medicine works from inside the body to transform the patterns of chi flow, especially with regard to the organs, or zang-fu. Herbs take longer to act but generally do so on a deep level. The practice of tui na, often called Chinese massage, is used as a form of body therapy to release bindings and blockages in the tissues, while simultaneously working with the acupuncture channels to effect change on a deeper level.

Traditionally a Chinese physician offers patients lifestyle advice, including dietary advice, and instructs them in chi kung techniques for self-healing. Often this includes a recommendation to take up t'ai chi as a way of maintaining robust health, as it utilizes the core principles of Chinese medicine, and is a powerful method of self-treatment.

Below Acupuncture needles and mugwort herb, burned in stick form or on the ends of needles to warm cold and deficient areas.

Chi Kung and Nei Gung

A person's chi energy can be stronger or weaker depending on their state of health – physical, mental and emotional – and also on their basic constitution. While Chinese medicine seeks to redress any imbalances in the flow of chi within a patient, chi kung ("energy work") practice enables a person to remove blockages in their own chi and actually increase their available energy, both immediately and in the long term.

Chi kung is a generic term for all types of Chinese energetic self-development work, and the practices it describes vary enormously in both underlying theory and application. The term is becoming increasingly familiar in the West, though Chinese energetic practices are latecomers compared to Indian yoga techniques, which established a foothold decades earlier. Chi kung is usually understood to imply methods that use a series of movements involving breathing work. In many ways this is not inaccurate, but as chi kung becomes increasingly popular in the West, the differences between the systems in existence will also become more evident. In fact, there are several chi kung traditions in China: medical, martial, Buddhist, Confucian and Taoist. Each has a distinct character and approach, reflecting its origins. Though some aspects of the systems overlap, others differ widely.

Below A core principle in t'ai chi is to integrate the inner with the outer, and internal practice with the external elements.

INSIDE AND OUTSIDE

The term nei gung, particularly Taoist nei gung, is much more specific. What most distinguishes nei gung from other chi kung practices is the difference between nei – the internal – and wei – the external. While nei gung methods work from the inside (the core of the body) to the outside, the opposite is true of other chi kung methods. Like acupuncture, which by accessing relatively superficial energetic channels seeks to have an effect on the organs and deeper systems of the body, chi kung often uses external movements and breathing techniques to do this. Chi kung also works one aspect of the body's energetic systems at a time, often building these techniques into a sequential set of movements.

Within each chi kung tradition there are many techniques, and some systems are highly effective, especially at removing chi stagnation, while others are not. The value of any chi kung system lies in how well it works in relation to the time and effort required from the practitioner. Many chi kung practices are easier to learn and apply than the more advanced nei gung methods. However, the potential benefits of nei gung practice are substantially greater than those available from more external chi kung practices.

An important principle of nei gung is that whatever you do at the deeper levels of your being has a great effect on all the more superficial levels: one unit of time and effort at a deep level can have ten units of effect on the shallower levels. Conversely, it takes ten units of time and effort at the shallower levels to achieve one unit of effect at the deeper levels. Therefore, according to nei gung theory, it is more useful to work directly at the deeper levels of your body and energy from the start. This is, of course, harder to achieve as the deeper levels are more "hidden", but it can be done, with a little application, by almost anybody.

One of the more immediate advantages of nei gung practice is that it allows for the release of deep tensions and blockages in the physical body, allowing the healing of even long-standing spinal and joint problems and also an improvement in the functioning of the internal organs. These benefits might never be attained with external chi kung

Right A movement from "dragon and tiger" chi kung. Practising chi kung alongside t'ai chi can greatly enhance a person's ability to work with chi energy.

Below Many of the nei gung components of t'ai chi are more easily developed separately, before being integrated into one's t'ai chi practice.

systems, many of which (though not all) are concerned mainly with developing chi – increasing the amount of power in the system. This is fine in a healthy, balanced body, but almost everybody has energetic (and physical) blockages that do not need to be "powered up", but instead need to be released. For most people the problem is not of a fundamental lack of energy, but of blockages in their energy flow, and this can manifest as a lack of available energy for a particular part of the body, or even overall. In a blocked water pipe, you would not want simply to increase the pressure, or the pipe might burst. Instead you would want to dissolve away the blockage to allow normal flow to resume. Nei gung methods seek first to release energetic blockages and correct physical misalignments before developing natural energetic capacity. Nei gung embodies the Taoist principle of naturalness – of regaining a natural healthy state that is inherently vibrant and powerful.

NEI GUNG TECHNIQUES

The techniques can be subdivided into several categories. They include opening and closing ("pulsing") of all the joints and tissues; spiralling of all the tissues; working with the energy flows of the deepest channels; dissolving blockages in all the energetic bodies; working with the energy of the spine and spinal cord; and breathing techniques (nei gung

does not rely on breathing to move the chi – the mind is used directly – but breathing may be used where appropriate). These are just a few of the Taoist nei gung techniques. Although they are usually learned singly, once mastered they are performed simultaneously. Thus nei gung practice may involve just one simple movement, within which all the nei gung methods are being applied at the same time. This creates a synergy that dramatically increases the effectiveness of the practice – it becomes more than just the sum of its parts.

NEI GUNG AND T'AI CHI

When performed correctly, t'ai chi is a nei gung practice – and this is also true of hsing-i and ba gua. After you have learned the t'ai chi form – the sequence of external movements – you will want to start introducing nei gung principles and components into your practice, one at a time. As you do this your form may change little on the outside, at least to the casual observer, but your personal experience of practising t'ai chi will change and evolve dramatically. Ultimately, a dedicated t'ai chi practitioner seeks to incorporate all the nei gung methods into their form, making it a very powerful and sophisticated nei gung practice. This is where the deeper benefits of t'ai chi are to be found, and where it truly becomes an internal art.

The Origins and Development of T'ai Chi

The exact origins of t'ai chi chuan are the subject of endless controversy, as there is no way of verifying which of the many theories about it are true. One thing is certain: t'ai chi first appeared in the Chen village in China at some time during the 16th century. Another certainty is that from the outset it had Taoist influence. The following story may or may not be true – but it is very likely.

A master named Wang Tsung Yueh arrived at the Chen village and visited the local inn. Over the course of an evening, the subject of martial arts was discussed – this was at a time when such skills were essential for survival in the face of organized banditry. The locals (all of the same clan) were very proud of their external Shaolin style martial art called pao twi or "cannon fist". Wang was unimpressed and told them so in no uncertain terms. Deeply insulted, the villagers attacked Wang, but he beat off his multiple attackers in a way they had never seen before. Amazed and humbled, they begged Wang to teach them his art. Wang agreed, but as he did not have time to teach them his complete system, he modified their existing external martial art to include Taoist nei gung methods – making it fully "internal". This new art – Chen style t'ai chi – continued to develop, and today is one of the three main styles of t'ai chi.

Where Wang Tsung Yueh learned his art will probably never be known. A well-known legend is that t'ai chi or its antecedent was created by the Taoist "Immortal" Chang San Feng after he watched a snake and a crane fighting. Whatever the truth, the involvement of Taoist sages in the creation and development of the internal martial arts can be taken for granted, as they all contain fundamental Taoist nei gung practices.

T'AI CHI EVOLVES

In the 19th century a master named Yang Lu Chan (1799–1872) further developed the art and spread t'ai chi beyond the Chen village. As a young man he had been tutored by the Chen clan – no mean feat, as t'ai chi was at the time their secret weapon, unique to the clan. Yang travelled all over China and accepted all challenges, never losing once, and never seriously injuring his opponents, no matter how violent. He became known as "Yang the

Below The art of t'ai chi, and the Taoist wisdom it embodies, has spread outwards from its origins in remote parts of China, to be practised by millions of people throughout the world today.

Right A female practitioner of t'ai chi straight sword. T'ai chi weapons also include the sabre, spear and wooden staff. Weapons practice can help develop strength, balance and spiralling energy.

Invincible". He was accepted as the finest martial artist in all China, and taught the Emperor's bodyguards. He also accepted other students, one of whom was Wu Yu Hsiang, whose "small frame" style of t'ai chi later became known as the Hao style. While a valid style of t'ai chi, Hao style is not considered to be one of the main styles, and neither is the Sun style of Sun Lu Tang, which is a fusion of all three of the Taoist internal martial arts.

Yang style flourished, and was known as Yang Family style as it was mainly passed from father to son: Yang Lu Chan passed it to his son Yang Pan Hou, who in turn passed it to his son Yang Chen Fu. It changed somewhat with Yang Chen Fu, losing some of its highly martial emphasis, and this is known as "new" Yang style. The changes were largely to do with the change in attitudes to the traditional martial arts in China after the Boxer Rebellion in 1900. This catastrophic event was a desperate attempt by the Emperor to expel foreign powers from Beijing, using martial artists ("boxers") from all over China. The foreign forces used machine guns and the result was carnage, and a total rout of the boxers. China was divided among the victors, and Chinese martial arts never regained their almost mythical status in the face of the stark reality of modern firearms. Yang style t'ai chi, however, survived, and continues to flourish.

WU STYLE T'AI CHI

Yang Lu Chan's top student, Chuan You, was adept at the most advanced, transformational aspect of t'ai chi energy work, and developed his art based on these principles. He later taught his son, Wu Jien Chuan (1870–1942), who also studied with Yang Pan Hou (Yang Lu Chan's son). Wu Jien Chuan taught with the Yang family in Beijing and he and Yang Chen Fu often demonstrated their t'ai chi side by side. Wu Jien Chuan, being 20 years the senior of the two, also helped Yang Chen Fu develop his skills.

Partly because of the transformational energy work that had been passed on to him by his father, and partly because he was also a Taoist spiritual practitioner, Wu Jien Chuan's interests lay increasingly in the inner aspects of t'ai chi, especially its potential for healing and meditation. This was in no way incompatible with the martial aspect, as the power, sensitivity and subtlety that can be accessed at the deeper levels of being inherently allow for superior martial ability. Wu consequently evolved his t'ai chi style to operate at the deepest levels, seeking to make its movements and energy flows originate from the practitioner's core. This was in keeping with Taoist nei gung principles of accessing the deepest levels possible at every stage. It could be said that Wu Jien Chuan was attempting to take t'ai chi closer to its

Taoist origins. He succeeded, as his style contains techniques that relate directly to Taoist nei gung, some of which are not so heavily emphasized in the other styles, or are entirely absent. The result was a "small frame" style of t'ai chi, where the external movements are not as pronounced but the internal movements are in fact larger.

LINEAGE

Wu taught openly, and as a result Wu style t'ai chi is widely known in China, and is arguably more popular than the Yang style in parts of southern China. The secretive days of the Chen village had passed and the art could be spread for the benefit of many. However, its deeper aspects and techniques would always be reserved for those worthy of the knowledge and capable of absorbing and understanding it. Thus the principle of lineage was, and still is, upheld.

The complete art was passed only to those few students whom the master accepted as formal disciples. The main reason for this was and is the importance of keeping the knowledge alive and intact, ensuring it is not "watered down", confused or lost. It is also a guarantee of quality – if you are training with a lineage master you know that what is being passed to you is authentic and effective. It is not always possible to train with such a teacher, but the closer your teacher is to a genuine lineage, the greater the likelihood that you will be well trained. T'ai chi will inevitably evolve in the future but, in the hands of talented masters, the knowledge and skill that has been passed down will provide the foundations for the art as it develops.

The Different Styles of T'ai Chi

Although there are differences between the various styles of t'ai chi, key similarities are shared by all the authentic styles. It is these similarities that distinguish t'ai chi from other martial, movement and energetic arts, and mark the authenticity of a t'ai chi style. If a style is lacking any of the core principles it cannot truly be said to be t'ai chi, though it might look like it: it will be only, as the Chinese say, "waving your arms in the air".

While many t'ai chi practitioners like to claim that their style is the "real thing", all genuine practitioners are essentially practising the same art, only with differences in emphasis. Just as the members of a family have different characters, interests and dispositions, so the various styles of t'ai chi have different emphases and approaches. The goal of all authentic t'ai chi is the same: the state of wu wei and the merging with the Ultimate, or t'ai chi. All styles also share the goals of superior personal health and energy, longevity, mental stillness and clarity, and effective self-defence.

Where the main styles differ is in their use of some of these principles, their approach to fighting techniques and, above all, in their approach to energetic development. A casual observer watching the three main styles being performed would be most likely to notice the following differences, which hint at quite dramatic differences in terms of the internal work of the following three styles.

Below Wu style posture "fan through the back" is a meditation point. The body is opened evenly to allow for a fuller sense of "letting go" from one's centre.

Below In the Wu style of t'ai chi the spine is allowed to lean on certain moves, while remaining straight along its length. Yang style adopts a more upright posture.

DIFFERENCES IN THE CHEN, YANG AND WU STYLES

Chen style has highly visible spiralling motions, both in the arms and the body as a whole. It is quite "gymnastic", involving jumps and leaps. The pace changes from very slow to very rapid. It employs visible shaking, vibrating moves when issuing energy, as well as stamping foot movements. It looks a little like Shaolin-type kung fu, which is apt, given its closeness to t'ai chi's "ancestor", pao twi.

Yang style appears much smoother than Chen style, without the acrobatic leaps and twists. Spiralling motions are hard to see as they are internal, and it usually maintains an even pace. It does not use the overt shaking and stamping movements of the Chen style. It typifies the popular image of t'ai chi – smooth, slow and peaceful.

Wu style appears to use much smaller movements than the Yang style, with both the stance and the arm positions less extended. It also appears to be "higher", as the practitioner may not bend the legs so much. Any spiralling motions are all but invisible in the Wu style. The practitioner appears to be doing less, and it may appear more "casual" than the Yang style. In certain postures the spine leans forward, whereas in Yang style it is nearly always vertical.

CHEN STYLE

The Chen style was originally used on the battlefield by armoured warriors wielding weapons. This shaped its form considerably, for instance, its gymnastic quality may be a result of the need to move quickly while encumbered by armour. Probably the most obvious difference between the Chen and later styles is in the visible use of chan ssu jin, or "silk-reeling" energy. The name refers to the way silk is drawn from a cocoon: it must be done with a smooth twisting action, or the threads will break. Chi moves in a spiral motion; to maximize the flow of chi in yourself you therefore need to use spiralling motions in the body. This is one of the key principles of t'ai chi, and in the Chen style it is highly visible as an external coiling movement. Energetically, Chen style seeks to develop "hard" or yang energy. This should not be confused with tensing the muscles as all styles of t'ai chi involve muscular relaxation.

Right The posture ji or "push" in the Yang style. Note the wider stance and position of the arms.

Far right Ji in the Wu style. Note the narrower stance and the hands located on the centreline.

YANG STYLE

T'ai chi was dramatically changed by Yang Lu Chan. Yang's was an age of firearms: armoured warriors became an anachronism, and the reasons for many of the Chen style's characteristics no longer existed. The spiralling elbow of Chen style became more dropped and relaxed; there were no jumps and leaps; stances were weighted 100 per cent on one leg and 0 per cent on the other. Chan ssu jin was achieved by spiralling the tissues of the limbs rather than the limbs as a whole; this became known as "pulling silk" because the emphasis was on directly drawing energy from and into the spine and lower tantien (the body's energy centre). Overall, the energetic work became more internalized, relying less on external motions and more on subtle motions within the body. Many Yang style masters went "smaller" in their form through the course of their lives. The energetic emphasis shifted from the development of hard, yang energy to soft, yin energy, eventually fusing the two. The Yang style works primarily on the external energy field of the body, which is useful for martial projection of energy, called fa jin, or "issuing power".

WU STYLE

The trend of internalization of t'ai chi methods continued with the Wu style, which incorporates Taoist meditation methods and a wider range of nei gung techniques. While spiralling actions are just visible in the Yang style, they are practically invisible in the Wu style, as they are done deep within the tissues. The Yang style opens up the outside of the body first, using large and extended postures, and later seeks to open the inside of the body. The Wu style, does the opposite, using smaller postures to access the inside of the body first, then letting those releases spread to the outside. This is the principle of "small on the outside, large on the inside": small external movements allow for larger internal movements, while large external movements usually allow only small internal movements.

While in the Yang style the progression is from external to internal, the Wu style starts with the internal. It works mainly with the deep side channels of the body, as it is more concerned with moving and transforming energy within the body than outside it. In the Wu style, described as "small frame", the hand positions relate to activating the deep channels of the body, rather than the external field. The elbows point down, creating a greater release in the deep side channels and greater internal pressures.

The Wu style places major emphasis on transforming energy rather than only moving it. This can make it superior for healing damage to the body's tissues and systems, which

need to be transformed and repaired and not just strengthened. Certain postures in the Wu style are designed to open and release the central energy channel – a Taoist meditation technique that is not found in other styles of t'ai chi. In its movements, Wu style t'ai chi generally uses more spheres, while the Yang style uses mainly circles. In Wu style the wrist pulse is often touched to lead into awareness of the internal organs. A very visible difference is the leaning forward on the bending moves in Wu style. This was introduced to allow a more natural action while maintaining an internally straight spine along the angle of lean. Some moves in Wu style use 45° angles in the hands rather than the flat planes found in the Yang style. Energetically, the Wu style seeks to develop soft, yin energy first and then to find hard, yang energy from the emptiness of the soft; this allows for a greater release of tension and healing from the start, but the Wu style is also somewhat harder to master than the opposite approach.

CHOOSING A STYLE

It would be true to say that the Wu style places emphasis on healing and meditation, while Yang style emphasizes the development of energetic power, but it is important to remember that the Wu style is an evolution of the Yang style, and not a radically different art. The postures and form sequence are largely the same, although their execution can differ. The true destination of t'ai chi is the same whatever the style, and the route you take depends on your nature and interests. Those who are yin by nature may find a yang approach works for them, and may be drawn to the Yang style. If you are more yang, or have an interest in meditation, you may be drawn to the yin approach of the Wu style.

Hsing-i and Ba Gua

Although all three Taoist internal martial arts share the underpinnings of Taoist nei gung methods, they appear quite different to the observer, and can feel quite different to the practitioner. This is because they utilize nei gung components in differing ways, each with a distinct approach and emphasis. Each has its own philosophical and spiritual approach, all with the same goal but taking different paths to reach it.

HSING-I CHUAN – MIND-FORM FIST

T'ai chi is based on yin/yang theory, and has an overall yin nature. Hsing-i is the opposite: both its energetic quality and its mental approach are very yang in nature. While t'ai chi has a yielding mental attitude, never meeting force with force but instead flowing around it and influencing it with the minimum of effort, hsing-i is aggressive, preferring to meet an opponent head-on and overwhelm them by greater force, applied correctly. Hsing-i is about imposing your will on your opponent. The "i" in hsing-i means "intent": you decide what you want to do, and do it; if your opponent is in the way, you simply crash through them. Hsing-i attacks continuously – even when you are retreating you continue to strike at your opponent. Yang energy is present constantly, never yielding.

Hsing-i tends to move in straight lines, even when changing direction: it zig-zags. This is visibly different from the circular movements of t'ai chi and ba gua. Hsing-i looks like an internal form of karate – linear and aggressive – but it differs in that it uses no muscular tension or anger (emotional tension). Its power comes from its nei gung, just like t'ai chi and ba gua. Unlike t'ai chi, however, it is almost always performed at high speed, with all movement originating in the fist or hand, as opposed to the tantien as in t'ai chi.

According to legend, hsing-i was created by Yue Fei, reputedly the greatest general in Chinese history. This hints at its aggressive, no-nonsense militaristic quality as a fighting art. In a sense, it is simpler than t'ai chi or ba gua, as it uses a minimum of techniques. Being based on Five Element theory, it possesses five main techniques: pi chuan or "splitting fist", which is Metal; tsuan chuan or "drilling fist", which is Water; beng chuan or "crushing fist", which is Wood; pao chuan or "pounding fist", which is Fire; and heng chuan or "crossing fist", which is Earth. Each develops the energy of its element within the practitioner and will benefit the corresponding organs: "splitting fist", for example, benefits the lungs, which are Metal in nature. In hsing-i fighting, these elemental techniques are used to defeat the opponent's techniques according to the ko (controlling) cycle

Above The pi chuan "splitting fist" technique of hsing-i is shown on the left, and the circle walking posture of ba gua on the right.

of the Five Elements; for instance, "splitting fist" (Metal) tends to overcome "pounding fist", which is Wood. The five main techniques can be linked and developed in what are known as animal forms.

Hsing-i is extremely effective as a martial art, placing its main emphasis on the development of internal power to deliver devastating strikes to an opponent. This power is mainly developed through the use of a standing posture called san ti. This is the "splitting fist" technique frozen in time, and is therefore Metal in quality. Over time, san ti develops the internal energy of the practitioner and also the mental focus, developing an iron will ("i"). This can then direct the body to produce a form ("hsing") that is infused with internal energy. Hsing-i does not appeal to the average person – it is overtly martial and its training methods are fairly arduous – but in the dedicated practitioner it can create a very strong mind and body. It is said of hsing-i that "It's not pretty, but it works."

BA GUA ZHANG – EIGHT TRIGRAM PALM

With a distinctly different quality and methodology to hsing-i and t'ai chi, the art of ba gua zhang surfaced in Beijing in 1852 with a master called Tung Hai Chuan. Tung never fully explained where he had learned ba gua zhang, but claimed

Above Hsing-i: on the left is tsuan chuan "drilling fist" – the Water element. Right is beng chuan "crushing fist" – the Wood element.

Above Hsing-i: on the left is pao chuan "pounding fist" – the Fire element. Right is heng chuan "crossing fist" – the Earth element.

that he learned it from an old Taoist sage in the mountains. It is certainly based on the ancient Taoist spiritual practice of circle walking meditation, but whether it was already developed as the complex internal martial art that Tung possessed will never be known. Tung Hai Chuan amazed the martial arts world of the time by beating all challengers with this strange and unique art. He became justly famous and passed the art on to a relatively small number of students, many of whose lineages survive to this day.

While t'ai chi has a yin quality, and hsing-i a yang quality, ba gua is concerned purely with change – it is not characteristically yin or yang, but flows between these poles with infinite permutations. Like hsing-i it is performed at speed, often lightning-fast. But unlike hsing-i it is extremely beautiful to watch, having a constantly flowing and coiling quality that does not resemble any other martial art – in fact it is quite unlike any other movement art.

This constancy of flow and change is perhaps the essential characteristic of ba gua – being the embodiment of change, it never hesitates and never stops. All the techniques, such as strikes and throws, are delivered on the move. While a t'ai chi practitioner takes a position, or "root", and executes a technique before changing position, a ba gua practitioner executes a technique as they are changing position. It is almost impossible to pin a good practitioner down – they are moving on at the very same moment that they are delivering a strike, throw or kick. This is made possible by the internal methodology of ba gua: there is a constant sense of coiling and uncoiling the body both internally and externally, and the practitioner is always "walking" – all movement originates in the feet. This allows for sudden changes of direction, allowing the practitioner to deal with multiple opponents simultaneously, flowing from one attacker to the next seamlessly and spontaneously.

The actual practice of ba gua zhang consists of "walking the circle". This opens the energy channels of the body and activates the upward and downward spiralling energy currents that pass through it. Then "single palm change" is practised, represented by chien, the trigram for heaven,

which is yang in nature. After this, practitioners develop the Double Palm Change, which is Earth and yin in nature. There are eight main or "mother" palm changes in ba gua, each symbolizing and embodying the energy of a trigram, with energetic qualities such as wind, thunder and fire. They are fast, complex changes of direction and energy that inherently contain martial techniques. Later these eight changes are developed into the 64 hexagrams of the I Ching, embodying all energetic change in the universe.

Higher levels of ba gua practice are linked to the principles of Taoist alchemy: transformation of the practitioner's internal energies, utilizing the energies of their surroundings and the cosmos. Crucial to this level of practice is the principle of spontaneity, merging with the Tao and allowing the flux of universal energies to determine the form that ba gua takes. Very few individuals reach this stage of accomplishment, but even at lower levels of skill, ba gua practice allows an understanding and acceptance of change to develop within, bringing about freedom from the rigid concepts that can limit creativity and human potential.

Below A detail from the second (double) palm change of ba gua, representing the trigram for Earth.

T'ai chi for mind and body

The reasons for learning t'ai chi apply to everyone. As human beings we all face challenges to our physical, mental and emotional health. It is simply a question of what form these problems take and when in our lives they appear. Learning t'ai chi is about taking responsibility for your own well-being and taking action to improve it to secure a healthy and balanced future. This chapter looks first at what makes t'ai chi unique as a mind–body practice, then compares its main benefits with those of other exercise regimes. This is followed by an examination of the role of the body and mind connection in relation to t'ai chi practice, and a look at how this relates to meditation practice. The chapter ends with sections on the use of t'ai chi for healing back and neck problems, energizing, reducing stress and stilling the mind, and balancing the emotions.

A Unique Approach to Self-development

There are many possible approaches to self-development: some ancient, some modern, stemming from many different cultures and traditions. Many share common tenets, others take radically different views of what self-development means and how we should go about it. They can be broadly divided into those that work primarily with the body, primarily with energy and primarily with the mind.

Most self-development practices take one of these three approaches, usually with the view that the level on which they are focusing is the "correct" one with which to work. This is not in itself wrong, as each aspect is indeed fundamental to human existence. Therefore any practice that genuinely accesses one of these levels and leads to development and evolution is important and valid – no matter where or when it originated. However, from a Taoist viewpoint, working with only one or two aspects of a human being is not a complete practice of self-development.

THE THREE TREASURES

The Taoists consider the three treasures of jing, chi and shen to be inseparable. Jing relates to the physical body, chi to the energy of that body, and shen to the mind. Just as all three are treated together in Chinese medicine, so in Taoist self-development practice you work with all three at the

Below Working with body, energy and mind simultaneously is an inherent part of t'ai chi practice.

same time. To omit one or more from your practice means that you are working not with your complete being, only with certain aspects of yourself. This is important both to achieve health and also in relation to your spiritual development. You cannot achieve true physical health if your energy is not balanced, and your energy cannot be truly balanced unless your mind is also balanced. Most people are all too aware of how mental stress leads to physical illness – this is a perfect example of the interrelationship between mind and body. Therefore, even if your goal is purely to achieve robust and lasting physical health, you need to include the levels of energy and mind in your practice. Conversely, even if your goal is purely that of spiritual development, you need the support of a balanced body and energy to stabilize the mind: you need only observe someone who is ill or in chronic pain to see the effects of physical ill health on the mind.

Where certain systems of self-development fall short is in a partial approach: believing that one can effectively ignore any of these aspects of oneself and yet still achieve balanced progress. Put simply, this is not possible. The Taoists have always understood this, as have many other ancient traditions. Practices that seek to develop only the "spiritual" aspects of a person, without also developing physical and energetic aspects, rarely succeed, because the foundations of a relaxed and healthy body and energy are not present. Practices that seek to find the spiritual solely through physical and energetic work, thus neglecting the mind, also tend to fail. The answer lies in working with all three aspects simultaneously, and this is what t'ai chi does.

THE T'AI CHI APPROACH

The practice of t'ai chi involves working simultaneously with your physical body, your chi, and your mind. While there are many training methods connected to it that involve working on specific aspects, the actual practice of t'ai chi should always involve all three at the same time. This is not only to develop all three levels – arguably that could be achieved by working with them separately. When you work with body,

Above A typical scene in China, where huge groups practise t'ai chi amidst the noise and movement of city life, an illustration of how the art offers a means of achieving stillness within chaos.

energy and mind simultaneously, something unique occurs: the integration of all three. A synergy takes place that dramatically increases the development of each of the levels. This is because in essence they are not separate; most people have just lost the natural integration within themselves and with the universe as a whole. By integrating your own existence, you begin integrating with all existence: this is spiritual development. However, even if you are not interested in spiritual development, but simply in obtaining better health and freedom from stress – and this is a perfectly valid motivation for wanting to learn t'ai chi – this integral method is invaluable in order to reap the greatest benefits from your time and effort.

T'ai chi involves movement and integration with the external world – the world outside of yourself, including other people – and therefore it can achieve something that purely inward-focused practices, such as many forms of sitting meditation, rarely do: the integration of your external (wei) and internal (nei) aspects. The practical effect of this is the ability to remain calm and centred even in the midst of stressful external circumstances, such as life in a big city or the work environment. In t'ai chi you learn to be inwardly and outwardly aware at the same time, and to retain stillness of mind within movement, both your own and that of the outside world. This is developed through solo

practice of the t'ai chi form, and through two-person push hands practice. T'ai chi is inherently a martial art, and so it also offers you an opportunity to identify and explore personal issues relating to the ego and your personal fears, in the context of a meditative practice. This can allow the release of tensions, including deep anger, that might otherwise be very elusive.

EVERYDAY LIFE

T'ai chi is relevant and timely in this increasingly hectic world. It provides a method of achieving inner and outer balance in the face of great pressures. It does not require you to abandon all worldly concerns and retreat to a mountain cave – in fact, that would not be considered a balanced approach to self-development as it would be excessively yin. Retreat may be an important part of your practice, whether for an hour or a month, but the art of t'ai chi evolved in the midst of life's swirling chaos, and as a practice it is quite comfortable there. It offers a means of achieving stillness within chaos, through patient daily practice. It is said, "One day's practice yields one day's results, one year's practice yields one year's results," meaning that by dedicating some time each day to t'ai chi practice, the benefits naturally grow. This has been compared to stacking one sheet of paper on top of another – each sheet seems to add almost nothing, but over time a tall pile of paper will be built up. Even half an hour of practice a day will yield excellent results over time. This is something that everybody can achieve, no matter how hectic their lifestyle, if they have a will to do it.

The Health Benefits of T'ai Chi

What distinguishes t'ai chi from other movement arts or forms of exercise is its use of the nei gung methods to release tensions within the body and to move and develop chi energy. This provides a host of benefits, many of which are not obtainable through ordinary exercise. T'ai chi is not simply a physical movement art: its movements and postures are the container within which you develop your chi.

Specific body alignments and movement patterns allow for the optimum flow of chi, and for releases to occur within the body, while avoiding chi "leaking" away. Because the physical movements are visible, they are the part that people recognize as "t'ai chi", but as your practice develops they will become only a part of a much greater experience. It is the internal work that distinguishes t'ai chi from other exercise systems and is responsible for its benefits.

T'AI CHI AND EXERCISE

Some exercise regimes adopt a "no pain, no gain" attitude that treats the body almost as an enemy to be vanquished, rather than as an integral part of yourself, and this can result in damage and accelerated ageing. In t'ai chi practice you always stay within your body's limits, not causing excessive wear, exhaustion or damage. The benefits of this approach can be seen in many practitioners in their 70s and 80s, who have physical flexibility, mental alertness and energy levels greater than most people half their age.

Below In t'ai chi one never locks any joints or induces any muscular tension, as this blocks the flow of chi in the body.

HEALTH

Fitness and health are not necessarily the same thing. You can become extremely fit, in terms of being able to run a marathon, and yet suffer ill health simultaneously, possibly as a result of the fitness training itself. Health is a state of balance, and you do not need extreme physical abilities in order to call yourself healthy.

The health benefits of t'ai chi can be divided into those relating to physical health, including energy levels, and those that relate to the mind and emotions. T'ai chi is known for restoring glowing health to the debilitated in a way that is hardly surpassed by any other system. Perhaps the most obvious feature of t'ai chi practice is that it involves constant gentle movement without strain. This allows for lubrication of the joints and regains space within them. A "drying up" and contraction of the joints occurs as you age, and t'ai chi can help to retain flexibility and general mobility

The pulsing (opening and closing) actions that take place within the joints and internal spaces of the body during t'ai chi practice cause body fluids, including cerebro-spinal fluid, to be smoothly distributed and circulated, nourishing all parts of the body, and allowing for the proper transportation of metabolic waste products, which can otherwise build up and cause disease. The constant bending and unbending of the limbs pumps the lymphatic system, helping to eliminate stagnation and boost and strengthen the immune system.

The rhythmic movements of the limbs towards and away from the body cause blood flow to increase to and from the heart, strengthening the major arteries and veins. Most heart conditions relate to hardening and blockage in these vessels, and not to the heart muscle itself (unless it is already damaged). Thus t'ai chi can play a major role in helping to avoid heart conditions. The Taoists consider that simply causing the heart to beat faster does not yield any great long-term benefits (and may even cause overuse and eventually exhaustion of the heart muscle) but that freeing up and strengthening the arteries and veins of the heart is most important. The use of internal spiralling actions throughout the body also assists in blood circulation, as it causes a gentle, rhythmic squeezing and release of all the

Right A yoga posture showing the use of maximum stretching and the locking open of the joints of the arms and legs. Many yoga postures are difficult for most people to achieve.

tissues. This can enormously benefit those with impaired circulation, a common condition in the elderly and those with sedentary lifestyles. Increased blood flow naturally benefits the brain, fostering mental acuity and alertness.

The Taoists say that "the chi is the commander of the blood" and this is one reason why energetic work surpasses purely physical work: when chi flows smoothly the blood does too, fully nourishing the entire body. The rhythmic compression and release of the internal organs, combined with internal twistings that can reduce adhesions of the organs to the ribs and spine, cause proper blood and fluid flow to be restored, and can greatly enhance organ function. The release of tension within the nervous system allows the muscles to relax; combined with the use of specific physical alignments, this can allow the correction of spinal and joint misalignments, healing many back, neck and joint problems. The gentle stretching and release of ligaments and tendons greatly assist in this. For the elderly and those with bad balance, t'ai chi develops a much greater physical stability, helping to avoid falls. It can give all practitioners a sense of having their feet firmly on the ground, and this has a correspondingly stabilizing mental and emotional effect.

All these actions, combined with the direct mental manipulation of chi, cause the energy of the body to become free and strong. In terms of physical health, this particularly benefits the internal organs and the glandular system. Medical studies have proved that regular t'ai chi practice boosts immune system function and endocrine levels relating to every system of the body. T'ai chi has also been shown to be effective in lowering high blood pressure, mainly due to its effect on the deep veins and arteries.

The effect of t'ai chi practice on the nervous system is harder to measure, but it is renowned for making practitioners feel "alive" and physically relaxed. It can also help to restore lost or diminished nerve function, for example following surgery or accidental damage.

T'AI CHI AND YOGA

Yoga, a physical and energetic self-development practice originating in ancient India, is also a type of internal art, and is very effective if properly taught and applied. Where t'ai chi and yoga differ is in their approaches and methods: whereas t'ai chi seeks to find stillness in movement, enabling the continuous flow and transformation of energy within the practitioner, yoga uses fixed postures to "dam up" and release energy in certain energetic centres. Whereas t'ai chi focuses on releasing the nervous system and the inside of the body, yoga focuses on stretching and releasing its outer structure. The result is that yoga practitioners often have

greater physical flexibility than t'ai chi practitioners, but the latter often have more relaxed bodies and nervous systems. They also have superior balance and movement abilities, and of course martial abilities, which are absent from yoga.

Yoga is an excellent practice for those with healthy spines and joints, but it should be approached with caution if problems exist in these areas, as it has a more "fiery" approach than t'ai chi and may not always fully take into account existing structural problems. The t'ai chi approach – of relaxing and releasing the body and always working within current limitations – is arguably superior if you wish to heal back, neck and joint problems.

SELF-HEALING

To list the many and various health benefits that regular t'ai chi practice can bring would take up many pages; to some extent every medical condition can be improved by it. This is because when the energy, blood, fluid and organ functions of the body are improved, it can begin the process of healing itself. T'ai chi is not a miracle cure, but in many areas t'ai chi practice can indeed work wonders. It is really a life-long health insurance policy.

The Mind–Body Connection

The Taoists consider that body and mind are not only related but inseparable. Of the eight energetic bodies that make up a human being, the physical body is the most gross, and the emotional, mental and psychic bodies are progressively more subtle and expansive, but all are interpenetrating and interrelated. Therefore anything that occurs within one level will have an impact on other levels as well.

In general, the more subtle bodies have a greater and more immediate effect on the less subtle, and vice versa: while your mental state has a great and immediate effect on your physical state, your physical state will not necessarily affect your mental state quite so immediately. The Taoists were not alone in observing this mind–body interrelationship; many traditions, both Eastern and Western, use different terms to describe it. The key principle is that mind and body are inseparable.

So-called "Western" thinking about mind and body is actually relatively modern, and can be seen as stemming from the work of the philosopher René Descartes in the 17th century. The key phrase in Cartesian dualism is: "I think, therefore I am." In other words, the thinking mind is set apart from all other aspects of being, including the physical body. The implications of this philosophy extend to our attitudes to the world around us – we see the world as separate from ourselves and no longer believe ourselves to be an integral part of nature. A pre-Cartesian attitude could

be expressed as "I feel, therefore I am," encompassing our whole experience of existence, not just the mental aspect. Prior to Descartes, Western philosophy was not so very different to Eastern traditions in this respect.

SCIENCE AND CHI

Many people now live in industrialized societies, the very foundations of which are based on Cartesian thinking. This permeates all aspects of our lives, especially science and medicine. Scientists and "Western" doctors are taught that all phenomena that exist can be measured and quantified, and if something cannot be measured it does not exist. This is highly relevant to the study of t'ai chi and the internal arts, because they are based on the existence of chi energy. Chi cannot be directly measured with scientific instruments, and will probably never be scientifically "validated". The reason for this is that chi relates to consciousness itself – it is a living force that can be felt and manipulated by the mind, but has no objective existence. This makes it no less real than a radio wave, but it exists in relation to our living bodies and our minds, rather than in the external world.

If we accept that Cartesian dualism is false, the fact that we can feel chi but not measure it does not invalidate its existence, any more than we would claim that our thoughts or emotions do not exist. Ultimately, from both a Taoist and Buddhist perspective, everything manifests from emptiness, and therefore nothing possesses concrete existence anyway. The branch of Western science called quantum physics entirely agrees with this, and goes so far as to state that phenomena exist only in relation to conscious observation.

BODY AND MIND IN T'AI CHI

The Taoists developed methods of working with the mind and body together; t'ai chi is one of those methods. In terms of the eight energy bodies, all energy could be considered to be some form of chi, but for the purposes of

Left The practice of t'ai chi and chi gung is about learning to feel rather than think. With time, you will gain direct and definite experience of your chi energy.

Above Learning to relax and develop open awareness while doing push hands practice with a partner.

Above Moving into a meditation point within the Wu style Form – integrating meditation with movement.

understanding t'ai chi the word "chi" is used here to refer specifically to the second of the energy bodies – the energy that circulates through the physical body and immediately surrounds it (the "aura"). The word "mind" means the intent or "i" (pronounced "yee"). This is the basic intent of your consciousness, which is involved in any action you perform. Often the simpler the action, the clearer intent is: picking up a teacup involves the intention to do that, but does not normally involve any logical thought process – you simply do it, rather than thinking about how or why you are doing it – whereas more complex actions may start to involve your thinking mind. Using the mind to move chi refers to pure intent and not to an analytical process of thinking about moving chi. It is intent – "i" – that connects with chi; the thinking mind actually hinders the process. This is a crucial point for t'ai chi practitioners to understand and develop. An oft-quoted phrase, "No 'i', no chi," means that if the intent is not present and clear the chi energy will not move as desired. Developing this clear intent, free of discursive thought processes, is a gradual process, but one that yields extraordinary results, both in chi development and in the development of a highly relaxed, yet highly focused, mind.

T'ai chi works with the body, chi and mind at the same time, each component augmenting the development of the others in a synergistic way. The alignments and actions of the body assist the flow of chi. The flow of chi helps the body to relax and energize, and the mind to become still. A still and focused mind can move chi at will, allowing the body to remain relaxed. T'ai chi practice should always involve body, chi and mind – take one component out and the circle is broken. While you may wish to emphasize or concentrate on one or two aspects in your training, you should always remember that this is just preparation for the performance of t'ai chi with your body, chi and mind working in harmony.

Your current experience will most likely not be that of the total integration of your body, chi and mind. If you perceive these aspects of your being to be separate, you will find it easier to refer to them that way for the purposes of working with them – and then as you become more experienced, seek to connect them and start to reintegrate them. Eventually, you may reach a stage of t'ai chi practice where they feel as if they are one – this is the point at which t'ai chi can become a truly mystical experience. This experience is not reserved for Taoist sages: it is potentially available to every ordinary man and woman.

THE MIND AND EMOTIONS

T'ai chi is superb as a relaxation practice. The emphasis on dropping and settling chi causes the mind to relax, and leads to increasing mental stillness. This in turn allows the nervous system to relax and release, which generates physical relaxation. The slow, rhythmic movements provide an antidote to frenetic daily activity and act as a metronome for your internal rhythms, allowing you to slow down and relax mentally. In addition, the physical movements and internal work allow for the release of bound emotional tensions, bringing about a sense of inner peace and emotional "smoothness". T'ai chi can develop a relaxed mental focus while fully exercising both sides of the brain with the coordination of simultaneous movement on the left and right sides of the body.

The Use of Meditation in T'ai Chi

T'ai chi is often described as a form of "moving meditation". Its mind–body synergy makes it a practice that is inherently meditative in nature. However, if we look more deeply at Taoist self-development practice we will see that t'ai chi is not in itself a meditation practice, but that it can be used in conjunction with meditation techniques. These techniques can then be incorporated into t'ai chi to make it a true moving meditation.

The common view of meditation is that it mainly consists of a practice that leads to relaxation, especially of the mind. It is usually assumed to be something that involves sitting motionless with the eyes closed. Both statements are true, but they do not give a complete picture of what meditation is. In the Taoist tradition, you are really practising meditation only when you are working with the energies of your consciousness, to transform blockage and tension in your emotional, mental, psychic and higher bodies. Simply becoming calmer is not meditation. However, this stillness is a prerequisite for being able to travel deeper within yourself and resolve tensions at these more subtle levels. T'ai chi practice can develop a degree of inner stillness as the foundation for deeper meditation practices. Some of these practices can be applied while doing t'ai chi: this then becomes t'ai chi meditation.

The Taoists recognize five modes of practice, relating to the basic activities of life: sitting, moving, standing, lying down and having sex. None of these modes is inherently superior to the others, but certain practices are easier to apply in certain modes. Sitting, for instance, facilitates

inwardly focused meditation practice; while standing facilitates practice relating to your physical and chi body. Once a practice has been well applied in the easiest mode for it, it is applied in all other modes. Inwardly focused practice is best learned sitting but is later applied during all the other activities, including t'ai chi form practice. The deeper Taoist meditation practices must be learned directly from a teacher, but some simple and effective practices are detailed in this book.

NORMAL T'AI CHI PRACTICE

T'ai chi has many different aspects; every practitioner will find their own personal areas of interest, and focus on them. It is possible to develop your body and chi, and achieve a degree of stillness, without venturing into the realms of meditation – there have been many t'ai chi masters who were not particularly interested in meditation or spiritual practice. This is a personal choice. True meditation practice can be a bumpy ride: to resolve deep-seated emotional, mental and psychic tensions you have to confront them nakedly. The phrase "face your demons" is apt. Not

Far left Meditation practice sitting in the lotus position. This is a useful and very stable position, but difficult for many people.

Left Sitting on a chair can be equally effective for meditation, and is more comfortable and familiar to most Westerners.

Below Meditating lying down allows for greater relaxation of the body, although there is a tendency to become drowsy.

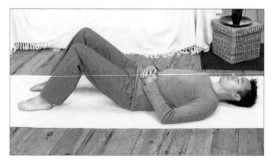

Right The Wu style posture "single whip". This posture and the posture "fan through the back" help to open the central energetic channel. These meditation points in the form enable the practitioner to release any tensions in his or her mind and energy into empty space, before continuing with the form.

everybody wants to do this, or feels ready to undertake this kind of work. For many, to become a little more relaxed and a lot healthier is enough.

Even without engaging in deeper meditation practices, the mind and chi work inherent in normal t'ai chi practice can have a profound effect on your mental and emotional world. It has a powerful effect in three specific areas: the nervous system (including the brain); the glands (endocrine system); and the main internal organs. Your nervous system is freed of tension and strengthened by practice. This reduces internal "noise" (a key symptom of prolonged and unresolved stress), bringing about a quietening of the mind and a sense of mental peace. Your glands are allowed to function smoothly, as they are boosted where deficient and calmed where overactive. The effects of this are very great, as the hormones secreted by the glands have a vastly powerful effect on the mind and emotions. For instance, overactive and "edgy" adrenal glands will mean that you are always "revved-up" mentally and emotionally. The main organs of the body relate to the basic "lower" emotions such as anger and grief, and imbalances here will cause corresponding emotional imbalances that will affect the corresponding organ. T'ai chi practice can break the cycle and restore balance.

THE DEEPER PRACTICES
One of the ways in which t'ai chi works to achieve internal transformations is through repetitive and rhythmic external motions. This is known in many traditions: Zen Buddhist monks, for example, are often given the task of polishing rice or washing dishes all day for many months. As they do this, their minds turn inwards and start to process their internal tensions, eventually releasing them and achieving stillness. The rhythmic motions of t'ai chi can have the same effect when linked to meditation practice.

In the context of the repetitive external activity in t'ai chi, meditation techniques can be applied, "dissolving" tensions inwardly, back into the emptiness that underlies all existence. This inner dissolving is distinct from the practice of outer dissolving, where the practitioner releases blockages in chi (relating to places in the physical body) outwardly until they become neutralized. Inner dissolving practice is applied to all the systems of the physical body, including the organs, glands, spinal cord and brain. Emotional, mental and psychic tensions can be stored in the physical body, and these can be accessed and released with the aid of the various

Right Push hands practice can provide a "reality check" for your levels of emotional smoothness and stillness.

postures and movements of t'ai chi. Eventually the inner dissolving practices allow for the practitioner to enter the central point (called t'ai chi) where there is no distinction between yin and yang, everything is inherently empty, and their true nature is revealed. A phrase used to denote this in relation to t'ai chi chuan practice is "stillness in movement, movement in stillness": stillness (yin) and movement (yang) become inseparable and indistinguishable from one another. This phrase has significant implications for meditation and spiritual practice.

PUSH HANDS AND MEDITATION
T'ai chi push hands practice is a very useful method for moving towards this state, as the two-person work provides a yardstick against which to measure and develop your ability to be truly relaxed and truly present while engaged in external movement and internal energetic work. If you become angry, fearful or upset when pushed by your partner, you may not be as emotionally relaxed as you think.

Healing Back and Neck Problems

Many people take up t'ai chi because they are suffering from stress and are looking for a relaxation practice, or are seeking long-term relief from back, neck and joint pain. These two problems often go hand-in-hand: stress generally leads to physical stiffness and pain, and prolonged spinal and joint pain almost always causes stress. As we age, our bodies contract. T'ai chi can help alleviate this tendency and enable mobility well into old age.

Occupations such as desk-bound office work may cause both stress and musculoskeletal problems. They are by far the most common health complaints in the developed world, and entire industries have grown up around them. From pharmaceuticals to relaxation tapes, from magnetic mattresses to on-site massage, there are hundreds of different "solutions" on offer. While some are more effective than others, most tend to focus on either back pain or stress, but not fully on both. T'ai chi is truly unsurpassed in helping to solve both of these problems simultaneously.

Spinal and joint problems can be roughly divided into two types: tension and misalignment. Like everything else relating to t'ai chi, neither really exists in isolation. Tension can be defined as tightness in the muscles, fascia and "sinews" (ligaments and tendons). A simple tension might be a knot (twisted muscle fibres) in the back muscles, which can be relieved, at least temporarily, by massage. Misalignment can be defined as imbalances in the skeletal structure, and misplacement of the ligaments and tendons.

A misalignment might take the form of one or more spinal vertebrae that are subluxated (twisted out of their proper place), or a tendon that does not run smoothly through the proper groove over a joint. Misalignments are typically treated by manipulation, such as that performed by chiropractors and osteopaths. These "adjustments" physically move the vertebrae back into their proper alignments. However, the vertebrae rarely stay there, but often return to misalignment. The reason for this also explains why t'ai chi is so effective at providing lasting correction of spinal and joint misalignments.

THE SOLUTION

Some approaches to back, neck and joint problems focus mainly on strengthening the relevant muscles. Strengthening healthy, unknotted muscles around well-aligned skeletal structures is fine, and can help to support the body. However, strengthening tense and knotted muscles surrounding misaligned vertebrae and joints is not fine: it will

Below The spinal alignments of t'ai chi encourage good posture, helping to reduce the likelihood of future back and neck problems.

Below A key part of t'ai chi alignments is learning to regain space in the neck vertebrae and open the occiput at the base of the skull.

Right As an arm rises in t'ai chi, the shoulder blade drops down the back like a counterweight, avoiding tension in the shoulders and helping to release shoulder, neck and upper back problems.

simply strengthen the problem itself, locking it more firmly into the body. Instead, you need release. You need to release the tensions that are causing muscles to be tight and pulling skeletal structures out of alignment.

Most people with spinal and joint misalignments do not have abnormal bone structure: the building blocks are not misshapen, just badly stacked. The skeleton cannot hold itself up alone. It is held up, and aligned, by the muscles attached to the bones. When they do not pull evenly or correctly on the skeleton, they will pull parts of it out of alignment. As a result, nerves will become pinched and there will be pain. Muscles do not have minds of their own; they act only in relation to the nerve signals they are given. If a muscle is "misbehaving" and pulling the spine out of alignment, it is because there is an incorrect nerve signal to that muscle. The nerves pattern the muscles – and chi patterns the nerves. When the flow of chi is not smooth and correctly patterned, the nerve signal will also not be smooth and correctly patterned, and the muscles will contract abnormally. This is why adjustment of the bones tends not to result in permanent relief: the muscles simply pull the bones out of alignment again. In order to restore the whole system to balance, the chi patterns of the body need to be made smooth again. Normal muscle function will result, and the muscles will hold the skeleton in its natural and correct alignment. This principle also applies to pain resulting from muscular tension, which restricts blood flow and pinches local nerves.

THE METHOD

T'ai chi practice heals these problems by relaxing the nervous system, smoothing and balancing the flow of chi, and gently stretching and releasing the internal and external muscles. The specific skeletal alignments of t'ai chi then allow the bones and joints to fall into their proper locations.

Tense muscles tend to lack sufficient blood flow, and this is a major cause of pain. The inward and outward movements of t'ai chi gently stretch and compress the muscles, "wringing" blood through them. The ligaments and tendons are gently stretched and released, and this restores lost flexibility and length, as well as healthy chi flow through the tissues. Tight, shortened ligaments and tendons are often a cause of problems around the joints. The spiralling actions of t'ai chi are a key factor in their release.

The fascia – a thin sheet of tissue that wraps around your entire body – is released through proper t'ai chi movement. When tight, it can act like a strait jacket, constricting the deeper muscles and joints. T'ai chi removes this strait jacket, allowing access to the deeper levels of the body. Once joint

pulsing has been learned, the opening and closing of all the joints from the inside dramatically increases the amount of synovial fluid, chi and space in the joints. T'ai chi is known for combating arthritis. Where there are spinal misalignments, pulsing gives vertebrae the space they need to return to proper alignment. In the case of a slipped disc, this will remove the pressure on the disc so that it is no longer forced out of the intervertebral space.

Where lower back (lumbar) problems exist, t'ai chi's emphasis on releasing and working with the kwa (the groin area at the front of the pelvis) will allow the pelvis as a whole to release and realign, releasing and stabilizing the sacrum, misalignment of which is often the source of lower back problems. Wu style t'ai chi places a strong emphasis on the kwa, and is known for healing lower back complaints in particular. In the case of upper back and neck problems, the release of the shoulder blades, called the "hidden joints of the body" by the Taoists, allows for the release of the entire area. Another common cause of musculoskeletal problems is the weakening of the insertion points where the muscles attach to the bones. These can tear away, resulting – in extreme cases – in complete loss of use of the muscle. Surgery is then the only recourse. T'ai chi stretches and strengthens these insertion points so that the problem is less likely to occur.

T'ai chi has much to offer in terms of health, longevity and well-being, but the most compelling reason for many people to start learning it is its superb record in healing back, neck and joint problems. Many Western doctors now recommend it to their patients for exactly this reason.

Energizing

At times, many people lack the energy they need to cope with the demands of everyday life. This feeling of low energy can result in a lack of enthusiasm for life, a feeling that it is all "too much". At the extreme, it can lead to despondency and even depression. This is a very common problem, especially for people who lead stressful lives. Often that stress causes insomnia, which prevents sufferers from replenishing their energy during the night.

Chronic tiredness is very common in people who have sedentary occupations, such as office workers. They are not expending large amounts of physical energy every day, yet are far more tired and de-energized than those who do expend energy in physical work. In terms of an "energy in/energy out" equation this seems to make no sense: if you are using less energy surely you should have more available. However, there is a factor at work that is the single biggest cause of most fatigue syndromes: blockage.

BLOCKAGE

The energetic system and its channels are like a network of water pipes connected to a reservoir. If the pipes are open and clear, water can flow through and out of them as fast as fresh water flows into them from the reservoir. You are constantly refilling your reservoir of energy from the air you breathe, the food you eat, and also from external sources such as sunlight and moonlight. If the pipes are partly blocked, however, then no matter how much water is in the reservoir, you will only get a trickle out of the pipes.

Clear the blockage, and the normal flow is restored, to be put to whatever use you choose. The desk-bound office worker may feel more exhausted than the bricklayer because his or her energy has stagnated. As with slowly moving water, which allows silt to accumulate, the channels have become blocked. Blockage can also occur for other reasons, such as physical damage to the body, or mental and emotional tension, but whatever the cause, the methods used to restore normal energetic flows are more or less the same. Also, you would focus on healing the root cause of the blockage, including harmful habits.

T'ai chi practice opens the energy channels of the body, both by correcting the physical misalignments and tensions that cause blockage and by directly opening the channels and causing chi to flow through them, thus "washing away" blockage. Every posture in the t'ai chi form causes chi to move in patterns that benefit specific channels and centres in the body. The constantly flowing nature of the form itself encourages chi to move freely where it may be stagnant. The mental and emotional relaxation that practice brings

Left Releasing chi energy in a posture from the Wu style long form. The martial origins of t'ai chi are clearly visible in this movement.
Below The storing (left) and release (right) of energy in the Wu style t'ai chi posture of "ji" (push). Note the compression and release of the kwa area at the front of the pelvis.

Left Stress causes your chi to "knot", blocking its flow. This leads to lethargy and inactivity, which then result in further stagnation of your chi. T'ai chi is an excellent solution to this common problem.

"unfreezes" chi, which can become frozen due to stress. Any physical exercise will help reduce chi stagnation, but because t'ai chi operates on a deeper level, and more directly with the energetic system and the mind, it brings proportionally greater results in this area.

HOW IT WORKS

There is a specific process that has the greatest effect in removing blockage: the gathering and releasing of energy. T'ai chi is based mainly on yin/yang theory, and the ebb and flow of its movements perfectly reflect this. Performing a t'ai chi form (and push hands), you move from yin postures and movements to yang postures and movements in a continuous, alternating flow. On a physical level, simply moving the arms towards your body, then away, then towards your body again, forms a cycle from yin to yang and back to yin again. You also open and close your joints, compress and release internal spaces in the body, bow and release your spine, spiral your energy out and back, and allow your mind – your intent – to go outwards and then inwards. All these actions take the form of a yin/yang cycle, as in the t'ai chi symbol. When you near the completion of yin, you start becoming yang, and vice versa, never stopping.

The continuous pulsing action of your body, your energy and your mind mirrors the pulsation that everything in the universe, from atoms to galaxies, constantly undergoes. Pulsation is life: stop pulsing (your breathing, your heartbeat) and you will die. This is an example of the microcosmic/ macrocosmic nature of t'ai chi practice: with it you seek to integrate more fully with, and reactivate, this natural pulsation within yourself. As a result you begin to feel more alive.

BUILDING YOUR RESERVES

Having removed the blockages in your energetic system, and regained the energy that should naturally be available to you, you can set about increasing your core reserves of chi. There are several reasons why you would want to do this: by

increasing your reserves, you also increase the energy immediately available to you; with a bigger reservoir you can draw more at any moment; you can sustain an output of energy for longer without becoming "drained"; and you have emergency reserves for those times, such as illness or great stress, when you really need extra energy. In terms of jing, this means that your post-birth jing is strong enough that you need not tap into your pre-birth jing, even in extreme circumstances.

During t'ai chi practice, you would choose to release proportionally more chi than you gather in order to eliminate stagnation in your chi. Once this has been achieved, you would seek to gather proportionally more than you release in order to build your reserves. The balance between gathering and releasing may vary from day to day, or from month to month, as the activities you take part in, and the condition of your energy and mind, will vary. Being sensitive to your internal state is an important skill to develop. As a general rule, you should seek to gather and release energy in a ratio of about 80:20, in order to build your reserves.

Chi that is gathered is stored in the lower tantien. This then naturally replenishes jing, which is stored in the kidneys. There are many elderly t'ai chi practitioners who, in their seventies and even beyond, possess the energy, mental acuity, sexual function and physical mobility of people half their age. These elderly practitioners also enjoy the mental, emotional and spiritual peace that should naturally develop with age, but so often does not. This is a direct result of the t'ai chi principle of regaining the natural freedom of body, energy and mind that we possess as babies. Observe a baby moving and you will see all of the t'ai chi principles at work.

Below A relaxed and healthy flow of chi energy enables you to enjoy life more fully, and it opens up your innate creative abilities that have the potential to make life truly fulfilling.

Reducing Stress and Stilling the Mind

Stress has become an almost universal complaint in modern society, to the extent that many Western doctors consider stress-related illness the "number one killer". In terms of costs resulting from lost working days and loss of skilled employees due to "burn-out", stress is a major problem for all developed nations. Stress negatively affects all the body's systems, and has been proven to dramatically reduce immune system function.

The costs to the individual suffering from chronic stress – loss of employment, relationships, and physical and psychological health – are compelling reasons to take action to reduce this burden.

It is natural to experience stress, whether physical or psychological, simply as a consequence of living. Problems arise only when stress is not released following the event that caused it, but retained within the body and mind; when new stressful events take place, tension begins to accumulate. Stress usually becomes chronic for one of two reasons: either the person is not able to relax following a stressful event, or so many stressful events occur in succession that there is simply no time to "unwind", and each event increases the stress burden. Either way, the solution is to learn to relax, and to be able to do so quickly and easily.

HEAVEN AND EARTH

T'ai chi practice works on the symptoms of stress, such as "frozen" chi and tensions within the body and nervous system. The feedback effect this causes allows for greater relaxation and, in turn, further release of tension. It also involves energetic work that directly causes the mind to relax and become still, immediately dissolving stress. The principles behind this work are very simple.

Two primordial flows of energy pass through the body in opposite directions: from heaven to earth, and from earth to heaven. They flow from above the body downwards and out through the feet, and vice versa, through the feet, up the body and out through the crown of the head. It is said by the Taoists that the energy of heaven descends and causes the energy of earth to respond (and rise), bringing about physical existence. The downward flow, yin in nature, allows for the release of tension and blockage throughout the system. The nature of the downward flow is like water, which seeks the lowest point and flows down without effort. The upward, yang, flow allows you to become energized and to maintain a physical body. It also has a "spiritualizing" aspect. Its nature is like fire, which leaps upwards and constantly seeks to move. In terms of reducing stress and stilling the mind, it is the downward flow that is of paramount importance.

The Taoists have a saying, "The brain eats the body", which refers to the propensity of an overactive brain (the thinking mind) to monopolize the energy available. When this happens there is insufficient energy available for the rest of the body, and it suffers as a consequence. The brain is being "greedy" and damaging the body. Occupations that

Below Using Taoist breathing meditation to release tension and start approaching stillness of mind. This is a powerful method of dealing with accumulated stress.

principally involve mental work can result in the overactivity of the brain. Once it has drawn a lot of energy upwards into itself, that energy tends to become stuck there. The result can be likened to a car engine with a stuck throttle: it revs out of control. This is a major cause of insomnia and anxiety. If you can get the excess energy to drop back into the body, the brain will calm down again.

Of the two major flows of energy, the upward flow is very easy to activate. The downward flow tends not to occur so readily in most people. It is relatively easy to become agitated and stay that way, with accompanying feelings of energy rising to your head, but much harder to become calm and stay calm. The common phrases "being grounded" and "being down to earth" perfectly express the importance of the downward flow of energy in achieving a relaxed and calm mind. It is important to understand that it is not the rising of energy itself that causes anxiety, but that energy becoming stuck in the upper body and brain, because there is not an equal, balancing downward flow of chi. The downward flow not only opens but also strengthens the channels, ready to handle the power of the fire-like, yang upward flow. For this reason, it is best to be cautious about undertaking any practices that heavily emphasize the upward flow before you have stabilized the downward flow. If this is not done, energetic "burn-out" can result, sometimes with serious consequences for mind and body.

T'ai chi practice heavily emphasizes developing the downward flow (in the initial stages), and regaining the ability to activate it fully at will. Ideally, this flow should be constant and automatic, and with practice it can become so. The practice of ba gua zhang, which tends to create a strong upward spiralling of energy, is best undertaken after some training in t'ai chi, or at least standing practice, so that the downward flow is continuously activated. (This is one of the factors that makes ba gua more difficult to learn than t'ai chi.) T'ai chi practitioners talk of growing a "root". Just like the roots of a tree, this means getting your chi to sink and connect into the ground beneath your feet. When this happens, not only do you clear blockages in your energy channels, and still your mind, you also connect fully with the flow of energy upwards from the ground, which can then move freely and smoothly through your open channels. This is a major source of power in the internal martial arts, so activating the downward energy flow is the key to utilizing the upward flow fully as well. The core practice for activating and developing the downward flow is standing practice, called zhan zhuang, or "standing like a tree". It is important to start with standing postures that emphasize the downward energy flow.

Above The "yin releasing" posture from the Wu form can be used as a standing posture to help release tension. It emphasizes the dropping of chi down the yin channels of the front of the body.

DROPPING THE MIND

As well as activating the downward, yin energy flow, in t'ai chi and chi gung practice you develop the ability to drop your mind into your lower tantien. This means that your awareness moves fully into that part of your body, where that energy centre is located. Found approximately four fingers' breadth below the navel, and on the central channel deep within the body, the lower tantien is the main energetic centre of the physical body. When your awareness moves into this centre, two things happen: your mind becomes still, and it connects with the chi of your entire body, awakening it. All movement in t'ai chi originates in the lower tantien, and your mind should be present there throughout your practice. As a result, you will have progressively deeper experiences of stillness, during which tensions and stress will dissolve and release effortlessly. The experience of "monkey mind", where the mind jumps constantly from one thought to another, will subside, and you will develop truly relaxed focus, your mind still and yet fully aware.

Balancing the Emotions

There are times when we feel that we have become ruled by our emotions, losing perspective and clarity with regard to the situation in which we find ourselves. The emotions that can overtake us vary widely, but the effect is the same: we can find ourselves acting in ways that are not beneficial to ourselves or others. A classic example would be becoming overcome by anger and saying or doing something that we later come to regret.

Strong emotions can blind us to what is actually happening, causing us to overreact or act inappropriately. From a Taoist perspective, emotions themselves are not enemies or things to be eliminated; it is a question of balance. We are not robots, we are human beings, and human beings have emotions. Those beginning meditation often ask, "If I eliminate my emotions, what will remain of my personality?" This question reflects a common misunderstanding of the process of working with emotions in the context of meditation and t'ai chi practice. We are seeking not to become unfeeling, but to achieve a state where we are not slaves to our emotions – where we can fully experience them without becoming conditioned by them. As a result we can discover our true personality, rather than one based on our individual emotional imbalances. This true personality is not only far stronger than the "imbalance personality" but is likely to be far more attractive to other people, especially those who are similarly balanced emotionally.

A person who seems angry and aggressive may actually have a true personality of great kindness and compassion, concealed (even from themselves) by the obvious imbalances.

If our emotional energy is truly balanced we will always experience emotions that are appropriate to a situation. When the situation that brought about that emotional experience ends, the emotional experience will also end. Without this balance we might, for example, get angry about something inconsequential, feeling overcome by rage, and then continue to feel angry after the situation has ended. This principle applies to any of the emotions: excessive sadness, for instance, can develop into depression.

THE EMOTIONS AND THE ORGANS

Chinese medical theory is very much concerned with the emotions, and it is considered that the energies of each of the main organs generate the emotions. This is related to Five Element theory, in which each element, or phase of energy, has its expression in a particular emotion. Each organ also houses an aspect of the shen, or spirit. In simple form, the correspondences are:

Heart
Fire; joy (enjoyment of life); pure consciousness
Spleen
Earth; caring (for yourself and others); intention ("i")
Lungs
Metal; grief (letting go); "earthly" spirit
Kidneys
Water; fear (self-reflection and re-evaluation); willpower
Liver
Wood; anger (ability to take necessary action); "heavenly" spirit

Each of the emotions has its proper time and place for expression, and its proper function. None is considered negative in itself: even anger is beneficial if it is applied correctly, for the correct reason – for instance, by a mother protecting her child. Joy provides the spark of life; grief is

Above Balancing the emotions is about avoiding the two extremes of emotionlessness and of excessive emotionality. A balance between these two allows for the normal expression of emotion, without the damaging effects of suppression or overindulgence.

Right Practising Cloud Hands chi gung. The t'ai chi principles embodied in this exercise represent the Taoist philosophy of balance in every aspect of your being: physical, energetic and mental/emotional balance.

required if we are to let go of people or things we have lost; caring for ourselves and others is essential; and it is through sadness that we know withdrawal and change is necessary. What is important is that these emotions are not inappropriately expressed or prolonged. Excess and deficiency of the emotions are equally harmful: excessive grief is an inability to let go, and becomes attachment, which often leads to anger; excessive caring becomes obsession, neediness and smothering; excessive joy becomes mania. Deficient joy becomes lifelessness, while deficient or unexpressed anger becomes frustration, and then depression. These are just a few examples: it is very useful to contemplate the beneficial and harmful aspects of all the emotions for yourself, and how they apply to you.

CORRECTING IMBALANCE

When all the emotions are balanced and properly expressed, the result is a "balanced person". As a personal practice, examine your own emotional responses throughout the day, trying to be aware of where and when your emotions are balanced, and when they are out of balance. This will give you a sense of where your focus should lie in your own emotional self-development practice. Also observe your partner and friends: the emotional patterns of people with whom you choose to associate will often mirror your own (like attracts like). Often, the very realization that you are over- or under-expressing a particular emotion can lead to a shift in your mentality, and a rebalancing of that emotion. This is particularly effective where the cause of the imbalance is mainly habitual – psychological conditioning rather than an organ imbalance.

Where there is an imbalance within the organs of your body, that needs to be addressed directly, through treatment such as acupuncture and practices such as chi gung and t'ai chi. If there has been a long-term pattern of a particular emotion being excessive or deficient, there will usually be an imbalance in the corresponding organ. The organ imbalance will cause a corresponding imbalance in the manifestation of the emotion, and the excessive or deficient expression of that emotion will in turn affect the organ negatively. So whether the root cause of the imbalance is at the level of the organs or the mind, both need to be addressed, as they are mutually dependent. Most people are born with an imbalance in one of their organs – and therefore in the corresponding element – and life-long emotional patterns may be directly caused by this. You may not be able to eliminate your hereditary imbalance completely, but you can practically eliminate its impact on your life using methods such as t'ai chi practice. When you discover what your

hereditary imbalance is, it can be a life-changing revelation, in terms of not only your health but also your emotional life.

T'ai chi works to calm your nervous system and mind, and to release emotional energies ("memories") that are stuck within your body. This smooths out your overall emotional state, allowing you to work more directly with the organs to release blockage, re-energize and balance them. The calming effects of t'ai chi on the glands help to unwind the addiction to very powerful hormonal secretions that usually accompanies an emotional pattern. For instance, a person who is frequently enraged will receive a large dose of adrenalin with each "freak-out", and this adrenalin "hit" can become addictive. All the emotions trigger glandular secretions, and some are opiates stronger than heroin. In the case of strong emotions, it is necessary to relax this glandular response. T'ai chi achieves this, largely as a result of its balancing effects on all the body's chi. Meditation practice can also be applied to specific glands and organs, to further the effects.

Preparation

This chapter starts with the fundamental principles of t'ai chi, with an overview of the energetic system of the body and how it functions, especially in relation to t'ai chi practice. It shows the precise body alignments that allow for optimum chi flow and release of physical blockages, and how to move in accordance with t'ai chi principles, unifying all parts of the body. The section on relaxing and releasing shows how to work solo and with a partner to loosen your body and release tension. Finally, the section on Cloud Hands chi gung gives a complete chi gung practice that embodies key Taoist nei gung principles, fundamental to t'ai chi. Practised alongside the t'ai chi form, Cloud Hands will greatly enhance your understanding of t'ai chi and speed up your development as a practitioner. Cloud Hands offers many of the physical, energetic and mental/emotional benefits of t'ai chi in an easy-to-learn practice.

T'ai Chi Principles

Taoist nei gung principles form the core of t'ai chi. However, because learning t'ai chi also involves learning many complex movements, it is much easier to learn nei gung principles outside t'ai chi practice itself, and then incorporate them into your t'ai chi form once you have mastered them. This is the main reason to practise secondary exercises such as those shown in this chapter.

The overriding principle in t'ai chi is to relax. This does not mean becoming floppy and collapsed, either physically or mentally, but becoming soong: a state of being unbound by any tension. A general guide is that you should use only enough muscle power to maintain the structure of your body and your postures. Feelings of strength in the body are actually indications of blockage at those places. For instance, if you raise an arm, you should use only the basic muscle power required to do that, and no more. This would be no more than about 10 per cent of your muscle power, possibly far less. When you relax this much, your chi flows very strongly through your body, and true internal power starts to manifest. However, becoming this soong is not so easy, especially for beginners. The more empty your body is, the more chi energy will flow through it. Try to keep this principle in mind at all times and it will naturally develop within you. Never get annoyed at yourself for being tense. Remember: you will not become relaxed by being tense.

ENERGETIC CHANNELS

For the practice of Wu style t'ai chi, you need to be aware of three main energetic channels in your body. The central channel runs from the crown of the head (baihui) exactly through the centre of the body on a straight line to the perineum (huiyin), and also through the bone marrow of the arms and legs. All three tantiens are located on the central channel, and this pathway is the main focus of Taoist meditation and spiritual practice.

The side channels run either side of the central channel, midway between the front and back of the body (like the central channel). As well as the central channel, Wu style t'ai chi works specifically with the side channels, and in many of the postures the hands are in alignment with them on their respective sides. The central channel is the primordial energetic pathway of the body, and is formed when the egg first divides in the womb. The side channels are formed with the next division, and from them all the other channels are spun out. Working with these deep channels affects all the other, more superficial, channels, and this is the primary reason for their emphasis.

Above As you relax more deeply into your body, you will start to have a sense of moving the outside of your body from the inside, without any feeling of using external muscles to do the work.

THE TANTIENS

There are three tantiens ("elixir fields") within the body: the lower, middle and upper tantien. The lower tantien is located approximately four fingers' breadth below the navel, deep in the body on the central channel. At first, you may not be aware of your tantien, but with practice it will "wake up" and you will start to feel a sense of energy there. Initially, this may seem like a "fuzzy" area of energy, but eventually it will condense into a precise sphere, and its location will become definite.

The middle and upper tantiens are not of such primary importance in basic t'ai chi practice, as they relate more to Taoist meditation practice. The upper tantien relates more to

Right Lying down, releasing the nervous system prior to beginning standing and moving practice. Note how the body is allowed to completely relax, without any holding of shape or position.

mental and psychic energies, and the middle tantien to "pure" emotions such as compassion, and your relationship with things or ideas. It is considered the residence of true consciousness – your hsin, or "heart-mind".

All three tantiens will be benefited by normal t'ai chi practice. However, the lower tantien, being the central point for your body's chi, is of primary importance in t'ai chi.

MAJOR GATES
Specific places within the body are of major importance in allowing the free flow of chi. These are sometimes known as "energy gates", as they can close or allow chi to pass. For the purposes of t'ai chi practice, those that you should be most aware of are: the crown of the head (baihui); the occiput, where the skull sits on the neck; the base of the neck at the seventh cervical vertebra; the armpits; the centre of the midriff; the inguinal, or groin, area (kwa); the perineum (huiyin); the hollow in the ball of the foot, or Bubbling Well point (yongquan); and the centre of the palms (laogung). All the joints of the body also act as energy gates. Finally, the tailbone (coccyx), which connects spinal energy into the ground, is one of the main pathways for connecting the energies of heaven and earth within you.

THE COMFORT ZONE
As a general rule, take your practice to only about 70 per cent of your ability, whether in terms of movement or stamina. The reason for this is that you are attempting to release tensions within your body, energy and mind. If you push yourself to the limit, there will be a subconscious tension response within you. Your body will tighten automatically if it thinks it is about to be damaged by being forced open. The same applies to your mind. If you stay just outside this "danger zone", you will start relaxing on every level, and your practice will achieve its aim. If you do this, your 70 per cent will become greater in real terms.

As part of this rule of moderation, do not demand perfection of yourself. You can do only what you have the ability for, at any stage. The Taoists use the phrase "more or less" in the context of self-development practice to indicate that you should never expect to be perfect. The balance between more and less will change over time, but nobody will ever do t'ai chi perfectly.

FEELING OR VISUALIZATION
Many people assume that they should try to visualize chi flows during practice, and sometimes t'ai chi and chi gung are taught this way. However, from the perspective of the Taoist nei gung tradition, feeling is far more important than

visualization. When you visualize energy flows within you they may happen accordingly, or they may not. You may simply generate sensations with your mind in a sort of self-hypnosis that misleads you. On the other hand, when you feel something happening you are in no doubt about its reality. You want to be able to forge a link between your "i" (intent) and your chi, so that you can move your chi directly without involving your thinking mind. By trying to make this connection occur, without visualizing, but being patient, you actually forge the link. Eventually you feel your chi, and are left in no doubt about what has actually occurred. This also enables you to be aware of the state of your energy, to feel blockages, and to feel your physical body more clearly. Many people have lost their natural ability to feel their own bodies and energy fully: they are over-visualized. Using this simple method, that process can be reversed.

RELEASING THE NERVOUS SYSTEM
The following technique is ideal as a preparation for practising t'ai chi or chi gung. If you are feeling stressed, the exercise may make you feel sleepy. This is normal and indicates that your nervous system is releasing tension: the more tired you feel, the more tension you have been holding within you. It is very important that you give your nervous system a chance to release before practising t'ai chi or chi gung. As you progress, you will find that your tension levels are generally lower, and this exercise is simply relaxing. Lie on your back and take a few moments to allow your mind and nervous system to settle. Then, starting at the top of your head, and moving down gradually through your body and limbs, let go of all feelings of strength and allow the floor to support you fully. Give yourself up to gravity and allow your body to become heavy, with a feeling of sinking into the ground. Take this process all the way to the feet and hands. Pay attention to your breathing and allow it to settle lower in the body, and to slow down naturally. When you feel calm and relaxed, rise and begin standing practice, followed by your t'ai chi form.

Taoist Breathing

The connection between breath, vital energy and consciousness is recognized by all the ancient spiritual traditions, and each has practices that work with the breath to achieve energetic balance and states of greater awareness. The expression "breath is life" is not an exaggeration: fail to take your next breath, and your life will soon end. Breathe well, and you will greatly enhance your life – physically, energetically and mentally.

Breathing is essential on a physical level, but its energetic meaning is also very profound – you gather and release energy with every breath in and out.

The state of your internal energy is instantly reflected in your breath: any emotion, such as anger, shock or sadness, immediately affects its quality. Conversely, the way you breathe has an immediate effect on your mental and emotional state. Try breathing rapidly and shallowly (from the chest) for a few moments, as if frightened or angry, then let your breath relax again and become slower and deeper (from the belly). Observe any changes in your mental and/or emotional state. This direct link between the physical breath, your chi and your mind is extremely useful in self-development practice. Breathing work is by far the single most powerful practice you can do.

In the Taoist tradition the breath is never held. Instead, absolute relaxation of the breath is cultivated, allowing it to become progressively smoother in its transition from yin (breathing in) to yang (breathing out) and back again. The breath is encouraged to drop to the lower tantien, making it the centre of your breathing. When this happens, your lower tantien is awakened and energized and your awareness enters it. This helps to cultivate mental stillness. The same approach exists in other traditions; there is a saying in Zen Buddhism that there is a "Buddha in your belly".

Above When sitting in a chair for breathing practice, align your limbs with your side channels. Check that your spine is straight, without being tense, your head "suspended", the occiput open. Relax your chest and belly, tongue gently touching your palate. Put your hands palms down on your knees, or rest them in your lap.

Above If you are comfortable sitting cross-legged on the floor, make sure you are symmetrical to left and right. Sit on a cushion so that your hips are slightly raised, and make sure your midriff and solar plexus area remains open, not collapsed. Your chest and belly must remain totally relaxed to allow your breath to drop.

BREATHING PRACTICE

Follow your breath in through your nose and down to the top of your throat. Be aware of all the sensations it generates, from the physical, to the energetic, to the emotional. As you breathe out, follow your breath back along this pathway, and relax and let go of everything you feel, allowing your energy to release fully. Continue breathing along this pathway until you feel your breath dropping lower, into your throat.

Let your breathing become more relaxed and continuous (from in to out, without holding or stopping), following the breath as it naturally drops through the centreline of your body. Continue to be aware of your internal sensations on each in-breath, and relax and let go of whatever you feel with every out-breath. It may take several weeks of daily practice to get your breathing to relax sufficiently to enter your lower tantien. Do not force the pace – it will only increase your level of internal tension, and is counterproductive. As you continue breathing you will find that your breath naturally becomes longer and slower, allowing the mind to relax and become still. Encourage this process, but without forcing yourself to breathe slowly.

Eventually, you will feel that your lower tantien fills and empties with every in- and out-breath, and that you are no

Breathing practice lying down
If you prefer to do the breathing sequence lying down, put your hands on your chest and tantien, and allow your body to sink deeper into the floor with every out-breath.

longer breathing from your chest. As the tantien fills, your breath (and chi) will "overflow" to energize the whole pelvic area, then the organs and spine. If you feel this happening, you can lead your breath to different parts of your body, but do not push it. Remember, as much as you breathe in and energize, you also relax and let go on the out-breath. If you feel that you are breathing through your legs or feet, without effort, just allow it to happen (this forms part of the more advanced process of "reverse breathing" alluded to in the Tao Te Ching: "The Wise Man breathes through his heels"). Never deliberately push your breath below your lower tantien as this can cause problems with your sexual energy. Follow the exercises, both on your own and with a partner holding the areas indicated and giving you verbal feedback.

1 Place one palm on your chest and one over your tantien to make you aware of the relative proportions of your breath in your upper and lower body. Relax your chest and belly, allowing your breath to sink. Then move your hands to just above your pelvic bone. Feel the front and sides of your abdomen – the tantien area – fill and empty with your breath.

2 Next place your hands near your kidneys, to feel the back of your abdominal area expand and release with your breath. Do not force your breath into your kidney area – be gentle. Try to achieve equal movement and relaxation on the left and right sides of your body.

Standing Practice

The purpose of this is to start feeling and releasing blockages and misalignments in your body, and to activate the downward, yin flow of energy within you, from heaven to earth. This assists in the dissolving of blockages as well as stilling the mind.

Standing practice is the foundation stone of the internal arts, essential to releasing blockage and building power. Ideally, you should stand for at least 10 minutes every day. It is not unusual for dedicated practitioners to stand for over an hour in one session, but you should build up your practice time very gradually.

TUCKING THE TAILBONE

The following pages detail the important body alignments of t'ai chi, and one of the major emphases is on "tucking" the tailbone. It is easy to misunderstand this principle. It does not mean that you should push or force your pelvis down and under, as this just creates tension in the very area that you are seeking to release. It means allowing the back of the pelvis to drop under its own weight. This requires you to relax your abdominal muscles, letting the front of the pelvis "hollow". At first this will result in a very small physical movement. However, it allows the sacrum and lower back to release, and over time the pelvis will drop considerably when allowed to do so. The end result is that the tailbone will naturally curve under the pelvic area, with a feeling as if it is threading through the back of the knees. When this process is complete, your spinal energy will connect from the tailbone through the back of the knees and the ankles, and through the Bubbling Well point on the foot, where it will join with the energy of the earth. The tailbone feels as if it is penetrating the foot. This is known as "rooting".

T'AI CHI MOVEMENT

The key principles in moving in a t'ai chi way are circularity and balance. Circularity means both moving the limbs in circles and curves – rather than in straight lines – and also moving continuously, flowing from yin to yang and back again without stops or gaps in the movement. This allows your chi to start flowing and continue flowing smoothly. The t'ai chi classics state: "From posture to posture the internal energy should be continuous and unbroken." This is one of the defining characteristics of t'ai chi.

MAKING PROGRESS

Many t'ai chi practitioners find that they go through periods of apparently little progress in their practice, followed by sudden "leaps". You may find this is the case with you. The "less rewarding" phases are actually very important, as it is during these times that you are integrating t'ai chi principles and your system is processing the new information. The leaps happen when the process of integration is complete. It is best to be neither disheartened by the less exciting periods of practice nor too triumphant or over-excited by

any sudden progress. Learning t'ai chi is a cyclical process, with one phase following another. Regular, relaxed practice is the best route to progress.

PREPARING YOUR STANCE

After preparing for standing practice by lying down and releasing the nervous system, you are ready to start the standing posture. Stand with your weight equally distributed on both feet. Your chest and belly should remain relaxed at all times, as this allows your chi to drop down the yin channels at the front of your body. It will then naturally rise up the yang channels in the back of the body. "Sink the chest to raise the back" is the phrase that expresses this. A sense of "melting" down the front of your body (including your face) is ideal. Pay special attention to the occiput at the base of your skull: gently draw your chin back and slightly downwards, as if you were tipping the brim of a hat. This opens the energy gate at the occiput. Keep space in your armpits – as if you had a golf ball under each one.

A partner should check you are not leaning back with your upper body, which is very common in beginners. Allow them to correct you, even if it makes you feel as if you are falling forwards (this feeling will pass). Your feet should be parallel even if it feels strange at first – this opens your sacrum. Always keep space in your perineum (between your legs). Feel as if your tailbone threads through the back of your knees, causing them to bend as you allow the back of your pelvis to drop. Feel as if you are sitting into your legs.

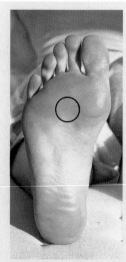

The Bubbling Well
Shown here by the red circle is the Bubbling Well point in the foot. You can find this point by curling your toes forward. The hollow that appears in the location marked is the Bubbling Well.

The Five Points
The five points are: the Bubbling Well in both feet, the laogung point in the centre of both palms, and the baihui point at the crown of the head. Maintain full awareness of these points during chi gung and t'ai chi practice to fully circulate chi.

Standing Posture

These illustrations show the major body alignments for standing practice and t'ai chi. This posture is called wu chi ("total emptiness"). Follow the annotations and, if possible, ask a partner to check your posture.

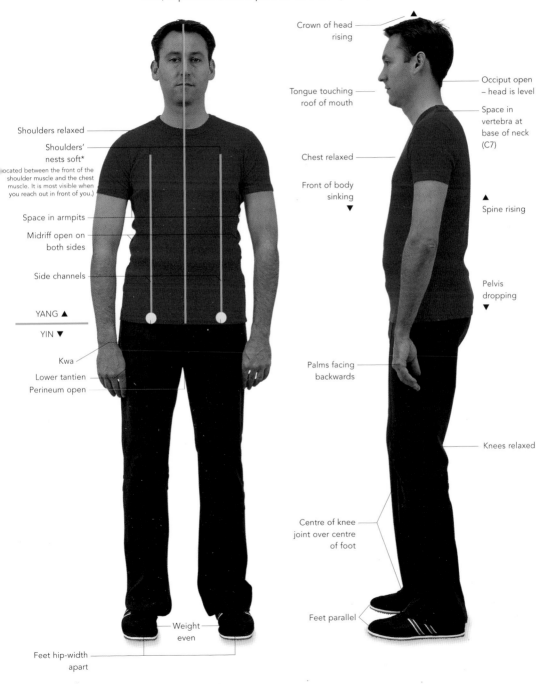

Crown of head rising

Tongue touching roof of mouth

Shoulders relaxed

Shoulders' nests soft*

*(ocated between the front of the shoulder muscle and the chest muscle. It is most visible when you reach out in front of you.)

Space in armpits

Midriff open on both sides

Side channels

YANG ▲

YIN ▼

Kwa

Lower tantien

Perineum open

Weight even

Feet hip-width apart

Occiput open – head is level

Space in vertebra at base of neck (C7)

Chest relaxed

Front of body sinking ▼

Spine rising ▲

Pelvis dropping ▼

Palms facing backwards

Knees relaxed

Centre of knee joint over centre of foot

Feet parallel

Kwa Squat and Tuck

The kwa is a key area in t'ai chi and all the Taoist internal arts. In anatomical terms, it is known as the inguinal fold, located at the front of the pelvis. It is easy to find, as it is the area that folds when you sit.

A relaxed kwa allows for strong chi flow through that area, for the efficient pumping of the fluids of the body, especially blood and lymph, and for the release of tension throughout the pelvis, especially the sacrum. As a general principle, the front of the body governs the back of the body – it is essential that you release the front of your body if you wish to release the back of your body. To find your kwa, first find your hip bones at the front of your pelvis. Now move inwards and downwards with both hands until your fingers fall into a softer area at either side of the front of your groin. This area will naturally fold as you squat or sit.

Do the following exercise several times until you gain a greater sense of blood and chi flow through your legs, and you can feel your kwa softening. When leaning forward, keep your spine straight, from tailbone to crown of head, along the angle of incline. Do not take your front knee beyond your front toes as this may strain the knee joint. If you find the heel of your rear foot rises, reposition your rear foot closer to the front foot (that is, shorten your stance). Repeat the forward squat and tuck on one side, then change legs and do an equal number on the other side.

1 Standing in front of a chair, use your fingers to find the kwa as you lower into a squat. Relax deeply into that place.

2 Let yourself fall gently into the chair, simply by relaxing your kwa.

3 Continue your kwa squats without a chair, allowing your upper body to lean forward naturally as you descend. Don't squat too low. Keep your spine straight, from tailbone to crown of head, along the angle of incline. Stand up again and repeat.

4 Take a step forward, keeping your feet the same width apart as in standing practice. With all your weight on your front leg, squat into your kwa. Let your left and right kwa fold equally. Make sure you allow your rear leg to bend, and note that the angle of your spine and the angle of your lower rear leg are the same. Keeping all your weight on your front leg, stand up, opening your kwa and bringing your pelvis forward.

Weight Transfer

This exercise will help you develop the smooth transfer of your body weight from one leg to the other, while remaining "rooted", or connected with the ground. Transfer your weight as if you were pouring water from one bottle into another.

When you transfer your weight smoothly, retaining this connection, it switches the up/down flows of chi to the opposite side of the body. Chi drops through the weighted leg into the ground and rises up the unweighted leg from the ground. Feel as if your weighted leg pushes you on to your unweighted leg.

1 Start in an equally weighted position with your feet about 1½ shoulder-widths apart. Transfer your weight smoothly from the right side to the left, maintaining the connection from your spine to the ground, and moving that connection to the left until it passes fully through your left leg. You have now transferred your "root" to your left leg. Make sure your left hip joint doesn't "pop out" to the side. Now transfer your weight back to the centre, and then to your right leg.

2 Ask your partner to apply steady resistance (making their body rigid as if it were a piece of wood) to the side of your hip as you transfer your weight. Notice how you need to stay "dropped" through your legs (rooted) in order to move them without effort.

3 Step forward and stand with your weight on your back leg. Keeping your spine upright and your head suspended, transfer your weight smoothly to your front leg. Feel your energetic "root" transferring from your back leg to your front leg.

4 Ask your partner to apply resistance at the front of your hips, and repeat, concentrating on smoothness and relaxing into your legs. Now practise shifting your weight alternately backwards and forwards. Change legs and repeat.

Unifying

These exercises help you unify your upper and lower body. The key to this is your spine – every part of your body should feel as if it is connected to it. When you unify your body your chi will also become unified and flow smoothly and strongly.

1 The "four points" (the shoulder's nest and kwa on each side) should always be linked as if they form a rectangle – you should not allow this shape to twist or distort. This means turning your spine as a unit along its length without twisting it.

2 Turn to one side, then the other, keeping your four points linked. Feel as if the movement originates in your lower tantien and your spine turns as a unit. Keep your spine vertical, without tilting to one side or the other.

3 Lock your elbows at your sides, your hands pointing forward, feeling the connection between your upper and lower body.

4 With your elbows still locked at your sides, turn to the left. Turn back to the centre and then to the right.

5 Hold your arms out in front of you, elbow tips pointing at the floor and palms down. This part of the exercise will help you develop the ability to link your arms to your spine, helping your chi flow smoothly from your tantien to your fingertips.

6 Turn to the left, keeping your arms linked to your spine, feeling that your spine is turning and your arms are simply attached. The movement should originate in the spine and not in the arms. Turn back to the centre and then to the right.

7 Take a step forward, keeping all your weight on your back leg, with the heel of your front foot resting on the floor, then turn in the direction of your weighted leg, folding into the kwa on that side. Let your unweighted leg turn as well, feeling the connection to your spine. Your tantien and spine are the origin of the movement, and your upper and lower torso do not twist in relation to one another. Keep your weighted knee fixed.

8 Turn 45 degrees from the centre in the opposite direction. Keep your weighted knee still, and don't let it twist. Turn back into your weighted kwa again, and repeat. Then change legs, and continue.

Stepping

When a cat steps, it carefully places a paw in front of it, not committing its weight until ready, then rolls through the paw surface from back to front. T'ai chi stepping is similar. The same principle applies whether you are stepping forward or back.

1 Start with your weight on your back leg. Shift 100% of your weight forward, transferring your root to your front leg, while maintaining an upright spine and proper alignments. As you move, try to maintain a level height. Look straight ahead and not downwards.

2 Peel your back foot off the ground and bring it level with your front foot. Have a sense of your kwa closing and "sucking" your back leg in and forward to this point.

3 Continue moving your unweighted foot forward and place your heel on the ground in front of you, without shifting your weight to it. Have a sense of your kwa opening and "spitting out" your front leg to bring it forward. Transfer your weight to your front foot, from your heel to the ball of your foot. Repeat with your other leg and continue stepping forward, alternating sides.

The Comfort Zone

Overextending the arms locks the joints and blocks the flow of chi, so approximately 30 per cent bend is retained in the extended arms, keeping within the comfort zone. The same applies to the legs. None of your joints should be locked open or completely closed at any time in t'ai chi or chi gung practice. When bringing your arms in towards your body, fold your joints to a maximum of only 70 per cent.

Raising the Arms

This sequence shows how to raise your arms during t'ai chi and chi gung practice.
Think of your arm as a lever, with your shoulder joint as the pivot and your
shoulder blade as a counterweight.

As your arm rises, your shoulder stays relaxed, not rising at all, and your shoulder blade drops down your back. Over time, this helps to release your shoulder blades, and thus your entire upper back and neck area. Keep a sense of your elbows being heavy, as if weighted down, throughout your practice. Raise your arms only as far as you can while keeping your shoulders relaxed and a sense of your shoulder blades dropping.

1 Start raising your arms with a partner touching your chest at the sternum (breastbone), to ensure that you do not raise your chest at any point during the exercise.

2 Relax the front of your body as your arms rise, ideally feeling that your chest and belly sink more the higher your arms go. A sense of dropping down through your side channels is ideal.

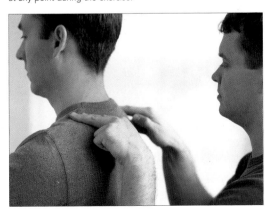

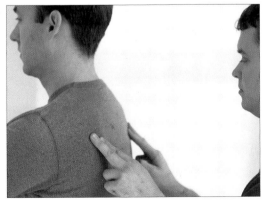

3 Raise your arms again with your partner touching your trapezius muscle, to ensure you do not lift your shoulders.

4 Raise your arms again with your partner touching the centre of each shoulder blade, to help you drop them down your back.

Relaxing and Releasing

T'ai chi is about learning to relax your body, energy and mind, and release tensions and blockages on all those levels. The techniques that follow help you with that process and prepare you for your t'ai chi form practice. You can continue to work with these exercises as secondary methods alongside your form practice. Remember that the most essential principle of t'ai chi is to relax and soften habitual tension, wherever you encounter it.

You can repeat the "washing downwards" exercise as many times as you wish. You may find you encounter and release different blockages with every repetition. If you find you start to shake spontaneously, allow this to happen, without manipulating it. This indicates the partial release of chi blockages and is perfectly normal. When your alignments are correct, it will feel as if your body holds itself up against gravity, with no conscious effort on your part.

WASHING DOWNWARDS

Align your body in the wu chi standing position. Consciously relax the soles of your feet, ideally until you lose any clear sense of where your feet end and where the floor begins. This will allow your chi to release through your feet and into the ground. Then relax your ankles, knees and kwa. Bounce a little on your legs to get a sense of being relaxed and springy in your kwa and your knee and ankle joints. Your lower body, from your tantien down, should feel heavy and sinking (yin). At the same time you should feel as if the crown of your head is floating upwards and your upper body from the tantien up is very light and empty (yang), but without raising your chest. This simultaneous sinking and rising opens your body between your head and your feet. The overall feeling is that you lengthen in opposite directions from your tantien: down through your feet, and up through your crown. Your tantien is the central point. This feeling should be maintained throughout all t'ai chi and chi gung practice. It ensures that your chi becomes full from the top to the bottom of your body. Be aware of the five points of t'ai chi: feet, crown and palms.

Once you feel settled in your posture, take your attention to the crown of your head and, as if you have a sheet of water there, allow it to start dropping through you, washing tension away. Allow it to wash through your arms at the same height as your body. Take this feeling all the way down, through your legs, out of your feet and beneath you, into the ground. Pay special attention along the way to releasing the main energy gates listed earlier. Always take this "washing downwards" process from the crown of your head fully into the ground.

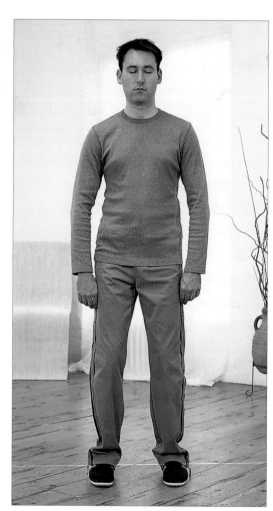

Above As you stand, have a sense of allowing release to occur only if it is ready, rather than expecting set results. This allows for greater relaxation and consequently greater release of blockages.

ARM DROPS

This exercise can be done solo or with a partner. If you are working on your own, raise your arms above your head and let them fall freely. Repeat several times, trying to let go of any tension in your arms as you let them fall.

If you are working with a partner, ask them to hold your arms above your head while you relax them completely. Concentrate on relaxing all the nerves in your arms and shoulders. Your partner can then release your arms, and, if they are relaxed, they will fall freely, swinging and "bouncing" at the bottom of their swing. If they do not, you are holding tension in them, so repeat until you release all residual tension in your arms.

DROPPING THE PELVIS

This exercise helps you develop a sense of letting go of your lower back and sacrum, to allow your pelvis to drop. Stand facing a wall with your toes about 30cm (12in) from it, and arms reaching upwards, palms on the wall. Progressively allow your pelvis to drop, and feel your spine lengthening downwards from the base of your neck, and the spaces between your vertebrae increasing. Return to your "normal" pelvic position and repeat. Get your partner to place a hand on your sacrum (at the back of the pelvis), to focus your awareness and encourage relaxation and dropping.

Below Dropping the pelvis is a core part of getting your spine to connect energetically with the earth.

Above Raise your arms above your head and then let them fall as freely as you can.

Above Try to let go of your arms completely so that they fall immediately when released.

SHOULDER'S NEST

Tension in your shoulder's nest locks tension into your upper back. Ask your partner to place two fingers in your shoulder's nest as they gently draw your arm towards them. Try to relax your shoulder's nest to allow their fingers to sink into the area, without your partner applying any pressure. This will result in your shoulder (including the shoulder blade) releasing forwards and moving off your back. Change arms and repeat.

Below Hollowing the shoulder's nest opens your back, giving your lungs more space and helping chi flow through the arms.

DRAWING THE ARMS

Stand with your back flat against a wall and have your partner hold both your arms at the wrists, supporting the weight of your arms. They should then very gently draw your arms equally towards them, opening your back and releasing your shoulders. When they start to encounter resistance, they should hold that position and very softly jiggle your arms (like jiggling a length of rope), until they sense your nervous system relax. They can then draw your arms out a little further, until your nerves start to tense again. Go through several cycles of drawing out and releasing, each time releasing your back a little more.

Eventually this releasing will extend through the length of your back, from your shoulder blades to your buttocks. See the arrows for the direction of release of your body's tissues.

SQUATS

Standing, raise your arms above your head. Then squat into your kwa, allowing the back of your spine to relax and curve open as you go. Finish with your hands behind your feet as shown, and tailbone curved slightly under your pelvis. This movement releases the back of your body and exercises your kwa fold.

Now open the front of your body, generating the movement from your kwa. As you raise yourself upright, raise your arms, palms facing out, until you are fully upright, with your hands above you. Feel the opening and stretching running from your toes to your fingertips (along your inner

Above The lengthening of the body's tissues horizontally is known as "wrapping". This wrapping can extend the entire length of the body, to include the legs and feet. It moves chi from the back of the body to the front, and vice versa (wrapping front to back).

Above Drawing the arms. Relax your nervous system so that the fascia of your back can release and wrap forwards. Your partner can actively help you relax your nerves and expand your back, while you remain relaxed and passive, just letting it happen.

Right and far right Squats open the front of the body from the tips of the toes to the fingertips. Keep the chest and belly relaxed as you do this, if possible opening the body in a wavelike motion from the feet to the fingers. Start with your hands together, above your head, then lean forwards and squat into the kwa. Only go as low as you feel comfortable, without putting any strain on your knees. Relax and let your head drop as you bend.

arms). Do not arch your spine more than a minimal amount. This movement releases the front of your body and your spine and opens your kwa. Relaxing the back of your body, squat again and repeat.

RELEASING THE HIPS

Lying on your back, bring your knees up and hold them in the palms of your hands. Relax your hip joints and legs, and using your hands – not your legs – to do the work, make circles with your knees, first towards each other, and then in the reverse direction. Allow this circular motion to move into your hip joints and sacrum, releasing them. During this exercise you may find that similar circling and releasing occurs spontaneously in your shoulders.

DRAWING THE LEGS

Have your partner raise one of your legs by the foot, and perform the drawing out/jiggling action they did with your arms, as if wiggling a rope to make a wave travel through it. This is to lengthen the tissues of your leg, hip and lower back, and release binding and contraction in these areas. They should not pull hard or jiggle forcefully. Ideally, this should create a wavelike motion along the length of your leg. After releasing one leg, repeat with the other. If your partner can support the weight of both legs, they can hold your feet parallel, jiggling them at the same time in a horizontal motion to get a wavelike releasing to travel from your feet through your legs and hips, up your spine, to your head. This can be extremely relaxing if done gently and well.

Above Hip joints tend to become stiff and blocked as they bear the entire body's weight. Circling your hips can help release these joints, allowing you deeper access while doing t'ai chi form.

Above When working with the legs, be very gentle, as they connect directly into the sacrum and spine. No force should ever be used while jiggling and releasing the legs with a partner.

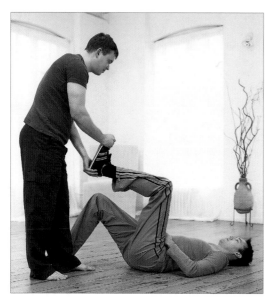

Above With misaligned leg joints, the line of force from walking and running will not pass through smoothly and over time joint damage will occur. Correct joint alignments will prevent this.

SPRING IN THE LEGS

Have your partner raise one of your legs by the foot, and align the centre of your foot with the centre of your ankle joint, the centre of your knee joint and the centre of your hip joint. They should then test the alignment by gently pushing along the axis of your joints while you gently push back. If the alignments are correct, there will be an easy springiness in all

the joints, which will rebound towards your partner once compressed. If incorrect, your joints will feel "dead", and you will feel that it requires some effort to push back at your partner. When you have achieved the correct alignment, remember how it feels so you can replicate it for yourself while doing t'ai chi (you can bounce on your legs while standing or doing t'ai chi in order to check this).

CIRCLES

Standing, interlock your fingers and circle your thumbs around one another in both directions. Then position one hand close to you and one further away, but both on the centreline of your body, palms facing you. Circle your hands around each other vertically, trying to make as perfect a circle as you can. Once you are comfortable with this, vary the diameter of your circles, from very small (fingers almost touching) to very large (arms' length). Then reverse the direction. Over time, try to make this movement originate from nearer your body (fingers to wrists to elbows to shoulder joints) until you are circling from your shoulders.

Next, place the palm of one hand over the back of the other hand and hold them out horizontally in front of you. Make circles in the horizontal plane, keeping the centre of the circles on your centreline (so your hands go to the left and right sides of your body and towards and away from you). Circle in both directions. Over time, bring the circles up into – and from – your shoulder blades.

Right and Far right Circling hands reflects the way t'ai chi involves making circles throughout the form. These circles start on a more external level, and then they become internalized, until you are making circles at increasingly deep levels within your body, and within your energy. This can have the effect of eliminating linear, "stuck" patterns in your energy and also in your mental processes, helping you to adapt to changing circumstances with an easy flow.

SWING

This exercise releases your lower back and pelvic area, as well as energizing the lower organs (the area known as the lower jiao). Pay special attention to the instructions on leg and hip alignments while moving and turning, as these apply directly to both the Cloud Hands chi gung exercise and t'ai chi form practice.

Stand with your feet parallel, 1½ shoulder-widths apart, and transfer your weight from side to side maintaining all the principles learned so far. Build up a regular, steady rhythm. Once this is well established, turn your centre (maintaining your "four points") to your weighted side as you shift your weight. Fold into your weighted kwa, as shown in the unifying exercises. As you turn, keep both knees steady, facing forward at all times – have a partner gently hold each kneecap, to assist in this. Never twist your knee joints or you may injure them. Leave your arms as relaxed as in the arm drop exercise; as you release your body and your motion becomes smoother, they will naturally swing towards and away from your body, gathering and releasing energy as they do so. Your weight shift should power the entire movement. Keep your head suspended and allow your pelvis to drop, letting tension release from your spine.

Above Swinging to the right. Note the folding into the weighted kwa, the spine turning as a unit, keeping the four points together. The head is suspended and the spine upright but relaxed.

Below Swinging to the left. As your arms relax and swing more freely you can allow them to tap your body gently as they come in. Make sure you keep your weighted knee still and do not twist it.

Below Working with a partner to ensure there is no twisting in the knees. By keeping the knees fixed and simultaneously turning to the side, the leg tissues are released by spiralling around the leg bones.

Cloud Hands

This complete chi gung exercise contains many key elements of Taoist nei gung, which are also fundamental to t'ai chi. It uses the weight shifting, turning and spiralling actions of t'ai chi, and teaches you how to spiral your arms in opposite directions simultaneously. It incorporates the key principles of t'ai chi, and therefore it is traditionally said that if you can do Cloud Hands well, then you can do t'ai chi well.

Cloud Hands works the upward and downward flows of energy in your body (on opposite sides), as well as the outward and inward flows from periphery to centre, and from centre to periphery. It activates spiralling energy in your body and releases your body through twistings of your tissues and pulsings of the joints and spaces of your body. It also activates the yin and yang meridians of your body, and unifies physical and chi movement into an integral whole. The way you shift weight, turn and connect your arms to your entire body through your spine is exactly the same as in t'ai chi. Cloud Hands embodies the essence of t'ai chi, and by practising it you will gain many of the benefits of t'ai chi practice in a very simple and easily learned form.

WHOLE BODY

During Cloud Hands your weight shift, turn and arm spiralling should be proportional: for example, at 20 per cent of your shift to one side, you will have turned through 20 per cent of your range of movement to that side, and will have spiralled your arms 20 per cent of their range. Make your movements flowing and continuous from one side to the other, and do not exceed your comfort zone of 70 per cent of your maximum range of movement. You are bringing energy up the unweighted side of your body to the fingertips of your raised hand, and dropping it down the weighted side, through the bottom palm. Turn your hands proportionately to the amount you raise and lower them.

1 Standing evenly weighted, hold your hands palms facing each other as shown here. You will move both arms simultaneously.

2 Bring your right hand up and out until your palm is facing your mouth. Lower your left hand until it is facing palm down.

3 Reverse your movement to return to the starting point, and then repeat with the arms moving in the opposite direction (left rises and right drops).

4 Standing with your feet about 1½ shoulder-widths apart, and parallel, start with your hands in the same position as before, in front of your lower tantien.

5 Transfer your weight to the left, and turn your centre to the left (folding into your left kwa). Remember to apply the t'ai chi movement principles that you have learned. As you shift your weight and turn, spiral your arms exactly as in the previous exercise. Do not bring your upper arm past your centreline.

6 Start shifting and turning back to the centre, spiralling your arms in reverse. When you return to the centre, start shifting and turning to the right, simultaneously spiralling your left arm upwards and your right arm downwards. Once you are fully shifted and turned, repeat to the other side.

The Wu style short form

This chapter contains a full Wu style t'ai chi short form, clearly illustrated and explained. The main practice in t'ai chi consists of a set, or form, of flowing movements. Each posture in the form leads into the next and each has a different function. The exact functions of each movement are best learned directly from a teacher, but by following the instructions here, and maintaining t'ai chi principles of body alignment and movement, you will start to gain the benefits of t'ai chi practice. Because the essence of t'ai chi is embodied in its principles, almost any physical movement could be adapted to become a "t'ai chi" movement. However, it is also inherently a martial art, so its postures relate to specific fighting techniques. The form is structured in such a way that these postures flow one into another to maximize the release of the body and the smooth flow of chi, as well as the gathering and releasing of chi.

Introducing the Form

The Wu style short form contains many of the postures of the long form and offers most of its benefits, but it is far easier to learn and much quicker to perform, and requires much less space. This makes the short form highly suitable not only for beginners but also for anyone with limited time and practice space. The short form can be extended by being practised back-to-back, flowing seamlessly from one form repetition into the next.

T'ai chi forms are generally divided into short and long forms. Long forms have certain advantages and also certain disadvantages, such as taking a long time to learn and requiring more time and space to practise.

BREATHING AND RELEASING

As you proceed through the form, relax your breathing. Do not impose a set pattern of in-/out-breaths on your movement. If you find that you naturally breathe in or out on certain moves that is fine, but it is very important that you allow this to occur automatically. This is because t'ai chi form practice causes release of emotional tension, and this happens primarily through the breath, as a vibration or charge within it. If you relax your breathing, the releases will occur naturally, but if you impose a pattern on your breathing, you may block releases of emotional energy.

EMPTY AND FULL

In the Wu style of t'ai chi, many postures involve gently touching the radial (thumb side) pulse of one wrist with the fingers of the other hand. This is visibly different to other styles. The reason for doing it is to make a connection with the energy of your internal organs, allowing you to release any blockages.

The yin/yang concept of "empty/full" is central to t'ai chi, and applies to the arms and legs as well as the left and right sides of the body. One hand/arm is full while the other is empty. The hand touching your pulse is empty, while the other is full. The empty hand/arm is supplying chi energy to the full. In relation to your legs, your full leg bears your weight and allows chi to drop down through it into the ground. Your empty leg is unweighted but still in contact with the ground. It is through the empty leg that chi rises from the ground, up through your body and out of your arms. Always keep your unweighted heel on the ground.

When moving outwards (releasing energy), allow your chi to release fully through your hands and fingers into the space outside you, but without "pushing out" mentally. This will help ensure that you eliminate chi stagnation from your system. Keep your eyes relaxed at all times – again, not

"pushing out" through them (which causes tension), but keeping them open so that your awareness is present both within you and in the space outside you.

At the end of your form practice, as you return to wu chi standing, feel that you are gathering chi from all parts of your body into your tantien. Allow any sense of agitation or excitement in your energy to settle down, until your chi feels calm and still. Then have a sense of condensing and storing that energy in your tantien. When you feel you cannot store any more, circulate whatever chi is not stored, throughout your body, to energize yourself fully.

Below An outward-moving t'ai chi form posture. Chi energy is circulated fully from the feet to the fingertips and the crown of the head. The gaze is relaxed and directed outwards.

The form is shown here from beginning to end, in sequence. The main pictures show the movements from a consistent angle to make it easier for you to understand in which direction you should be facing at any given point. Where the position of the arms and/or legs is obscured, for example by a turn, refer to the smaller images in the Alternative View boxes, which clearly show the side of the body hidden in the main image.

The most important thing to remember when following the steps is that t'ai chi is a movement practice, and that the pictures show only set points along a continuum of movement. Some of these points are the "final" positions of the postures, others are transitional points. However, even the "final" positions are in themselves transitions into the next posture: in t'ai chi you never stop, but flow continuously from posture to posture.

The arrows on the pictures indicate the direction of movement from the previous position into the current one. Study the positions of the arms, legs and body, in relation to both the previous picture and the surroundings, and relate this to the directional arrows and the text describing the movement. Imagine the movements between the images shown, moving from the last posture to the next, along the direction of the arrows.

MOVING THROUGH THE FORM

Apply the principles that you have learned regarding body alignments, weight shifting, turning, and kwa squat and tuck. Try to coordinate the movements of your arms, legs and body, as you did in the Cloud Hands chi gung exercise. Throughout your t'ai chi form, have a sense of your spine moving as a unit, and being the core of the movement.

Start with at least a short standing practice, allowing your chi to drop into the ground beneath your feet before you begin moving. Once you start moving, proceed at whatever pace you find easiest while maintaining awareness and being physically comfortable with the movements. T'ai chi is generally practised at a slow pace (extremely slow when practised for meditation), but you will want to adopt a medium pace to start with, just slow enough to coordinate your movements. You should expect to take about 5 minutes to complete the short form, once you have learned the movements. Then you can start to slow down, until the form takes about 10 minutes to complete. Once you feel comfortable with this slower pace, you can move as slowly as you wish, while maintaining maximum awareness and not "spacing out". Be aware that the slower you move, the more stamina it will require: faster is generally easier.

KEY PRINCIPLES

The following are some key points to remember:
- Flow continuously through the movements.
- Move your body and limbs as a unit, with the spine directing all movement.
- Direct a relaxed gaze in the direction of your movement.
- Do not cross the centreline of your body with your hands.
- Maintain a sense of heavy elbows and relaxed shoulders.
- Your elbow tips should remain at 45 degrees to the vertical, or lower, pointing at the floor, unless specified.
- Keep your head suspended and your upper body light, while your lower body is relaxed and heavy.
- Keep the space at the base of your skull open, never tipping your head back, especially when leaning forward.
- Never lock any of your joints, either open or closed.
- Keep your weighted knee fixed above the centre of your foot as you turn; do not let your knee joint twist.
- Keep your chest and belly relaxed, but do not slump.
- Keep your head suspended and your spine rising while the front of your body drops.
- Use only as much strength in your arms as you need to hold them in position.
- Keep your hands very relaxed, even when making a fist.
- Do not hold your breath, or impose a breathing pattern. Breathe through your nose, with your tongue gently touching your palate.
- Keep the heel of your back foot on the floor when tucking after a squat.
- When tucking, and at other times, do not force your pelvis and tailbone downwards or forwards.
- Remember to keep within the comfort zone.
- Keep space in your armpits at all times.
- Keep your hands at least a fist-distance from any part of your body, unless otherwise specified.
- Do not try to force your body open. Create space by relaxing, then move into that space.
- Direct your chi to your five points: the top of your head, both palms and the soles of the feet.

Commencement

The following exercise, as well as being the start of the t'ai chi form, is an excellent chi gung practice in its own right. It consists of four sequential movements that can be practised in a continuous cycle. Each of them embodies one of the four main energies of t'ai chi. These are known as "peng" (ward off), "ji" (press), "lu" (roll back) and "an" (push downwards). You can perform "commencement" repeatedly before the main form.

"Peng" energy has a quality like wood floating or a balloon expanding. "Ji" energy is like a spear moving out in a straight line. "Lu" energy is soft and yielding, or like a strong vacuum, and is the characteristic, yin, energy of t'ai chi. "An" energy is heavy and crushing, like a weight dropping. These four energies are different ways of manifesting your central or true chi. The movements of "commencement" enable you to manifest them relatively easily: in the rest of the t'ai chi form, they are applied in more complex ways that are not necessarily as clear-cut. There are four additional energies: "tsai" (pull down), "lieh" (split), "kao" (shoulder stroke) and "jou" (elbow stroke). Tsai is a combination of "lu" and "an", and "lieh" is the combination of "peng" and "ji" energy. The shoulder and elbow strokes bring energy to those parts of the body.

Allow your arms, legs and body to move simultaneously. This principle is described in the t'ai chi classics as: "One part moves, all parts move. One part stops, all parts stop." No part of your body should move in isolation, but you should feel that your whole body moves as one unit. This unifies the chi of your entire body into an integrated whole, and is a very important concept in t'ai chi.

During "commencement", in order of the movements you will be: raising chi from the ground "peng", then extending it into space in front of you "ji", then drawing it back into you "lu", and finally dropping it back into the ground "an".

By alternately bending and opening your limbs and kwa you are forming a cycle from yin to yang and back again. You are also alternately gathering energy and releasing it – again in a yin/yang cycle.

As you begin, you may find it useful to perform this several times before you move into the rest of the form. The function of "commencement" is to "start your engine", getting your chi to start flowing and settling you mentally and physically into your practice. Repeat it as many times as you need, until you feel relaxed and your awareness is connected with your movements and your chi, and then proceed with the rest of the form.

1 Wu Chi Start from the wu chi standing posture. Ideally do at least 10 minutes of standing practice before proceeding. In any case, establish correct t'ai chi alignments, then allow your chi to drop into your tantien, and from there into the ground beneath your feet.

2 Peng Sit into your kwa, allowing your knees to bend as you bring your wrists upwards and outwards in an arc. As your arms rise, keep your wrists totally relaxed and bend your elbow joint, bringing your elbow tips to vertical (pointing at the floor). Your wrists should move in from your sides until they are aligned on your side channels.

3 Ji Open your kwa and stand up as you unfold your arms in a wave-like motion towards your fingertips. Allow your hands and fingers to open, and keep a 30 per cent bend in your arms and legs. Keep your elbow tips pointing vertically downwards, and your palms facing the ground. Do not raise your chest; soften and hollow your shoulders' nests. Keep your eyes open and gaze in a relaxed way into the space beyond your fingertips.

4 Lu Sit again into your kwa, bending your knees while dropping your elbows vertically, bringing your hands in towards your body at shoulder's nest height. Bring your wrists straight in, to about a fist's distance from your body, keeping your wrist joints completely relaxed. Feel as if you are drawing energy inwards through your fingers. Have a very "empty", yin, mental attitude as you do this: a sense of effortlessly drawing everything into yourself.

5 An Open your kwa and stand again, as you drop your hands straight down the line of your side channels to the level of your lower tantien, where they move round to your sides; keep your fingers pointing forward and your hands about a fist's distance from your body as you move your chi to the soles of your feet.

6 An Beware of raising your chest during this move. As you stand up, relax and drop your chest. Once you have brought your hands to your sides (by the sides of your legs), then maintain the feeling of dropping your chi for a few moments, then completely relax your hands, going "neutral" and fully releasing your chi beneath your feet.

Raise Hands

With this sequence you begin moving into the main part of the form. You will now start to move your body in more complex patterns. Review the t'ai chi principles set out earlier, and try to incorporate these in all your movements.

1 Shift your weight to your right, doing "peng" to the sides, wrists rising as your arms and legs bend. Do not pull your arms too far back – your chest should stay relaxed.

2 Open into "ji" as you stand up, keeping your weight 100 per cent on your right leg. Do not lock your elbows or knees.

3 Sit into your kwa as you allow your left leg to swing forward, placing your left heel slightly in front of you, toes up. Keep 100 per cent of your weight on your rear leg. Simultaneously bring your arms in front of you in a hugging motion until your palms are aligned with your shoulders' nests. Elbows point downward at 45 degrees: feel as if they are resting on your hips.

4 Keeping the roundness in your arms, press your palms toward each other on your centreline until you are touching your left pulse with your right fingers. This action opens the space between your shoulder blades. This opening may extend further down your back. As you end the movement, allow the front of your body to relax and sink as your spine rises.

Play the Lute

Here you will start turning your body in coordination with arm and leg movements. Remember to make all turning originate in the spine, with your arms and legs turning like the spokes on a wheel (the spine is the axle).

1 Staying rear-weighted, fold into your right kwa as you turn 45 degrees to the right. Allow your left leg to turn with your spine. Slide your left hand underneath your right hand as you turn, so your wrists are crossed.

2 Shift your weight to your left side and slide your right hand over your left hand until you are touching your right pulse with your left fingers. Turn the back of your right hand to face outwards as you move. Look in the direction of your right hand.

3 Stay left-weighted as you sit into your kwa and turn a further 45 degrees to the right as you allow your right leg to swing in front of you, placing your right heel on the floor slightly in front of you, toes up. Simultaneously drop your elbows as you bring your hands towards you until your right fingers are pointing vertically upwards, at face height and on your centreline.

Hand detail step 1
As you turn your body 45 degrees to the right keep your right hand fixed and slide your left hand underneath it until your wrists are crossed.
Note: this image is a left side view.

Hand detail step 2
As you shift your weight to your left leg (body still turned 45 degrees to the right) keep your left hand fixed and slide your right hand over your left.
Note: this image shows your point of view.

Grasp Sparrow's Tail

This sequence incorporates all the main energies of t'ai chi. In sequence, you will do "peng", "lu", "ji", "lu" and "an" energy. This will give you a feeling for the way in which you transform your chi as you move through the form.

1 Staying rear-weighted (left leg), open your kwa and limbs as you turn 45 degrees to the right, touching the back of your right wrist with your left fingers as your hands move out and up in a clockwise circle. Turn your right leg with your body. Feel that you are expanding your energy outwards ("peng" energy).

2 Turn back to the left (staying rear-weighted) as you bring your hands in and down towards you, sliding your right hand under your left. Feel that you are drawing energy inwards ("lu" energy).

3 Turn to the left until you are folded into your left kwa. Your forearms finish in a straight line, left palm over the back of the right hand, then turn your right hand palm up. Your hands should be no lower than your elbows in order to release your shoulders and neck.

4 Turn your right palm upwards and turn your centre 45 degrees to the right (90 degrees from the commencement position). Shift 100 per cent of your weight to your front (right) leg and squat into your kwa, keeping your palms together. Reposition your back foot so that your stance is comfortable.

5 Stand up on your front leg – without shifting your weight back – as you open your kwa and tuck your pelvis. Touching your right pulse, "scissor" your arms up and out to heart height with the centres of your palms on your centreline. Release your energy in a straight line into space in front of you ("ji" energy).

6 Shift your weight to your back leg, sitting into your kwa as you allow your elbows to drop and fold, still touching your right pulse. Allow your right wrist to relax completely as you move back, as if carrying a plate on your palm. Feel that you are drawing energy inwards ("lu" energy) through your hands.

Alternative view steps 4, 5 and 6

4 Squatting as you gather energy. Note that the hands remain on the centreline of the body. The head is not tipped back, but looking downwards.

5 The posture "ji". Note the centre of the hands are on the centreline of the body at heart height, the arms at 45 degree angles, hands also inclined.

6 Drawing chi in with "lu". Note the 45 degree outward turn, dropped elbows and relaxed wrists. The hands are still on the centreline of the body.

7 Once fully back-weighted (left leg), turn your centre 45 degrees to the right, keeping your hands on your centreline. Maintain the feeling of turning from your spine, with your unweighted leg and your arms linked, like the spokes on a wheel (the spine is the centre of the wheel).

8 Flip your right palm vertically and turn a total of 90 degrees to the left, turning your right foot with your body. Keep your hands on your centreline as you turn. When you are fully turned, shift weight to your right leg as you push heavily ("an" energy) from the heel of your palm and forearm. Do not overextend your arms.

Single Whip

Along with "fan through the back", this is the most open posture in the form, and it allows for the release of not only physical tightness and contraction, but also energetic tension. It is a meditation point, so take a few moments to relax fully once you are in the final posture.

1 Form a "beak" with your right hand by bringing the fingertips together as shown in the hand detail box below, turning your left palm to face you and touching your right pulse. As you do this, "wind up" slightly into your right leg (turning very slightly to the right), with no weight on the left.

2 Releasing the "wind-up", open your body from your centre. Your right hand and right knee should not move at all. Your left hand and left foot move outwards in an arc together. Allow your back to open out and your elbows to move slightly away from your spine.

Hand detail step 1

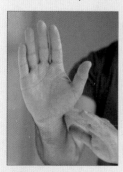 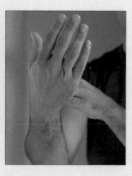 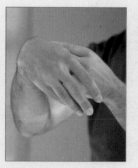 

The final hand position of "grasp sparrow's tail".

Turn the palms of both hands towards you.

Circle your right hand anticlockwise, leading with the little finger.

Finish with your right hand dropped, wrist relaxed, and all four fingers touching the thumb, forming a beak.

3 Shift your weight to the left, as you fold slightly into your left kwa. The edge of your left hand points in the same direction as your left foot.

4 Shift and turn to the centre (evenly weighted left/right). Keep your hands at or below shoulder height, elbows dropped. Sit into your legs, keeping your spine straight. Release outwards.

Diagonal Flying and Hold Ball

"Diagonal flying" moves chi from one extremity to another, lengthening the body.
"Hold ball" develops the ability to issue chi from your hands.

1 Shift your weight to the left. Turn 45 degrees to the left, swivelling your right foot on the heel to point in the same direction as your left foot. Simultaneously turn your left hand palm up, and bring your right hand palm down to the level of your right kwa. Feel as if you are pushing energy down with the right hand, which then rises up and out of your left arm.

2 Staying left-weighted, wind up a little into your left leg (into your left kwa) as you turn your hands over, left palm down, right palm up, as if holding a large ball. Allow your right hand to move slightly left to your centreline. Feel as if your palms are energetically connected to one another.

Yin Release and Shoulder Stroke

The "yin release" posture releases and drains the yin channels of the front of the body, and is highly effective when used as a standing posture for stress relief. "Shoulder stroke" opens the pelvis, and is a main martial move of t'ai chi.

As the front of your body "sinks" in the first move of this sequence, allow your spine to rise proportionally. This activates the "microcosmic orbit" of energy within you, which is a naturally occurring circuit of chi that goes down the front of the body, loops through the tantien and perineum, and up the spine and over the head. The descending phase of this circuit is yin, and the ascending is yang. The place where your tongue touches the palate (roof of the mouth) is the changeover point, and acts as a switch to allow the chi to flow more strongly. It is for this reason that you should have your tongue touching your palate the entire time you are practising t'ai chi or chi gung.

1 Keeping your right hand fixed in position, and your weight on your left leg, turn your centre 45 degrees to the right and allow the right leg to swing in front of you, placing your right heel on the floor slightly in front of you, toes up. Relax the inside of your right arm and your chest as you turn. Bring your left hand around with your centre, to finish with it in front of your heart (or throat), directly above your lower (right) hand, which is in front of your tantien. Relax the entire front of your body, from the crown of your head down to your toes, allowing all tension and blockage to melt downwards into the ground.

2 Shift your weight to your front (right) foot. Then open your right kwa as you turn your centre 45 degrees to the left, spiralling your right hand downwards to open your right shoulder blade.

3 Keep your right knee fixed, kneecap facing forwards as you turn. Your right hip and right shoulder should move forward (in the direction of your knee) as you turn. Keep your head suspended and spine upright.

Elbow Strike and Wrist Strike

Another main martial technique, "elbow strike" follows "shoulder stroke" in a wavelike motion, finishing at the end of the arm with "wrist strike". These postures will help move chi from your spine through your arm to your fingertips.

1 Stay front-weighted as you turn 45 degrees back to the right and squat into your kwa, while bringing your right hand up your centreline, turning your palm upwards as you move. Bring your left hand with your centreline as you turn.

2 As you turn and squat your right hand proportionally spirals up your centreline. This will bring your elbow out to your right side and energize it. When you have completed the move, while squatting, reposition your back leg closer to you with your back foot parallel to your front foot.

3 Stand up while remaining fully weighted on your right leg (tucking your pelvis under you), keeping your back foot on the floor. As you rise, allow your right hand to move out in front of your tantien, as if tossing a coin away. Keep your left hand on your centreline. If you cannot keep your back foot on the floor, this means your stance is too long and you should bring your rear foot further forward. This a general rule in t'ai chi. Over time, your leg sinews will lengthen and release and you will be able to adopt a longer stance.

White Crane Spreads Its Wings

This posture moves chi up and down your centreline simultaneously. Overall the shape your hands make is like a smooth rectangle: up your centre, across the top to the right, down the right, across the bottom, up the left and back to the centre.

1 Sit in your kwa, drawing up your rear foot to bring it parallel to your front foot, normal standing width apart.

2 Return to an upright position, while dropping your left hand down your centreline and bringing your right hand up your centreline, in front of your left hand. Continue moving your arms as you drop your weight down your left side.

3 When your left hand reaches your lower tantien it should move round to your left side. Your right hand finishes above your head. Look upwards at your right hand as it rises (without tipping your head back). Weight is on the left leg.

4 Shift your weight to the right and turn into your right kwa. Keep your left hand fixed by your left side, and bring your right hand to your centre as you turn.

5 Still turned to the right, squat into your kwa evenly on both sides and lower your right arm until it is at thigh height, fingers pointing forward.

6 Turn and shift your weight back to the centre as you slide your left hand forward, to finish parallel with your right hand and at the same height.

8 Remaining turned to the left, stand as you do "peng".

9 Open into "ji", still turned to the left.

7 Shift your weight to the left and turn into your left kwa, keeping your arms linked to your spine. You knees should not twist at all, keeping the space between your legs. You may find you can make only a very small turn here.

10 Turn back to the centre as you "sit in the wrists", drawing energy in through your fingertips, down your arms (allowing your elbows to sink), into your spine and down through your body. As you sit in the wrists, allow your pelvis to relax and drop, while keeping your head suspended. This increases the space between your spinal vertebrae.

Brush Knee and Twist Step

In this sequence you will perform the same movements alternately on your right and left sides, a total of three times. It is excellent for opening your shoulders and hips and developing good balance and left/right coordination.

1 Shift your weight to the right and turn 45 degrees into your right kwa, as you bring your right hand down to your right side, palm up, bringing your left hand to your centre, palm facing to the right.

2 With your weight on your right leg, open your right kwa and turn your centre 90 degrees to the left, bringing your left heel in an arc, slightly behind your right heel. At the same time, bring your right hand up to ear height, palm facing you, and your left hand down your centreline, palm down at tantien height. Your left foot points in the same direction as your centre.

3 Turn your centre and your left foot (swivelling on the heel) a further 45 degrees to the left, bringing your left hand to the side of your left leg. Transfer your weight to your left leg and squat into your left kwa, bringing your right arm down and forwards in front of you, fingers pointing forwards. Reposition your right foot closer and parallel to your left foot. Stand up on your left leg (tucking your pelvis), turning your right hand palm out as if pushing forwards, keeping your elbow tip down.

4 Keep your weight on your left leg and turn 45 degrees into your left kwa, bringing your right hand across to your centre, palm facing left, and turning your left hand over, palm up, as if holding a large ball at your side. Stay turned to the left and step through with your right foot, resting your right heel on the floor in front of you, foot angled with your turn. Stand up, your left hand rising to ear height, palm facing you, your right hand moving down your centreline, palm down at tantien height.

5 Staying rear-weighted, turn your centre and your right foot (swivelling on the heel) 45 degrees to the right, bringing your right hand to the side of your leg. Transfer your weight to your right leg and squat into your kwa as you bring your left arm down and forwards in front of you, fingers pointing forwards.

6 Stand up on your right leg, and turn your left hand palm out, keeping your elbow tip pointing vertically down.

7 Keep your weight on your right leg and turn 45 degrees into your right kwa, bringing your left hand across to your centreline, palm facing right, and turning your right hand over, palm up, as if holding a large ball at your side.

8, 9, 10 Continue the sequence from here in a mirror image of what you did on the left side, until you finish with your left foot forward, pushing with your right palm.

Alternative view steps 3 and 4
Tucking and pushing forward, turning to the left and holding a ball, stepping through.

Hand detail step 3
A relaxed and open hand.

Needle at Sea Bottom

In this sequence, you will first send your energy straight upwards, above your head, and then straight downwards into the ground. This move will help strengthen your legs and release your kwa, hips and sacrum.

1 Shift your weight to your back (right) leg as you bring your right hand in towards your heart (palm facing left), keeping your left hand, palm down, by your side, and sit into your kwa.

2 With a sense of pushing energy down with the left hand and pushing downwards with your tailbone through your right (weighted) heel, open your kwa and limbs as your body rises and your right hand ascends your centreline to finish above (and in front of) your head. At the same time, lift your unweighted left heel until only your left toes touch the ground. Follow the right hand with your eyes; do not tip your head back.

3 Sit in your kwa as you bring your right hand downwards and your left hand out and up, as if your hands are circling each other, palms facing. At the point where you are fully sitting in your kwa, your hands are at the same height. Open your kwa, but not your legs, as your right hand continues downwards on your centreline, fingers pointing down and your left hand rounds the top of the circle and moves in towards your heart.

4 Shift the weight to your left foot and squat as your hands circle to bring your left fingers to your right pulse. Your arms and legs bend at the same time. Tuck your pelvis and stand up on your left leg, stabbing your right fingers upwards.

Alternative view "needle at sea bottom"

1 The left hand remains by your side as you move.

2 Your right hand ascends your centreline.

3 Opening the kwa as the right hand descends.

4 Squatting on the front leg as your hands join.

Fan through the Back

Along with "single whip", "fan through the back" is the most open posture in the form. It is a meditation point where you allow release of your body and mind.

1 Without shifting your weight, turn your left foot and centre 45 degrees to the right. Stay weighted on your left leg. Bring your arms with your turn, and turn your right hand palm down.

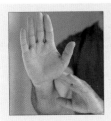

Hand detail step 1
Gently touching the back of your right wrist with your left hand. As you open in step 2, your left hand will remain fixed and your right hand will move with your body until you finish in the position shown in 2.

2 Keeping your left hand fixed in space above your left leg, open your body from the centre, bringing your lower body into an identical position to "single whip" (centre-weighted), but with your arms asymmetrical: your left hand in line with your left knee and your right hand aligned with your right shoulder's nest. Both hands should be at the same height and the same distance from your body. Feel as if you are drawing a bow as you move: your left hand is holding the bow (fixed), and your right hand is drawing the bowstring. As you finish in the central position, allow your arms to release outwards from your spine, opening your body from the centre, as if letting the arrow fly. Eventually you should also feel that your legs release in the same way. Release your central channel as in "single whip".

Turn and Chop with Back of Fist

This sequence will give you a strong sense of alternately opening your body, closing it, and opening it again. It will help you be aware of your centre, and develop stability and balance while turning.

1 Shift your weight to the right and turn 45 degrees to the right, swivelling your unweighted left foot on the heel to point in the same direction as your right foot. Simultaneously move both your hands up, inwards and down in an arc until your arms are parallel in front of you, elbows down and palms facing each other at shoulder height, at the width of your side channels.

2 Shift your weight backwards to your left leg and fold into your left kwa, swivelling your right foot on the heel. Feel as if you are folding into your centre. Allow your left hand to follow your centreline as you move, and your right arm to spiral down to finish with your hand in front of your tantien. This is the most closed posture in the form. Your right foot turns inwards.

3 Staying weighted on your left leg, open your left kwa, lifting your right foot off the floor, as you turn your centre 90 degrees to the right. As you move, strike outwards with your right elbow.

4 Unfold your arm and strike out with the back of your (relaxed) fist as your right heel touches down. Your left palm projects chi into your right fist.

5 Shift your weight to your right leg and start to squat into your kwa. Reposition your back foot when necessary. As you squat, bring your right fist down your centreline, as if it is very heavy ("an" energy).

6 When you are reaching the limit of your squat, start tucking and standing up again, weight on your front leg. Your right fist arcs upwards, to finish at your side just above your hip bone. Your left hand turns outwards in front of your heart, as if you are pushing something away from you.

Alternative view steps 4, 5 and 6

4 As you chop outwards with the back of your fist it remains on your centreline. In martial terms, the front heel is stamping to a shin or instep.

5 Keeping both hands on your centreline as you shift your weight forward and squat. Make sure your head does not tip backwards.

6 Tucking and standing up on your front leg, right fist at the top of the hip/base of the liver, and left hand on the centreline in front of the heart.

Parry and Punch

During the following movements, up to the punch, your right fist continuously circles your liver. This releases energetic blockage in that organ. Keep the contact between the side of your fist and your body very relaxed and light.

1 Sit into your kwa and swing your back (left) leg forwards until your left heel is resting on the floor in front of you. At the same time, bring your left hand in towards your heart.

2 Stand up on your right leg, opening your kwa, and push out in front of your heart with the outside edge of your left hand, gently pushing downwards with your left heel.

3 Staying on your back leg, lengthen from your left foot, up your left leg, through your body and along your left arm to the tips of your fingers, allowing your left hand to move outwards and your body to turn naturally to the right.

Alternative view step 3
Keep your back leg stable and rooted as you lengthen up from your front (left) leg, through the left side, and along your left arm to your fingertips.
This will naturally cause your spine to rotate to the right.
Allow your head to turn with your spine, but gaze in the direction of your left hand.
Do not lock your left elbow - keep a 30 per cent bend.

4 Bring your left hand back in towards you and turn your centre back to the left. Your right fist continues to circle your liver as you are moving.

5 Shift your weight to the left leg and squat into that side, repositioning your rear (right) foot when necessary. As you squat, bring your circling right fist downwards and forwards, bending the elbow, fist still turned fingers up.

6 Tuck and stand on your left leg as you unbend your arms and legs, allowing your fist to move out and turn over, thumb up, on your centreline. Project chi from your left palm into your right fist. Keep your fist (and your mind) very relaxed at all times.

Alternative view step 5
Shifting to the front leg, preparing for the punch. Your elbow moves downwards and forwards as you squat.

Alternative view step 6
As you tuck and stand up on your front leg, your elbow unbends in proportion to your legs, hips pushing your arm forwards.

Close Up and Step Forward

This sequence involves the closing and opening of your centre, then the washing downwards of chi through your side channels. This helps clear any stagnation in your chi, first through the horizontal, then through the vertical line of your body.

Alternative view
Keep your front (left) knee fixed as you turn.

1 Keeping your right fist fixed in space, and your weight on your left leg, open your left kwa and fold into your right kwa, turning your centre to the right without moving your right fist at all. This requires you to relax the inside of your right arm and your chest as you turn. Bring your left hand with your turn, on your centreline, until your left fingers are partly under your right arm, behind the elbow.

2 Open up again, turning back to the left, as you wipe along the underside of your right arm with your left hand, turning both left and right palms upwards as you turn. Finish with palms up at shoulder height, elbows down, on your side channels.

3 Shift your weight back, sitting into your kwa, bringing your palms towards you, keeping your elbows fixed.

4 Take your elbows out to the sides, turning your hands around your laogung points. Allow your shoulders to open.

5 Shift your weight forwards as you bring your hands down your side channels, as if washing downwards through your body. Keep your shoulders relaxed. As you shift forwards fully, step through with your rear (right) leg and shift your weight on to it, squatting as you do so. As you step through, your hands wash down to tantien level, and then turn, fingers forwards, palms down, to release your energy outwards and downwards.

Tiger and Leopard Spring to Mountain

During this sequence, you tuck your pelvis three times in a row, moving it forward progressively more with each tuck. Over time, this will help release tension in your sacrum and tailbone, as long as it is performed gently and without strain.

1 Keep your weight on your right leg and tuck slightly, doing "peng" as you did in the "commencement", but keeping 100% of your weight on your front leg.

2 Drop into your front leg without bringing your pelvis back, and sit in your wrists, bringing your palms to vertical as if sliding them down a sheet of glass. Tuck again and open your palms, especially the kou area between thumb and index finger. Allow chi to issue from your laogung point, in the centre of your palm.

3 Drop again into your front leg (without bringing your pelvis back), and pull your hands downwards and back to your sides, doing "tsai" (pull down).

4 As you drop into your front leg, raise your wrists, doing "peng" to the side.

5 Tuck a third time as you do "ji" to the side.

Closing

This is the final part of the form, as you return to the same place on the floor that you started from. As you turn, remember the concept of making your spine the axle of a wheel, with your arms being the spokes that are attached.

1 Staying weighted on your right leg, open your right kwa and turn your centre 90 degrees to the left (to your starting direction), swivelling on your left heel. As you turn, proportionally pull your hands inwards, dropping your elbows and pulling energy into your spine ("lu").

2 When you have turned fully, transfer your weight to your left leg, and start closing into your left kwa as you swivel your unweighted right foot to point in the same direction as your left. Continue to pull in with your arms as you move.

3 Open your kwa and unbend your limbs, doing "ji" to the side.

4 Sit into your kwa and slide your rear (right) foot forward, parallel to your left, at shoulder width. As you do this, your arms hug until your wrists are crossed.

5 Stand up, opening your kwa, moving your weight to the centre and widening the circle of your arms from your spine, keeping your wrists crossed.

6 Sit in your kwa and separate your arms until they are parallel, wrists relaxed. Feel that the outside edges of your hands and forearms are energized with "peng" (horizontal peng). Then do "ji" straight ahead (as in "commencement").

7 Perform "lu" and "an" exactly as in "commencement".

8 Finish your practice in the same wu chi standing posture you began in at the start of the form.

Taking it further

Your practice can develop and deepen perfectly well using just the short form, because the essence of t'ai chi is to be found in the Taoist nei gung principles, which can be learned and applied fully in the short form. Eventually you may wish to learn a long form, as the repetition and flow can allow for greater development of your chi. However, for a beginner, learning a long form can be a daunting undertaking, and a short form is also far more practical for busy people with little free time. Other practices that take your t'ai chi experience further are push hands and meditation. These will not only help your t'ai chi develop, but are powerful techniques for personal development. When practised side by side, they can assist you in the process of releasing emotional tensions and even in dealing with ego-related issues. In this respect they can be linked to spiritual practice, and assist on that path.

When and How to Practise

Progress in t'ai chi comes through regular and sustained practice. How much or how little you train depends on how quickly you wish to progress and how much opportunity you have for practice, but some practice is always better than none. Daily practice, even for short sessions, is far more useful than occasional marathons, because it will help integrate t'ai chi principles into your mind, nervous system and body far more easily.

Forging the link between your awareness and your energy is a gradual and sustained process, but very little time is really needed on a daily basis. If you do have a gap in your regular practice, restart at the last point you felt confident.

EXPERIENCING CHI

At first, you may not feel your chi moving during practice. This is normal. It is often said that it takes six months to a year to "wake up" your chi. This is not an all-or-nothing experience; your awareness of chi develops and deepens over time and there is no end point. Even if you cannot feel chi moving during your practice, it will be; it is taking place below the level of your conscious awareness. If you persevere, you will become consciously aware of your chi, and at that point you can start to work with it more directly. How you experience chi is individual: you may feel sensations such as heat, magnetism, wind, cold, static electricity or tingling, and all are equally valid. The important thing is that you are feeling something. The specific sensations you encounter will vary from day to day, minute to minute, and posture to posture. Try to avoid attaching any great significance to these sensations, and simply be present in the experience.

DEVELOPING YOUR SKILLS

Patience is truly a virtue in learning t'ai chi. Certain t'ai chi skills will take time to develop, no matter how intensively you practise, just as it takes a set time to digest a meal, and this cannot be rushed. As you practise, you will have moments where you gain abilities, or your body or mind release, only to lose that experience again. This "now you see it now you don't" experience is perfectly normal, and over time you will "see it" more than you don't, until that particular ability or experience becomes commonplace to you. Patience and perseverance will always yield results.

Learning t'ai chi is like learning to drive a car: at first it seems impossible to perform and keep in mind all the actions and principles that are required simultaneously. The brain is not good at focusing on more than one thing at a time – and more than three is impossible for most people. However, you focus mostly on a specific action at any particular moment until this starts to become more automatic for you. You can then focus on another simultaneous action until that too becomes automatic. Those two actions now become one, in that they no longer require your full attention, so you can focus on another action. Eventually all the actions become so automatic that they require no conscious effort: driving is just one thing. You can then listen to the radio or have a conversation while driving, something inconceivable in the early stages of learning. The parallel in t'ai chi is being able to add deeper nei gung techniques, one by one, so that what seemed like separate parts become a whole ("separate and then combine"). With this approach, there is no need to feel daunted by the seeming complexity of t'ai chi.

A very useful exercise to help make your form movements more automatic is to practise the entire form without using your arms. Place your hands over your tantien and keep them there, as you run through the form using only your lower body. This will build a solid foundation for all your movements. The t'ai chi classics say: "If there is a problem,

Left Relaxed t'ai chi practice before bedtime can help release nervous tension and prepare you for restful sleep.

Right Shown here is t'ai chi being practised with an emphasis on full awareness of chi flows through the body, and of internal relaxation and development, rather than a concentration on the precision of external movement.

look to the waist and the legs." This means that misalignments and errors in the lower body are usually the cause of errors in the upper body. Most people find it harder to focus on their lower body than on their arms, and training in this way will help correct the situation.

NIGHT AND DAY

New students often ask when is the best time of day to practise t'ai chi. The answer is: whenever they can. Practising first thing in the morning is very beneficial, partly because of the yang energy of that time of day, but if you are too busy then, practise when you can. T'ai chi will not lose its efficacy. Practising last thing at night is also very beneficial as it relaxes your nervous system and releases physical tension before you sleep.

You should not practise when very full or very hungry, though you can practise after a light meal. Practice is not recommended while you are intoxicated, exhausted or ill, as it is best not to manipulate your chi in these circumstances. Men should not practise within one to two hours of sexual activity (orgasm) as their sexual energy needs to restructure without interference. This is less of an issue for women. For women, practising during menstruation, while not harmful, may cause heavier bleeding, as the chi moves or "governs" blood. This could actually be a desirable effect in cases of menstrual cramping, when the blood is not moving freely.

RELAXING INTO YOUR PRACTICE

"Rome wasn't built in a day" – this Western saying is perfectly applicable to t'ai chi and all Taoist self-development practice. Let your practice be a holiday from the pressures of daily life. Ultimately, in t'ai chi there is nothing to achieve: you are simply returning to your natural state, free of your previous tensions. This happens through sustained practice, done without attachment to results. Demanding results of yourself inevitably leads to self-criticism and more tension, and so in the context of t'ai chi practice it is counterproductive. Keep up your regular practice, but relax and, above all, enjoy it. Let t'ai chi become a source of joy in your life, and you will find that your practice naturally develops in ways you never expected.

T'AI CHI THEORY

If you want a better understanding of the theoretical and philosophical underpinnings of t'ai chi, you can study the relationship of the "thirteen postures" of t'ai chi to yin/yang, eight trigram, and Five Element theory. This can lead to insights into the nature of the postures found in t'ai chi and their corresponding energies. It is best undertaken later in

your practice, as you should learn to feel t'ai chi from the beginning, rather than make it an intellectual study. You may also wish to read commentaries on the t'ai chi classics, and commentaries by various t'ai chi masters, for their insights into the theories and methods of practice. This book is intended to give you a foundation in the main principles of t'ai chi, after which you will be better equipped to understand the meanings of the classics and other commentaries, which, if studied at the very beginning of your t'ai chi journey, can be somewhat bewildering, and therefore daunting. Once you have become more familiar with t'ai chi, however, you will find they are more easily understood and helpful to your continued development.

THE IMPORTANCE OF A TEACHER

This book is intended to give you a good understanding of what t'ai chi is about, and to get you started in your practice. If you follow the exercises in it carefully, you will progress well. However, if you wish to continue with your t'ai chi practice, you should find a competent teacher. Apart from the fact that some techniques are hard to learn without personal guidance, there may be errors in your practice that could be easily corrected with input from a teacher. Additionally, some energetic techniques are best learned directly from a teacher who can perform them themselves. A teacher can guide you to new levels of t'ai chi practice that you would otherwise never even guess existed. This will make your journey into t'ai chi evolve and deepen far beyond your initial expectations.

Deepening Your T'ai Chi Practice

At the heart of t'ai chi lie the methods of Taoist nei gung, and these provide the real benefits of t'ai chi practice. The more nei gung in your t'ai chi, the deeper your practice becomes and the greater the benefits. Some nei gung techniques are harder to master than others, and some offer relatively greater benefits. The best method of progressing is to first learn the movements of the form well, and then start adding nei gung techniques to it.

It is not that some nei gung techniques are more important than others, as ultimately they are synergistic – each aspect of Taoist nei gung helping every other aspect to function fully. However, there are two techniques that can dramatically enhance your t'ai chi practice, in terms of how efficiently you work with your chi, and the degree of energetic and physical releasing that you achieve. These are pulsing and spiralling.

PULSING

Using the technique of pulsing, or "opening and closing", you open and close your joints (and your internal body spaces, such as the kwa) from the inside. This is not the same as bending and folding your limbs at the joints. You cause the space within each joint to change. This is a naturally occurring action, but one that becomes severely diminished as you age. Pulsing not only frees constriction and increases the health of the joints themselves (for instance, increasing the synovial fluid in the joints), but also enables you to gather and release chi very strongly. This in

Below Pulsing the wrist joint. Here the wrist is shown at its most open point. The next action is to release the pulling open, and then to push inwards, closing the joint. The forearm is held fixed.

turn releases blockages in the joints, which are the major energetic gates of your body. (The spine is added to this process eventually, using a more advanced nei gung practice known as "bend the bow and shoot the arrow".)

PULSING WITH A PARTNER

If this is done correctly and gently, your wrist will relax substantially and you will feel a greater sense of chi moving through your wrist, hand and arm, in coordination with the pulsing. This will improve your t'ai chi practice.

1 Holding your forearm fixed with one hand, your partner uses the other to pull your hand gently outwards, increasing the space in (and therefore opening) your wrist joint.

2 Your partner returns the joint space to "normal".

3 Your partner gently pushes your hand towards your forearm, decreasing the space in (closing) your wrist joint. When they have found 100 per cent of your range of movement in both directions, they should open and close (pulse) your wrist joint rhythmically, keeping to 70 per cent of that range. Repeat with the other wrist.

T'AI CHI RULER

This exercise allows you to develop joint pulsing within yourself. It is best practised immediately after you have had your joints pulsed by a partner.

Stand normally, arms and legs slightly bent, and bring your hands to about waist height. Open your arms and legs as you stand higher, and allow your hands to move out and up in a circular motion to about shoulder height. As you open up, feel your wrist joints opening internally. Bring your hands back towards you and down to starting position, continuing the circular motion, and bending your arms and legs. As your hands come inwards, feel your wrist joints closing internally. Repeat without stopping, finding your natural rhythm. If you achieve pulsing in your wrist joints, let it spread to your finger joints, then progressively along your arms, through your body and into your legs, until you feel all

Right This is the most open stage of the t'ai chi ruler exercise. From this point the arms and legs bend as your hands come towards your body. Try to open and close your hands from the centre of the palm (laogung) as you move outwards and inwards.

your joints pulsing in coordination, opening and closing with your movements. Feel as if you are drawing energy inwards through your hands on the closings, and releasing energy outwards on the openings. You can then apply opening and closing to the outward and inward actions of the form.

SPIRALLING

The actions of spiralling activate the naturally spiralling flows of chi within you. They also free your muscles, fascia and ligaments, increase blood flow within your tissues, and help your internal organs to move naturally. Once you have a clear understanding of spiralling in your arms and legs, you can combine it with pulsing of the joints, to maximize your energetic work and physical releasing. This will be easier to achieve in Cloud Hands practice (closing as you move towards the centre, opening as you move to either side) than during t'ai chi form practice, but once you have a clear sense of it, you will find it starts to occur naturally in your t'ai chi form. A good teacher can provide further instruction on pulsing and spiralling in t'ai chi.

As you slowly perform Cloud Hands, have your partner help you spiral the tissues of your arms (one arm at a time) in the same direction as the turning of your hands. You should feel your muscles and ligaments twisting around your bones, rather than the bones themselves being twisted by your partner's hands.

While practising Cloud Hands, have a partner spiral the tissues of your legs (one leg at a time) in the same direction as your turn. You should feel your muscles and ligaments twisting around your bones, rather than the bones themselves being twisted. Your partner should spiral the tissues first in your lower legs, and then in your upper legs. With two partners, your lower and upper legs on one side can be spiralled simultaneously, and then both legs can be spiralled at the same time (at the same level). Feel as if the spiralling of your tissues around the bones generates your turn. Your knees should never be twisted in any way. Always exercise caution when spiralling your legs – keep to 70 per cent of your limit, and do not allow your joints to twist.

Below Spiralling the tissues of the arm as it rises in Cloud Hands. Note that the elbow remains dropped, pointing downwards.

Below Spiralling the legs in Cloud Hands. It is vital that the knee joint is not twisted at all – only the muscles of the leg should twist.

Being Creative – T'ai Chi as an Art

T'ai chi training starts as a science, with many precise principles to learn and apply, but once the science is assimilated, it becomes an art. It can be compared to learning painting techniques or musical theory, and then using those skills to paint or compose freely, applying them in a harmonious and creative way. Advanced principles of t'ai chi – nei gung techniques – are accessed by approaching your practice with a creative mentality.

The creative mind is a natural gift that can become blocked by tensions and fixed ideas about what is possible and how things should be achieved. When you enter your deeper, creative mind, the answers manifest themselves spontaneously. The way you enter this deeper mind is by relaxing and letting go of the desire for specific results, opening yourself to whatever may occur. This is a very important aspect of intermediate and advanced t'ai chi practice.

ADVANCED T'AI CHI PRACTICE

As you become familiar with the form and the main principles of t'ai chi, additional practice methods will help you develop. One of these is to use t'ai chi form postures as standing postures. This means holding a posture for some time (anything between a few minutes and an hour) in order to allow your body to release in that posture and your chi to develop. This can be a painful experience, as you start to feel existing tensions within your body. However, it is a very fast and effective method of releasing those tensions. As a starting point, try standing in the "single whip" posture, and

Below The "single whip" posture is ideal for standing practice. As you stand, maintain your external structure but relax internally.

also in the "yin release" posture. Both these positions will help develop your chi and release tension in ways that will benefit you generally. Another useful method is to do your form with your eyes closed. We normally use vision to help with our spatial awareness and balance. Doing t'ai chi with your eyes shut will develop your balance and physical awareness and help you find your internal stability.

RIGHT- AND LEFT-HANDED FORMS

All t'ai chi forms are "handed", meaning that the movements and postures are not symmetrical: you will work one side of your body comparatively more than the other. Normally, you will learn a right-handed form to start with. You should train with this for approximately three years before learning to perform an exact mirror image of the form. After this, you may choose to perform both equally, or to emphasize either the left- or right-handed form to open up that side of your body. If you choose the latter, you would practise a ratio of at least 2:1 on the side you want to work on. It is important that you become very confident with the initial, right-handed form before attempting a left-handed form. If you are genuinely left-handed (rather than only writing with your left hand) you may want to reverse the order and start with a left-handed form, in which case you should seek the guidance of a teacher.

Most people have imbalances between the left and right sides of their body. One side will be more tense or blocked, energetically and/or physically. You should always play to your weaker side, moving only as much on your stronger side as you can on the weaker side. This way, your weaker side will draw energy from your stronger, and will improve, rather than the opposite. This principle also applies when doing a moving chi gung such as Cloud Hands.

NEI GUNG TECHNIQUES

T'ai chi is principally about implementing Taoist nei gung principles within yourself. The form exists to help you do this in an efficient way (as well as having martial functions). The physical movements of the form are not t'ai chi. They are what an untrained observer will see as t'ai chi, but as you

Right Playing with the form. Although the movements may not correspond to specific postures in the form, all the t'ai chi principles of alignment and movement are present. As you learn nei gung methods this can be a powerful way of developing these techniques in a freer, more spontaneous way.

progress you will come to realize that t'ai chi is really what is going on within you. This is, of course, all but invisible to the average outside observer.

Every posture in the form has several variations; some relate to your level of practice, others are simply different ways of performing a technique. Nothing is written in stone apart from the fundamental, underlying principles of t'ai chi. Once you are very familiar with the form, you will start to work on various nei gung techniques, adding them to your form practice one by one. Pulsing and spiralling are two very important examples, but there are many others. They include the stretching and release of the ligaments, which also brings about strong emotional release; the movement of the fascial tissues and chi in wavelike motions up and down the body, activating the yin and yang meridians; the "wrapping of tissues" from the back of the body to the front and vice versa, activating horizontal flows of chi; the deliberate movement of the fluids of the body; the incorporation of circles and spirals into all your movements; the movement of energy both up and down in the body, and from centre to periphery and back again; and the movement of energy into and out of the spine and tantien.

FREEING YOUR FORM

As you continue with your t'ai chi form practice, you might find that your experience of it becomes a little rigid and lacking in spontaneity. Ultimately, spontaneity in practice comes from what is happening within your body. In order to break free of any feeling of rigidity it can be very useful, and enjoyable, to "play" with the form.

A good starting point for this is "drunken" t'ai chi. In this method of practice, your main focus is on completely releasing the nervous system, including the brain. As you run through your form at a slow pace, allow your nervous system to relax and release as completely as possible. The result will be movement that flops and jiggles as you release tensions in your nerves. If you succeed in releasing tension in the brain as well, you will find that your eyelids flutter. Allow yourself to stagger and lose balance, if that occurs spontaneously. Do not give any thought to t'ai chi principles or being "correct" in your form. This method is extremely relaxing and very useful if you are stressed and holding nervous tension. It is especially beneficial when practised immediately before going to sleep.

SPONTANEOUS MOVEMENT

Once you have learned to relax your nervous system through "drunken" t'ai chi, you can start to play with your t'ai chi form. At first, try varying the movements: see if you can alter

a movement while retaining a sense of flow and adhering to t'ai chi principles. Try making your movements more circular, even if this means doing an "incorrect" move. Try to get the circles you are doing with your arms to spread into your shoulder blades, moving and releasing these "hidden joints of the body". Take the circles and spirals into all parts of your body, especially parts that feel stuck or relatively lifeless, to wake up and release those areas. Eventually, try not only to take the circles and spirals to your lower tantien, but to make them originate from it, and spread to all parts of your body. In t'ai chi, all movement, both energetic and physical, originates in the tantien.

At this point in your practice, you may find that you are doing "spontaneous" movements that allow you to carry out this internal work, and no longer doing a t'ai chi form. Continue with this, being creative and letting your body show you how you can manifest these circles and spirals. Now be conscious of your alignments, and, as you move, be aware of when your body feels open and correctly aligned, and when it closes down. Learn from this with an open mind. Play with these alignments, and find what works best for you. Be conscious of gathering and releasing energy as you move, in an alternating, pulsating way. Let your chi move out from your centre (tantien and spine) and back again. Find which sort of rhythm enhances this.

After you have practised in this spontaneous way, go back to your form practice, relaxing and observing any changes in the way your form feels. It should feel freer and more alive. You will have gained a much greater understanding of some of the nei gung principles of t'ai chi.

Exercises for Meditation

The following exercises will help you explore meditation practice more deeply and start to integrate it with your t'ai chi practice. They mainly involve using your awareness of your breath in order to lead your mind inwards and release tensions on your emotional level (although your mental and psychic energies may also be accessed). Sitting meditation is an excellent adjunct to t'ai chi, both before and after practising the form.

Your breath is the most direct link between your mind (awareness) and your energy, whether physical (chi) or emotional. Using breathing meditation techniques, you can connect with progressively deeper levels of your energy. Initially, you might feel slightly more nervous, but this means that your awareness is going deeper and you are noticing internal tensions that already exist. Persevere, and these tensions will dissolve.

FOLLOWING THE BREATH

Sitting comfortably, follow your breath progressively down your central channel to your lower tantien, as in Taoist breathing practice. However, this time focus more on your emotional (and mental, and psychic) energies as you breathe. Throughout your downward progression be especially aware of the quality of your breath – whether the breath itself is smooth and "neutral", or whether it contains some vibration, charge, tension or agitation, however subtle.

Anything in your breath that is not completely smooth is an indication of internal tension, most often in your emotional energy. The breath is the principal medium whereby emotional tension can release; it is also the principal means by which you can become more aware of emotional tension. Let your breath be the guide to your deeper emotional states, and let it be the means to you becoming emotionally "smooth". Allow any tension or vibration in your breath to release of its own accord as you breathe out. Use your in-breath to become aware of emotional tension (within your breath), and your out-breath to allow it to release, by relaxing the breath itself and letting it become smooth and "empty". Continue this process as you follow your breath down your central channel. If you experience any sort of vibration, charge or sensation in the breath (or in any part of yourself) that you find impossible to understand – because it does not seem to relate to any form of emotion or anything you can "identify" – this may mean that you have encountered blockage or tension in your psychic energy. In any case, apply the same method of allowing your breath to become smooth as you breathe out,

Below Breathing meditation practised lying down allows for more physical relaxation. Make sure your awareness remains focused.

Above Meditation with the eyes open. Taoist practices combine internal (nei) with external (wei) awareness. Sitting meditation is an excellent starting point for this.

in order to release that tension. Throughout this practice, adopt an attitude of being willing to experience whatever "comes up" while you are practising, with the knowledge that whatever is inside you must be experienced fully in order for it to be released fully.

MEDITATION WITH EYES OPEN

Once you feel comfortable with this method of breathing meditation, practise with your eyes open, keeping them very relaxed and neutral. Allow the images of your surroundings to come into you, through your eyes, rather than projecting your mind outward through your eyes. Maintain full awareness internally, while simultaneously being aware of your surroundings. After practising sitting, with your eyes open, practise standing in the wu chi standing posture, eyes open. Then practise while walking slowly, with full awareness. Following this, practise while doing Cloud Hands chi gung. If you practise the open-eyed method of breathing meditation well, you will find that you can achieve an effortless, relaxed focus in all activities. You will gain a sense of equanimity, regardless of what takes place around you, greatly reducing your stress response to outside events.

T'AI CHI MEDITATION

After you have become familiar with eyes-open practice while sitting, standing, walking and during Cloud Hands, you can apply breathing meditation while performing your form. Avoid correcting your form while practising t'ai chi meditation. Allow yourself to relax fully, letting your body perform the movements automatically while your awareness

is on your breath. Be especially aware of the places where you change from yin to yang and vice versa, both in your physical movements and your breathing.

You may wish to slow your movements down considerably as you approach these yin/yang changeover points, to allow release to occur and to enter deeper levels of stillness. It is at the changeover points that you are most likely to encounter stillness, and release deeply held tension. Allow your form to become naturally smaller and "looser". If you find you need to concentrate on the sequence of movements of the form, practise using only the commencement until your form movements are truly automatic. As a general rule, the more slowly you move the deeper your awareness will go, allowing for deeper release. Adopt a gradual approach to slowing your practice speed; experiencing and releasing emotional tension can be an intense experience – stay within the comfort zone.

Below Practising t'ai chi form for meditation. Note that the body and limbs are looser and the posture smaller than in normal form practice. Total release of tension is the goal.

Push Hands

Tui shou (push hands) training is indispensable for furthering your t'ai chi practice. It also forms the bridge to the practice of t'ai chi as a martial art. However, it is not a martial practice in itself, and should be used even if you have no interest in the martial aspects of t'ai chi. Done correctly, it embodies the t'ai chi philosophy of relaxation, yielding, sensitivity and appropriateness of action.

Its benefits derive mainly from the fact that in push hands practice you are working with a partner, in a way that can be either cooperative or challenging. The interplay of chi between push hands partners allows for very efficient release of chi blockages in both practitioners.

BASIC PRINCIPLES

As you practise push hands exercises, try to remain as relaxed as possible. Adopt the attitude that even if your partner is trying to push you, this is by mutual consent, and is in order to help you develop your skills. Be aware of any emotional response that the exercises evoke, and try to relax that. Push hands is not sparring, and should not be practised with any "hard" martial intent, or you will not benefit from it fully. If you have an interest in t'ai chi as a martial art, the relaxation under pressure that you gain from push hands will form a foundation for t'ai chi fighting.

Retain all the key t'ai chi alignment and movement principles as you go through these exercises. Try to use a minimum of physical strength and maintain contact at all times, "listening" to your partner's movement and chi and not opposing it. Maintain awareness of your breathing: never hold your breath, and allow any emotional tension to release, as in t'ai chi form practice. Bear in mind the principle, "Four

Benefits of push hands
Push hands is important for all t'ai chi practitioners for the following reasons:
- It tests your ability to gain and develop an energetic "root", as well as helping you develop your root.
- It highlights those areas of your body that may be stiff or tense, and allows you to relax them consciously.
- It tests and develops your application of the key t'ai chi principles regarding alignment and movement.
- It provides an environment in which you can become more aware of tension in your nervous system, and allow it to release.
- It highlights emotions such as anger and fear, and allows you to relax and reduce your glandular response to external pressure. In conjunction with meditation practice, it makes you more aware of your ego and your need to win.

ounces can defeat ten thousand pounds," meaning that a very light force applied correctly can divert a very large force, without trying to oppose it. This is like leading a large bull by the ring through its nose – it cannot resist.

PUSH HANDS PRACTICE
As you repeat these exercises, focus on relaxing your nervous system and mind, on rooting, alignments and weight transfer. Your partner should feel as if they have nothing to push on – like pushing at thin air – and you should feel as if you have used no effort to yield to and divert their force. Neither person should push or yield further than correct alignments will allow. When you have finished the following sequence, change legs and arms. You can also do this exercise with the opposite leg and arm combination, and turning/diverting inwards rather than outwards.

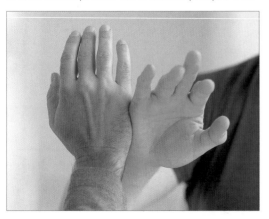

Left Making contact at the wrists. Try to feel as if you are "stuck" to your partner's wrist, always maintaining light and relaxed contact.

1 Start with both partners adopting the stance shown here, opposing feet stepped towards each other and opposing wrists lightly touching, back to back. Put your other hand in the small of your back.

2 As your partner shifts their weight fully forwards, turning their palm outwards to push the back of your wrist, start to shift your own weight back, yielding to your partner's pressure, but keeping your "courtyard" – the space between your arm and body – intact.

3 As you shift your weight fully to your back leg, turn your centre outwards as shown, keeping your arm connected to your spine and bringing it with the turn. Turn up to 45 degrees, diverting your partner's force away from your centre.

4 As you reach the end of your yielding and diverting movement, start turning back to the centre, turning your palm towards your partner and beginning to push as they turn the back of their wrist towards you.

5 As you return to the centre (facing your partner), start shifting your weight forwards, pushing towards your partner's centre at heart height.

6 As you do this, your partner should yield to and divert your push just as you did theirs. At the end of their movement, they will start pushing back towards you. Repeat the cycle.

Push Hands Training Exercises

The following training exercises will help you develop rooting, yielding/diverting, body and leg alignments, and stability in the upper and lower body. The push should be slow, with force building gradually.

YIELDING AND DIVERTING

These exercises are designed to develop further your ability to remain stable and rooted even while you are being pushed. The force of the push is either yielded to and diverted by turning the spine, or at a more advanced level, is yielded to internally – the energy of the push is allowed to travel unhindered down through the body and into the ground. Your partner will feel as if they are either pushing on thin air, or that they are pushing against the ground.

1 As you stand in a front-weighted stance, your partner pushes slowly on your shoulder. Yield to this force, while maintaining alignments. Repeat on the other side, then change legs and repeat, then do the same with a back-weighted stance.

2 Return to a front-weighted stance while your partner pushes slowly in the centre of your chest. Change legs and repeat, as before, and then do the same with a back-weighted stance.

3 Repeat the exercise with your partner pushing on your belly, in the centre just below your ribcage. Once again, change legs and repeat, and then repeat on a back-weighted stance.

4 Starting in a front-weighted stance, have your partner push straight forwards at the centre of your chest. Without shifting weight or diverting the push by turning, try to sink the force of the push downwards through your body and legs into the ground. This is yielding internally (downwards).

5 If this is successful, try standing normally in an even-weighted "wu chi" posture and repeat. Let this exercise help you feel where you are internally bound and blocked: try to relax those places inside your body so the energy of the push can pass through you and drop into the ground.

ROOTING EXERCISES

The following three exercises help you develop your rooting skills and body alignments. Standing in wu chi posture, take a few moments to become as rooted as possible, getting your chi to sink to your tantien and into the ground. Have your partner test your alignments and rooting by pushing gently and slowly (not abruptly) at the sides of your body, arms, legs and even your head, one side at a time. You will easily feel where your alignments are correct and it requires no effort to resist the push (other than the basic energy required to maintain your structure), and where your body "jams up" and you need real effort to resist a push. Adjust your alignments at those places and retest the posture. In a more advanced practice, using your intent, try to bring your chi to the site of the push, minimizing the physical effort needed to resist. Repeat the previous exercise with pushes

Below The posture "double an" from the "grasp sparrow's tail" sequence of the t'ai chi form, being tested by a partner.

Above Rooting exercises basically test how secure your stance is, and whether your body is aligned correctly.

on the front and back of your body. Once you are comfortable with these exercises, have your partner gently push randomly on any part of the body, at any angle. You will find that some of the angles will naturally be harder to resist than others.

Assume a posture from the t'ai chi form, and have your partner test it by pushing and pulling on you from various angles. This type of static posture testing is very important in t'ai chi as a means of discovering the precise body alignments that allow your chi to flow fully in each posture. By doing this you will also discover the relative strengths and weaknesses of each posture in the form, and better understand the characteristic energies of each posture.

When you do this posture testing you will find that if your arms are overextended or too withdrawn, the posture is weak – in other words, your chi is not flowing strongly. What you are seeking is an ideal balance of yin and yang within each posture, which gives it a natural and effortless strength, both structurally and energetically. Understanding the nature of each posture will greatly help you understand t'ai chi in all its forms and principles.

Push Hands Variations

The single push hands exercise is the foundation of push hands practice. Once the basic skills have been developed you may wish to learn other variations, such as double push hands, and push hands at different heights, such as high push hands and low push hands.

These advanced push hands exercises train different parts of the body and develop different forms of yielding, diverting and pushing, as well as helping you to release different parts of your body. Martially, they train your awareness and movement skills at different heights and in response to a variety of potential techniques an opponent might employ.

One of the key skills that push hands training develops is that of "ting jin" (listening energy). This involves being sensitive to your partner's movement, energy and even mental intent so that you react appropriately to their actions, always one step ahead of them. This ability to be sensitive to and interpret other people's intentions, and then act appropriately and with perfect timing, is a very useful skill in many areas of life outside of t'ai chi practice. Once you have developed your "listening" skills, you can develop your "jan" (yielding), "lan" (merging) and "nien" (adhering) skills. The highest level of this progression is "suei" (magnetizing), but this is a very rare skill indeed.

FA JIN

Fa means "issuing", and jin means "power", and "fa jin" relates to the fast release of energy, in order to uproot, move and/or strike an opponent. It can also be used in healing practice (such as chi gung tui na, or massage) to clear energetic blockages in a patient. In the context of t'ai chi practice, and specifically push hands, it is used to push a partner/opponent away from you. It can also be used to clear chi stagnation from your or your partner's body.

There are many levels of skill in "fa jin". The highest levels rely almost solely on chi projection, rather than biomechanical action (such as joint compression/release and

Below Double push hands in the Wu style is a set sequence that manifests "peng", "lu", "ji" and "an" energy in sequence.

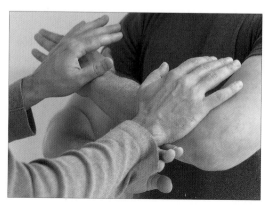

Above High push hands. As your partner pushes towards your head, shift your weight back and yield and divert upwards and out.

ligament release). At a very high level, fa jin seems mysterious when experienced. It can feel as if you are being picked up and moved a large distance as if by a wind, with no real force having been applied to you. Use the squat and tuck that you have learned already to develop your gathering and release skills. Do not tense or "push" as you release – simply let go outwards, and fa jin will start to occur.

VARIATIONS

T'ai chi push hands uses specific training methods to develop your skill in relation to different areas of the body and (with a view to martial skill) in relation to different techniques you might encounter. Double push hands develops the ability to coordinate both hands in relation to a double-handed push or technique from your partner. The specifics of this method need to be learned from a teacher. High push hands relates to a push or strike aimed at the head, and helps you remain "dropped" and relaxed while raising your arms. Similarly there are low push hands training methods, relating to the lower body, as well as specific variations dealing with other angles.

Above Gathering chi energy (including your partner's chi) as you squat in preparation for issuing in "fa jin".

CIRCLING HANDS

This freer, more spontaneous form of push hands can provide a transition into t'ai chi sparring (martial practice). The use of circles is strongly emphasized: your arms and those of your partner circle continuously, touching at the wrist. These circles are mirrored in your body, eventually originating from within your lower tantien as internal movements that cause external circles to manifest.

At first, circling hands should be practised with a view to developing listening energy in relation to your partner's movements, and using circular movement to release your body. Once you have established a relaxed rhythm, you can try pushing your opponent when an opportunity presents itself. You can push on any part of your partner's body, and at any angle. Find out by trial and error what does and what does not work in terms of both timing and technique.

Above Tucking the tailbone and standing up as you release gathered chi rapidly with "fa jin". Note that the partner has become uprooted.

Aggressive, rapid pushing is not required if you use good timing and judgement. Try to maintain a flow, even when you attempt to push. If your partner attempts to push you, use circularity of movement and the skills you have gained so far to yield and divert their force.

As a transition into t'ai chi sparring, you can also attempt to slap your partner (gently) at various places on the body, rather than just pushing. You can also apply t'ai chi techniques such as "shoulder stroke", "elbow strike", "split" and "pull down". It is a good idea to discuss the rules of this practice before you begin, to establish whether you both consent to pushing, gentle slaps or harder contact, so that neither of you will feel aggrieved if you are on the receiving end of a push or slap. You are engaging in this practice to help each other develop, not to make enemies, or hurt each other. Try to stay relaxed, whatever happens.

1 For circling hands, stand as shown and circle your hands, wrists touching.

2 Shift your weight and turn your body as appropriate.

3 Open your partner's centre with the left hand and push with the right.

T'ai Chi as a Martial Art

Though t'ai chi chuan is a practical martial art, the vast majority of people who practise it today do so for its benefits in health and stress reduction, rather than as a self-defence or fighting practice. T'ai chi does not yield martial ability easily – it requires prolonged and intensive practice to become a proficient t'ai chi fighter. This is because it requires development of Taoist nei gung skills in order to fight without using any tension or anger.

From a purely martial perspective, the benefits of this method of fighting are greater awareness, responsiveness, appropriateness of action and power. These skills grow over the years, as opposed to waning with age – a common problem for external martial artists.

EXTERNAL AND INTERNAL

The external martial arts are so-called because they do not use internal, nei gung principles. Instead they rely on muscular strength, speed and aggression. Most popular martial arts are of this type, such as karate, jujitsu, taekwondo, Thai/kick-boxing and kung fu. Interestingly, Western boxing adopts a more relaxed and circular fighting method than many of the Oriental external martial arts. The development of strength, speed and aggression can make you a very good fighter, sometimes in a relatively short time (depending on your ability). However, there are several disadvantages to this type of training: regular practice involving the deliberate use of aggression (anger) does not allow for the smooth release of this type of emotion. On the contrary, it tends to power-up existing emotions within you,

which is not helpful for your personal development. Physical tension is not released, and may even increase as a result of training. Damage may be inflicted on the body (especially the joints) over time, which can lead to problems such as arthritis later in life. These factors depend on the severity of your training regime, but in order to become a "serious" martial artist, you must train hard. Almost none of the deeper self-development benefits of the internal martial arts are gained with external martial arts training.

If you genuinely feel the need to defend yourself against aggression, an external martial art may provide the answer. If not, then you would benefit from examining your motivation for wanting to practise a martial art. If it is principally for self-development, an internal martial art such as t'ai chi may be ideal. When practised correctly it can make you more relaxed, healthier and more emotionally balanced as you age, and, in time, a proficient martial artist.

Below A classic image of external martial arts: power, speed and aggression are being used to overwhelm the opponent in this women's taekwondo competition.

Right A Chinese Shaolin monk practising kung fu. There are chi development practices in Shaolin styles but they do not adhere to the t'ai chi principles of relaxation. External, muscular strength and tension are deliberately employed to generate power.

KUNG FU

Most of the kung fu style martial arts do not share any of the core principles of t'ai chi chuan, hsing-i chuan or ba gua zhang. Kung fu (pronounced "gung fu") means "work" (or "effort") and "time" – in other words, skill gained from prolonged practice. The phrase can be applied to any activity, from that of a chef or a carpenter to a martial artist. A better term is "wushu" (fighting method). There are many highly developed and colourful "wushu" styles in existence, such as "praying mantis". These are effective martial arts but they use external principles and training methods, and should not be confused with the internal martial arts simply because of their Chinese origins. Semi-internal or external/internal Chinese styles also exist, such as "monkey boxing" and "eight drunken immortals". These are closer to the internal styles but still use some external training methods and principles.

T'AI CHI FIGHTING

Push hands and circling hands practice forms a bridge to martial t'ai chi practice, as it develops your ability to root, relax under pressure, interpret and respond to an opponent, understand fighting angles and use them to your advantage, and issue power. Less obvious is how t'ai chi form practice relates to real-life fighting.

The slowness of t'ai chi form practice allows for the release of tensions at every level – especially of the nervous system. The limiting factor on speed of movement is tension in the nervous system. When the nerves relax, not only do the muscles relax, but nerve signals can flow more freely and rapidly. This allows for much faster movement when fighting. T'ai chi masters are known for possessing extraordinary speed of movement, being able to change from one technique to the next with lightning speed. This ability is enhanced by the use of circles in movement, and circularity of thinking – not becoming mentally "stuck" at any moment. The greater awareness that t'ai chi practice brings – a truly relaxed focus – allows for the exploitation of an opponent's mental "gaps". You do not gap, or do so significantly less than your opponent. The exploitation of these gaps – moments when someone loses awareness of what is happening – is a major factor in high-level martial arts of any kind. A boxer who says, "I didn't see it coming," has been hit while he was gapping. Some t'ai chi masters can directly (psychically) induce an opponent to gap.

T'ai chi form postures and movements programme various martial techniques into your system, which can then emerge spontaneously during sparring or fighting. These techniques, whether throws, kicks or strikes, can be further developed while sparring with a partner. The sequence of techniques – indeed the techniques themselves – used in the form do not imply that you would use exactly those techniques while fighting. T'ai chi is about principles, and at an intermediate and higher level t'ai chi fighting is extraordinarily spontaneous, the only rule being that the key principles are maintained.

The use of chi energy is central to t'ai chi strikes and kicks – using the same external technique, this energy can be focused either to move an opponent harmlessly or to cause serious internal injury. The amount of power generated by a true internal strike far exceeds that from any "external" strike, and has to be experienced to be believed.

T'ai chi fighters make use of the principle, "start after your opponent, arrive before him". This skill has been likened to the way a cat waits until after a mouse starts to run, and then intercepts it further along its trajectory. It is initially developed through push hands practice. A good t'ai chi fighter always seems to be at least one step ahead of their opponent. Additionally, the saying, "give your opponent what they want, but not the way they expect it," means not opposing them head-on, but luring them into a trap. "Forget yourself and follow the other" applies here (and in push hands), where the "other" is your partner or opponent. T'ai chi fighting skills can seem mysterious to the uninitiated – almost supernatural – but in reality they are abilities that most people can develop, with sufficient application.

FIGHTING WITHOUT ANGER

Assuming that you are not expecting to need to defend yourself against a physical attack, you might ask why you should be interested in practising t'ai chi as a martial art. From the point of view of advancing your t'ai chi practice in general, martial training can provide a clear test of your development. Martial practice gives you a greater understanding of your t'ai chi form practice in terms of the chi movements and transformations that take place in it.

FIGHT OR FLIGHT

The principal benefit of martial training lies in developing the ability to remain calm under extreme pressure. There is arguably no greater stress-causing event than having a person try to hurt you physically. Naturally, you would not train to this extreme under normal circumstances. Sparring would not be escalated to the point where your opponent was genuinely trying to cause you injury unless you were training for real life-or-death conflict, in which case the realism of an all-out attack would be an essential part of your training. Nevertheless, having a sparring partner attempting to make even light contact will almost certainly trigger your

natural fear response (often known as "fight or flight"). The moment this response is triggered, your adrenal glands "fire up", secreting large amounts of adrenalin. Your vision narrows, your heart beats rapidly, your breathing becomes shallow and rapid and your nervous system becomes over-stimulated, resulting in physical tension. At the emotional level, a common response to the fear stimulus is anger. This fear/anger response is deliberately utilized in the external martial arts. One of the reasons that the internal martial arts are superior from a fighting perspective is that this adrenalin response actually limits speed of movement and perception (even though it does provide an initial "boost"). The relaxed and open mental awareness and powerful and quick movements of a good internal practitioner provide an edge when fighting a "fired-up" external practitioner.

The fight or flight response sets in motion a set of bodily responses that can lead to a number of serious stress-related diseases. Even a moderate triggering of this response, when repeated regularly, will degrade your health, and many events in daily life can cause it. Adrenalin is secreted quickly, but eliminated slowly from the body. Your system needs sufficient time between stressful events to reduce your adrenalin levels. The constant secretion of adrenalin will keep your body in semi-permanent stress mode, exhaust your adrenal glands, and from a Chinese medical viewpoint,

Below Responding to a punch with yielding, turning and sticking; applying a joint lock/break, while remaining centred.

Below Following up by trapping the opponent's arm and using the body to apply a lock/break while attacking the opponent's throat and taking his balance. From here he could easily be thrown back.

Above Brushing away (diverting) an attack and simultaneously striking the side of the opponent's head. Note his balance has been taken. T'ai chi specializes in swift counter-attack techniques.

Above Moving swiftly to step to the side of an attacker and subtly control his arm. This would be especially useful if he was armed with a knife. He is now vulnerable to attack from behind.

will deplete your kidney energy (your core energy). Adrenalin can also be addictive, leading you to seek out stressful situations or stimuli, despite the negative effects on your physical and mental health.

During t'ai chi martial training you learn to relax the adrenal response, under the pressure of your training partner's attacks, by using techniques such as releasing emotional tension through the breath, and relaxing nervous system tension as it occurs. In this respect, t'ai chi sparring is an extension of the work you do in push hands practice. The result is that you are able to remain free of the fight or flight stress response even in "stressful" situations. Not only does this benefit your health, but it makes it more likely that your reaction to everyday situations will be calm and appropriate, and that you will not respond in ways that you might later regret.

FIGHTING AND MEDITATION

T'ai chi martial training brings up latent, deeply hidden emotional tensions, often in the form of fear or anger. Once recognized, they can be released during meditation practice. Sometimes, a t'ai chi martial practitioner who is also a meditation practitioner will stop sparring or training when they experience these emotions, and they will then practise a sitting meditation for a while in order to release the unwanted emotional tensions, before going back to martial sparring or training.

After you have practised meditation for some time, you will find that because you have released many of your more surface-level tensions, what remains is deeper, more hidden and harder to identify. Martial training can help you find where these deep tensions lie. Ultimately, martial training confronts you with your own ego, and is in many ways a short cut, albeit a challenging one, to accessing this level of meditation practice.

SELF-DEFENCE

Although your main motivation for martial practice may be its self-development aspects, there is the added benefit of gaining self-defence skills. This is particularly suitable for women, as t'ai chi does not rely on muscular strength, an area where many women are at a disadvantage. The development of internal power can give a woman the ability to defend herself against a physically stronger attacker. There have been many proficient female t'ai chi fighters throughout China's history. T'ai chi martial training gives many women a very welcome sense of self-confidence in relation to their physical safety. Additionally, it can help anybody respond appropriately in physically challenging situations – for instance, you may simply want to restrain or control a person who does not have truly malicious intent. You will have the presence of mind, ability and confidence to use much less force than you would need to if someone was trying to cause you serious harm.

The T'ai Chi Lifestyle

T'ai chi is very much about achieving balance on every level of your being – physical, energetic, mental and emotional. This philosophy of balance can be extended to encompass all aspects of your life, from the moment you wake in the morning to the time you go to sleep. Since t'ai chi is more than just a specific practice that you do for a set time every day it can become an invaluable guide to leading a healthier, more balanced life.

The principles that you learn and practise in your t'ai chi form and push hands sessions can be applied generally, sometimes with dramatically positive results. If you re-examine your lifestyle, behaviour and habits in the light of your t'ai chi knowledge, you can see where imbalances exist, and their consequences. This can cause you to re-evaluate certain long-term habits and attitudes, and bring about positive change in those areas of your life that you may have found less than satisfactory. Just as in your t'ai chi form practice you seek to balance the releasing and gathering of energy, so there should be a balance between these two in other areas of your life. Naturally, change will occur only if you want it to – your intention is everything.

WORK AND MONEY

One of the major areas of your life that can become a cause of imbalance, and even ill health, is that of work. Most people need to work to earn a living, and in fact work can give you a sense of purpose and direction, self-worth and achievement. Work can be seen as a yang activity, just as resting can be seen as yin. It is appropriate to have a balance of the two: all rest and no work can result in stagnation of your energy. Work involves an expenditure of energy, whether physical or mental, and resting involves the replenishing of energy. Work is probably the greatest expenditure of energy in your life, and your approach to it is a major factor in leading a balanced life.

If you overwork, you expend more energy than you replenish (this could be said to be the definition of overwork) and, just like spending more than you earn, you end up in debt. In this case the debt is energetic, and in order to settle it you have to tap into your deepest reserves – your pre-birth jing. This is like selling the family silver: once it is gone, it is gone for ever. The longer you sustain this level of overwork, the greater the problem. In Taoist terms, the only valid reason for depleting your essence is if your life immediately depends on it: for instance if you are stuck on a mountain freezing in a blizzard. If you are tapping into this essence for any other reason, you have to re-evaluate those aspects of your life that are causing you to do so.

Above Work is an essential part of life, but it must be balanced with the need for rest and recreation if we are to truly enjoy our lives. Material desires can often distort this balance.

Some people overwork because they have genuinely difficult lives – they may be struggling to support a large family – but many others overwork for less critical reasons, such as excessive ambition or in order to sustain a luxurious lifestyle. This is not to say there is anything wrong with wanting physical comforts and luxuries, but from a Taoist perspective to pursue these at the expense of health and mental/emotional well-being is an unbalanced attitude. Any attitudes or habits that seriously threaten your health should be carefully examined. It is essential to find a balance between the desire for money and a successful career, and the maintenance of mental and physical health. Where this balance lies varies from person to person, but the principle can be very useful in finding it for yourself.

CONFLICT

Mental and emotional stress does not come only from overwork. Your home life might be a major cause of stress, resulting from bringing up children, dealing with partners and lovers, friends, parents and relations. Often these issues

Left The principles of push hands embody the core philosophy of t'ai chi and can teach you to lead a more harmonious emotional life both at work and at home.

can be less clear-cut and harder to resolve than work issues. From a t'ai chi perspective, you need to work with your current circumstances to find balance: it is an evolution that is needed, and not a revolution.

In order to deal with difficult situations involving those close to you, you can apply the t'ai chi principles of yielding and appropriateness. This means relaxing the ego-driven need always to be right, and giving way on issues where conflict would not be helpful. Just doing this will start to defuse the tension between yourself and others, and make it much more likely that both sides can find common ground. This does not mean being weak or a pushover, any more than yielding in push hands implies weakness, but it is all about appropriateness of response. When it is appropriate to stand your ground and "fight", then from an energetic standpoint you are working with the flow of the Tao and are much more likely to succeed. And because you have not overreacted to every challenge, your "opponent" knows that you are now serious about achieving your aim. This naturally engenders respect. This principle can be applied in all your dealings with other people, whenever there is the potential for some form of conflict.

DIET

An individual's diet is a major factor in achieving balanced health. Western medicine fully acknowledges this, but the Chinese medical view of diet is incredibly sophisticated, as it takes into account both the physical and the energetic properties of all foods, as well as the timing of meals and cooking methods. A full examination of Chinese dietary theory would require an entire book, but by applying some of the key principles you can help yourself regain and maintain good health.

Foods are categorized according to whether they are predominantly yin (cooling) or yang (heating); nourishing of blood or chi; causing "damp" and "phlegm" to form or disperse within the body; and which internal organs they most affect. An optimum diet is one that contains a balance of yin and yang foods, does not promote dampness or phlegm, and nourishes blood and chi. Steaming is a yin method of cooking. Boiling is more yang, grilling or baking more so, and frying is extremely yang, so you can affect the yin/yang balance of a food by the method of cooking.

While it is best to consult a Chinese medical practitioner to find out exactly what foods would most benefit you individually, there are a few general rules about what to avoid. Foods that promote phlegm, such as dairy foods, are best avoided, as well as foods that encourage dampness to form in the body, such as yeast (and therefore beer), heavily fried food of any sort, and wheat. This is especially relevant if you live in a damp climate. Fried food is also very "hot", however, and this can cause problems of internal heat if you live in a warm climate. In general, very spicy food should be avoided for the same reason. Heavily processed food should not be eaten as, apart from the chemical additives, the living chi energy of the food is diminished by the processing. Microwave cooking of food also disrupts chi.

Overall, a diet very much like that recommended by Western nutritionists is fine, with the exception of cold raw foods such as salads, or excessive amounts of raw fruit, which are seen as harmful to the transformative function of the spleen. Vegetables should be lightly cooked or steamed.

Below Food is truly your foundation, physically and energetically. A nutritious and balanced diet is a solid foundation for a long, healthy and happy life.

The Chinese often put ginger with steamed vegetables, as its gently warming yang nature balances the cooling, yin nature of the vegetables. Chicken is considered a well-balanced foodstuff, nourishing chi and being fairly neutral in terms of yin/yang. Chicken also nourishes the spleen, which is key to absorbing the energy of food. Beef is considered yang, and can generate internal heat in the body. This may be appropriate for a person who is internally "cold", but not for a person who is "hot". It is a good blood tonic, and this may be useful for many women who tend towards "blood deficiency" due to their menstrual cycle. If you are a vegetarian, blood-nourishing vegetables such as beetroot and spinach should be included in your diet.

The timing and regularity of meals is also seen as important. The ideal is a main meal some time between 7am and 11am, the period when the stomach and spleen are most energetically active. Following that, smaller meals can be eaten during the day, but only light snacks in the evening. This is because stomach and spleen energy is at its lowest ebb at night, and a large meal will not be properly transformed; the spleen can become "bogged down" and unhealthy weight gain may follow. A large meal late at night can also result in disturbed sleep. This accords with the principle that you should eat "breakfast like a king, lunch like a rich man, and dinner like a pauper". Achieving a balanced diet can help you resolve even deep-seated health issues, especially when combined with Chinese medical treatment and personal chi practice.

Below The early part of the night is particularly important for replenishing your yin energy.

SLEEP

Proper amounts of restful sleep are essential to your well-being; what constitutes restful sleep and how to achieve it is not always so obvious.

Just as eating meals late at night can disturb your sleep, drinking alcohol at night can have the same effect – in Chinese medical terms, it can disturb the shen, or spirit. Mental tension is an obvious factor in insomnia: from a Taoist perspective it is the result of (and causes) energy becoming stuck in the brain, over-energizing it and causing repetitive and excessive thinking, with the mind "whirling around". This is a condition that is particularly prevalent in those who spend the day involved in mental work. The brain becomes so energized that mental activity refuses to subside when it is time to sleep. In chi gung terms, this is the result of energy not dropping from the brain to the lower tantien and feet. A simple but highly effective remedy is to roll your ankles at least 50 times in each direction – this brings your chi down to your feet and allows your brain to de-energize and calm down. Standing practice and gentle t'ai chi practice before bedtime also help enormously.

It is important to allow a winding-down period before going to bed. Try to avoid any mental work late at night, including the taking in of new information such as reading and watching the television immediately before bedtime. Listening to music, massage (especially of the feet), a warm bath – all these can allow your mind to settle prior to sleep, helping to counter insomnia. It is also very important, in terms of the natural energetic cycle of day and night, that you go to sleep before midnight if possible.

TAOIST SEXUAL PRACTICE

The Taoists have a matter-of fact attitude to sex: they see it simply as one of life's natural activities and do not impose any moral judgements upon it. Some people are more interested in sexual activity, some less – this is a personal preference. Where the Taoists do distinguish sex from other activities is in relation to energy: it is probably the most energetically "alive" experience that most people have. As a result of this it is seen as a very powerful practice, where those taking part can work with the strong energies involved to heal, release blockages and tensions in any of their energetic bodies, develop and strengthen their energy and, of course, enhance sexual pleasure. A range of techniques can help to achieve this; some are concerned more with the physical and chi levels, and some with meditation.

All the Taoist nei gung practices that underlie t'ai chi are applicable during sex. Sexual chi gung is very powerful and best approached gently. As with anything else, excessive

Above Every object has its own energetic quality and can influence your energy. Colours can strongly influence your mental and emotional state.

Right Filling your living space with light and life will have a corresponding effect on you.

activity leads to imbalance. What constitutes excess depends on the individual; as a general rule if you feel energetically "drained" rather than just relaxed after sex, it may mean activity has been excessive, or your approach to it has not been sufficiently relaxed.

EXERCISE

The best exercise you can engage in is t'ai chi or another Taoist internal art, but in fact, any gentle exercise is beneficial, helping to eliminate stagnation of chi and blood, and keeping your body flexible. Over-strenuous exercise can be energetically draining, and damaging to your body. If you do other exercise, especially weights, do it with relaxation. T'ai chi is ideal because it is not only a gentle physical exercise, but also works directly with your energy and mind. The body abhors inactivity – energy and blood stagnate, and the joints and tissues stiffen and contract. Constant gentle movement is ideal, and is one of the keys to longevity.

DRUGS

Just as the Taoists do not form moral judgements about sex, they also do not ascribe any moral attributes to drugs, but consider them to be substances that have a strong effect on your energy and mind. So-called recreational drugs are not considered "evil", they just do not bring the user any benefits, and cause greater or lesser degrees of harm to the body, energy and mind. Because drugs do not promote balance, they are not considered useful, and are best avoided. Caffeine and alcohol are seen to be less harmful, and acceptable as part of a balanced lifestyle. Nicotine is not considered a useful substance.

OTHER FACTORS

Many aspects of your life, such as whether you maintain clean and tidy living spaces, what sort of clothes you wear, and your general mental attitudes towards yourself and others, can have a profound effect on your health and well-being. A home full of clutter and mess invokes scattered and disordered energy, and this will have a corresponding effect on you, in terms of both your internal world and the things that happen to you. Similarly, a dirty and neglected home will attract negative energies that will promote illness, both physical and emotional. Conversely, a clean, ordered home, full of life, will encourage a positive energy response, as well as simply making you feel more cheerful.

Wearing drab, worn or dirty clothes can also have a negative effect in terms of the energies you attract. This does not mean dressing like a harlequin – simply introducing some life and colour into your wardrobe. It can also be beneficial to consider which colours have a positive effect on your energy and mind, and dress accordingly. Experiment to find out for yourself how different colours can affect you.

How you behave towards other people determines not only how other people treat you but invokes a subtle energetic response from the universe as a whole. The phrase "Do unto others as you would have done to yourself" sums this up.

You should try to make every aspect of your life reflect the way you would like to live – bringing a sense of balance, liveliness and joy into all aspects of your day-to-day life. This means nurturing and respecting yourself, being aware of your inherent self-worth and celebrating it every day.

The Short Form

The short form is shown here from start to finish, it is best used as a quick reference once you have become familar with the positions.

Commencement

Raise Hands

Play the Lute

Grasp Sparrow's Tail

Single Whip

Diagonal Flying / Hold Ball

Yin Release / Shoulder Stroke

Elbow Strike / Wrist Strike

White Crane Spreads its Wings

Brush Knee and Twist Step

Needle at Sea Bottom

Fan Through the Back

Turn & Chop with Back of Fist

Parry and Punch

Close up & Step Forward

Tiger & Leopard Spring to Mountain   Closing

AIKIDO

DEVELOPMENT OF MIND & BODY THROUGH GRACEFUL AND POWERFUL DEFENCE TECHNIQUES

An Introduction to Aikido

Aikido is a Japanese martial practice that operates on many different levels. At a basic level it teaches that you can overcome an aggressive attack by harmonizing with it, as opposed to meeting force with force. The defensive movements are designed to blend with an attack, lead it until neutralized and then apply a controlling technique. You learn to apply pinning, locking and throwing movements and combinations of these against any attack.

The strategies of defence are drawn from several of the classical martial arts of Japan, such as jujutsu (grappling), kenjutsu (swordsmanship) and yari jutsu (spearfighting) and, when coupled with the aikido founder Morihei Ueshiba's concept of "aiki" (way of harmonizing the spirit), the techniques crystallize into powerful linear, circular and spiral movements that are beautiful to watch, but devastatingly effective when applied.

People usually start aikido in order to learn something of self-defence, improve their physical fitness or learn a little about Japanese culture. People also tend to be drawn to aikido because of its spiritual dimension – among other benefits, it is possible to apply the philosophy of the practice to bring about a more fulfilling quality of life. At its highest level, aikido becomes a vehicle for physical and spiritual integration to a degree that individuals can clearly see themselves as being at one with humanity, nature and the universe itself. When you go to a dojo, or training hall,

Below Chiba Sensei in action at the United Kingdom Aikikai Summer School at Birmingham University, August 1988.

for the first time you embark on a journey that will take you through all the standards of, and approaches to aikido, as long as the individual commitment is there.

BENEFITS OF AIKIDO TRAINING

When looking for ways to become physically fit, most people think in terms of their local gym or leisure centre. Some people consider swimming, dancing or step-aerobics classes; some recognize that they need to build up their strength, so enrol at a local weight-training facility; others may need more stamina, and so join a running club. As a means to an end, there is nothing wrong with any of these disciplines. And while they will yield the desired results if approached with commitment, some people may feel that they need a sense of direction, something to occupy their mind as well as their body.

Unfortunately, training in aikido, or in any of the martial arts for that matter, does not immediately spring to most people's mind when considering a physical-training regime. Many have a misguided impression that the martial arts are only for those who want to dominate or control others or to inflict pain. In fact, quite the opposite is true. As you learn the many throws, pins and projections, it becomes evident that their execution actually promotes health. There is no fighting with your partner, no trying to beat him or her; there is only a harmonious blending of movement that results in a feeling of exhilaration and self-control. If the instructor has taught the concept of ukemi properly – this is the art of learning to fall safely – when you leave the dojo you should feel as if you have had your whole body gently stretched and massaged.

A NON-VIOLENT PRACTICE

Most people who stay with aikido are looking to perfect the art and have no desire to hurt anybody. What is unique to aikido is the attitude with which you train. There is no competition in the traditional form of the art, and the feeling during practice is one of mutual co-operation for the successful completion of a particular technique. The partner who applies the technique is called tori, while the one who

Above Tamura Sensei, 8th Dan Shihan, Aikikai Hombu representative to France, teaching at a seminar in Bristol, England.

Above Yamada Shihan, 8th Dan, Aikikai delegate to the USA, demonstrating sankyo at the National Sports Centre, Wales, 1985.

receives it, uke. Uke's intention is to maintain as close a contact as is possible with tori so that the sensitivity to neutralize the effect of the movement can be developed, and in this way the situation "recovered". Training like this means that the muscles are stretched and joints are put through a wide range of natural flexion – almost like a massage. Couple this with learning how to fall safely, so that you develop the confidence to respond to the throwing techniques, and you have a complete exercise system in which strength, stamina and suppleness are simultaneously developed. All this and self-defence, too! This attitude, and the relationship between the two practitioners, means that there is no conflict, no dualism and, therefore, no violence, making it perfectly safe for men, women and children to practise.

It is true that martial arts from all over the world were devised to kill or to inflict injury on the battlefield. Many of these arts are extant today, even though they are no longer of any practical use, and are practised largely for reasons of cultural heritage. What tended to happen with many of the Japanese martial arts was that they underwent a socio-political change and evolved from "arts" concerned with the destruction of life into "ways" of integrating the physical and spiritual beings of practitioners to make them into better people. Thus, the art of Japanese archery kyujutsu, or "art of the bow", became kyudo, the "way of the bow". Similarly, kenjutsu, "art of the sword", became kendo, the "way of the sword", and jujutsu, "art of gentleness", became judo, the "way of gentleness". The techniques of aikijujutsu, "art of aiki", became aikido, the "way of aiki".

This aikido guide is predominantly aimed at individuals with an interest in aikido who would like to make that crucial first step of joining a dojo. It gives a comprehensive overview of the subject, with individual chapters designed to promote interest without being overly involved and off-putting. Most of what constitutes traditional aikido is touched on in a way that should engender enthusiasm, while the exercises and movements are shown in a clear, simple step-by-step format.

It should be pointed out that the techniques shown in the following chapters are just a few of the hundreds that constitute aikido, and they have been picked to give an indication of the variety available in training. Virtually every defence technique has an omote (a motion to the partner's front), and a ura (a motion to the partner's back) variation, but it is beyond the scope of this book to be fully comprehensive. For clarity of understanding, some of the techniques also contain inset pictures to show the finer, sometimes unseen, aspects of the techniques.

After referring to this section it is hoped that readers will understand the extraordinary scope of aikido. We live in a world preoccupied with war, strife and technology, where the all-pervading idea reigns that to win you need to be the biggest or the fastest or the strongest. This leaves a welcome place for aikido with its philosophy of non-violence and emphasis on the spiritual. This guide will have served its purpose if it inspires just one single reader to search out a qualified teacher and begin training – for that is the only way to grasp the meaning of this fascinating art.

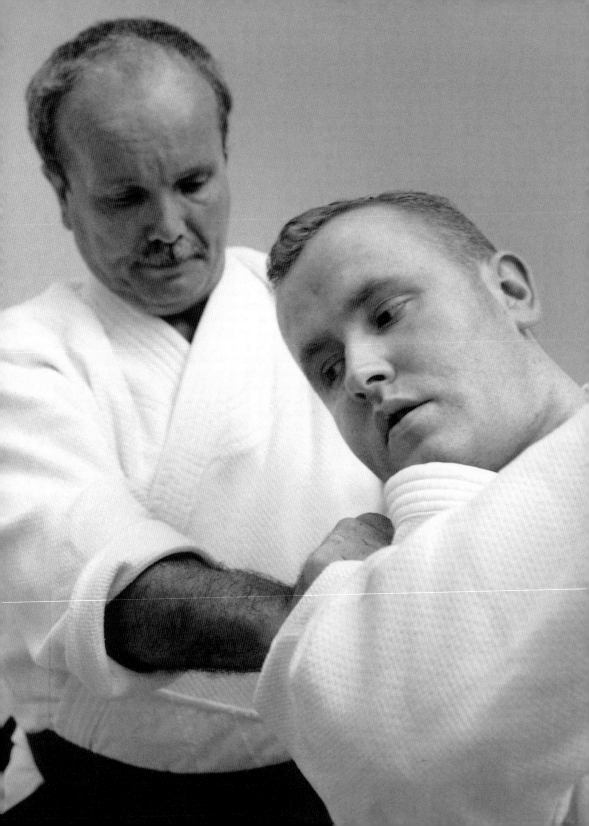

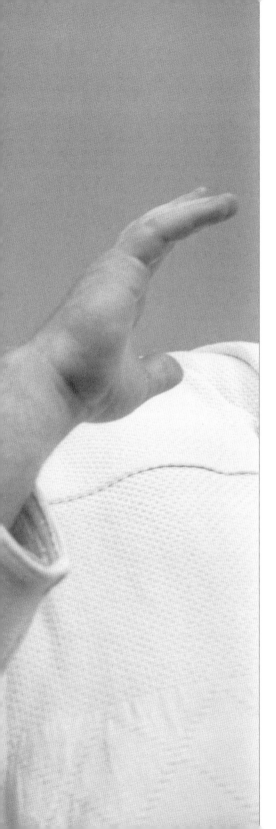

Aikido
in context

This chapter looks at the contextual framework of aikido. The historical roots of aikido are traced through the technique of Daito ryu-aiki ju-jutsu, which has a lineage stretching back to the 9th century. Morihei Ueshiba's role in developing the philosophical, spiritual and physical concept of aikido is covered here in detail, including the significant relationships that he had with other key figures and the strong aikido heritage that he left on his death. The traditions and etiquette integral to aikido and the way they are practised in modern dojos are also explained, along with the formal postures of the art. A section on principles and philosophy looks at centred power and the importance of mental focus and, to finish, an outline of required clothing and equipment.

Historical Background

While the name aikido came into use only in the 1940s, its origins can be traced back to the Minamoto family in 11th-century feudal Japan. Passed through the generations of this family, the principles of the art were the heritage of 19th-century Daito ryu master Takeda Sokaku. Initially a weapons art, under Sokaku Daito ryu transformed to focus more on the grappling arts. These influences all leave their legacy in the practice of modern aikido.

The roots of aikido began about a thousand years ago with Prince Teijun, the sixth son of Japan's fifty-sixth ruler, Emperor Seiwa. He is believed to have passed on secret information concerning the principles of aiki to successive generations of the Minamoto family. Known as Seiwa Genji, the descendants of the clan kept this knowledge as their personal family art throughout the centuries. In 11th-century Japan there were two main samurai families, or clans – the Heishi and the Genji. The leader of the Genji clan was Minamoto No Yoriyoshi, who was a very powerful force on the eastern side of the country. He had two sons, one of whom was called Yoshimitsu – it is this man who is widely accepted as the founder of the tradition that

Below Minamoto No Yoshimitsu (1045–1127), son of the leader of the Genji clan, is thought to be the founder of Daito ryu-aiki ju-jutsu.

ultimately became Daito ryu-aiki ju-jutsu. Yoshimitsu is reputed to have cut up the bodies of dead soldiers in an attempt to understand the bone structure of human anatomy to enable him to create more effective jujutsu techniques. Legend also has it that he once watched a spider making a web, observing that the spider could catch prey that was bigger than itself. This led him to the notion that size and strength were not so important, and that with guile it could be possible for a small person to defeat a much larger opponent.

Yoshimitsu meditated over these concepts for years and realized that the principles that made his techniques work were based on movements that occur in nature – he had discovered aiki, and in so doing had laid the foundation of Daito ryu, a tradition that still exists today. Years later, Yoshimitsu moved to a place called Kai in the Yamanashi Prefecture and took on the family name of Takeda, creating a dynasty that took control of the area until the late 16th century. The martial art started by Yoshimitsu underwent several changes and was passed on to the Aizu clan by Takeda Kunitsugu.

The Aizu was one of several warring clans and they adopted Daito ryu as their secret art, permitting only high-ranking samurai, courtiers and people of wealth to study it. The system incorporated swordsmanship, spearfighting and certain unarmed combat forms based on Aiki in-yo-ho, the doctrine of "harmony of the spirit", based on the complementary but antagonistic opposites yin and yang. The most secret of these arts was called the Oshikiuchi, taught only inside the castle to the elite warriors. The training at this time came under the authority of the head of the Shirakawa Castle and former chief councillor of the Aizu domain, Saigo Tanomo.

In 1867–8 there was civil war in Japan between the Tokugawa shogunate, or military government, and the forces of Emperor Meiji. The Aizu clan had stood with the Tokugawas, and were consequently defeated. This confrontation brought to an end more than 700 years of clan feuding and heralded the start of a ten-year period of change, the end of which saw the abolition of the wearing of two swords and, thereby, the end of samurai doctrine as it was. Many martial ryu, or schools, disbanded as there was no longer any use for the swordsmanship techniques that had been part of daily life for

Above Four men in traditional samurai costume.

centuries. Some staunch traditionalists went underground and trained in their arts to keep the traditions alive. It was from this environment that one person was to emerge who was to have a profound influence over the creation of aikido – Takeda Sokaku.

TAKEDA SOKAKU

It was Takeda Sokaku who resystemized Daito ryu and is credited as its founder. Born in Aizu Bangemachi in Fukushima Prefecture in 1859, the son of Takeda Sokichi, as a boy he learned kenjutsu (art of the sword), bojutsu (art of the staff) and other jujutsu forms. He was also skilled in sumo, and apparently there is to this day a sumo ring in the house where he was born as a testament to the family connection with that art form.

After the Meiji Restoration there was an effort to suppress the practice of martial arts in an attempt to curb any future civil insurrection. Sokaku, however, coming from a staunchly traditional samurai family, continued to practise ono-ha-itto kenjutsu under Shibuya Toma, one of the old Aizu warriors. Later, Sokaku began travelling the country searching out leading martial artists and learning all he could from them. In 1873 he became an uchideshi, or live-in student, of Sakakibara Kenkichi of the Jikishinkage ryu of kenjutsu. After the death of his older brother, Sokatsu, in 1875, Sokaku was expected to take on the role of leader in the family tradition of Shin Shoku – a Shinto tradition in which he would be expected to prepare and participate in shrine ceremonies. Sokaku, however, was not a good student – so bad was he, in fact, that he was said to be totally illiterate. Not long after this time, Sokaku resolved to forego his religious duties with the family and devote his life instead to the pursuit of martial arts.

Above Japanese print of a samurai warrior on the battlefield.

Above Takeda Shrine at present-day Yamanashi Prefecture.

While there are no written records, it is said that this was the period when Sokaku was first introduced to Aiki jujutsu by Hoshina Chikanori, otherwise known as Saigo Tanomo, head of the Shirakawa Castle, who had been taught the art by Sokaku's grandfather, Soemon. Others have said that it was actually Sokichi, Sokaku's father, who taught him the arts. What is certain is that Saigo's philosophy had a profound effect on Sokaku and made him think deeply about the value of swordsmanship in a society that was beginning to evolve without practical need of it. Saigo paradoxically hired Sokaku to be his bodyguard and also to transmit to him the secret arts of the Aizu clan, known as Oshikiuchi, as he recognized within him great potential as a martial artist. Barely 1.50m (5ft) tall, Sokaku devoted his entire life to bujutsu and acquired teaching licences in okuden, or secret teachings of the ono-ha-itto-ryu (swordsmanship) and sojutsu (spearfighting) in 1877, along with Aiki jujutsu. Sokaku spent a lot of his life travelling Japan taking on anyone wishing to test his fighting skills – he was never defeated. His legendary skills gave rise to many stories – such as one where Sokaku was on a train and he became involved in a disagreement with an American teacher, Charles Parry, over the seating arrangements. Parry was a large man, but even so when tempers flared Sokaku easily restrained him using Daito ryu techniques. Impressed with this Japanese man's ability, Parry informed his superiors and word filtered through to American President Theodore Roosevelt, who requested a demonstration. A teacher was dispatched, who, after the demonstration, established a teaching regime in America. Charles Parry himself became a student and was given a teaching licence by Sokaku himself.

Left Saigo Tanomo, Sokaku's mentor who made him consider the role of weapons in a society that had rejected them.

It is clear that Sokaku was the consummate martial artist, a man always on his guard and totally alert. Even on social occasions, he assumed the hanmi (back triangle stance), as can be seen in some photographs taken of him. Based mainly in Hokkaido, in the most northern part of Japan, Sokaku only occasionally visited Tokyo and the West, continuing his own austere training and teaching well into his eighties. He died in 1943 after suffering a stroke. Although Sokaku could hardly write his own name, he insisted that all students he taught record their names in his ledger (called the Eimei Roku) and considering that he is said to have taught more than 30,000 students in his lifetime, including Morihei Ueshiba, founder of aikido, this is an impressive ledger.

Below Daito-ryu master Takeda Sokaku (1859–1943), whose practice influenced the development of aikido more than any other martial art.

Aikido founder, Morihei Ueshiba, was drawn as a young man to religious mysticism and the martial arts. He later met Takeda Sokaku, master of Daito ryu aiki jujutsu, and then Onisaburo Deguchi, leader of the Omoto-kyo movement, both of whom had a profound influence on him. Ueshiba developed his accumulated knowledge into a new art that combined his philosophical principles, immense spiritual powers and physical technique.

Aikido's founder, Morihei Ueshiba, was born on 14 December 1883 in Tanabe, present-day Wakayama Prefecture. According to his son, Kisshomaru, when Ueshiba was a small boy he saw his father being beaten up by thugs in the pay of a local politician. This experience had a profound effect on the young Ueshiba, who vowed that one day he would become strong enough to take his revenge. At the age of seven, Ueshiba's father sent him to school to study the classical Chinese texts, but he became bored with this style of education, choosing instead to engross himself in esoteric Shingon Buddhist rites and various meditative practices. Despite an interest in science and mathematics, Ueshiba felt himself increasingly drawn to religious mysticism and the martial arts. He devoted himself to hard, physical training and developed an interest in sumo to improve both his physique and his spirituality. Ueshiba started his formal education at 13 but left just a year later. He returned after a while and enrolled at the Yoshida abacus institute and, upon graduating, took a position in the Tanabe tax office, where his duties involved the assessment of land values. Much to the annoyance of his father, Ueshiba resigned his position over a local dispute about fishing legislation, and went to Tokyo to make a living in business. With his father's financial backing he established a stationery business in 1901, and it was around this time that Ueshiba began his martial arts training in jujutsu and kenjutsu. The following year, however, he contracted the vitamin-deficiency disease beriberi. As a result of this, he closed the store and moved back to Tanabe, where, on his recovery, he rekindled his relationship with Hatsu Itogawa, a childhood girlfriend, whom he subsequently married.

MILITARY SERVICE AND HOKKAIDO

In 1903 Ueshiba joined the army, where he was nicknamed "king of soldiers" due to his prowess with the bayonet, and for his dogged determination and honest character. The Russo-Japanese war broke out in 1904 and Ueshiba was sent to the front, returning as a sergeant having been promoted for bravery in the field. It was said of him that if others would do twice as much work, then he would do four times – such

Above Morihei Ueshiba (1883–1969), the founder of aikido, shown in his mid-fifties when he was considered at his prime.

was his character. During this time Ueshiba received instruction in yagyu ryu jujutsu. In 1907 his discharge from the army came through and he returned to Tanabe to take up farming, becoming involved with local politics as leader of the young men's association. At this time, his father had a dojo built on the family property and engaged the services of a high-ranking judo expert who was visiting the area to teach kodokan judo to Ueshiba. In 1910 Ueshiba embarked on an ambitious government plan to settle land in Hokkaido, an island in the north, and asked for volunteers from the young men's association. In 1912 he led a group of 54 families to start a new life in the wilderness of Shirataki. The settlers endured severe hardships during the next few years due to the hard climate and poor land, but gradually – due in no small part to Ueshiba's efforts – they began to reap rewards. And a timber business they had set up also began to return a profit.

Above A picture of Morihei Ueshiba and Onisaburo Deguchi. It was Deguchi's teachings that began to steer Ueshiba away from the pragmatic approach of Takeda towards a more spiritual dimension.

MEETING WITH TAKEDA SOKAKU

While in Hokkaido in 1915, during a stay at an inn at Engaru, Ueshiba was introduced to a man who was to change his life – Takeda Sokaku , master of Daito ryu aiki jujutsu. Immediately impressed with Sokaku, Ueshiba asked if he could become his student. He stayed at the inn for the next month and received his first teaching certificate of proficiency in Daito ryu. On his return to Shirataki, Ueshiba built a house and a dojo for Sokaku on his property and took private lessons from him every morning for many years. Historical evidence suggests that although there was a great deal of respect between them, there was no affection, and this was probably due to their differences in outlook. Sokaku was a pragmatic martial artist who had been something of a street fighter all his life, had a reputation for arrogance and was ill-tempered. Ueshiba was a deeply spiritual person whose view of martial arts was becoming channelled towards the physical and spiritual integration of the individual. Sokaku expected total loyalty and obedience from his uchideshi, or live-in students, in return for his teachings. Ueshiba gave his total dedication to Sokaku during the next four years.

MEETING WITH ONISABURO DEGUCHI

In 1919 Ueshiba received a telegram informing him that his father was gravely ill. He immediately left Hokkaido, leaving all his property to Sokaku. However, instead of travelling straight

to his father's bedside in Tanabe, he stopped at Ayabe to pray for his father's recovery at the headquarters of Omoto-kyo, a new religion in Japan. Here, Ueshiba met another individual who was to influence him greatly and was to have an enormous input in the development of aikido – Onisaburo Deguchi, the charismatic leader of the Omoto-kyo movement.

The son of a student of Kotodama – the belief that the sound of certain words can result in physical manifestations – Onisaburo displayed a genius for classical study at a very early age and had a seemingly insatiable thirst for mysticism. In his lifetime he is said to have authored a massive amount of work on the subject, including one piece that numbered 81 volumes. Known as the *Reito Monogatari*, or "Tales of the Spiritual World", it concerns itself with Onisaburo's travels in the cosmos interpreting the past, present and future in terms of the Kotodama, as well as giving advice on a wide variety of mundane things, such as personal hygiene: "Men do not have an absolute right to enter the bath before women; it depends who is the dirtier." Such esoteric concepts were apparently gleaned from conversations he had with various gods and Buddhas, who had divulged their secrets to him.

Onisaburo married into the family of another mystic, a man who had developed the Omoto-kyo religious movement, and adopted their family name of Deguchi. He took over the movement and fashioned it to suit himself. He was said to have been an extremely flamboyant character, a man with a penchant for fine clothing and the company of beautiful women. With a mane of hair capped by a shaman's hat, he must have cut a dashing figure – a man who was both charismatic and irresistible as a leader.

Along with the development of the chinkon-kishin meditation techniques, Onisaburo was interested in music, composing ballads, folk songs and even dance music, including waltzes and tangos. He was also involved with calligraphy, painting and sculpture and, for a time, dabbled in directing movies. With such a wide range of interests and his charismatic qualities as a spiritual leader, it was hardly surprising that Onisaburo attracted more than just ordinary country people to his teachings. Government officials, intellectuals, aristocrats and high-ranking military men all became fascinated with this new religion, with the result that the sect expanded rapidly in popularity and became increasingly wealthy. During the period between 1919 and 1921 the cult had attracted several million devotees.

UESHIBA AND OMOTO-KYO

It is said that while Ueshiba was in meditation at the Omoto-kyo temple he had a vision of his sick father, but was advised by Onisaburo that his father was happy and that he should let him go. So under the spell of Onisaburo was Ueshiba that he stayed for a while talking with the guru and taking part in chinkon-kishin meditation sessions. When he returned to Tanabe he found that his father had indeed passed away peacefully. After a brief but intense period of misogi, or purification, involving Ueshiba going into the mountains every night and training himself like a demon swinging his bokken, or wooden sword, Ueshiba decided to move to Ayabe to avail himself more of Onisaburo's Omoto-kyo teachings. He remained there for the next eight years. Taking Onisaburo's advice, Ueshiba built a small dojo on his property to continue his martial training and to train other Omoto-kyo followers.

Early in 1921 the Omoto sect came under scrutiny by the local government, which, for political reasons, attempted to close the sect down. Onisaburo, along with several other members, was arrested. Ueshiba immersed himself in his martial training and farming, and by so doing discovered a profound connection between agriculture and the martial arts, a connection that was to remain with him for the rest of his life. After the abolition of feudalism, dating from the late 19th century, many samurai turned to farming. In this they found a spiritual connection and strong affinity between budo (literally, the "way of the combat") and working the land, as the two have traits in common, such as living honourably. Onisaburo was released on bail within two years and Ueshiba helped him rekindle interest in the Omoto-kyo religion.

SPIRITUAL ENLIGHTENMENT

Around this time Ueshiba began to move away from the pragmatic and austere qualities of the traditional martial arts and more towards spiritual ideals in his search for something to unite mind, body and spirit, as he saw this as the way forward. In 1922, after intensive study of Kotodama, he renamed his art "Ueshiba ryu aiki bujutsu". In 1924 Ueshiba and Onisaburo left for Manchuria and Mongolia to establish a "new world order" based on the ideals of Omoto-kyo. Known as The Great Mongolian Adventure, this brief period had a marked effect on Ueshiba's spiritual development. He became embroiled in several desperate situations – he was attacked with swords, shot at, arrested by a Chinese warlord and then chained and threatened with execution. He escaped death only as a result of the very fortunate intervention of the Japanese consulate. On his return to Japan Ueshiba resumed his training and farming and also began training in the art of the spear. It is said that his experiences in Mongolia had given him almost magical powers of perception, with stories of him being able to dodge a bullet. This type of intuition was to show itself many times in his later life.

Above This fine picture of Ueshiba in his later years has a serene quality, depicting a man totally at peace with himself.

Above Ueshiba in his eighties, effortlessly dispatching a young uke during a demonstration.

In 1925 Ueshiba received a visit from a naval officer, a man who was also an expert in kendo, or Japanese swordsmanship. The two of them apparently had some sort of disagreement, tempers flared and a physical encounter then ensued. The officer attacked with his bokken (wooden sword), but was unable to land a blow, as Ueshiba was able to perceive the direction of every cut before it actually happened. In the end, the officer was forced to sit down exhausted and Ueshiba went off to wash himself in a nearby well.

What happened next is an extremely well-documented experience of enlightenment for the aikido founder. While washing at the well he felt that he was bathing in a golden light pouring down from heaven. It was a revelation and he felt reborn, as if suddenly his body and spirit had been turned into gold. At the same time, the unity of the universe and the self became clear to him and he came to understand the philosophical principles on which aikido is based. It was at this time that Ueshiba changed the name of his art from aiki bujutsu to aiki budo, as aikido had now begun to transcend the boundaries of mere martial art, becoming more of a spiritual discipline. The prefix *jutsu* refers to physical technique or art, whereas *do* (pronounced *doh*) means "way" (in terms of a spiritual path).

The next few years saw Ueshiba teaching his new art to high-ranking personnel from the army and navy and the world of politics – he even spent a brief period teaching at the crown prince's palace in Tokyo. After deciding that his future lay in the teaching of martial arts, he obtained a property in Ushigome, in Wakamatsu-cho, in 1930 where he embarked on building a dojo. This was a massive undertaking, and during the construction phase he built a temporary dojo, and this is where Ueshiba received a visit from judo founder, Dr Jigoro Kano. Kano was so impressed with aikido, apparently declaring it as "my ideal budo", that he promptly dispatched two of his high-ranking students to train with Ueshiba. One of these was a man called Minoru Mochizuki, who remained with the founder and became one of only a handful of people ever to be awarded the rank of 10th Dan in aikido.

THE KOBUKAN DOJO

In 1931 the mighty Kobukan was built in Tokyo, on exactly the same site as the present-day facility. Consisting of an 80-mat dojo, the Kobukan attracted people from all over Japan, and in the next ten years many notable students began training there, including Shigemi Yonekawa, Rinjiro Shirata and Gozo Shioda, the latter who went on to create his own style of aikido called yoshinkan. Another student to train there was Kiyoshi Nakakura, who was to become the founder's son-in-law, but he was primarily a kendo practitioner and went on to become Japan's top exponent of the art. With the outbreak of World War II there was a dramatic effect on membership of martial dojos across the country as many of the students left the area to go off to war. The Tokyo dojo was left in the charge of Ueshiba's son, Kisshomaru.

THE MOVE TO IWAMA

Ueshiba had become physically and emotionally drained by the carnage of the war and so, with his wife, he moved to a small farm in a rural location called Iwama, which was about 130km (80 miles) or so from Tokyo. There the two of them lived a Spartan existence, but they were perfectly happy living off the land, not missing at all the frenetic activity of city life. Ueshiba had been acquiring land in the area since 1935 and now, in 1942, he owned quite a sizeable plot. He decided to build there what was to become the spiritual home of aikido – a shrine that was dedicated to the philosophy of aiki and an outdoor dojo in the Ibaraki Prefecture. And it was at about this time that Ueshiba formally changed the name of his art from aiki budo, the "aiki martial way", to the modern name of aikido, the "way of harmony".

Above Morihei Ueshiba, founder of aikido, with Hatsu, his wife and companion for over 60 years.

THE SPREAD OF AIKIDO

The devastation caused during the war meant that essential services – transport, food supply and communications – were all badly affected resulting in very little activity in martial arts dojos. This, and the fact that the occupying military authorities had banned the practice of all martial arts, had closed the Tokyo dojo. The building itself was used as a shelter for people made homeless during the Allied bombing raids. In 1948 permission was given by the Japanese ministry to create an aiki foundation to promote the principles of aikido, as they were non-violent, and a year later the Tokyo dojo reopened.

Initially the dojo struggled financially, but as normality gradually returned and some of Ueshiba's pre-war students resumed their training, conditions began to flourish and new dojos were opened up all over Tokyo, including, for the first time, universities. The first public demonstration of aikido was held in 1956 and now there was interest beginning to be shown by foreign students.

A few of Ueshiba's senior students had travelled internationally and had begun to attract followers. One such senior, Abbe Kenshiro, was in Britain in the mid-1950s and is credited with being the first to show aikido in London at a judo tournament. Judo was an art in which he also excelled, along with kendo and karate. During the mid-1960s, the founder (also referred to as O'Sensei, which means "great teacher") dispatched many of his uchideshi to countries throughout the world to spread the word of aikido and establish a link with the hombu, or world headquarters, in Tokyo.

Above Budo master Abbe Kenshiro, seen here executing a judo throw, was the first to introduce aikido to Great Britain.

In the latter years of his life Ueshiba began to take things easier, immersing himself in farming and developing his own personal aikido. In addition to prayer and meditation, he became involved more with calligraphy and studying religious scriptures. He still taught aikido, mainly at the hombu and Iwama dojos, and he began to travel more – and expected his uchideshi to follow him to look after his needs. Apparently, this could be more difficult than it sounds, as Ueshiba would jump into a taxi or a train, not explaining where he was going and expecting his hapless kaban mochi, or bag carrier, to arrange tickets and expenses. Testimonies from his students reveal that acting as kaban mochi was harder than the training itself! In his final years, Ueshiba taught aikido more by example than physical demonstration, suggesting that students should make up their own mind about what they had been taught. His long lectures would be expressed in such a way that they could be interpreted at different levels. Thus Ueshiba would encourage the students to think for themselves and not to be continually led.

As founder of aikido, Ueshiba received many awards from various organizations in Japan and from abroad – he was even recognized by the emperor in 1964. But on 26 April 1969 Morihei Ueshiba died at the age of 86. On his deathbed he is supposed to have said that aikido was for the whole world and that he himself had only scratched the surface.

Above The founder executing the ikkyo arm pin in suwariwaza, or kneeling technique.

Traditions and Etiquette

To understand the culture of aikido, students must have sympathy with the ritualized traditions that were practised in feudal Japan. This is why, in so many ways, aikido is unique in its outlook compared with other martial arts that use more direct fighting skills. The strict rules of behaviour and comportment in aikido also help to reduce the practitioner's sense of ego, a state of mind that should be at the core of any serious aikido student.

A NON-AGGRESSIVE APPROACH

It is not uncommon to associate martial arts with the idea of using greater skill, speed, strength and aggression to subdue an attacker – understandable considering how many martial arts such as karate, judo, kendo and kung fu, to mention a few, encourage this outlook. There is nothing wrong with healthy competition as a measure of the success of one's personal training compared with another's. However, problems arise when the obsession to win becomes greater than the winning itself. Unfortunately, this can be a consequence of competitive training and, if the martial artist is not aware, can result in the overdevelopment of the ego with its "win at all costs" regime.

THE RATIONALE OF AIKIDO

Most martial arts deal with conflict in terms of the physical encounter, exponents using their skills to overcome a situation once it has begun. Where aikido differs dramatically is in its ethic of not dealing with conflict. Aikido does not seek to engage in conflict at all, preferring to stifle an aggressive intent long before it develops into physical confrontation.

Below Principal and founder of the UKA, Shihan W. J. Smith executing kokyu-nage against a punch, UKA Summer School, 2004.

The aikidoka (a person who practises aikido) believes that the highest level of martial art is when an aggressor is defeated without that person realizing it has happened.

The aim of the aikidoka is to diffuse an encounter in such a way that a potential foe is transformed into a potential ally, without ever surrendering or capitulating in any way. Of course, it may not always happen this way and confrontation may become inevitable – in which case the aikidoka is armed with technique. To the exponent of aikido, the physical encounter is a much lower-level use of aikido strategy, and is consequently only ever used when all else has failed.

Aikido believes that weakness is not an answer to conflict, and neither is excessive brutality. Consequently the techniques themselves are applied with an attitude of controlling an attacker without causing undue harm. This ethic can be confusing for the casual observer. On the one hand, aikido is a martial art, or is it? Some noted texts on aikido suggest that it isn't a martial art in the generally accepted sense because it does not condone conflict and does not talk of cutting down an enemy. If you move harmoniously with an attacker, then you are not entering into a conflict. Similarly, if one neutralizes an enemy, then why is it necessary to destroy him? If you make a friend out of an enemy, how is this just martial art?

CONTROL WITHOUT DAMAGE

Aikido is more than a martial art, it is a martial "way" (or *do* in Japanese, indicating an art that has transcended just physical technique, incorporating various spiritual and philosophical ideals) and embodies the highest levels of ethics in martial training. It centres on controlling and neutralizing one's opponent. This focus distinguishes aikido from competitive arts that teach exponents to punch or kick another competitor. Aikido teaches that conflict is to be avoided – this in itself is extremely rare in martial arts. The ideal is that an opponent is controlled without necessarily causing injury. Many of the techniques were modified by the founder at different stages of the art's development. In later years, as he became more spiritual, he took away some of the more dangerous elements of technique so that they could embody his vision of harmony and peace. Very few techniques involve direct pressure against regardless – this also applies to weapon training. Chiba Sensei, a Japanese aikido teacher and an internationally acknowledged master of aiki weapons, once said during a seminar that: "If you know how to do shomen-uchi [a frontal cut with a sword or empty hand], then you can do aikido." And the truth is that so much that is done in aikido depends on understanding this relatively simple action.

The effectiveness of aikido develops from controlling the course of an attack from when it is perceived, preferably before it is launched, then blending with it, rather than blocking it, and coming back with a countermove. One harmonizes with the attack and leads it to a point of exhaustion before applying a technique of neutralization. This is one of the cornerstones of aikido practice, the principle permeating every aspect of aikido strategy.

THE SWORD OF THE SAMURAI

In feudal Japan when a samurai visited another's house, he would surrender his long sword and retain his short sword. If you entered someone's house and their wall-mounted sword was hung with its tip facing the door, you had to be careful because this person did not trust anyone. A sword mounted with its handle facing the door meant that its owner trusted the people admitted. This same etiquette is observed today in dojos that display a katana kake, or sword rack. If a samurai allowed the saya, or scabbard, of his sword to knock the saya of another samurai, it was considered a gross insult that could be resolved only by the drawn sword and the spilling of blood. To be invited to inspect another samurai's sword at his home was considered an honour. But if you got it wrong, it was considered an insult.

Typically, you were offered the sword held in its owner's left hand in its scabbard with the cutting edge facing him. The sword held in the owner's right hand with the cutting edge towards the recipient was considered an offensive act.

Above Future masters learning their craft – two young enthusiasts practise aikido at a children's class in Birmingham, England.

the natural movement of the joints. The idea is that the joints are stretched in a natural direction a little farther than they could go on their own. Consequently, after a practice your body feels revitalized as opposed to uncomfortable.

A PRACTICE FOR ALL

Although aikido can be practised by men, women and children, research has shown that repetitive stretching of young joints can result in problems in later life. So in Great Britain, for example, certain joint techniques are eliminated from children's practice. The founder taught that one should move so as to close off all openings for attack when engaging an opponent and he structured the techniques to incorporate this ideal. This meant that all techniques, whether basic, intermediate or advanced would be the same in terms of body movement. This, coupled with the concept of musubi, or "tying together", laid the foundation for a defence system that is comprehensive in the way it deals with an attack. In the mind of the aikidoka, all techniques are one, as the body moves in the same way

Below The katana kake, or sword rack, is used to exhibit the katana (long sword) and the saya (scabbard).

Above Tamura Sensei demonstrating a move in front of his attentive students.

The recipient would accept the sword as it was given him, by the left hand, turning the cutting edge towards him quickly. The person inspecting the sword would by now have placed a special cloth in his mouth to absorb the moisture in his breath – lest it go onto the blade. Allowing the breath to reach the blade would almost certainly have transmitted damp and bacteria and so begun the process of rusting – and would not have been taken lightly. The inspector of the sword would then slowly draw the blade from its scabbard with his left hand and, with a piece of washi, a type of paper cloth, wipe away any oil or deposits from the bottom to the top of the blade. Then he would apply some uchiko powder to absorb any moisture on the blade and wipe from bottom to top. After completing his inspection he would wipe the blade again and apply a light coating of oil before slowly returning the sword to its scabbard and returning it to the owner, as described above. The slightest deviation from this etiquette would not be tolerated.

OBSERVING ETIQUETTE

The etiquette used in traditional aikido dojos is a distillation of that used in feudal Japan – the difference being that in feudal times, non-observance of certain etiquette could result in a fight to the death. While contemporary aikidokas may not be under that pressure, disregarding dojo etiquette contributes to a watering down of tradition and an erosion in the transmission of the art. When we disregard etiquette we lose some of the oriental quality of aikido, and what it is that separates what we do in the dojo from what goes on in exercise rooms elsewhere. Etiquette is discipline and respect, and a dojo without these qualities is a dangerous place to be, particularly when weapons are involved. Japan's infrastructure was based very much on the sempai/kohai (senior/junior) relationship, a strict hierarchical system. Originally, the samurai (whose name means "one who serves") would be employed by a daimyo, a feudal lord, to fulfil their every demand. If he ever brought his lord into disrepute or grossly failed in a task, he would ask for permission to commit suicide (formally – seppuku) or ritual suicide, which entailed him disembowelling himself with a knife seconds before a helper (the kaishaku) beheaded him with a sword to end his agony.

BASIC DOJO ETIQUETTE

It is difficult for the Western mind to comprehend this behaviour, yet in those days it was considered honourable. Yet we see many examples of indigenous customs that we may find strange. We accept these as being "different" from our own and acknowledge that traditions are a trait that distinguishes one culture from another. If we disregard these traditions we lose sight of what that race is and how it has evolved. In traditional aikido dojos the etiquette is stringent when compared with other martial arts, and aikido has retained its Japanese quality all the more for it. If you join a club that is affiliated to the International Aikido Federation (IAF), it does not matter if you live in Europe, Asia, North or South America, the etiquette is the same. Here are some examples:

- When entering a dojo, a tachi rei (standing bow) is performed in the direction of the kamiza, meaning "seat of the gods", an area usually in the centre of the wall opposite the entrance. There may be a wooden structure to house a picture of aikido's founder and perhaps a scroll containing calligraphy of the Japanese kanji for "aikido". There may also be a katana kake (sword rack) and wooden weapons. Sometimes flowers are displayed, or simply a picture of the founder.

- The class lines up, kneeling, with the sensei (teacher) at the front and the students in front of the shimoza (opposite wall), with the sempai (senior students) to the right of the dojo facing the kamiza. The instructor uses the command Hai, which means "Yes". (At some dojos, "shomen ni rei" is said, which means "bow to the front".) The whole class responds by bowing while saying "onegaishimasu", which means "please teach me". The sensei then faces the members of the class, who then all bow to him or her. At some dojos the sempai say "sensei ni rei", which means "bow to sensei".

- If you are late for a class, you must wait at the side of the tatami (mat) until given permission to join the class by the sensei. You then perform a seiza (formal kneeling) bow in the direction of the kamiza.

- Engage in some warm-up exercises and then join the class by saying to a fellow practitioner "onegaishimasu", meaning "please teach me".

- The sensei indicates the end of the class with a hand clap, when everyone lines up as before. The etiquette is the same as at the start, but the utterance is now "domo arigato gozaimashita" ("thank you very much"). A lower-ranked student will generally fold the sensei's hakama (pleated, pants) after practice, and this is considered an honour.

During practice, talking is kept to a minimum with full focus on what is being said and taught by the sensei. Aikido is taught mainly by demonstration, with students copying what they see to the best of their ability and repeating it over and over.

A bokken (wooden sword) is treated as a live blade, as is the jo (a staff). The bokken was a practice weapon for the samurai, who used it rather than a real sword to avoid the lethal cutting power of a live blade. It can still cause damage, however, and has to be respected. When making the salutation at the start of the class, the handle of the bokken is held in the left hand, cutting edge toward you, with the right hand underneath holding the blade near the tip. A standing bow toward the kamiza is then made. The students make the same bow to the sensei.
At the end of the class, the same thing happens in reverse – everyone bows first to the sensei and then to the kamiza. You do not touch someone else's bokken without invitation. When the weapon is at its owner's side, it is bad manners to step over it and you should not touch its cutting edge.

Above Students sitting in seiza as they watch their instructor demonstrating.

Below left and right Two practitioners face each other, before bowing in seiza rei – the bow of a student to their teacher or of two students showing respect to each other before or after training.

Seiza (Formal Kneeling)

These front, side and rear views show the formal kneeling posture known as seiza. There should be a feeling of stability as you mentally perceive the two knees and the feet behind as a triangle – the most stable form in nature.

Hold the hands either in a loosely closed fist or with the fingers straight, pointing slightly inwards and resting on the thighs. The knees should be about two to three fist-widths apart.

Keep the spine straight and the chin tucked in.

The big toes can either touch, as here, or be crossed.

Seiza Rei (Formal Kneeling Bow)

This sequence shows the correct way to execute a formal bow from the kneeling position.

1 Start off in the seiza position, shown above.

2 Place the left hand on the tatami.

3 Place the right hand on the tatami, fingers angled in towards each other. You have formed a triangle with your elbows, hands and forearms placed so that should an enemy try to push your head to the floor your hands would cushion the impact.

4 As you lean forward to bow, remember never to show the nape of your neck to your opponent – it was considered bad manners, not to mention dangerous, to lose sight of him. Reverse these steps to return to the start position.

Tachi Rei (Formal Standing Bow)

This is the formal standing bow that is used as an everyday standard in Japanese society. The tachi rei is a polite, courteous greeting and has more or less the same meaning as shaking hands in Western culture.

1 Begin by standing straight with the palms of both hands resting on the front of the thighs and fingers pointing slightly inwards. Your eyes should be looking forward, directed at the object, or person, to which you are bowing.

2 Bending from the waist, keep the upper body straight and bow forward. Lower your eyes as you make the bow and then return them to looking forward at the object of your bow as you straighten again to the start position.

The kamiza (seat of the gods)

This is the focal point of the dojo, usually consisting of a wooden structure styled with a Japanese feel. It traditionally houses a picture of aikido's founder, Morihei Ueshiba. A scroll with the kanji of aikido can also be hung in this area. Weapon racks containing bokken (long wooden swords) or jo (short swords) are also common, as are flower arrangements. The whole class faces the kamiza when the session begins and at the command "hai" everyone bows to O'Sensei's picture. The attitude is of thanking the founder's spirit for showing the way to enlightenment.

Principles and Philosophy

There are a number of key principles to absorb as a new student of aikido. The idea of centred power, enabling coordination of mind and body, is a core concept, along with the importance of using circular, spherical and spiral moves rather than blocks, and the emphasis of non-resistance over technique. Finally, there is the inspiration drawn from the harmonies evident within the natural world, and the influence of the principles of yin and yang.

CENTRALIZATION

When you begin aikido training you will be guided through a system of exercises – physical and mental – designed to make you "think from your belly", meaning the centre of gravity of the human body, which lies bout 5cm (2in) below the navel and a little way inward (depending how big your belly is). This central point, known variously as the tanden, hara or seika no itten, is considered in the Far East not just as the physical centre of the body, but also its spiritual centre.

Below The seiza, or formal kneeling posture gives a feeling of stability from the balanced, triangular position of the knees and feet.

Awareness of the tanden is the first leg of the journey to becoming a physically and spiritually integrated human, and the goal of your training is the total coordination of the mind and body. Imagine a central axis from the top of your head down through your body and out through the floor, with the point of emphasis being the tanden – it is with such awareness that all movements in aikido are made. This idea of the "centre" is then expanded to include one's relationship with the environment and, ultimately, the universe. It is not only the Japanese martial arts that have awareness of the centre as a prerequisite, but also Chinese, Russian and Indian arts. Indian yoga teaches us of the "serpent power of the Kundalini", which equates to the same thing.

CENTRED POWER

The power that can be generated by a person who is centred can be extraordinary, with adepts being able to resist being lifted, pushed over or moved in any way. The founder of aikido can be seen famously on film sitting down cross-legged, resisting the attempts of several students simultaneously pushing on his forehead to unseat him. They all end up on the floor with a shake of his head.

Having developed awareness of your centre, the next step is to maintain that awareness while executing techniques with a partner. Sitting silently meditating in a room is a far cry from dealing with several attackers – this is the real test of your ability to reach into the power of the centre.

EXTENSION

Having found your centre you then have to learn how to extend power from it. The traditional way is to experience this within the framework of the techniques. If a technique fails, it is usually down to a lack of centredness and, thus, no extension of energy. A Japanese sensei would probably say that a student has "no kokyu", or no breath power, if this happens – breath power being the vehicle that transmits ki, or spirit energy, from the centre.

Aikido holds that this energy can be harnessed in the centre of gravity and then channelled through the body to the fingertips into technique. Aikidokas aim to keep this extension

Above The bokken cut is made up and down the body's centre line. The blade is projected above the target and cuts along the backstroke.

Above The final cut of irimi-nage where tori is about to take uke down by rotating his arm and sticking his thumb into the floor.

turned on at all times so that they are always generating power. This extension of energy can be likened to the emanation of water from the ground that runs into a spring that feeds into a river. As long as the water exudes continuously from its source no impurities from the river can get to that source. So, if you extend your mind forcefully your arms will not bend and they will become like a shield against attack.

Many practitioners of traditional aikido like to practise the weapon work associated with it: the bokken (a wooden sword), the jo (a 1.2m/4ft long oak staff that replaces the traditional spear) and the tanto (a wooden or rubber knife that replaces a real blade). These weapons complement perfectly the idea of extension from the centre, particularly the bokken and jo, which require both hands to hold the weapon. In this way, the hands are automatically held in line with the centre line of the body, making it easier to imagine extension from your centre and up through the weapon towards your partner.

If your partner grabs your right wrist and you assume the hanmi posture (shown on page 420), and extend that arm in line with your central axis in a particular direction, as long as you concentrate forcefully on the idea of energy coming up through the floor, through your centre to your fingertips, your partner will be sent hurtling away with a surprising force. The ultimate use of extension is within a multiple attack, where you are at the centre of the action whirling in their midst like a tornado, repelling the aggressors in the same way.

CIRCULAR, SPHERICAL AND SPIRAL MOTION

There are few examples of straight-line movement in aikido. Even when we move directly forward it is with a slightly circular body motion. The reason for this is that the basic strategy for dealing with a straight-line attack, such as an overhead strike to

the front of the head or a direct punch to the face, is to move in a circular fashion off that line. When the attack itself is more circular, as an attack to the side of the head or face, then the evasive movement is either to move off the centre line and overwhelm the attack before it has generated any power (if the attack has launched), or step inside it with a circular motion to neutralize it (if the attack is well into motion).

There are no blocks in aikido, only parries and deflections. Blocking goes against the flow of energy and may not work if the attacking force is too great. With aikido strategy, it does not matter how much attacking force is used, as you are not there to receive it. If we take the example of shomen-uchi irimi-nage ura (the front-head strike shown on page 432), the initial movement is to parry the attack and step circularly around it to a position whereby you are right behind and close to your attacker, effectively with your attacker's back on your chest and both of you looking in the same direction. From here it is easy to lead his energy in a large circle destroying his balance (kuzushi). As his weight falls, you add your own body weight to the motion and send him spinning around your centre. At the point where he tries to regain his balance, you switch your body weight from one foot to the other, causing him to lose his balance the other way. It only remains to step in and cut across his neck and face to effect a throw.

These circular, spherical or spiral movements are irresistible. If we draw on our experience of the natural world, the spiral is seen as a most powerful force. If we look at phenomena such as tornados, hurricanes and whirlpools and, further afield, at black holes and galaxies – they are all examples of forces generated by, or containing, circular and spiral motion. At the other end of the scale, all molecular activity is circular with atoms spinning around a nucleus.

Right This tranquil scene shows the sky (yin), the land (yang) and water. When agitated by lunar movements and the weather, the water can produce great force (yang), but otherwise is calm (yin).

When confronted with gyaku hanmi katate-dori (a wrist grab), for example, at the instant you are gripped you make a tenkan (turning movement), leading your attacker's energy by extending your energy from your centre and joining with that of your attacker's. You move with the idea that you are centred and that the central axis of your movement is a straight line from your head through to the floor. Next, your own body becomes the overall centre of the entire motion with your attacker spinning out of control on the periphery.

Instead of prioritizing strength, speed and force, aikido emphasizes non-resistance, saying "when pulled, enter; when pushed, turn". Every technique, body movement and cutting motion with the arms operates in circles and spirals. Standing alone with their arms extended, aikidokas extend their consciousness all around themselves in a protective sphere, and any attacker entering that sphere will be repelled.

PHILOSOPHY OF AIKIDO

Phrases used to describe the basic doctrine of aikido include "To practise aikido is to learn how to harmonize with nature" or "Aikido is the budo of love." They all encompass the real spirit of aikido. Problems can arise in interpretation, however. Many people ask themselves how a martial art can be related to love, or how the subjugation of another individual can be in harmony with nature? It is only by interpreting the words correctly that the answers reveal themselves. If we look at the land, sky, seas, trees, grass and listen to the winds and feel the heat of the sun, we see that this is nature in all its glory. But how do we reconcile this to aikido?

Right The rotary movement called kaiten (see page 422) exemplifies the concept of yin and yang. When faced with a strong attack the idea is to parry, not block, the force. By turning off the line of the attack and letting it carry on, the parry harmonizes with it.

YIN AND YANG

For thousands of years in the East there has been the belief that all phenomena are governed by antagonistic but complementary opposites, known as "yin and yang" in China, "in and yo" in Japan and "tamasic and rajasic" in India. The yin-yang symbol shows a circle divided by two shapes of identical size – one black, one white. We also see a small circle of black in the white part and of white in the black. The outer circle represents "the whole" – call it god or nature or whatever – while the black and white "fish" shapes represent the two opposites of the whole that interact and cause it to exist. The symbolism denoted in the small, opposite-coloured circles in each segment states that nothing in nature is *completely* opposite, and contains elements of its opposite.

This concept is borne out on every level of existence. The white shape within the circle is known as yin, and associated characteristics are: expansive, upward, lightness, cold and fast. The black shape is yang and is characterized by contraction, downward, heaviness, heat and slow. When you think about this you realize that virtually every natural phenomena can be explained in terms of yin and yang.

MUTUALLY DEPENDENT FORCES

Many forces of nature exist in a state of flux, opposite yet mutually dependent, drawn to each other yet repelled. Some are obvious, while others require more thought when applying the yin-yang principle. Think of the relationship of man and woman. As a general classification, women are yin with characteristics such as: feminine, gentle, soft, receptive, quiet, hairless and passive. Men are generally yang, with the following traits: masculine, violent, hard, aggressive and loud. But these are crude categorizations; what makes the whole thing so fascinating is that in reality men and women exhibit qualities of yin and yang in varying degrees. It is perfectly normal to have men with many of the attributes of yin and women with varying degrees of yang attributes. When you consider the yin-yang symbol, this notion falls in line with the thinking behind the two small circles in their respective halves – nothing is completely yin or completely yang, merely varying degrees of both.

Ki and Kokyu

Ki is a profound concept, one not easily grasped, and has stretched the abilities of undoubtedly intelligent and lucid people. It is the force that gives life to every living thing; the essence that makes us breathe, that makes our blood flow; that maintains all molecular activity. The word kokyu refers to breath power in terms of respiration. It is the process of breathing, but it can also be interpreted as the respiration of the universe and the flow of the opposing forces of nature.

The word aikido loosely means "way of harmonizing the spirit". Ai is "harmony"; ki is "spirit"; and do is "way". In a much grander sense, it is the power that energizes nature and the universe itself. Ueshiba's message through aikido was to harmonize one's own ki with the ki of the universe. He felt this was the way for humanity to reconcile itself and become one with nature and, thus, make the world a better place in which to live. To do this, we have to try to understand what ki is within the individual, how to experience it and how to channel its force.

USING KI IN YOUR DAILY LIFE

The person who can explain ki and how to develop it in an A+B+C=D manner has not been born yet and anyone who makes that claim is to be treated with suspicion. There are, however, a few mental and physical exercises you can do to promote its development. If you look at people who are experts in any field, you will see that they make what they do look easy. Take an electrician, for instance; he could be

Left The instinctive power generated by an infant's grip can be intense, and an excellent example of the power of the unconscious coordination of mind and body, or ki.

engaged with you in conversation while he is putting the wires into a plug and the part of the brain looking after the plug is on autopilot and so he is effortlessly able to complete this task and talk, too. This is an example of mind and body coordination. When you begin something new you have to work hard learning all the steps necessary to complete the process. Then you need to repeat it again and again until it becomes second nature. Only then will the skills you have acquired come out naturally. This is the natural learning process, and is particularly apt when talking about martial arts, as repetition is vital to your ultimate success.

RELEASING THE POWER OF KI

The power we are talking about can show itself in different and dynamic ways, such as in situations of stress. One woman in America managed to lift a truck off her small son and so save his life after he had become trapped. She cracked several vertebrae in the process, but it shows the power that is within the human body. There have been many documented cases of people tearing doors off their hinges to save people trapped inside burning buildings, and then ignoring the pain of severe burns to perform their acts of heroism. Where does this power come from? Very young children are also capable of generating enormous power – if you have ever held out a finger and let an infant grab hold of it you will know how true this can be.

These are examples of ki – a power that can be tapped only with unconscious coordination of mind and body. If you try to rationalize or intellectualize in a stressful situation, the force will not emerge. It has to be instinctive, with no gap between perception and reaction. So, a young infant has no information to draw on, its mind is a clean slate and any actions it takes are instinctive. When the child grabs your finger it probably is not even aware of doing it as it gazes around not looking at anything particularly, but taking in everything in general.

The conclusion from this must be that everyone has an extraordinary power inside that may only surface naturally in extreme circumstances. Alternatively an expert or master in any field can exhibit ki as a result of not having to think

consciously about what they are doing, in other words when mind and body are as one. So when you hear of a karate master breaking two house bricks with one blow, or an aikido exponent resisting the attempts of several people to move him, know that you are witnessing the power of ki.

DEVELOPMENT OF KI

Aikidokas attempt to harness the power of ki and to use it at will. This is not an easy endeavour, but one that must be undertaken if progress is to be made. It is too simplistic to assume that if you practise diligently, ki will emerge automatically. You have to cultivate the right mental attitude for that to happen. One of the biggest problems you will encounter in the quest for ki is bringing the wandering mind to rest. Some people can do this more easily than others. Before you can contemplate ki you need to be able to focus your mind. If you feel that you need it, there are ways you can learn to concentrate more effectively. Zazen (seated meditation) is one way; the ancient Indian system of yoga is another.

CONCENTRATION AND IMAGINATION

During the breathing process described opposite, you must imagine that the exhalation represents an expansion feeling from your centre of gravity, coupled with the notion that all the impurities of the day are being expelled with the breath. When any thoughts come, try to deftly turn them away, but not with any sort of forceful effort, as this will disturb a focused mind. In time you will be able to reach a calm and serene state of mind and, effectively, think of nothing. Of course, during the act of breathing, breath only goes in and out of your lungs. The route it

Above The ebb and flow of the tides in all the seas of the world are examples of kokyu respiration in the grand sense.

takes in the exercise is purely imaginary, but this awareness is essential to achieving the desired results. While zazen is not practised to achieve anything other than zazen, it does develop single-minded concentration and a sense of understanding of where the tanden, or your centre of gravity is.

This is a major part of Zen Buddhism, where exponents can sit looking at a plain wall for hours at a time. You may think this seems a waste of time, but in reality it is time very well spent as the degree of single-minded concentration that can be achieved is awesome. One of the difficulties in any martial art is maintaining a calm, clear mind in the midst of a frenzied onslaught from multiple attackers. If you are able to switch your consciousness in any direction instantaneously, and with total commitment, you will be coordinated and able to liberate ki energy. We have to develop a strong centre and be able to extend power from that place. Some Japanese masters recommend zazen meditation, although it is by no means essential. You may have good powers of concentration naturally, in which case it is not necessary. And there are large, very successful aikido organizations that do not include zazen in their curriculum. However, as an individual you need to develop single-mindedness to the extent that you are not readily distracted, particularly in stressful situations, and zazen practice is an excellent discipline to help you achieve this goal.

Once Chiba Sensei, the first official UK representative from the Aikido World Headquarters in Japan, was asked what ki is. His reply was that ki is the physical

Right This exercise for developing kokyu involves two people holding the other. Tori needs to harmonize with and deflect their power, otherwise he will be overcome.

manifestation of the power of the imagination. The more positive the mind, the greater the degree of imagination and, therefore, the ki that is generated is more powerful. The mind can be exercised like the body, and the more it is exercised the stronger it will become.

KOKYU (BREATH)

In the physical sense, kokyu is understood as the process of breathing which, of course, is inhalation and exhalation. In another sense, as mentioned earlier, it can be interpreted as the respiration of the universe, the natural flow of the opposing forces of nature, positive and negative. You may view the flow of day into night and the tides of the sea coming in and going out as perennial examples of kokyu. To employ kokyu successfully within aikido you must learn to harmonize your body with that of an attacker, in the same way that the forces of nature harmonize with each other, for only then is the whole achieved. These forces do not collide with one another; instead they work together to achieve harmony. A mighty oak tree that has stood for hundreds of years can be uprooted when hit with the force of a whirlwind, yet a blade of grass at the tree's base will toss and turn in the direction of the wind and consequently not be destroyed. In this sense, the grass is stronger than the tree. If we can think like this when practising aikido, what kind of power do we possess?

CULTIVATING KOKYU RYOKU (BREATH POWER)

To understand kokyu, you need to develop an awareness of the tanden, your centre of gravity, also referred to as "the one point". Zazen (seated meditation) is good for this, as are the following exercises. There are also specific exercises within the framework of aikido to help you understand the concept of kokyu. Called kokyu-ho, or breathing method, they enable you to generate the power used in all aikido techniques.

Breathing and zazen

First, find somewhere that is warm and comfortable where you will not be disturbed – preferably a matted area. Traditionalists use a zafu, which is a small round cushion, placed under the buttocks, though you should sit only on the edge of the cushion rather than square on, so that your knees can drop down towards the ground. The posture of either the full or half lotus can be used, but equally good is the seiza posture (pictured right), although this can be hard on the knee joints initially. Whatever method you use, make sure that you mentally perceive a straight line from the top of your head, through your chin to your centre of gravity.

Half close your eyes and fix your gaze on the floor about 1.5m (5ft) in front of you. Close your mouth and place your tongue

on the upper palate. Try to clear your mind and think of nothing, which is not as easy as you might think. Relax all your muscles, starting from the feet upwards. When you reach the head, sit and simply

be aware of your posture and breathing – long breaths, in through the nose, and long breaths, out from the mouth. Do not sniff as you inhale, but control the inhalations with the epiglottis at the back of the throat. Enter totally the world of breathing and direct the breath through the nose and (in your mind's eye) up to the top of your head. The breath travels down your spine to its midpoint, then across to the tanden, a point about 5cm (2in) below the navel and the same distance inward (this equates to a person's centre of gravity). At the tanden, imagine that your breath is coiling up, just as if it were a spring – a contracting and, at the same time, a cleansing process. Exhalation is the reverse: your breath goes back the way it came, but instead of being expelled through the nose, you use your mouth.

Suwariwaza Kokyu-ho

The most basic of the exercises for developing breath power is called suwariwaza, or seated kokyu-ho. Remember, this exercise is not a test of strength, but an extension of the power from the tanden.

1 The uke (the practitioner who receives the technique) is holding both wrists of the tori (the practitioner who applies the technique). In the basic form, the wrists are held at chudan (middle) height. There are several variations.

2 Tori leans his body weight forward and raises his arms, as if cutting up with two swords, causing uke's elbows to be raised and destroying his power. This takes away uke's capacity to generate any strength.

3 Finally by cutting over uke's left hand with his right and spiralling his left handblade toward uke's armpit, tori is able to displace uke's centre of gravity and cause him to fall. Uke rolls naturally to the side.

4 Tori extends from his centre imagining that he is holding down the centre of the earth, and disregarding uke's hold. Uke offers token resistance to test tori's stability.

Tachiwaza Kokyu-ho

The next stage is to practise the standing form of the same exercise, which is called tachiwaza, or standing kokyu-ho. These are the basic forms of kokyu-ho practice, but it can be practised from a variety of attacks.

1 Uke holds tori's right wrist with both his hands.

2 Tori steps to the side of uke, aligning his body, and begins to cut upwards as if raising a sword in the centre line of his body. This enables tori to lift up his arms using his centre of gravity.

3 Tori now steps behind uke and by extending his arm across uke's body destroys her balance. By turning his hips and leaning his body weight forward, tori causes uke to fall.

THE TANDEN AND THE CENTRE LINE OF THE BODY

It quickly becomes clear from practising these kokyu methods that the power supplied for every technique comes from the tanden, which is on the centre line of the body in the lower abdomen. From this it follows that in order to move someone you have to displace that person's centre of gravity with your own. In the case of the sitting kokyu-ho, your posture, when kneeling, automatically assumes a triangle composed of your two spread knees and the feet behind.

From the stability of the triangle (the most stable form in nature) we generate power through the tanden and extend it through the arms to the fingertips, as if projecting a high-pressure stream of water from the centre of gravity. As we lean our gravity forward with these ideas in mind, we generate an incredible force on our partner as he tries to maintain a grip on the wrists. The net result is that he is moved without any recourse to muscular power from the arms or shoulders.

The same applies to the basic standing technique. Here we lean our centre of gravity into our partner's grip from an initial triangular posture, turn to the side, deflecting her force, and then, by cutting up the centre line of the body from the centre and aligning the feet by her side, you create too much force for her to maintain her grip and posture. It only remains to continue cutting upwards and over her neck in a spiral motion to cause her to lose her balance.

RELAXATION AND ALIGNMENT

No matter how you are attacked, it is crucial to harmonize with that attack and then align your body in such a way that you can use your centre of gravity, your tanden, to generate the power necessary to effect a technique. Only in this way can a smaller, weaker person overcome a larger, stronger opponent. This is a practical application of kokyu and one reason why so many women are attracted to aikido, as women, in the main, do not have the physical strength to cope with a male aggressor.

Extending power from the tanden only ever works when the body is relaxed. Putting muscular tension into these movements only serves to shut the power off – much as would happen if you kinked a hose while water was surging through it. The kokyu-ho movements are natural in that they promote the idea of deflecting your opponent's power, not receiving it. It follows, therefore, that you must practise in a relaxed manner and not try to force your partner down, otherwise your partner will sense this and fight against your technique. When you drink a glass of wine, you don't grip the glass with enough force to break it. Similarly, when you

Above In hidari hanmi, or left posture, the hands are held in the centre line of the body. The body itself is angled at 45 degrees to the front. From this position rapid front and rear movement is possible.

hold the steering wheel of a car, you don't grip it so strongly that you lose manoeuvrability. If you stand and tense your body you may feel strong and stable, but in reality you are weak and can be very easily moved. In aikido, the more relaxed you are, the more stable you are and, consequently, the more power you can generate. It is vital, however, to be centred by being aware of your tanden and that every movement (in your mind's eye) originates from there. Through repetitive practice you will come to realize that if you have the centre behind every movement you make, then you maximize your body's potential to generate power.

In summary, when we stand in the triangular posture of aikido, with hands extended on the centre line of the body, we are in the most stable form possible. We learn to concentrate our mind in our tanden through a variety of means: meditation, breathing exercises, torifune and furitama (see pages 412 and 413) and the kokyu-ho exercises themselves. We can then move on to the next stage, which is to extend power out from our newly discovered centre. If we imagine with full commitment that power is extending from the tanden out of the fingertips then it will really happen.

Clothing and Equipment

It was Jigoro Kano, the judo founder, who first initiated the design of a long-sleeved, long-trousered suit for practitioners, later adopted by aikido professionals. The long sleeves and trousers he devised were to replace earlier suits where the sleeves came above the elbows and the trousers above the knees, a design that caused many scrapes and cuts during practice. The hakama, worn only by senior grades, was originally used to protect clothing and the samurai's legs from painful friction when on horseback.

KEIKOGI

The standard practice suit, or keikogi, used for aikido is generally the same as that used in judo. The wrap-over jacket has to be able to withstand the rigours of being gripped at the collar, shoulder and sleeve during training and is consequently made of a thicker, more robust cotton than, for example, the karate-style suit, where gripping is limited. The trousers again are usually reinforced at the knees and are tied around the waist by a drawstring fed through the waistband. The suit comes complete with a white obi (belt) made of thick cotton. When you buy a keikogi, it is best to purchase one at least a size bigger than for normal clothing, as it can shrink dramatically on its first washing.

HAKAMA

The hakama, or divided skirt, is traditionally worn on formal occasions only by the upper classes of Japanese society. In aikido, it is worn only by yudansha, or dan grades, although permission to wear it is sometimes given to a person who has provided an outstanding service to a club or organization, and women can be given special dispensation, too. The hakama can be made of cotton or a mixture of cotton and polyester or Rayon, and it is available in heavy or lightweight grades. The traditional colours are black or blue. With some you must be careful that the dye does not transfer to the keikogi during a hot practice session. At the end of a training session it is traditional to fold the hakama on the tatami (practice mat) to preserve its shape, and this takes quite a while to do properly. It is considered an honour to fold the sensei's hakama after a class.

ZORI

A traditional type of Japanese footwear, zori, are similar to a Western sandal. Usually made of straw, they have a thong that fits between the large and second toe and over the inside and outside of the foot to keep the footwear securely in place. This simple design emerged as a result

Above The modern keikogi, or practice suit, is made from heavyweight cotton.

Above The hakama, or divided skirt, is traditionally blue or black, although high-ranking aikidokas often use other colours.

Left Traditional zori, or straw sandals, are worn to and from the practice tatami, or mat.

of the requirement in Japanese society that one should remove footwear before entering a house. Modern variants are made of rubber or leather and are worn either as fashion accessories or as beachwear.

Above The jo (staff, top) and bokken (wooden sword, bottom) are both traditional aikido weapons.

Above The tanto or tanken is a knife used in tanto dori, or knife taking. It is vital to imagine that the blade has the power to cut.

AIKIDO WEAPONS

Shown here are the weapons most commonly used in aikido. The bokken, or bokuto, meaning wooden sword, is approximately the same shape and length as a real Japanese sword. This is used to practise the sword techniques left as a legacy by the founder of the art, which include suburi, or solo exercises; uchikomi, or basic one-step cutting and thrusting with a partner; awase, or basic paired blending practice, and kumitachi, which is a more advanced paired practice that begins to bridge the gap between pure swordsmanship and the practice of aikido. The ultimate practice is tachidori, or sword taking, in which the unarmed aikido exponent faces an attacker who is armed with a sword.

Next is the jo, or short staff. This weapon is approximately 1.25m (4ft) long and 25mm (1in) thick and is used to realize the spearfighting heritage of the art. Disciplines practised include: suburi, or solo exercises; awase, or basic paired blending techniques; kumijo, or advanced paired techniques; and jo tori, techniques for taking a weapon from an attacker. Some aikido schools also practise jo kata, in which imaginary attackers are dealt with in a series of flowing movements. Next down is the tanken, or tanto, which is a wooden knife used to practise defence techniques, using a variety of thrusts, slashes and cuts as if the knife were a small sword or dagger.

HEALTH AND SAFETY

Thankfully in recent years there has been an emphasis on teaching aikido to children, so they can benefit from these new skills and, in the process, ensure the popularity of aikido in years to come. However, with a view to safety, certain techniques should be eliminated from children's practice because of the risk of joint problems occurring in later life. In Britain, for example, children under 14 years of age must practise only with children of a similar age and children aged 14 and above can practise with adults providing that they are segregated within the mat area and a qualified coach is put in charge of the group.

Contact any of the international organizations for specific guidance and recommendations (see useful contacts on pages 498–9).

- Another essential for any aikido organization is the recommendation that all aikido instructors who are qualified coaches – and, therefore, able to teach the art unsupervized – should be qualified in basic first aid.

- There should always be a fully stocked first-aid kit readily available and an accident book in which details of any accident can be recorded. There are also formal documents for this purpose.

- Dojo heads should ensure that the building itself is well maintained and in a good state of repair so that it is a safe place in which to practise.

- Objects such as radiators, chairs, wall corners and stanchions should be made safe to avoid injury.

- Tatami (mat) and canvas should be monitored regularly to ensure there are no rips or tears that could snag someone's fingers or toes, and that they are laid properly with no spaces or gaps.

- Any jewellery worn by a student must be taken out or off to avoid harming themselves or others.

- Fingernails should be clean and short, and long hair tied back.

- The practice suit, or keikogi, should be clean and the student must exhibit a high standard of personal hygiene.

- Weapons should be checked for cracks and splinters before every session.

- Dojo heads need to be made aware of any physical or medical problems students may have.

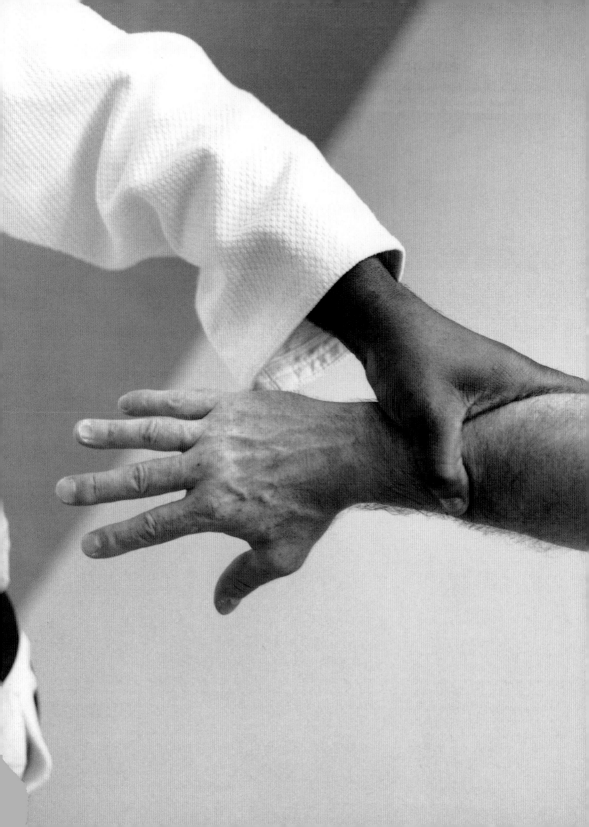

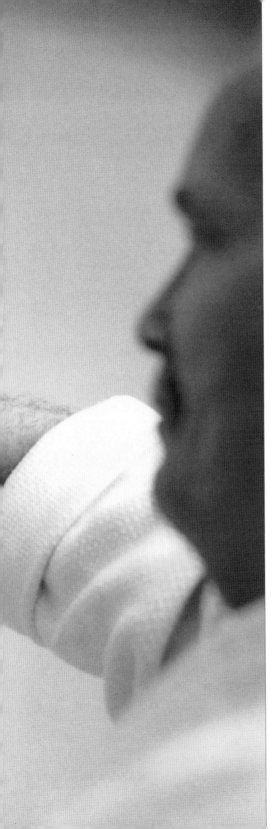

Preparatory movements

In aikido, as in any other form of physical training, the body has to be prepared. Muscles need warming and gently stretching and the joints need to be put through a range of movements to enable them to accommodate the rigours of practice. What differentiates these exercises from those used in athletics, gymnastics, football and so on is that the mind as well as the body is conditioned. In this chapter a range of conditioning exercises are set out in the order they are normally taught in the dojo. These exercises, however, are by no means definitive, and you may find that they vary in both form and order depending on which country you are in and, indeed, which region.

Breathing

There is a Chinese saying that breath is the lord of power, and a glance at any of the kung-fu fighting styles dating back to the times of the original Shaolin Temple in AD495 will reveal the great emphasis that was placed on proper and controlled breathing. Followers of the Indian practice of yoga also stress the importance of prana, or breath, and almost any physical endeavour such as aikido can be enhanced by being aware of the difference that controlled breathing can make.

Deep abdominal breathing techniques perform two distinct functions. They imbue the body with oxygen, which relaxes the muscles and prepares them for stretching. They also direct the mind to the tanden in order to develop the mindset necessary to understand the concept of extension of energy from there. During the breathing exercises that follow use the visualization techniques referred to in ki and kokyu (see pages 399–403) as well as the box below.

Inhalation and exhalation
In the illustration to the right, the directional arrows flowing in through the nose show the path of the breath during inhalation. Physically, you need to put your tongue against the roof of your mouth and then inhale through the nose, with the feeling of drawing in purifying energy from the whole universe. Imagine that you are controlling the inhalation of air with the epiglottis at the back of the throat, rather than merely sniffing it in. The breath is then directed (in the mind's eye) to the very top of the head and down the spine to a point about 5cm (2in) below the navel and 5cm (2in) inwards. This is the approximate centre of gravity in the human body and is also regarded as the spiritual centre. Commonly referred to in aikido as the tanden, this point has a similar importance in most of the major doctrines of the Far East. When the breath reaches this point, hold it and imagine that it is coiling up and tensing, in just the same way as a spring would.

The blue directional arrows flowing out through the mouth indicate the path of the exhaled breath. As you start to exhale, contract the cheeks of your bottom (This act, along with the tongue on the roof of the mouth, represents the spiritual closing of the openings of the body.) The breath uncoils in the tanden with a feeling of expansion and follows the same path as the inhalation, but in reverse. The other difference is that the breath that is expelled through the mouth has the quality of emptying all the impurities of the day that have been gathering in the body.

Single-cycle Breathing Exercise 1

All the following breathing exercises follow the same inhalation/exhalation techniques as those outlined opposite. This first single-cycle breathing exercise is one of the more commonly used ones in aikido dojos.

1 To start this exercise, stand in a relaxed position with your feet a shoulder-width apart, hands in front of your thighs with your fingers extended.

2 Inhale as you raise your arms above your head, as if you were cutting up with a sword, to the position shown.

3 Continue inhaling as you lower your arms to shoulder height, palms up.
As if pushing up with both hands, raise your body onto the balls of your feet.

4 Turn your hands palms down and effectively swallow your breath. Then begin the exhalation process, with the feeling of pushing down with both hands.

5 Lower your body and feet to the floor gradually and return to the start position, as in step 1, to complete the exercise.

CAUTION
If at any time as you perform these breathing exercises you feel dizzy, faint or see spots of bright light, then stop immediately. These symptoms may indicate problems and you should seek medical advice before continuing.

Single-cycle Breathing Exercise 2

This is a simple breathing exercise that makes you aware of your tanden or centre of gravity. It should be done while imagining cutting up and down with the sword as you raise and then lower your arms.

1 To start this exercise, stand in a relaxed position with your feet a shoulder-width apart, hands slightly to the centre of your body. Always begin breathing exercises by exhaling at the start.

2 Inhale as you raise your arms above your head, as if you were cutting up with a sword, to the position shown.

3 Continue inhaling as you draw your arms down to just above shoulder height. As you do this, make fists and imagine you are pulling down a heavy shutter. Hold this position for three seconds.

4 Begin exhaling and allow your arms to relax and slowly return to the start position. Gradually unclench your fists as you feel your tanden expanding.

5 Return to the start position.

Double Inhalation/Exhalation Exercise

This is one of a series of double inhalation/exhalation breathing exercises taught by Tamura Nobuyoshi Sensei from France, perhaps the most senior teacher in Europe and a favourite uke of aikido's founder, Morihei Ueshiba.

1 To start this exercise, stand in a relaxed position with your feet a shoulder-width apart, hands slightly to the centre of your body and with fingers extended.

2 Position your hands just below the navel, palms up, with the fingertips pointing towards each other. As you inhale, draw the hands upwards to the height of your nipples.

3 Turning both hands over, exhale. With a sense of pushing down, extend your hands down to below your navel once more. Try to develop a sense of rhythm and a smooth, uninterrupted movement.

4 This is the hand position of the finished cycle. Prepare to move your right hand across to the side of the hip.

5 Move your right hand across to the side of the hip with the fingers turned inward. As you make a second inhalation, begin a large circular extension with your left hand from the centre line of the body, cutting upwards and outwards. As your hand reaches the apex, pause, then exhale, extending fully outwards until your hand returns to the position in the previous step.

6 From this finish position, begin the same sequence for your other side, swapping hand positions as necessary.

Torifune

Part of misogi, a Shinto purification exercise, torifune is also known as the "rowing exercise". It is used to row spiritually to utopia, or "from this world to the next" in the mind of the practitioner. It is also an excellent way to train to become aware of your tanden.

1 Assume a left hanmi posture, extend the arms and make your hands into fists, with the middle knuckles protruding. Feel as if you are forcefully pushing your arms out with your tanden and shout "Hei!" as you bend your front leg and straighten the back one. Kiai is the expulsion of air caused when you tighten the abdominal muscles.

2 Make sure you pull your arms back with the same intensity used to push them forward. Imagine that you are making two elbow strikes to someone standing behind you. Bear in mind that the energy for this movement comes from the centre of the body in between the hips, just below the navel. As you go back into this position make a kiai shout of "Ho!"

Movement repetitions
Some teachers recommend doing more movement repetitions than others so it really depends on the philosophy of your teacher. Recommended here is doing enough repetitions to last 20 seconds or so.

Side view step 1
This side view allows you to see the depth of the stance in step 1. It is important to have a positive attitude when practising this exercise and to make the kiai shout as loud as is practicable, as the whole idea behind this movement is to summon up an indomitable spirit, gradually increasing in intensity as you perform your repetitions.

Side view step 2
This side view of the step 2 posture shows how in this position the front leg is straight and the back leg is bent. The hands are pulled back in a clenched, but relaxed manner onto the front of the pelvic bones. This exercise is normally done at the start of the class and the repetitions for each posture are practised on both the left and the right sides.

Furitama

The accompanying exercise is known as furitama, or "shaking the ball". It is a calming exercise and its purpose is to vibrate energy from your centre to all parts of the body after the vigour and vitality of torifune (see opposite), and is done immediately afterwards.

1 Stand in a relaxed position, feet about a hip-width apart, hands by your sides with fingers extended.

2 Extend the arms out in a large circle above the head with a view to clasping the hands together overhead.

3 Close your eyes and imagine that you are taking in energy from the universe itself as you draw your hands to your tanden or centre of gravity.

4 This picture shows the final position of the hands. From this position the hands are shaken vigorously up and down, at the same time imagining a ball being shaken in your centre. This movement agitates the energy you have received and dissipates it to all extremities of your body. On completion of this exercise, stand as you are with your hands together and mentally fix your gaze between your eyes. Breathe normally. This exercise lasts about 20 seconds in total.

Warm-ups and Stretches

The solo exercises in this section are just a selection of the many available. There is no hard-and-fast rule regarding which warm-up exercises to use and some teachers, depending on their own experience, have created their own. The movements that follow have been recommended by various shihan or master teachers.

The body needs to be warmed sufficiently to avoid any pulls and tears of muscles and ligaments. It is a good idea to practise breathing exercises before you warm up and stretch – this oxygenates the blood that feeds the muscles. Warming up should also increase the heart rate. This will also allow the muscles to stretch by an extra 20 per cent, highly recommended considering the range of sudden stretching that can occur within aikido training. Always be mindful, too, that the warm-ups should aim to mirror the actual training. The exercises shown here condition the back, stomach, hips and knees – all vital elements within training. The wrist exercises in particular stimulate the muscles and tendons of the wrist and forearm in exactly the same way as any aikido technique.

If it is cold you should always perform additional exercises, such as running on the spot or jumping for a couple of minutes, to raise the heart rate more and warm yourself thoroughly before you start stretching. The duration of warm-ups and stretching will depend on your experience. Some aikido organizations emphasize the body conditioning more than others. Generally, though, a reasonable warm-up routine should last 15–20 minutes.

This set of calisthenics is designed to warm the muscles and condition the joints. The exercises include movements adopted by many disciplines as part of their warm-up routines, as well as conditioning exercises that are specific to aikido. Perform all of these exercises with your mind at your centre of gravity.

Muscles and Joints

To avoid injury you must ensure that your muscles are relaxed and warm before you begin stretching in preparation for training. The first exercise stimulates blood flow and wakes up the muscles and joints. Open palms can also be used in a slapping action for the same result.

Stimulating blood flow

Hand detail step 1
You only want to stimulate blood flow and not cause bruising, so note that you strike gently with a half-formed fist, the flat of the fingers making contact rather than the knuckles.

1 Stand with your feet hip-width apart, feet facing forward. Half close your right hand into a fist (see detail) and begin gently striking at your left shoulder, gradually working down the inner and outer arm.

2 After repeating the same procedure for your right shoulder and arm, move on to the upper chest muscles, working down to the abdomen, and inner and outer thighs and calves.

3 Working back up the body, stimulate your buttocks and lower back. Work on your back and the sides of your neck to resolve this part of the exercise. Repeat the movements for two minutes.

Twisting upper body

1 Stand naturally, widen your stance so that your feet are a shoulder-width apart and raise and extend your arms.

2 Twist your upper body left and right, pivoting from the hips with your feet facing forward. Begin twisting to the right.

3 In a flowing movement, twist your upper body to the left, keeping your feet facing forward. Repeat for 15 seconds.

Body Stretches

The following are typical body stretches practised in many dojos that follow the traditional art of aikido.

Side stretch

Rotary body stretch

1 With feet apart and a straight back, incline your body to the left with the right arm extended overhead. Exhale.

2 Repeat this movement on the opposite side, this time with your left arm extended. Repeat for 15 seconds.

1 Start with both hands above your head and describe a large circle with your arms, with the tanden as the centre.

2 Be aware of your breathing pattern. Exhale as you go down and inhale as you come up. This is actively harmonizing your breathing with your body movement.

3 Fully extend the arms and touch the mat with your fingertips, if your suppleness will permit. Do not overdo this movement and strain your body.

4 Repeat the movement, describing a circle in the opposite direction. Repeat for 15 seconds.

Back Stretch

If carried out with commitment, this simple back-stretching exercise is an excellent whole-body workout. To avoid injury, work within your abilities and don't take the movements farther than your body will readily allow.

Side views of steps 1 and 2
These two side views show the first part of the exercise from a side-on position, allowing you to see the complete depth of the stretch you should be aiming to achieve. Depending on your degree of suppleness, this could, however, take weeks of daily practice. Don't rush the process.

1 Stand with your legs wider apart than in previous movements, as shown, and with both hands above your head. Bend forward, extending your arms so that your fingers touch the floor. Exhale at the stage. Stroke the floor between your legs, ensuring that the final stroke is farther back than the others.

2 Reversing the movement, extend back up and open your arms wide with your head right back so that you can see the ceiling directly above you. Inhale deeply at this stage.

Hip Rotation

This simple warm-up exercise stretches the central muscles around the hips and waist. In combination with the other warm-up exercises shown here, this sequence helps to prepare the whole body for general aikido techniques.

1 Place your hands on your hips and push your centre forward as far as is comfortable, while keeping your feet flat on the floor.

2 Incline your body to the right, imagining your body is rotating in a circle.

3 Now project your bottom to the rear and straighten your legs as you complete a full circle.

4 Finally, incline your body to your left and complete the circular movement of the whole exercise. Repeat for 20 seconds.

Knee and Calf Bends

These exercises are designed to condition the lower limbs. Aikido can take its toll on the knee joints so it is important to keep them supple. Please take your time with these bends and do only what you can manage.

Knee circles

1 Place your hands on your knees with knees loosely bent and rotate in a circular motion by bending the knees farther forward as they move to the side. You should aim to keep gentle pressure on the front and sides of the joints. This is the basic way, although a variation of this exercise is to open the knees away from one another in to out and out to in.

Calf workout

1 Place your hands on your knees, bend your knees and bring your chest down. Try to keep the soles of your feet flat on the floor. If your knees are stiff, you may have to extend your arms out in front to act as a counterbalance. Otherwise, keep your hands on your knees. As well as exercising the knees, this movement gives your calf muscles a good workout.

Side view for calf workout

This shows the depth of the squat required to stretch the calf muscles fully. Take your time, and as your suppleness grows, deepen the position little by little.

Knee stretch

1 From the start position shown above for the calf workout lower your weight onto one knee, as shown. Make sure that the opposite leg is fully extended and that you make contact with the floor only with the heel of that extended foot. Either extend your arms to maintain your balance or place one hand on your knees and the other on the floor. Hold for five to ten seconds.

2 Repeat for the other leg, again holding the position for five to ten seconds. Do not attempt this exercise if you have a knee problem of any description.

Neck Conditioning

Neck-conditioning exercises are crucial in the preparation of the body. Centre the head between each side-to-side movement and don't rotate it in a complete circle as this can damage the vertebrae and, in some cases, the arteries in the side of the neck.

Neck conditioning 1

1 This first step is simply to turn to the side and look slightly behind while not moving your shoulders.

2 Bring your head back into central alignment momentarily before repeating this movement on the other side. Make sure you keep your shoulders still.

Neck conditioning 2

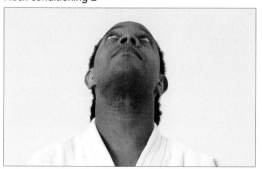

1 Look upwards and then bring your head down to a central position, hold this momentarily.

2 Now move your head so you are looking downwards, effectively putting your chin on your chest.

Neck conditioning 3

1 Bring your head up again and then, facing directly forward, pick a point on the wall to focus on. While still able to see that point, turn your head to the right.

2 Next, rotate your head downwards in a half circle to the same point on the left side. Repeat steps 1 and 2.

3 Rotate your head in a semicircle from left to right, pausing momentarily, and then right to left. Try to touch your chin on your chest in between movements.

Wrist Flexibility

You must exercise your wrists vigorously, known as tekubi kansetsu junan undo, before every aikido training session. This special emphasis is due to the fact that many of the techniques are directed at the wrists, forearms and elbows.

Nikkyo

1 Place one hand over the back of the other, as shown, and with a curling motion draw the hand back towards your chest. This flexes the wrist and also conditions the back of the hand.

2 In this position you can see the hand fully drawn back and at maximum stretch.

Sankyo

1–3 These three images show the conditioning exercise for a technique called sankyo. Take your hand, as shown here, and using a type of wringing action, stretch the wrist outwards, away from the body.

Kote gaeshi

1–2 For this conditioning exercise take your hand in the other and twist it inwards and downwards in front of your body. Imagine that your mind is a high-pressure water jet blasting up your body from your centre and through the arms and fingers.

Basic Movements

This section introduces the hanmi stance and deals with the basic aikido body movements: tandoku dosa, solo exercises, and sotai dosa, exercises with a partner. Tandoku dosa teaches the student how to stand up properly and, using certain body motions, how to distribute their weight to allow rapid movement in any direction. In sotai dosa you are able to test your stability and "centredness" with a partner holding you strongly to enable you to learn to displace your partner's balance without recourse to physical strength.

USING THE TANDEN

A student first has to become aware of the tanden, or centre of gravity (see page 403). Doing this is largely a spiritual exercise where breathing techniques and a strong imagination play an important part. Initially, one has to learn to contemplate this centre in a quiet environment. It is much more difficult to "keep centred" when moving around.

Hanmi is the basic kamae, or posture, that the aikido practitioner assumes in which they stand as if holding a Japanese sword. The bokken, or wooden sword, is held in the same way as in kendo, and the difference lies in the kamae. Kendo and its subordinate art iaido, or way of drawing the sword, involve the feet pointing directly forwards, parallel to each other. Hanmi involves positioning the feet apart with the back foot pointing outwards at approximately 60 degrees to the forward foot. Tandoku dosa, or solo training, helps the student to move from the centre. One learns that the centre moves first and then the body follows. Sotai dosa is a more advanced level where the student learns to move in a centred way, while also dealing with another person holding with full strength.

Hanmi

This is the basic stance of aikido and is called hanmi, which means "half stance". This is a reference to the angle the body assumes in relation to an attacker – about 45 degrees to the front.

Hidari (left) hanmi

Turning at 45 degrees to an attacker, your feet assume the back triangle stance, or ura sankaku. Hold your hands as if you were gripping a Japanese sword (though with fingers extended), with, in this case of left hanmi, the left hand at approximately the height of the solar plexus and the other at the height of the navel.

Migi (right) hanmi

This right hanmi posture shows how with 60 to 70 per cent of your body weight on the front foot, and the back foot at an angle of approximately 60 degrees to the front foot, this is a versatile posture that permits rapid movement in any direction.

Tandoku Dosa

These solo exercises are unique to aikido and involve repetition of the art's core movements. Their aim is to teach you to move your body evasively while maintaining hanmi, or the half-stance posture (see opposite).

This is where you first become aware of the importance of maintaining a stable posture and of the centre line of the body, and its role in moving you out of the line of an attack.

The following movements occur naturally in the techniques themselves but here they are taken out of context so that you can practise them until they become second nature.

Irimi ashi: tsugi ashi

1 This is the right hanmi posture. From here the idea is to push forward off the back foot with both feet, gliding across the surface of the floor and advancing across the dojo in the same right posture. The back foot follows behind.

2 The back foot has followed up closely behind the front foot and the whole movement is about to start again. At this stage the knees are slightly bent and the hands and forearms are extended as if cutting upwards with two sword blades.

3 Perform continuously until you reach the other side of the dojo, where you make tenkai ashi (a 180-degree pivot) on the balls of your feet. Continue until you get back to where you started from.

Irimi ashi: ayumi ashi

1 As before, the posture is right hanmi, but this time the back foot comes forward in the same way as it does for normal walking. It is important to practise repetitions in both postures.

2 The body weight starts to transfer from the right to the left foot as the left foot comes forward. Keep the balls of both feet in contact with the floor for stability and to move off the attacking line.

3 With left foot forward, the student is in left hanmi and ready to bring the right foot forward to repeat the movement on the other side. Practise this up and down the dojo, turning in tenkai ashi each end.

Tenkan ashi

1 Start in the hanmi stance, as shown here, and prepare for the tenkan, or turning movement, which is one of the cornerstones of aikido.

2 Pivoting on the front foot by 180 degrees, pass through the kaiten, or rotation movement. Keep the ball of your rear foot in contact with the floor at all times.

3 By drawing the right foot circularly back the student faces the opposite direction to where he started. It is important to keep your weight on your front foot.

Kaiten ashi

Tenkan

The tenkan, or turning movement, is one of the cornerstones of aikido. It involves passing through the kaiten movement shown to the left and pivoting on the front foot by 180 degrees, remembering to keep the ball of your rear foot in light contact with the floor at all times.

Irimi tenkan

For irimi tenkan, take a large step forward, as shown in irimi in step 1 on page 421, before making the pivot described here. For irimi tenkan where you enter with the back foot, step forward with the back foot and then perform the pivot.

1 Pictured here is the kaiten, or rotation movement. From the hanmi stance, step off the central line – the imaginary line of an attack that is aimed at the centre of your body, whether the face or the stomach – with your leading foot.

2 As you place that foot, rotate your hips so that your body is now facing in the same direction as the attack. Your left hand here is used not to block any movement, but to parry or deflect it. The idea is to get behind the attack and allow it to carry on.

Shikko

Unique to aikido, shikko, also known as samurai knee walking, derives from Japan's feudal history where there were no chairs, and all social activity – doing business. eating a meal or sitting in conversation – was carried out in the formal kneeling position known as seiza.

A samurai had to be ready for sudden attack, even while seated, and although etiquette meant that he had to surrender his katana, or long sword, at the door of a host's house before entering, he was entitled to retain his kodachi, or short sword. Defence from a kneeling position with a sword was one of the samurai's essential skills. Called iai jutsu, or the art of fast sword drawing, it enabled an exponent to react swiftly to sudden aggression, very often cutting down an assailant without even having to stand up. The knee movements first used in this way form the basis of samurai walking in aikido.

Physically, shikko is also very beneficial, exercising many parts of the body at the same time – the waist and hips, knees, ankles and toes are all stimulated. By far the most important reason for practising shikko is to become aware of the importance of using your hips and your body's centre of gravity, or tanden, to facilitate economy of movement. Because you do not have the same mobility on your knees as you do on your feet, if you can perform techniques well on your knees, the improvement in your standing techniques becomes more marked.

1 Start in right hanmi position, with your weight on the toes and knee of your left leg, incline your weight forward and go down onto the right knee.

2 Swivelling forward on that right knee, and with a strong hip movement, bring your left knee forward while keeping both feet together, as shown here.

3 Place your left knee on the floor and begin the whole motion again, swivelling on your left knee this time. Ensure that each forward motion originates from the hips and that you maintain the defensive position of the hands: in other words, make sure that your leading hand is the same as your leading knee.

Sotai Dosa

In paired exercises you are able to test your stability and "centredness" with a partner holding you strongly (usually by the wrists), the aim being to learn to displace your partner's centre and, therefore, balance, with a variety of extension techniques.

Sotai dosa are paired exercises designed to familiarize you with aikido movements. In the basic exercises shown here, learn how to move your partner's body using kokyu, or breath power, as opposed to strength, as well as move off the centre line of your partner's attack. These exercises vary from school to school, but the principles are the same. This sequence shows the gyaku hanmi katate-dori irimi exercise practised at jodan (upper level), chudan (middle level) and gedan (lower level).

Gyaku hanmi katate-dori

In this starting position the uke holds his partner's wrist and tries to keep the grip all the way through the movement.

Irimi jodan

This exercise moves your partner's centre of gravity without recourse to physical strength. Tori steps forward with the leading foot and pushes off with the back foot. The same entering movement is used at three levels – jodan (upper), chudan (middle) and gedan (lower). These are selected according to whether your opponent is taller, the same size or smaller than you. The levels also show the motion to deal with an attack to the head, to the midsection and below the belt. Here (left) tori cuts upwards while bending his front knee and leaning his gravity into the cutting motion. Uke is driven away with great force. He maintains a strong grip, but relaxes his shoulders to harmonize with the force rather than resisting it.

Chudan

From the starting position the same movement is repeated, but now tori enters with his extension at chudan or middle level.

Gedan

From the starting position the same movement is repeated, but now tori enters with his hands at the gedan or lower level.

Kaiten

Kaiten is a movement used to deflect an opponent's energy sideways. Tori steps slightly to his right, then turns his hips left-wards, deflecting uke's power.

Uchi kaiten

1 From the starting position tori cuts upwards with a spiral motion to raise uke's elbow, entering slightly with his forward foot.

2 Tori then enters with his back leg passing inside underneath uke's arm.

3 With a sharp turn of the hips tori cuts downwards, projecting uke's elbow forward and causing loss of balance. Tori needs to cut with the gripped arm as if it were a sword. This extension causes uke's raised elbow to project forward and takes away his capacity to generate strength.

Gyaku hanmi katate-dori tenkan ho

This is the reverse-stance one-handed-grip turning movement, which is also called the tenkan, and is one of the most fundamental movements in aikido. The successful execution of the body-turning motions shown here rely on understanding the mechanics of the movement and also keeping aware of your centre of gravity, the tanden.

1 With your right hand, take your partner's left wrist, or vice versa. Incline your body weight forward, establishing good contact with your partner's extended energy.

2 Turning your hips to the right, drop your bodyweight on to your partner's grip. Imagine you are uniting with his power. Pivot on your leading foot and draw the rear foot 180 degrees to the back of your partner.

3 Extend the hand that is being held forward and your free hand as well. This creates the feeling that energy is being extended from your tanden and that your body is working as a whole unit.

1 Your right wrist is gripped by your partner's right hand.

Ai hanmi katate-dori irimi

Illustrated here is ai hanmi katate-dori irimi, a one-handed mutual-stance entering step. In ai hanmi the contact is right hand to right hand, or vice versa. This sequence shows tori entering with the forward foot, keeping his back foot in balance with his partner's. Some schools call this attack kosa dori, meaning a crossed-hands grip. This movement is not so practically relevant to a contemporary fighting context, and originates from the fact that both ai hanmi and gyaku hanmi wrist attacks were used in many of the old grappling arts. It is important for uke to try and maintain a flexible grip throughout these exercises.

2 (first variation) As you step forward with your right foot, raise your right arm, as if you are cutting upwards with a sword and then push forward with your centre. This is irimi with the leading foot in front of uke.

2 (second variation) Place your left hand on the attacker's neck or shoulder and pull her backwards slightly, taking her balance. Then extend your sword arm to weaken the attacker's grip. This is the classic shikaku, or blind spot position, in which uke's back is directly in front of tori's chest. This is irimi made with the rear foot coming forward and behind uke.

Ai hanmi uchi kaiten

This movement is known as an uchi kaiten, or inward rotary exercise. Shown here is ai hanmi when both uke and tori are in a right hanmi stance. It involves rotating inside and underneath uke's arm. Tori's attitude when cutting up with her right hand is that the underside of her hand and arm is the cutting edge of a sword. Tori does not lift her hand to raise uke's arm, but leans her body weight into the cutting-up motion. This provides far more power than just muscular strength.

1 In this situation, the uke (the person receiving the technique) is attacking the wrist of the tori (the person delivering the technique).

2 Tori steps in with her right foot and raises her hands as if cutting upward with a sword. Tori's left hand is here shown inside uke's right arm.

3 She steps under the uke's raised arm and rotates her body inwards with a turn of her hips. At the same time she pushes down on the uke's arm, as if cutting downwards with a sword.

Irimi issoku

This routine involves entering with one step into the side of your partner. The attack here is gyaku hanmi katate-dori, but this movement can be adapted to any attack and serves two purposes: to enter into the attacker's shikaku, or blind spot, neutralizing the attack; and to disengage the attacker's grip.

1 As your partner grabs you by your right wrist, resist the temptation to pull your hand back.

2 Instead, enter with your right foot and rotate your hand in a spiralling movement. Using your left hand to cut off his remaining grip, enter deeply behind him.

3 In this final position you are in your partner's shikaku, or blind spot. From here it is possible to execute a wide variety of disabling techniques.

Ukemi

Literally defined as "the art of falling", as in a forward or backward roll, ukemi is probably the first thing that you will be taught how to do when you join an aikido club. The reason for this is that you must learn how to neutralize the effects of aikido techniques and build up the confidence necessary to fall to the floor without injuring yourself. Only by doing this will you be able to learn the art and so make progress.

The concept behind ukemi is actually a lot deeper than this rather simplistic explanation implies, and it can be more appropriately described as "the art of recovery". This is because every technique applied on you in aikido requires you either to neutralize or recover from it – this principle is true no matter what situation you have been put in – be it a throw, an arm lock or a pinning technique. Being able to recover, or take ukemi, is central to learning aikido, because when techniques are applied with full commitment they can be dangerous if the practitioner cannot take ukemi.

Mae Ukemi

This sequence demonstrates the mae ukemi, or forward roll. It is a basic movement in aikido that will help to ensure your safety from the outset. All ukemi techniques require making your body as free of tension as you can, here achieved by losing your balance into the roll.

1 In the start position for the front roll, place the little finger of your hand on the tatami (mat), and adopt an attitude of extending yourself forward.

2 From the front foot, push off and roll along your leading arm, diagonally across your back and then up the other arm. As you push yourself forward, adopt an attitude of losing your balance into the roll, rather than mechanically placing yourself in it. In this way you are "recovering" from the situation.

3 This is the position you are in as you come out of the roll. When performed correctly, it will involve contact with the outside muscles of your arms, shoulder, back and leg, and it acts almost as a body massage. As a result, at the end of a practice you should be enjoying a feeling of well-being, though the function of the movement is, perhaps, one day to save your life.

Ushiro Ukemi

This sequence demonstrates the ushiro ukemi, or backward roll. Again, as with mae ukemi, aim for an attitude of actually losing your balance into the roll so that you create the feeling of recovering it again. This prevents you becoming too mechanical and tense.

1 Stand as shown, with one foot behind the other and your arms extended out in front of your body.

2 Lower your weight onto the outside of your calf muscle (not your knee), and project your bottom out as if making yourself into a ball.

3 Roll back onto your outer thigh and diagonally across your back, kicking your legs over your shoulder. It is important to tuck your chin in as you roll. This keeps your head off the mat and ensures that you roll across the back of your shoulders and end up on the leg you started with.

4 During this movement, your body should make contact with the floor as it did for mae ukemi, but this time in reverse order – leg, back, shoulder and finally your arm.

5 This is the position adopted after the roll and prior to the standing up position shown in step 1.

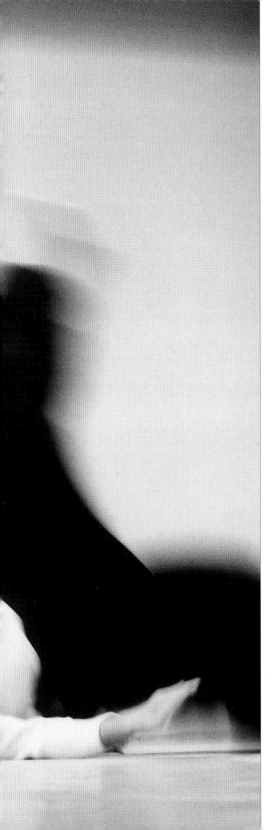

Aikido techniques

There are literally hundreds of techniques within the framework of aikido, and in a book of this scope it is only possible to show some of them. Because the art of aikido is based on certain core principles, it is possible to interpret instructions in a variety of ways. It is wise to be wary of an instructor who says that there is only one way to do things because as long as something makes sense within the framework of aikido, it is likely to work. The one thing most true aikidokas attempt to relinquish through their training is their ego. Included in this section are some of the classic attacks within the aikido repertoire. Some styles are more martial than others and feature strong attacks, while others modify the intensity and are used more as a medium of contact between partners to facilitate the practice of technique.

Striking Methods

The following techniques are the basic strikes most commonly used in aikido. They are taken from classical Japanese attacks with the sword, spear and knife rather than contemporary fighting attacks. All attacks in aikido – even a grip on the wrist – are made with full commitment. Without this, the techniques cannot be practised. This is because without a committed, spirited attack there is no force to harmonize with, no energy to deflect – quite simply, no aikido!

Aikido techniques are executed when two partners come together and a contact is established. When that contact is ai hanmi, both partners have the same foot forward – right foot to right foot. When the contact is gyaku hanmi, the partners have their opposite feet forward – right foot to left foot. This idea permeates all aikido technique in that as the attacks become more advanced the postures of both partners remain the same. Let us take the example of shomen-uchi, a strike to the front of the head with the blade of the hand (see below).

As contact is made, the partners end up in the same posture as in ai hanmi katate-dori. Conversely, yokomen-uchi is a similar strike, but the target is the side of the head. As contact is made here, both partners come together in gyaku hanmi. This principle applies to every technique and is the main reason why ai hanmi and gyaku hanmi techniques constitute the majority of what is practised in a typical dojo. Repetitive training in basic technique from these two postures, therefore, prepares practitioners for more advanced training.

Shomen-uchi

This first sequence of images is shomen-uchi, or front-head strike, based on the basic overhead cut with a Japanese sword. Tori protects his head against a possible thrust to his face, prior to extending his handblade in a large circle towards the front of uke's head.

1 As its name suggests, this attack is made with the blade of the hand held as if it were a sword striking the centre of uke's head.

2 Tori brings his feet together while simultaneously protecting his face.

3 As he steps onto his right foot, he launches the attack. This all happens in one flowing motion, with the strike quickly executed and aimed above the target as if cutting on the backstroke in the same way as a sword. You should adopt the feeling of "cutting" and not "hitting" the target.

Yokomen-uchi

This sequence shows yokomen-uchi, or side head strike. Steps 1 and 2 for shomen-uchi (see opposite) are repeated; but in step 3 the cut is aimed circularly at the side of uke's head/neck. The power is generated by a hip turn.

1 This attack begins in the same way as shomen-uchi, with the blade of the left hand held as if it were a sword, but this time the strike is slightly diagonal to the side of the head or neck.

2 Tori brings his feet together while simultaneously protecting his face with his right hand.

3 As he steps onto his right foot, tori launches the attack. This happens in one flowing motion, and the strike is executed quickly, aimed to the side of the head or upper neck. Adopt the feeling of "cutting" and not "hitting" the target.

Chudan Tsuki

The middle thrust, or chudan tsuki, is a modern punching technique. The original punching style was based on a knife thrust to the midsection called furizuki, or upward circular thrust, performed as if holding a knife and hiding it, and then striking towards the solar plexus.

1 This attack begins in the same way as shomen-uchi, with the blade of the left hand held as if it were a sword. The punching fist is held underneath the right ribcage with the shoulder pulled in.

2 Tori brings his feet together, extending his left hand as a protection against an attack.

3 As he steps on to his right foot, tori launches the attack in one flowing motion, with the strike executed quickly. As the forward step with the right foot is made, the left hand pulls back and the right fist travels out.

Chudan tsuki thrust
When tori's attacking arm is two-thirds extended (the stage shown between step 2 and step 3), the wrist rotates sharply so that the right-hand palm is face down. Step 3 illustrates how the impact is made with the knuckles of the index and third fingers and the fist makes contact at the area between the left and right ribs, just below the breastbone. The power of the punch is generated by a turn of the hips.

Grabbing Techniques

Shown below are some of the classic grabbing attacks. The attitude when grabbing should be one of trying to control your partner's whole body. It is also important to attack off the centre line of your partner, positioning yourself so you are difficult to hit.

Ai hanmi katate-dori

Also called kosa-dori, this is a mutual-stance one-hand hold. Both uke (the person receiving) and tori (the person delivering) are in the same stance and making contact with the same hand left to left, or right to right).

Gyaku hanmi katate-dori

Here uke and tori assume an opposite, or reverse, posture to each other. Contact is made with opposite hands (right hand to left). Uke must grip with the little finger first quite strongly, then each successive finger with a little less power.

Sode-dori

In this attack called sode-dori, or sleeve grab, uke grasps tori's sleeve. It is a more practical attack than the wrist grips already shown here, and gives tori an opportunity to practise the same techniques as in gyaku hanmi.

Kata-dori

Uke grabs tori at the shoulder in kata-dori, or shoulder grab. The contact is the same as in gyaku hanmi (see above), so this attack enables training in the techniques from that posture. Uke can attack with a free foot or hand, and so tori must move off that line of attack and out of danger as a defence technique is applied.

Morote-dori

Uke grips tori's wrist with both hands in morote-dori, or two hands holding one wrist. From tori's perspective, although the stance is gyaku hanmi (see above), it is possible to practise both ai hanmi and gyaku hanmi style techniques because there are now two hands to choose between.

Rear-attack Techniques

Some of the simpler rear-attack techniques, or ushirowaza, can be taught at a beginner or intermediate level, but the majority are for intermediate to advanced training. Traditionally, ushirowaza techniques begin with uke and tori in ai hanmi stance with their hands crossed and fingertips pointing at each other's eyes (see step 1 below). This equates to the position in aikido swordsmanship of seigan, or crossed swords pointing at the eyes. The most basic attack is uke gripping both of tori's wrists from behind (ushiro ryote-dori) as shown below.

Always remain aware of your tanden when practising ushirowaza. This ensures that you are as stable as possible and that your balance is difficult to disturb. Constant tanden awareness also means that you can extend your energy forwards, essential in the execution of many techniques from this attack, as your body actually moves backwards. Practising renzoku uchikomi, or continuous stepping and striking practice, with a partner in aiki ken (aikido swordsmanship), up and down the dojo, is an excellent way of understanding this concept (see pages 474–5).

There are many techniques within ushirowaza. In ushiro ryo sode-dori both sleeves are gripped; in ushiro ryo hijitori both elbows are gripped; in ushiro ryo kata-dori both shoulders are gripped; in ushiro katate-dori kube-shime one wrist is gripped while a choke hold is applied with the other arm; and in ushiro munedakishime a bear hug is applied from behind. All of these movements begin from the crossed-hand position below. The attacker never approaches from behind. Virtually all aikido techniques can be practised from ushiro attacks.

Crossing hands

1 In this posture, uke and tori are in ai hanmi stance (see page 426) crossing hands as if they were two swords. This is the classical beginning of all ushirowaza, or techniques from attacks to the rear.

Entering behind

2 Here uke cuts tori's arm down with his leading swordhand, gripping the wrist at the same time and moving the balance forwards. This makes it easier for uke to advance round the back of tori.

Ushiro ryote-dori

3 Uke takes a large step with the rear foot around the back of tori and grabs the other wrist. The aim is to grasp the other wrist and immobilize tori's arms. In the original grappling arts the intent would be to pull the arms back together and strike the centre of the spine with the knee causing damage. The most basic of the ushirowaza attacks, ushiro ryote-dori, or two hands on two hands from behind, is also known as ushiro tekubi tori, behind wrist hold.

Applying the Techniques

The diversity that exists when it comes to the application of aikido techniques can be confusing for new students. However, no matter what style of instruction aikido teachers adopt, all are united by the principles that the founder taught. On the next few pages there follows a selection of techniques picked from the hundreds available, and these include many of the classic attacks in the aikido repertoire.

As well as the variety of teaching styles, dependent on the perspective of the individual teacher, aikido has large and flowing techniques as well as those that are short and sharp. Remember also that there are both traditional and non-traditional forms of the art and it makes you realize the variation that is out there. The techniques that follow represent only a fraction of what is available. Some of the techniques are in omote form, which means movements initially towards the front of an attacker, and others are in ura form which are movements towards the back of an attacker. These concepts roughly equate to irimi and tenkan, or entering and turning in relation to your partner.

SWORDSMANSHIP WITHOUT THE SWORD

This phrase is sometimes used to describe the rationale behind aikido techniques. Whether you are an advocate of weapons or not, it is plain to see that the various thrusting, spiral and circular arm and body movements are based on the movements found in Japanese swordsmanship (also, to a lesser extent, in Japanese spearfighting, as typified by the jo). When looking at the techniques on the following pages look carefully at the postures, arm movements and positions and if you place an imaginary bokken (wooden sword) or jo in the hands of tori – the person executing the technique – you will often see the relevance of the actions.

Suwariwaza Kata-dori Ikkyo Omote

Suwariwaza, or seated techniques, are a throwback to old Japan when business was conducted in the seated seiza position. Defence techniques were developed to counter attacks to someone in seiza by either an armed or unarmed aggressor.

1 Uke attacks using a kata-dori (shoulder grab). Tori and uke are in gyaku hanmi, or reverse posture, in relation to one another. Uke positions himself as he grabs tori's shoulder so that he must take one step forward in order to be able to strike tori with the other hand. This is the correct ma-ai or combative distance. Tori needs to move as if he were going to be hit with uke's free hand.

2 Tori moves his body to the side with shikko (knee walking), stretching his right arm outwards and cutting down on uke's arm with his left, causing him to lose balance.

3 Tori takes uke's wrist, pressing it against his right shoulder. Simultaneously, tori enters into uke's side, applying handblade pressure to uke's elbow.

4 Entering by stepping forward with his right leg, tori controls uke's elbow and pushes him down with power from the hips. It is important to relax the shoulders and move from your centre.

5 Tori pins uke's arm and wrist with power from his tanden, or centre of gravity. Always pin uke's arm higher than 90 degrees to the body. This is to prevent uke gaining leverage to resist.

Suwariwaza Shomen-uchi Irimi-nage Ura

This seated front-head-strike technique encapsulates the idea of harmonizing with an attack, neutralizing it, and then applying defence. Throughout the movement tori is a whirlwind in the centre of the action, sending uke spinning around his centre of gravity.

1 Uke and tori start this sequence in hanmi when uke and tori face each other in a half stance or 45 degrees to each other.

2 Uke enters with his rear foot and makes a shomen-uchi strike. Tori enters with his rear foot and deflects with his sword arm, gripping uke's collar.

3 Tori continues to turn, swivelling on his knee and dissipating uke's energy. At this stage tori and uke are facing the same direction.

4 Tori withdraws his right foot in a circular move and drops his weight on the collar grip made in step 2. Uke follows trying to retain his balance.

5 Tori reverses his stance and body weight by swivelling on his right knee and raising his left leg. Then, withdrawing his left knee, tori projects uke to the mat.

6 Restraining uke's neck with his left handblade, tori uses his right hand to control uke's free arm.

Suwariwaza Shomen-uchi Kote-gaeshi

The actual body movement of this front-head-strike technique is almost identical to irimi-nage. The focus now, however, is on uke's wrist. The idea is to place your hand on the back of his as a perfect match and to turn it sharply outwards and downwards.

1 Uke (the person receiving the technique) and tori (the person delivering the technique) start off in hanmi.

2 Uke attacks with shomen-uchi, or a front-head strike, and tori deflects the strike with his sword arm.

3 Tori simultaneously takes uke's wrist with his left hand. This enables tori to control uke's hand prior to tori placing his other hand on the back of uke's hand. Tori extends power from his tanden, making it impossible for uke to lift his arm.

4 Placing his hand on the back of uke's wrist, tori swivels on his right knee and applies pressure on uke's wrist, causing him to fall to the mat. The sudden inward twisting of uke's hand causes uke's wrist to buckle – the discomfort he feels makes him lean forward to compensate and therefore he loses his balance. Uke must harmonize with tori.

5 Tori applies strong pressure on the back of uke's elbow and, maintaining the grip with his left hand, forces uke to spin over onto his front.

6 Tori applies an immobilizing pin with both arms. This is done by tori hugging uke's arm against his body, the lower arm just below uke's elbow and the upper arm gripping uke's wrist. Pressure is applied by a total body turn towards uke's head – this can result in dislocation of the shoulder joint if applied too hard.

Hanmi Handachi Shiho-nage Ura

Hanmi handachi techniques involve one sitting and one standing, practised to simulate tori dealing with a taller opponent. The technique here is shiho-nage, or four-corner throw from behind. The principle is to fold the attacker in half to bring him down to your size.

1 Uke and tori start off in hanmi handachi with tori sitting and uke standing. The full name for this position is gyaku hanmi katate-dori, or one-handed grip.

2 Tori makes a tenkan movement, cutting forward with her sword arm to take uke's balance.

3 Tori cuts upwards and enters under uke's arm, simultaneously taking uke's wrist with her other hand.

4 With a strong turn of the hip, tori swivels on her left knee and cuts down the centre line of her body with both of her hands holding uke's wrist.

5 Entering deeply behind uke, tori drops onto her right knee and pins uke's wrist, as shown.

Hanmi Handachi Uchi Kaiten-nage

This is an example of the rotary or spin throw with one sitting and one standing. The idea is for tori to spin uke onto his back and not to throw him into a forward roll. Uke manipulates his own body to roll to safety in a kind of half forward, half sideways ukemi.

1 Uke and tori begin this sequence in hanmi handachi.

2 Tori raises uke's elbow by cutting upwards with her gripped hand in a kind of spiral motion. Having raised uke's elbow and broken the power of his grip, tori then enters underneath his arm.

3 Drawing uke's arm back, tori keeps uke's head down with her left hand.

4 Tori grips uke's left wrist with her right hand from underneath while maintaining the pressure on uke's neck. At this stage tori is not throwing uke directly forward – the idea is to spin him onto his back so tori is extending across uke's body.

5 Stepping forward with a strong turn of the hip, tori throws uke with a spinning motion – this is achieved in the following way. Tori's right hand, while still being held, cuts upwards from underneath and takes a strong grip on uke's arm. While keeping uke's head down with her left hand, tori then enters with her right foot onto her right knee in shikko, or knee walk, driving forcefully with her right hip. By tori extending her right arm, uke's arm is pushed forward creating pressure on his shoulder from which ukemi is the only answer.

Hanmi Handachi Yokomen-uchi Shiho-nage

Yokomen-uchi, or side-head strike, features a strike to the side of tori's head with the handblade. No block is involved. Tori extends his arms to meet uke's attack and harmonize with the movement. Then uke's attack is neutralized and her balance extended forward.

1 Uke and tori start here in hanmi handachi. Uke attacks in a circular motion and tori moves off the attacking line inside of uke's motion. Tori extends his arms as if raising a sword to parry an attack.

2 As uke attacks with yokomen-uchi, or side-head strike, the target of which is the side of the head, tori moves in a circular fashion inside the strike, parrying with his left sword arm and trapping uke's attacking arm, drawing her balance towards him.

3 Tori raises uke's arm by cutting up in a spiral as if raising a sword. Then, controlling uke's wrist with both hands, tori enters under the arm with his rear foot and, swivelling 180 degrees on his left knee, cuts down.

4 Now, facing uke, tori enters with his right foot dropping onto his knee. Cutting down as if with a sword, tori destroys uke's balance as she begins to topple back.

5 The final pinning position. Tori pins uke's wrist to the floor, with his body weight ensuring that there is no gap between uke's elbow and her head. In the original jujutsu form the technique would include a finishing blow to the head.

Ai Hanmi Katate-dori Shiho-nage Omote

The most basic way to practise this one-hand grab technique, this represents the principle of cutting up and down with a sword. From the initial grab tori cuts across uke's belly with a sword, steps in while raising the sword, turns by 180 degrees and cuts down again.

1 Uke starts this attack by grabbing tori's right wrist with ai hanmi katate-dori, or a mutual-stance one-handed grab.

2 Tori takes uke's wrist and, reinforcing with the left hand, deflects uke's energy sideways. Because tori stretches uke's arm in front of him and to the side, a dead side is created so that uke cannot retaliate in any way.

3 Tori steps forward with his back leg and raises uke's arm as if raising a sword. This causes stress on uke's wrist which he cannot resist and facilitates tori's movement underneath uke's arm.

5 As if cutting down with a sword, tori leans his centre of gravity forward and takes control of uke with strong pressure on his wrist and elbow.

Step 5 pinning technique

When applying the final pinning movement, don't allow any gap between uke's elbow and his head. If there is a gap then uke can generate more power to resist the pinning effect and potentially wriggle out of the grab.

4 By turning 180 degrees with a powerful twist of the hip, tori controls uke's elbow and wrist, causing him to lose his balance backwards.

Gyaku Hanmi Uchi Kaiten-nage Omote

This is a basic way of doing this inward rotary throw technique and is another good example of the idea of cutting up and down in the same way as with a sword. It is vital for tori to push forward with the elbow as he cuts upwards, otherwise uke will be able to stop him.

1 Uke begins this sequence by attacking tori with gyaku hanmi katate-dori. This is when uke and tori are in reverse postures and uke is gripping tori's wrist with one hand.

2 Tori raises uke's elbow by cutting upwards with his arm, as if raising a sword. This takes away uke's capacity to generate strength in that arm and enables tori to slip underneath it.

3 Tori steps under uke's raised arm with his rear leg and applies a strong hip turn, cutting forwards across uke's body.

4 Stepping back with his right leg and cutting low to the floor, tori takes uke's left wrist and, with his left hand, prevents uke from standing up.

Step 4 firm control
In step 4, keep uke's head under control with your centre of gravity rather than with upper-arm strength.

5 Entering with his whole body and turning his hips, tori extends his right arm and exerts pressure on uke's left shoulder. As tori is already controlling uke's head, uke's body is compelled to spin onto his back. Rather than crash onto his back uke extends himself half forwards, half sideways and takes ukemi, rolling out of danger.

Ai Hanmi Katate-dori Udegarami-nage Omote

This one-hand grab technique begins like the ikkyo arm pin, taking uke down prior to the throw. As he does this, tori takes his own wrist for added power. Uke's wrist control and body position are very similar to shiho-nage but the effect is amplified by the arm twining.

1 Here we see uke attacking tori with ai hanmi katate-dori, or mutal-stance one-hand grab (see page 426).

2 Tori cuts upwards with his right sword hand while controlling uke's right elbow with his left. So, with his held right hand tori uses his handblade to cut into uke's wrist, breaking his grip. This raises uke's elbow, which tori takes with his left hand and then steps in and drops his weight onto uke's elbow.

3 Tori steps in deeply towards uke's armpit with his left foot. While uke is low down, tori takes his own right wrist with his left hand prior to the entering movement of the next stage.

4 Tori takes a sweeping, circular step with his right foot around the front of uke with the attitude of hitting his face with his own hand.

5 Tori makes a tenkan movement with his right foot and applies pressure to uke's arm. Here tenkan, or a turning movement, is shown from steps 4–5 as tori steps in front of uke and makes a 180-degree turn on his right foot. This has the effect of forcing him downwards where tori can finally control his arm by his head.

6 This is the final pinning position of the technique. Uke's wrist and elbow are bent (see box to right). Tori extends his two hands away from himself, causing uke to submit.

Ai hanmi katate-dori pin
The pin shown here is similar to that for shiho-nage, except that both hands are used. Tori's left hand grabs his own right wrist for added leverage and power. Tori extends downwards, exerting strong pressure on uke's wrist and elbow.

Gyaku Hanmi Irimi-nage Ura

This is a basic way to do the entering throw from a reverse-stance one-hand grip. Tori disengages the grip and enters behind uke into the shikaku, or blind spot. The priority is to keep turning, staying in the centre of the action, with uke spinning around tori's centre.

1 Uke attacks with a wrist grab in gyaku hanmi katate-dori, or reverse stance one-hand grab.

2 Tori disengages uke's hand. To do this, tori rotates his gripped left hand/wrist inwards and at the same time cuts off the remnants of that grip with his right handblade. Tori then enters deep behind uke using the irimi issoku movement, entering into the side of uke with a single step.

3 Looking in the same direction as uke, tori turns by pivoting on his left foot, turning uke with him and destroying his balance.

4 Tori takes uke's collar and, by reversing his body weight, turns to face in the opposite direction. This involves the tenkai ashi movement, a 180-degree pivot on the balls of both feet, transferring the body weight from a frontal direction to behind.

Step 2: the power of weight transfer
Tori transfers his weight from his right foot to his left in step 2 as he turns. This completely destroys uke's balance prior to the throw in steps 3 and 4.

5 Tori, stepping in with his rear foot, cuts down across uke's neck to bring him down. The power of the throw is effected by a strong turn of the hips, plus an attitude of cutting down the centre line of your own body, rotating the arm as if sticking the thumb into the mat.

Irimi-nage
The movement of irimi-nage is executed across uke's body. Tori enters more into the side than directly to the front as he cuts to fell uke. Tori extends his fingers and cuts down as if trying to dig his thumb into the mat.

Shikaku
In the gyaku hanmi irimi-nage ura waza sequence shown here it is important that tori enters deeply behind uke into the position known as the shikaku, or blind spot. In this position uke's back is effectively in front of tori's chest.

Shomen-uchi Shiho-nage Omote

The execution of this front-head-strike four-direction throw technique is the same as for ai hanmi katate-dori shiho-nage (see page 442). The difference is the attack, so once tori has parried the initial strike and extended uke's arm, the concluding movements are the same.

1 Uke prepares to step forward and make a strike at tori with shomen-uchi (a front head strike).

2 Tori extends her right sword arm, harmonizing with the blow. Stepping off the central line of the attack, she uses both hands to grip uke's wrist.

3 Tori diverts uke's energy with a turn of her hips. At this point uke cannot generate any power in his arm and is thus powerless to resist tori's technique.

4 Tori follows up the manoeuvre by stepping in with her rear foot, stepping under uke's arm, and pivoting 180 degrees.

5 Tori cuts down with her whole body causing uke to fall backwards. Tori does this by imagining uke's elbow as the tip of a sword and his wrist as the handle of that sword and then cuts as if she is cutting from her centre of gravity.

Shomen-uchi Irimi-nage Ura

The difference between this front-head strike technique and ai hanmi katate-dori irimi-nage is the attack. Shomen-uchi is a strike, katate-dori is a grab. After the strike has been parried, the actual body movements of the two techniques are the same.

1 In this sequence, uke prepares to launch a strike with shomen-uchi.

2 Tori "blends" with the attack by entering forward and deflecting the blow with her raised sword arm.

3 Tori enters deeply behind uke, cutting his arm down and breaking his balance, making him start to fall backwards. In this position tori has grabbed uke's collar from behind with her left hand, and is pulling backwards and controlling his right arm with her right handblade.

4 Pivoting on her left foot, tori draws uke's energy out in a circular fashion, causing him to lose his balance.

5 By transferring her body weight from one foot to the other, tori is able to cut down across uke's neck with her arm, gaining full control.

6 Finally, tori steps in with her rear foot to bring about a throw.

Yokomen-uchi Udekime-nage Ura

This side-head strike technique involves crossed arms and a throw from behind uke. This shows the control of yokomen-uchi by entering rapidly and dominating before the attack has generated any power. Tori's left-hand contact is a parry deflecting uke's power backwards and downwards.

1 Uke prepares to launch a strike with yokomen-uchi, or a side-head strike. There are three ways in which this attack can be dealt with: stepping underneath it; stepping inside it circularly; or entering and dominating.

2 Tori enters with tsugi ashi and cuts down on the attacking arm before it can generate power. This is basically a follow-up step whereby the forward foot enters sliding on the balls of the feet and the back foot "follows up" behind it. The idea is to overwhelm an attack at the moment it starts.

3 Cutting down with her left hand and gripping uke's wrist, tori makes tenkan and extends her left arm under uke's elbow.

4 Tori drives her left hip forward and levers uke's elbow, causing him to roll forward to escape the pressure.

Shomen-uchi Kokyu-nage

A kokyu-nage, or breath throw, is usually a formless movement practised to understand timing, coordination, ma-ai (combative distance), extension and correct breathing. There are many types and styles and they can be executed against any attack.

1 In this exercise, uke attacks tori with shomen-uchi (a frontal head strike). Tori must be ready to move forward rapidly to dominate the attack as the arm raises.

2 Uke makes shomen-uchi. Tori enters slightly with tsugi ashi using the leading foot and cuts upwards with her sword arm, deflecting uke's energy. Tori enters with ayumi ashi using the rear foot, a movement similar to normal walking.

3–4 Tori continues to step in with her rear foot. From this position, she cuts upward and then downward rapidly with her left arm inside uke's elbow, while simultaneously striking uke's midsection with her palm hand, thus sending uke into a forward flip ukemi (see also step 4 to right).

Throwing technique
In step 3, it is important to enter close in to your partner, using your body motion, not your arms, to produce the throw.

Gyaku Hanmi Katate-dori Ikkyo Omote

Ikkyo is a key technique in aikido. Subsequent techniques such as nikkyo, sankyo and yonkyo depend heavily on understanding the movements of ikkyo. This movement is a basic arm pin using a reverse-stance one-hand grab with the arm pin at the front.

1 In this sequence, uke attacks tori by gripping her in gyaku hanmi katate-dori, or reverse-stance one-hand grab.

2 Tori steps sidewards, drawing uke's balance with her, and cuts down with her left hand on his arm. This takes the power from his grip. Tori also grips uke's wrist with her left hand.

3 Tori extends both of her hands, changing her grip to control uke's elbow and wrist, while pushing with her hip across uke's line of balance.

4 Tori enters with a strong hip turn towards uke's armpit with her rear foot in a powerful movement designed to propel uke away from her.

5 Dropping her centre on uke's arm, tori causes uke to fall to the mat on his chest. Instead of relying on muscular power, this result is achieved by tori manipulating uke's arm in front of her and then extending her arms so that she can drop her body weight.

Cut back to centre
In this detail of step 2 tori is cutting back towards her centre with both hands, as if cutting with a sword. The leading handblade is more positive than the rear one – this ensures that uke's power is taken away and his balance is destroyed. As a result of this uke cannot generate any power in his grip and is therefore rendered vulnerable to the technique that follows.

Ai Hanmi Katate-dori Nikkyo Ura

In this mutual-stance one-handed grab, tori's handblade rolls across the forearm. Nikkyo is a powerful technique that can be painful if uke does not take ukemi properly. He should neutralize the movement by accepting the wrist torsion and pushing his forearm towards tori's body.

1 Here, uke (the person who receives the technique) launches an attack on tori (the person who delivers the technique) with katate- or kosa-dori, meaning a one hand, or crossed hand, grab.

2 Tori traps uke's hand against her wrist (see detail below) and changes her posture, cutting into his wrist with her right handblade.

3 Tori cuts down on uke's wrist using her handblade with a kind of cutting/rolling of the radius bone in uke's forearm. This forces uke to the floor.

4 Tori changes her grip to gain control of uke's elbow, and makes tenkan, a basic body turn, to bring him in front of her.

5 Tori drops her body weight onto uke's arm, taking him to the mat.

6 Tori effects an arm pin, turning her hips and forcing uke to tap the mat in submission. Tori achieves this by hugging uke's arm close to her body, capturing uke's wrist in the crook of her left elbow and restraining his elbow with her other forearm.

Hand detail

This close-up of step 2 shows how to trap the attacking hand. Tori traps uke's fingers against her forearm, therefore preventing his escape. Tori then just has to roll uke's forearm with her handblade to conclude the movement effectively.

Ai Hanmi Katate-dori Sankyo

Sankyo is a powerful wrist-twisting technique often used by police departments as a restraining movement. From the moment tori takes uke's hand he effects an inward-twisting motion against the hand and fingers, which is maintained until the end of the technique.

1 Uke grabs tori in katate-dori, or one-hand grab.

2 On contact, tori cuts upwards with his right sword arm cutting into the back of uke's wrist and, taking uke's wrist and elbow, leans his weight forward to unbalance uke.

3 Tori steps forward, taking uke's wrist and elbow (see detail bottom far left).

4 Keeping pressure on uke's elbow, tori manipulates uke's grip on his hand (see detail bottom middle).

5 Keeping everything else the same, tori changes hands, maintaining the twisting pressure on uke's wrist.

6 Tori steps around uke's arm, taking the back of her elbow. A combination of pressure and circular motion disorients uke.

7 Dropping his weight onto uke's arm, tori takes her to the mat (see detail below right).

8 Tori applies an immobilizing pin. He changes the hand that grips uke's, keeps the wrist twist and uses his other arm to hug uke's at the elbow.

Step 3 detail
Tori's body weight is extended onto uke's elbow. The right-hand fingers are extended backwards to loosen the grip.

Step 4 detail
Tori, having detached uke's grip, takes uke's hand and fingers and twists them inwards as he maintains left-hand contact.

Step 7 detail
Tori has changed hands but keeps the same pressure on and drops his body weight onto the back of uke's elbow.

Kata-dori Nikkyo Ura Waza

This shoulder-grab attack is more practical, involving uke grabbing tori's shoulder with one hand and potentially striking with the other. The first priority, therefore, is for tori to move off the line of attack and stretch uke sideways to unbalance him (kuzushi).

1 Uke grabs the clothing at the point of tori's shoulder.

2 Tori extends the gripped arm sideways and uses his left handblade to cut down onto uke's elbow, drawing him off balance.

3 Taking uke's wrist with both hands, tori changes his posture and, placing uke's thumb on his collar bone, then cuts down with his whole body targeting the wrist. This causes uke to fall to the mat.

4 Tori follows through, dropping his body weight onto uke's elbow.

5 Tori arrests uke's shoulder by gripping it with both his knees. He controls uke's arm by hugging it against his lower abdomen, ensuring the arm is bent and tori can see the palm of uke's hand.

Pinning action
This pinning action is used for nikkyo and kote-gaeshi. Both of tori's arms arrest uke's arm and hug it tightly. Both of tori's arms are positioned with the palms upwards. Tori tries to grip uke's wrist with the crook of his own elbow.

Yokomen-uchi Ikkyo Omote

This strike to the side of the head combined with an arm pin is a practical attack and can be likened to a strike with an implement or a punch to the side of the face. Uke attacks with his handblade and tori's objective is to control the attack before any power can be generated.

1 Uke prepares to launch an attack on tori with yokomen-uchi (see page 433).

2 To counter this attack, tori enters with tsugi ashi, which is a gliding follow-up step, extending her leading arm and cutting down with her handblade on uke before much power can be generated.

3 Sweeping her right hand over her left, tori cuts uke's arm away in a circular motion and takes uke's arm and wrist with both of her hands.

4 Entering strongly towards uke's armpit with her left foot, tori thrusts him away with her hip and takes uke down to the floor.

5 Tori pins uke's arm, extending energy to her handblades from her tanden, or her centre of gravity. This is achieved by tori placing her left knee against uke's ribs and her right knee by his pinned wrist. Tori then pins uke's arm above the elbow and at the wrist.

Chudan Tsuki Uchi Kaiten Sankyo

This middle-thrust inward rotary wrist twist involves punching the midsection of the body. Originally this attack was known as furizuki, an upward circular thrust which developed from a knife attack. Shown here is the karate-style punch that is practised in most dojos.

1 Uke prepares to punch chudan tsuki, a middle thrust, at tori's midsection.

2 Tori evades the thrust by entering with her rear foot around the attack, parrying with her left hand and grasping uke's attacking wrist with her right.

3 Tori cuts up into uke's elbow with her left handblade and passes underneath his arm, manipulating the grip into the sankyo wrist twist. This is achieved by tori holding the back of uke's hand with her left and twisting his fingers up towards his own armpit with her right.

4 Tori applies the wrist twist and cuts down as if treating uke's elbow as the tip of a sword.

5 Tori steps around uke's projected elbow with a large entering and turning motion called irimi tenkan and ends up by uke's head. Tori changes hands simultaneously keeping the pressure on the wrist and elbow, stepping in a circular movement behind uke. Grasping his elbow, uke is brought down onto the mat.

6 Tori immobilizes uke, swapping hands simultaneously, while maintaining the sankyo grip.

Morote-dori Yonkyo

This two-handed grab wrist pin aims to control the whole of uke's body by applying pressure to nerves in the forearm. Tori's grip on uke's wrist is the same as if she were holding a sword. The technique is to project uke's arm forward as if cutting with that sword.

1 Uke takes hold and grips tori's wrist with both hands as if holding a sword.

2 Tori first makes tenkan. Because she cannot lift her left arm, held by both of uke's hands, she has to pivot on her left foot to a position whereby she can deflect uke's power to the side by cutting upwards with her sword arm. This breaks the power of uke's grip. Tori then aligns herself with uke, while cutting upwards and raising uke's elbows.

3 With a powerful irimi, or entering and hip turning movement (see page 422), tori enters towards uke's armpit and cuts down with both hands, controlling uke's elbow with one hand and his wrist with the other.

4 Tori locates the nerve in uke's forearm just above his wrist pulse with the root of her forefinger and applies pressure to it with a hip-turning motion (see detail below left). This is exactly the same grip as that used on the handle of a bokken in weapon training.

5 Unable to withstand the grip, uke falls to the mat where he is pinned (see detail far right). Tori's foot is close to uke's armpit as she applies pressure to the nerve.

Step 4 detail
Here you can see how the wrist is pinned in yonkyo, with the wrist held as if it were a Japanese sword. The leading hand grips just above uke's pulse point and applies pressure with the root of her forefinger. Tori imagines uke's elbow to be the point of the sword and cuts down.

Step 5 detail
As you can see here uke is on the mat as tori continues to apply the wrist pressure to make uke submit. Tori applies pressure by turning her right hip downward and outwards. This adds her body weight to the existing pressure on the nerve.

Jodan Tsuki Rokkyo

Rokkyo, also called ude-hishigi and literally meaning "arm smashing" is one of the few aikido techniques remaining unchanged from its original aikijujutsu form. It is the only technique that goes against the natural movement of a joint and needs care during application to avoid injury.

1 Uke prepares to attack tori by making jodan tsuki, or a thrust to the face. This is basically a straight punch to the face.

2 Tori cuts upward with her left hand, deflecting the punch, and grabs uke's wrist.

3 As tori cuts downwards she makes tenkan, a 180-degree turn pivoting on her right foot, and revolves uke's arm, effectively hugging it against her upper body.

4 Tori uses her other arm to reinforce her grip on uke's arm. In this position, she can now exert strong pressure on the elbow joint by turning her hips inwards.

Ai Hanmi Katate-dori Kote-gaeshi

This movement, literally translated as a mutual-stance one-handed grab outward wrist turn, provides an immobilizing pin to control the wrist and elbow. It is an example of nage katame waza, or throwing and pinning technique.

1 Uke grabs tori in ai hanmi katate-dori, meaning the mutual-stance one-handed grab (see page 426).

2 Tori makes the first part of tenkan by taking uke's wrist with her left hand and disengaging her right hand by rotating it. She completes the tenkan movement and drops her weight onto his wrist (see detail below), taking his balance and continuing to move.

3 Tori switches her balance and places her hand on the back of uke's hand. As if rolling uke's fingers and hand into a ball, tori applies the kote-gaeshi wrist, in turn transferring her weight from the right foot to the left.

4 Uke falls to the floor while tori maintains the pressure on his wrist.

5 Moving around uke's head, tori applies pressure to the back of uke's elbow, with her left hand pushing his elbow towards his face, causing him to roll over.

6 Tori finally applies an immobilizing pin by hugging uke's arm close to her body ensuring that the arm is bent and that the wrist and elbow are controlled. It is advisable for tori to position herself so that her body is at 45 degrees to uke's, with her right knee close to uke's head.

Step 2 detail
This close-up detail of the second step shows how tori has disengaged her right wrist from uke's grip and gripped uke's wrist with her left hand, prior to placing her hand on the back of uke's hand in order to effect the kote-gaeshi throw.

Gyaku Hanmi Katate-dori Kote-gaeshi Gyaku

In this movement, literally translated as a one-handed grab with a reverse outward wrist turn, tori combats an attack by breaking the power of uke's grip, rolling her hand and fingers inward and forcing her to submit.

1 Uke launches an attack on tori in gyaku hanmi katate-dori, or reverse-stance one-hand grab.

2 Tori enters strongly with his leading foot straight towards uke, leaning his weight into the movement while cutting upwards with his left swordhand. This breaks the power of uke's grip.

3 Tori grabs the base of uke's thumb as he steps around the front of her (see detail below).

4 As tori withdraws his left leg, he places his left hand on the back of uke's hand and cuts down on the back of uke's hand rolling uke's fingers inwards.

5 To avoid the pain, uke falls to the mat. Tori keeps the controlling pressure on the wrist the whole time.

6 Finally, tori immobilizes uke by stretching her arm and drops his body weight onto uke's elbow, causing her midsection to lift. The pressing down on uke's elbow and the pulling up of her hand causes immediate discomfort and her back arches as a reflex action. The result is rapid submission by uke.

Step 3 detail
Tori disengages uke's grip by drawing back the fingers of the gripped hand and simultaneously gripping the base of uke's thumb with his right hand.

Chudan Tsuki Kote-gaeshi

This middle-thrust movement is almost identical to that of ai hanmi katate-dori kote-gaeshi (see page 458). The difference is how tori harmonizes with uke's attack. This application, basically a stomach punch, is also effective against a knife (tanto) attack.

1 Uke stands ready to make a chudan tsuki, or a middle thrust, attack on tori.

2 As uke thrusts forward, tori enters by stepping forward into the blind side of uke. Deflecting the thrust with his left handblade, tori then makes tenkan by pivoting 180 degrees on his left foot and parrying the thrust.

3 Tori grips uke's wrist and continues turning, leading uke's energy and unsettling her balance (see detail bottom left).

4 At this position, tori drops his centre of gravity slightly, preparing to switch his balance. It is vital for tori to keep uke's wrist in front of his centre so that he can use the centre to control uke.

5 Tori steps back, opening his body by stepping back in the opposite direction with his left foot and transferring his weight to that foot. Tori simultaneously places his hand on the back of uke's hand (see detail below right).

6 When uke falls to the floor, tori puts his right hand on her elbow and drops his body weight. Uke rolls over onto her front, where tori immobilizes her by pinning her arm against his body and controlling the wrist and elbow (see step 6 on opposite page).

Step 3 detail
This close-up detail shows the grip that tori has on uke as he begins to lead her around his centre.

Step 5 detail
Here you can see tori gripping uke's wrist with his left hand, with his right hand placed on the back of uke's hand. As tori turns and twists the wrist outwards, uke loses her balance as she tries to compensate for the discomfort.

Kata-dori Kote-gaeshi

This one-hand shoulder grab is slightly more advanced as tori does not wait for uke to make contact with her shoulder, but deflects the attack with her right handblade before uke is able to grab her.

1 Launching an attack, uke attempts to grab tori by her shoulder.

2 Stepping back just before uke can grab, tori harmonizes with the movement and cuts down uke's hand with her right handblade before contact is made. This is a deflection of uke's power.

3 Tori grips uke's wrist with her left hand and draws uke's energy forwards, causing him to lose his balance.

4 Tori places her hand on the back of uke's hand and applies kote-gaeshi by twisting his wrist outwards, as if rolling uke's fingers and hand into a ball. The pressure needs to be constant, not allowing uke to straighten his wrist and generate any power to resist.

5 Stepping around the top of uke, tori applies pressure to the back of his elbow, causing him to roll over.

6 Tori immobilizes uke's arm. As long as uke's arm is bent against tori's body and the wrist is gripped by tori's elbow, uke will be unable to resist and will submit.

Ushiro Ryote-dori Ikkyo Omote

This rear two-handed grab and arm pin is one of the ushirowaza techniques. Tori must have good balance so as not to be easily pulled backwards. Mentally tori projects uke forwards as she steps backwards. This is the basic tenet for all ushiro techniques.

1 Approaching her from the rear, uke grabs and holds both of tori's wrists – uke must ensure that he establishes a good grip on her wrists.

2 Stepping back with her leading foot, tori extends strongly forwards with both arms. Uke loses his balance forwards, a position required prior to the execution of most ushirowaza.

3 Tori straightens up and grips uke's wrist and elbow as shown. At this stage tori is preparing to enter with a gutsy thrust of her right hip as she steps in, which will send uke forwards and sideways and completely destroy his balance.

4 Taking a step forward, tori drops her body weight onto uke's arm, causing him to fall. Finally she pins his arm with extended power from her centre. There is no tension in the shoulders. Tori aims to pin uke's arm slightly higher than 90 degrees to his body.

Ikkyo arm pin
This two-handed arm pin involves pinning the arm at a position greater than 90 degrees to uke's body, higher than the shoulder. The grip has a slight push and twist. Tori imagines that the power comes from her centre of gravity.

Ushiro Ryokata-dori Sankyo Ura

Using the same principle as ushiro ryote-dori ikkyo omote, tori extends – her wrists are not gripped, but the movement is the same. Tori does not try to wrest the grip, but pushes it against her shoulder so that the shoulder's power effects the wrist-twisting motion.

1 Approaching from the rear, uke grips tori by both shoulders.

2 Tori immediately steps forward with her rear foot, simultaneously extending both of her arms to unsettle uke's balance and bring him forward.

3 Stepping back with her right foot, tori holds uke's wrist as if it were a sword. Turning her gripped shoulder inward powered by an inward hip turn, power is generated onto uke's wrist. Tori takes uke's wrist in a wringing motion with her right hand, and with her left hand applies her body weight just above uke's elbow. This wrist twist causes uke to release his grip.

4 Tori steps in a circular fashion behind uke and grips his elbow, then drops her body weight onto his arm (see also close-up detail to right).

5 With uke now on the mat, tori immobilizes his arm, maintaining the wrist twist.

Step 4 detail
In this close-up you can see the detail of the grip just prior to tori dropping her body weight onto uke's arm.

Ushiro Katate-dori Kube-shime Kokyu-nage

In this rear one-handed grab and choke-breath throw uke grips one of tori's wrists and steps behind to apply a choke with the other arm. He grips tori's collar high up and applies pressure against the carotid artery with the collar. Tori leads uke before his grip consolidates.

1 Approaching from the front, uke grabs tori's wrist and steps behind her in an attempt to apply a choke hold.

2 Tori harmonizes with the movement, turning and extending the gripped hand over her head. She does this, not by opposing uke's power, but by leading it as she extends uke's arm over her head, continuing in one circular motion with the intent of wrapping uke's arm across his other one.

3 Tori now grasps uke's upper right sleeve and extends her left hand across her body to completely take his balance.

4 Tori now drops onto her left her knee and extends forward, projecting uke to the mat.

Ushiro Katate-dori Kube-shime Koshi-nage

The defence for this one-handed hip throw comes from koshi-nage, or a hip/waist throw, where uke's body is loaded onto tori's hips and then flipped over. The attitude for tori is not to lift uke's body, but to extend and lead his energy and present her hips for him to ride over.

1 Approaching from the front, uke grabs tori's wrist and steps behind her in an attempt to apply a choke hold.

2 Tori turns, harmonizing with uke's energy, and extends her gripped hand over her head.

3 By extending her right arm underneath uke's, tori is able to neutralize her attacker's power.

4 Now, by bending her knees and lowering her centre of gravity, uke effectively rides over tori's hips.

5 Uke flips over tori's hips and lands on the mat. Tori is not gripping uke at this stage. However, depending on how well uke has been led, there may be a need to grip uke's right elbow (as shown here) to ensure he flips over naturally and does not hurtle head first onto the mat.

Futaridori Kokyu-ho

This technique, involving tori and two ukes, is a good way to test your kokyu-ryoku, or breath power. With one attacker holding each wrist, you need to manipulate the attackers in such a way as to be able to use your tanden and hips to drive the cutting motions of the hands.

1 In this encounter, tori's wrists are held by two ukes. The ukes are there to help tori train his breath power and not necessarily to struggle against everything that tori does.

2 Tori, using a strong hip-turning motion, steps forward and cuts upwards with his left sword arm as if raising a sword.

3 Withdrawing his right foot in a circular movement backwards, as if drawing a bowstring, tori takes his right arm back and cuts across both of his partners with his left sword arm. It is important to keep both ukes close together.

4 Tori draws his partners underneath his left arm, stretching them both fully and compromising their balance. This is achieved using circular movement and extension of ki.

5 Finally, tori leans his centre of gravity forwards and fells both of them.

Futaridori Nikkyo

This is a defence technique against two attackers holding both of tori's wrists. It relies on a rapid and forceful step forward to draw the attackers forward, and then another step quickly backwards so that they do not have time to regain their posture.

1 Tori's wrists are held by two attackers. Tori extends both arms, imagining ki is flowing through his fingers.

2 Stepping quickly forward with his rear foot, tori leans his body weight forward to draw his partners in front of him.

3 Drawing his elbows together, tori cuts upwards from his centre of gravity. He does this with his two sword arms close together, driven by a strong hip lift, in a similar movement to the way a weightlifter would get his body underneath a weight. This has the effect of bringing the two partners together.

4 Tori simultaneously extends both hands over the top of his partners' wrists without actually grabbing them. Tori's shoulders must be relaxed and his attitude one of cutting over the top of both ukes' wrists.

5 With a type of cutting roll of both of ukes' radius bones in the forearm, tori exerts a painful impulse with his two handblades, forcing his partners' forearms down. Don't try to force the ukes' forearms down with direct pressure on the wrists – this will never work. The movement has a rotating cut which is difficult for the ukes to resist, so they are forced to harmonize with the movement.

Weapons and advanced training

This chapter includes a brief overview of weapons training from the many approaches that are available. Subjects covered include how to hold weapons and the postures and attitudes to use; how to use weapons with examples of basic cuts and thrusts with the bokken (wooden sword) and jo (wooden staff); basic partner practices such as uchi komi, awase or blending exercises; and disarming a knife-wielding aggressor, or tanto dori. The chapter also looks at kicking techniques, or geri waza, which are suitable for more advanced students because of the danger of injury, and self-defence techniques, also an advanced training method because classic aikido movements need careful adaptation to suit the requirements of contemporary self-defence.

Handling and Using Weapons

The first thing you learn with weapons is how to hold them. You have to hold the bokken and jo strongly with the little finger and the next finger up of each hand. The middle and forefingers hold in a loose manner. This grip permits rapid manoeuvrability and the ability to parry and strike quickly. It approximates to the same grip you have on the steering wheel of a car when driving or when you hold a knife and fork.

The tsuka, or handle, of the bokken is held with the left hand and with the little finger parallel to the bottom. The right hand should be about three-widths of a finger up from the left hand, so that the forefinger can just touch the tsuba, or the protective handguard. The grip on the jo is the same as with the bokken, but you need to spread your hands wider apart.

One of the biggest problems you will encounter is how to generate the necessary power for the sword to cut properly. The rule is that "the sword cuts, not you". Even though the bokken is wooden, you have to treat it as if it were a live blade – otherwise the whole concept of sword training loses reality. The cut with a live Japanese blade always occurs on the backstroke, so you have to project the blade over the top of the intended target and then allow the speed and gravity of the weapon to slice through it effortlessly.

LEARNING THE BOKKEN, OR BOKUTO
The traditional division of weapon techniques can be classified as follows:
- **Suburi:** Solo exercises designed to help you understand how to hold the sword, how to do basic cuts and thrusts, how to change direction and maintain your balance and how to harmonize body and weapon so that they feel as one.
- **Uchikomi:** Encountering a partner for the first time. You learn five sets of movements that allow you and your partner to practise timing, coordination and the concept of ma-ai, combative distance awareness. You are also introduced to the idea of avoiding the central line of attack. The practice involves moving up and down the dojo with a partner cutting and thrusting in different combinations.
- **Awase:** A blending exercise. Here you and your partner remain in one place and practise simple one- or two-step cutting and thrusting movements.
- **Kumitachi:** In this more advanced partner training, movements become more complex and contain variations that go some way to bridging the gap

between weapon training and body art (tai jutsu). Some of these advanced techniques involve throws and joint locks and promote the concept of riai, which means "blending of truths". At this level of training, one learns to move as if weapons are an integral part, or extensions of the body.
- **Tachidori:** This is the highest level of weapon training in which an unarmed individual learns to face a sword-wielding aggressor.

LEARNING THE JO
The sequence of learning the jo is very similar to that of the bokken.
- **Suburi and jo awase:** Both these terms have the same meaning as the sword (see above).
- **Kumijo:** These more elaborate movements are practised for the same reasons as for the bokken.
- **Jo kata:** Continuous cutting, thrusting and striking movements that are performed solo with the jo. These can be performed only once the basics of suburi are fully understood.
- **Jo dori:** Again, the highest level of training within aiki jo whereby an attacker thrusts and is disarmed with a variety of throwing and pinning techniques.

Weapon terminology
Throughout this chapter you will come across the traditional Japanese terms used to describe the names of the techniques and the names of the partners in the scenarios.

Uchitachi: The partner who attacks with the bokken.

Uketachi: The partner who performs the technique.

Uchijo: The partner who attacks with the jo.

Ukejo: The partner who performs the technique.

The Five Postures of the Bokken

These are the five basic ways of holding the bokken (wooden sword) in traditional aikido weapon training: held along the centre line, held above the head, held to the right of the head, hidden from your partner and held low.

1 The first posture is chudan no kamae, the most basic of all the postures. The bokken is held in the centre line of the body with the tip pointing toward your partner's eyes. **2** The second is jodan no kamae, where the sword is held above the head.

3 When the sword is held at the right side of the head, it is called hasso no kamae. **4** The fourth posture, wakigame no kamae is, in effect, hiding the sword. **5** When the sword is held low, as shown here, the posture is known as gedan.

The Five Postures of the Jo

These are the five basic ways of holding the jo (short staff) in traditional aikido weapon training: the basic posture, held in front as a sword, held high as a sword, held vertically, and held in readiness on the ground.

1 The basic jo posture chudan no kamae. **2** Chudan no kamae where the jo is held in front of you as a sword. **3** The third posture, where the jo is held as a sword above the head.

4 In hasso no kamae the jo is held vertically to the right side of your head. **5** In the fifth posture of readiness, the jo rests on the floor and the hand position can vary according to the context.

Weapon Attack: Shomen-uchi

When practising this front-head strike, it is good ma-ai, or combative distance awareness, to be able to take one step to reach the target. The area that cuts, called the monouchi, is on the cutting edge of the blade 4cm (1½in) from the tip to a further 20cm (8in) downwards.

1 Uchitachi, the attacking practitioner, stands in chudan no kamae opposite uketachi, the person who receives. Uchitachi extends his ki down the blade.

2 Uchitachi raises his sword as he steps back. From here uketachi has no idea whether the attack will be shomen or yokomen-uchi.

3 Stepping forward, uchitachi cuts to the centre of uketachi's head.

Weapon Attack: Yokomen-uchi

The attack movement of this side-head strike is the same as shomen-uchi (above), but the target area of the cut is to the side of uketachi's head. Because the sword is raised in the same wasy as shomen-uchi, it is difficult for uketachi to forsee the direction of the attack.

1 Uchitachi, or the attacking practitioner, stands in chudan no kamae opposite uketachi.

2 Uchitachi raises his sword as he steps back. From here uketachi has no idea whether the attack will be shomen- or yokomen-uchi.

3 This time the cut is directed at the side of uketachi's head.

Weapon Attack: Tsuki

This movement, meaning "thrust", is a similar attack to a punch to tori's midsection. For those familiar with the tsuki "kendo", thrust (where the body is held square on to uketachi), this thrust differs as it has uchitachi moving into hanmi, or half stance, to deliver the thrust.

1 Uchitachi stands with both his feet together, with his sword pointing at uketachi. This is a practice for uchitachi to execute tsuki in hanmi (left or right).

2 Uchitachi, sliding his front foot forward, prepares to thrust.

3 Uchitachi completes the tsuki attack by targeting the side of the neck, as shown, or uketachi's throat. Uchitachi reverts back to step 1, then makes tsuki in left hanmi.

Counter Attack: Kirigaeshi

Kirigaeshi, or countering cut, is a defensive, as opposed to offensive, cut. It is a response to an attack and involves moving off the line of a straight cut or thrust, parrying the strike and then responding with an attack yourself.

1 The partners face each other. It is essential to have an appropriate distance (ma-ai) between partners.

2 Uchitachi steps off the line of an imaginary attack, and protects his body and head with his sword.

3 Uchitachi changes posture and raises his sword. He steps off the attacking line with his left foot, bringing his right foot to his left and then stepping back with that right foot as he cuts with the sword. Uchitachi is here learning to step off the line of potential attack and deliver the counter attack.

4 Stepping back, uchitachi makes a defensive shomen-uchi (front-head strike).

Renzoku Uchikomi: Shomen Uchikomi

The movements of renzoku uchikomi, continuous stepping and striking practice, are traditional partner exercises practised up and down the dojo in left and right hanmi. Usually there are five renzoku uchikomi, of which the first three are shown here.

1 Chudan no kamae is the basic posture of partner sword practice. It is also called seigan, and is employed when both partners' weapons touch about 5–7.5cm (2–3in) from their tips, and while the tips point at each other's eyes.

2 Uchitachi steps forward and raises her sword to cut with shomen-uchi. Uketachi extends his sword towards the attacking sword to meet it and steps backwards in a circular manner.

3 Uketachi draws his sword down to the centre of his body, neutralizing the attack. This continues as uchitachi in step 2 steps forward onto her left leg and strikes again. Uketachi repeats, but this time in left hanmi. This continues up and down the dojo.

Renzoku Uchikomi: Tsuki Uchikomi

This movement is a basic attack-and-defence scenario involving tsuki uchikomi (continuous thrusting and stepping). The body moves in the same way as the previous technique, and as above it involves parrying rather than blocking or trying to stop the movement.

1 This exercise starts in the seigan posture. Uketachi extends his sword across uchitachi's weapon in an attempt to lead her into an attack. Uchitachi maintains contact with uketachi's sword until it passes across her centre line, when uketachi can no longer control it.

2 As her blade is now not under control, uchitachi is free to attack. She steps forward with her left foot coming up underneath uketachi's parry and makes the tsuki attack, stepping off the line.

3 Uketachi steps circularly back with his right foot, cutting up the centre line of his body, and deflects the thrust. Uketachi leads uchitachi's blade as in step 1, but from the opposite side, enabling continuous practice up and down the dojo.

Renzoku Uchikomi: Kirigaeshi Uchikomi

This is the basic way to practise kirigaeshi, a countering technique with a partner using the same body movement as the previous techniques. This enables the practice of musubi or tying together, where partners try to maintain weapon contact for as long as possible.

1 Uchitachi and uketachi face each other in seigan. This is also known as chudan no kamae, or middle posture and is the start position for all aikiken practice.

2 Uketachi presses down on uchitachi's blade with his own. This is a way to lead your partner into a practice. Originally, in a real combat situation, this movement would have been used to knock down uketachi's blade prior to a direct attack.

3 Uchitachi maintains the contact between the weapons and steps beneath and to the side of uketachi's blade, parrying, protecting and cutting in a single movement called kirigaeshi.

4 Uchitachi raises her sword to make a counter attack.

5 Uchitachi makes a left-foot shomen-uchi, meaning a strike to the front of uketachi's head.

6 Uketachi steps back circularly, drawing his sword back to his body's centre line and parrying the strike. This final position illustrates how, by moving off the attacking centre line, it is possible to deflect an attack enough to eliminate danger.

Jo Awasewaza: Makiotoshi Against Shomen-uchi

This jo awasewaza (staff blending) movement called makiotoshi (twisting down movement) is a powerful defence. It aims to propel uchijo's weapon back towards him and to strike his leading hand. Ukejo should visualize dropping her centre of gravity down her partner's centreline.

1 Ukejo, the partner who performs the technique, and uchijo, who attacks with the jo, initially face each other in ai hanmi, both holding the jo in gyakute, or reverse hand.

2 Uchijo makes shomen-uchi, a front-head strike with the jo, raising it up his left side to an above-head position.

3 Ukejo moves slightly to the side raising her jo to parry the attack.

4 Ukejo propels the attacking jo away by rolling her jo down her partner's jo with a wrist action, while leaning her body weight into the action to cut the thumb or fingers of the attacker. Uchijo's attitude should be to neutralize this action by letting go with the target hand and then allowing the weapon to flow backwards.

Jo Awasewaza: Makiuchiotoshi Against Tsuki

This second jo awasewaza movement is called makiuchiotoshi (twisting-down striking drop). While the intent is clearly martial, safe practice requires the targeting of an area on the jo as near to the hand as possible to avoid causing injury.

1 As uchijo prepares to thrust at ukejo, ukejo steps slightly off the attacking line. Turning her body, she revolves the jo, parrying the thrust, using the left hand as a fulcrum.

2 Ukejo continues to make a large, circular strike against uchijo's leading hand. The idea is to strike the hand and the weapon down – uchijo is aware of this and lets go before impact.

3 As uchijo's attack nears its target and she drops her weight onto the attacking weapon, uchijo lets go with his leading hand and allows the impact to drive his jo downwards.

Jo Awasewaza: Junteuchiotoshi Against Kesa Giri

Junteuchiotoshi (front hand-striking drop) involves turning the upper body and meeting the attacking jo, but not blocking it. Kesa giri is a diagonal strike to the side of the head/neck that follows the angle of the gi jacket as it is wrapped around from the left shoulder to the right hip.

1 Uchijo and ukejo face each other in ai hanmi. Note the different ways that both partners are holding the jo.

2 Uchijo raises his jo to make kesa giri (a diagonal cut) – the target being the side of the head or neck.

3 Ukejo raises her jo to meet the attack, turning her body to face it and parries the strike. The impact of an attack like this can be great. Ukejo's grip on the jo must be strong enough not to allow the weapon to give way, but resilient enough not to generate stiffness.

4 With a feeling of dropping her body weight and rolling the jo down that of the attacking weapon…

5 … ukejo makes a large circular movement, protecting herself and propelling the attacking weapon away. Her attitude is to strike uchijo's leading hand in the process. He, in turn, must adopt an attitude of neutralizing the attack by harmonizing with it, so he lets go of the weapon with the targeted hand.

6 From above her head, ukejo makes a tsuki thrust in one movement. She does this, having knocked down the attacking jo, by thrusting her own weapon towards uchijo's midsection causing him to bend backwards to avoid it. Ukejo's whole body is behind this thrust, making it a formidable strike.

Tanto Dori: Tsuki Kote-gaeshi

Tanto dori is a knife defence and must be taken seriously. Although wooden weapons are used, the tanto has to be handled as if it were a live blade where the slightest touch of the blade would cut. Tori's prime directive is to wrest the tanto from uke.

1 Uke prepares to thrust at tori's midsection using a chudan tsuki, or middle thrust.

2 As uke thrusts, tori enters around the attack using irimi ashi (see page 421), stepping in with his rear foot, and parrying before then gripping uke's wrist (tori must parry first).

3 Tori makes tenkan, pivoting on his leading foot by 180 degrees, and drops his weight on the captured wrist.

4 Stepping back with his right foot behind uke and transferring his weight forward, tori places his hand on the back of uke's and makes kote-gaeshi, turning uke's wrist and arm outwards and downwards, causing them to buckle and uke to fall to the mat.

5 As uke falls to the mat tori pins her arm, making sure that the tanto is taken away as soon as possible.

Tanto Dori: Tsuki Katagatame

Another tanto dori, or knife-defence action the success of this technique relies on controlling the weapon quickly and hugging the arm against the body, controlling uke's wrist and elbow and keeping the blade facing away.

1 Standing in ai hanmi, or mutual stance, tori prepares for uke's thrust with the tanto. Tori must be alert and ready, as at this stage it is difficult to determine what attack is coming.

2 Tori turns his body (kaiten) and deflects the attack. Kaiten is a rotating movement of the hips, pivoting on the balls of the feet so that you are facing the same direction as the attack. Tori uses his right handblade to deflect the attacking arm.

3 Tori cuts down with his right hand and arrests uke's knife-wielding arm with both of his arms. Once the tanto is controlled, tori drops his centre of gravity. While uke's arm is bent against tori's body she will be unable to generate any power.

4 This movement causes uke to drop to the mat.

5 Tori immobilizes uke's arm by hugging the arm close to the body and turning his right shoulder towards uke's head. This creates strong pressure on the shoulder and forces uke to submit or risk a potential dislocation of the shoulder. At this point tori takes away the tanto, ensuring that it is safely out of the way.

Tanto Dori: Yokomen-uchi Gokkyo

This knife-defence action is carried out in combination with a side-head strike and arm stretch. The attack here can be when the tanto is held as if to stab like a dagger or to slash like a small sword.

1 Uke prepares to launch a strike at the side of tori's head or neck using yokomen-uchi, or a side-head strike.

2 Tori enters with ayumi ashi. He steps forward with his rear foot in a movement similar to normal walking, but moves both feet across slightly to keep out of uke's centre line. Tori then cuts down on uke's arm with his right handblade, while taking her wrist with his other hand. This grip has tori's thumb underneath uke's wrist and therefore applies forward pressure on the wrist – preventing any movement of the blade in uke's grip.

3 Having controlled the tanto, tori extends his arms in front in a large sweeping motion as he turns, controlling uke's arm. Tori steps forward and drops his centre of gravity onto uke's arm. From here tori continues forward towards uke's armpit, taking her balance slightly sideways.

4 This movement causes uke to drop to the mat. Tori's reverse grip with the left hand, which remains the same throughout this sequence, is essential for this technique.

5 Tori stretches uke's arm outwards and then bends her wrist back, as shown. Strong pressure is then exerted on the wrist against the mat – this causes the fingers to open so that the tanto can be removed.

Tanto Dori: Yokomen-uchi Shiho-nage

This knife attack uses a side-head strike. Generally the knife is held as if it is a small sword. The secret in this sequence is to step inside the circular slashing movement and parry, rather than block, uke's movement.

1 Tori (on the left) prepares for uke's yokomen-uchi with a tanto.

2 Uke makes a large circular slash at tori's head. Tori steps inside of the attack, parrying it with his left handblade.

3 Cutting down with his left hand, tori takes uke's wrist with both hands and extends in front, taking uke's balance.

5 Tori makes tenkan, pivoting 180 degrees on his right foot, while gripping uke's wrist with his right hand. With a cutting-down motion tori wrests the tanto from uke's grip with his left hand, pinning her wrist to the mat (see detail below).

Step 5 detail

This detail shows the final pin on uke's wrist after the tanto has been taken away. Tori bears his weight onto the wrist and pushes slightly inwards to ensure there is no gap between uke's wrist and her head. This immobilizes uke.

4 Tori steps in with his back foot and passes under uke's arm, turning 180 degrees. At this point, tori controls uke's wrist and the tanto and begins to cut downwards causing uke to fall to the mat. The knife handle must be controlled to turn uke's wrist inwards.

Kicking Techniques

Kicking techniques, or geri waza, represent more advanced aikido training, and they can be dangerous if not practised properly. Because nearly all require a fluent understanding of ushiro ukemi, or backward breakfall (see page 429), they are often omitted from training. Some factions of aikido do not recognize geri waza as orthodox, although the exercises that follow were taught by a uchideshi, or live-in student, of aikido founder, Morihei Ueshiba.

Kicking techniques represent a fascinating insight into the practical applications of aikido. In any study of traditional aikido, you cannot understand how it has evolved if you do not go back to its roots. If the martial heritage of aikido is ignored then it ceases to be a budo, or martial way, and becomes nothing more than an elaborate system of exercise.

By their very nature kicking techniques are martial. Practice therefore must be conducted in a positive but controlled manner. Kicking is a very real threat in today's society, but by applying the core principles of aikido body movement, kicking attacks can be easily controlled.

The following techniques are three variations on irimi-nage, or an entering throw. There are many more defences against kicks that cannot be included. The examples here involve defences against maegeri, or a front kick. There are also defences against other kicking attacks, such as mawashi-geri, or a roundhouse kick, but in an introduction to aikido such as this they are not covered.

Chudan Maegeri Irimi-nage – Variation 1

The kicking area used in chudan maegeri, or middle front kick, is the ball of the foot. The knee is lifted in front of the body and then the lower leg is launched from that position. In aikido you never try to block such an attack, but always to parry or deflect it.

1 Tori faces uke in gyaku hanmi, or reverse stance.

2 Uke strikes with chudan maegeri by lifting the knee in front of the body and then kicking the lower leg. Tori deflects the kick with his right hand as he makes irimi issoku, or one-step entering.

3 Entering deeply with his left foot as he parries the kick to uke's side, tori places his right hand under uke's leg and extends his left hand across uke's front to dominate any strike from his right hand, and to cut across his neck. With his leg in the air and leaning back as a result of the dominance of tori's hand movement, uke is totally off balance.

4 Tori extends his body weight forward to bring uke down to the mat.

Chudan Maegeri Irimi-nage – Variation 2

This is another variation of the chudan maegeri, or middle front kick. The movements below could be just as easily applied to a front strike to the head (shomen-uchi) or a punch to the face or stomach (chudan-/jodan-tsuki).

1 Tori and uke face each other in ai hanmi, and uke prepares to strike tori's midsection with a front kick.

2 As uke steps and kicks with his right leg, tori deflects the attack and enters with his back foot with ayumi ashi, in a slightly exaggerated walking movement that also moves off the line of attack. Tori avoids blocking the kick, which would result in a broken forearm.

3 Continuing the entering momentum, tori cuts across uke's neck, causing him to lose balance, or kuzushi. With a feeling of dropping his centre of gravity, tori can then bring uke to the mat.

4 Tori has executed irimi-nage in the same way as he would from any other attack – avoiding the central line of attack, then entering and throwing.

Chudan Maegeri Irimi-nage Ura

This is the third way of executing the principle of irimi-nage, or entering throw. The first two techniques are examples of omote, or movements directly to the front of uke. This is an example of ura, where completion takes place behind uke.

1 Tori and uke confront each other in gyaku hanmi, or opposite stance.

2 Uke kicks and tori parries uke's kick sideways, therefore avoiding its force. He then steps in deeply with his front foot and then onto his left foot to get behind uke.

3 Tori takes uke's shoulders. If this is done while the kick is still happening, the combination of pulling him backwards and downwards makes it easy to fell uke. Tori is in the classic shikaku or blind-spot position, where it is difficult for uke to retain his balance, or to launch any kind of counter-attack.

4 Tori drops his body weight onto uke's shoulders while pulling back and pushing down. This causes uke to lose his balance, after which tori is able to bring him down.

Aikido and Self-defence

When considering taking up aikido, ask yourself what you expect. It is a traditional art, one that incorporates training against the weapons already described, as well as nearly every type of unarmed attack. The founder also wove his religious and philosophical beliefs into aikido, giving it spiritual aspects that have become a magnet to those not necessarily interested in pure combat, but also to those who want something they can apply in their daily lives.

Many people cite self-defence as the main reason for beginning aikido, so it is the responsibility of instructors to make sure that prospective candidates are aware of what self-defence means in the context of the art.

A PRAGMATIC AND CO-OPERATIVE ART
In the early 1970s, Chiba Sensei, the technical director for the Aikikai of Great Britain and the official delegate from the Hombu in Japan, was asked about aikido and self-defence: "How, if aikido is an art that teaches us to harmonize with an attack, can victory be secured against several people coming at you if all you do is harmonize with them and you don't try to hurt them?" Sensei's answer was: "You are thinking too much in terms of the religious side of the art. Aikido is a martial way that recognizes individuals' rights to defend themselves, and to do what is necessary to control a situation."

If we look back to the days of the samurai in feudal Japan we see that the martial arts they practised had to be effective on the battlefield. Society was governed then by military

Below The final stage of hanmi handachi shiho-nage where tori approaches the kneeling uke from behind. Here, uke bends with the movement prior to taking ukemi.

warlords who employed samurai warriors as retainers, and these warlords had to find ways to train their samurais to be unbeatable. Thus, a huge number of martial ryu, or schools, sprang up. If the warriors in your service were the best trained, then you won and accrued land, property and wealth.

When you begin your training it should be made clear to you that most of the regular practice in the dojo is what is called "conditioning training". It is geared towards conditioning the body in terms of understanding the mechanics of the techniques and in physical training – conditioning the mind in terms of understanding kokyu and ki (see pages 399–403) – very little training in actual self-defence movements takes place. The thinking behind this is that you are conditioning your body in preparation for the martial art, not in the martial art itself. So you should not be surprised to find that practice is conducted in a spirit of co-operation between partners, and that you never try to compete with or resist your partner during practice. This is in line with the founder's philosophy of harmony and non-violence and reflects the fact that aikido movements are the same movements that are seen in nature.

DIVERSITY
Aikido is taught traditionally through the dissemination of core principles from which all of the movements and techniques stem, rather than by showing masses of techniques, and it is this commonality that, paradoxically, enables the art to be interpreted in many ways. It is fascinating to note that the world's greatest aikido masters, men who have sat at the feet of aikido's founder, Morihei Ueshiba, through differences in build, temperament and motivation came away with, in some cases, unique ideas on aikido and went on to develop their own styles of the art. This is one reason why different people are attracted to different shihan, or master teachers. Regarding weapons, some advocate that it is not necessary to train with them at all, while others follow the classical weapons style of the late grandmaster Saito Shihan. There are several prominent shihan who have gone on to create entirely new weapon systems and styles that incorporate elements of other martial arts the shihan have studied. It is likely that Ueshiba would have been happy

Above Ukemi, the art of falling or recovery, is vital in developing the confidence to neutralize the effect of a throw. Students need to learn to fall both forwards and backwards, the latter shown here.

Above Kung-fu master Bruce Lee introduced the martial arts into popular Hollywood culture. Here, he executes a mawashi-geri, or roundhouse kick, in his film *Fist of Fury* (1972).

with these differences in interpretation of his art. He is said to have stated on his deathbed that "Aikido is for the World", and that he had only scratched the surface of what was on offer.

LEARNING THE ART

When beginners enrol at a dojo, they will be taught how to roll forwards and backwards and how to do taisabaki, or body movements. Next they will begin partner practices that lead to kihon waza, or basic technique. This training teaches you how to harmonize with an attack, redirect it and then apply a technique to neutralize it. When receiving the technique, you will first attack your partner with full commitment. Then, as the technique is applied, you will neutralize its effect by blending with it rather than trying to escape from it. As you progress to more advanced training, the movements become more sophisticated – but it is essentially the same as that encountered in basic training.

When you tell people that 90 per cent of aikido is conditioning training, in which you train with a co-operative partner, many draw the conclusion that the art is impracticable. Even 30 years of slow-motion training in wrist-grabbing techniques will not prepare you for a street mugger. You have to train for the situations you think you might have to deal with. Aikido is as good, if not better, than most martial arts for self-defence, but you have to change the training criteria in order to be successful. Techniques against a punch, for example, have to be modified, as there was no concept of this in the original art. The attack we know today as chudan tsuki (see page 433) was originally called furizuki, which is an upward circular thrust with a knife, so we have to take account of this and modify the training where necessary.

You have to ask yourself if you are ever likely to be assaulted with a sword, spear or halberd. The answer is likely to be "No". A street fighter will have no understanding of harmony,

musubi, contact or ukemi. He will try to resist anything you attempt and will not necessarily make a "committed attack", preferring to adjust his balance as and when, much as a boxer would. Cross-training with other martial arts is a must if self-defence is your priority. If you want to use aikido to defend yourself against a boxer, then train with a boxer – but one you know! If you want to defend yourself against a street attack, train with a street fighter. You have to become familiar with the situation that you are training for, and it's important that you do that by experiencing the situation in a controlled environment with somebody who will point out the problems with your defence strategies.

In this scenario it is fairly certain that aikido is sufficiently resilient to contain any situation. Any quality martial art will give exponents an advantage over an untrained attacker – with physical fitness, mental and spiritual training, stamina, co-ordination and timing providing that all-important edge. Public perception of martial arts is a major contributory factor in their credibility. Over the years, Hollywood films, and the media in general, have not done martial arts any favours. The notion of one man taking on and defeating 20 armed villains has done precious little for local dojo instructors trying to recruit members, as the public perception is that the martial arts are only for the lunatic fringe, for people who think they can run up walls and fly through the treetops.

Anybody looking for self-defence techniques must be aware that it is necessary to train realistically to be successful in real situations, so expect the odd bloody nose or black eye in the dojo. Many people expect too much for too little effort: they join a dojo and if they cannot fight like Bruce Lee in two weeks they throw in the towel. Committed individuals need to find an experienced instructor who understands their self-defence needs, and who will work with them to devise extra-curricular training to concentrate on achieving their goals.

Self-defence Techniques

The following sequences show scenarios where aikido techniques have been modified to suit particular situations where self-defence is required, such as defending yourself from a bag snatcher, or a punch to the face. It is essential that a student must have a thorough knowledge of the techniques that these movements are based on in order to adapt them successfully and carry them out in a non-controlled environment.

All these techniques come under the category of oyowaza, or applied techniques, and, as the name suggests, are practical applications where the intent is to enable an escape from a potentially serious situation. In each case their application would be short and sharp and with no consideration for uke

(as there would be in general practice). These movements have been chosen because they are relatively simple and quick to apply and because it is easy to see at a glance which techniques they are derived from. As a general rule simple manoeuvres are better in a self-defence situation.

Defending a Head Attack from Behind

This sequence, the first example of oyowaza, is an application of nikkyo and shows a method of defending a hair-grabbing attack from behind. The mechanics of nikkyo, or wrist in turn, need to be understood before this technique can work.

1 In this attack from behind, uke grabs tori's hair.

2 Tori traps uke's hand with interlocked fingers (see detail below) and pushes his hand against her head while turning to face uke.

3 Drawing her leg back sharply, tori cuts into the back of uke's wrist by turning her head down and inwards. It is quite possible, at this point, that the sudden pressure on the wrist would cause the assailant to let go immediately. In this case tori could get away without necessarily having to hit uke with her knee.

4 The pressure on the wrist brings uke's head down and forward, enabling tori to strike his face with her knee. The purpose of aikido is not to cause injury if at all possible. However, here is a situation where the youth may not let go of the girl's hair immediately, in which case the girl can bring her knee full force into the attacker's face.

Step 2 detail
This shows a close up of the interlocked fingers pushing uke's hand onto tori's head. Tori needs to cut into the back of uke's wrist sharply before he realizes what is happening.

Defence from a Bag Snatcher

This sequence, which is an application of kote-gaeshi, is an effective method of defending an attempt to snatch your bag. It involves taking control from the bag snatcher so that you are controlling him, as well as securing the bag.

1 Tori searches through her bag as she is approached by uke.

2 Uke makes a grab for the bag but tori holds on with her right hand.

3 Tori pulls with her right hand to enable her to take uke's wrist.

4 Without wresting uke's grip from the bag, tori grabs the back of uke's wrist and applies the kote-gaeshi wrist turn (see detail).

5 This pressure causes uke to fall. Tori maintains the wrist action.

6 While stepping around uke's head tori switches hands and applies strong pressure on the back of uke's elbow which, coupled with the twisting action on the wrist, causes extreme discomfort to uke (see detail).

Step 4 detail
Holding uke's right wrist with her left hand, tori places her right hand around uke's fist on the strap, as if she is embracing uke's hand. With a sharp inward squeezing and rolling action, tori breaks the power in uke's grip.

Step 6 detail
Applying strong pressure on the back of uke's elbow as well as a wrist-twisting action, tori causes extreme discomfort to uke. This, along with a few harsh words requesting the handbag's release, should prove to be all that is needed.

Defending a Neck Grab

This sequence is a practical application of rokkyo or arm smashing. Because it is applied directly against the natural movement of the joint, if uke's arm is pinned against tori's body and an inward hip movement employed, the elbow can be broken.

1 Tori takes in a view at a park when she is approached by a stranger who realizes that she is alone. It is difficult at this stage to know what the stranger's intentions are.

2 Uke, or the stranger, attempts to grab her by the neck, so tori takes the underside of uke's wrist with her right hand.

3 Reinforcing her grip by bringing her other hand up, tori rotates uke's arm as she turns away from him.

4 Tori hugs uke's arm against her body keeping it straight and effects a powerful hip turn applying strong pressure directly against the elbow joint.

Defending a Punch to the Face

This sequence is an application of ikkyo, or the arm pin. The final pin is executed with strong pressure against the back of uke's wrist and just above the elbow to the ground. The pinning pressure comes from the tanden, or centre of gravity.

1 As uke steps forward to strike tori's face, tori parries the thrust, keeping his right hand in contact with the back of uke's wrist while simultaneously positioning his left hand to grasp uke's elbow (see detail).

2 Tori grips uke's wrist and elbow and exerts a leading and bearing-down pressure. It is important to to draw uke forward slightly to take his balance, and take away his capacity to generate strength in his arm. Then it is a matter of applying your full body weight suddenly and directly on top of the elbow joint.

3 Tori steps back with his leading leg and drops his weight onto uke's arm causing uke to crash to the ground very hard, potentially face first. The technique can be used to restrain the assailant, or if he cannot, or will not, be reasoned with – to incapacitate him as necessary.

Step 1 detail
When tori parries uke's punch, it is not a blocking movement, but a deflection where tori's intent is to stick the back of his hand to uke's wrist/forearm. This movement is used here to facilitate the easy transition of tori's right hand from a parrying position to a position where he can grab uke's wrist.

Defining an Attack with a Weapon from Behind

This technique is an applied version of shomen-uchi irimi-nage. Because this would be a potential life-threatening situation the applications here have to be short, sharp and quick, and not allow uke any time to recover.

1 Tori takes in the tranquil scenery of parkland as uke hovers behind. Uke approaches tori from behind, threatening an overhead strike with a wooden club.

2 Tori turns to face uke and steps in with his left foot while raising his right sword arm to deflect the blow sideways. The contact should never be a full-on block using power against power. So here the sword arm (as the sword would be) is held at an angle to deflect the energy of the attack sideways.

3 Tori enters more with his left foot, then turns his body to face in the same direction as the attacker while at the same time cutting the attacking arm down in front of him with his right arm and trapping it against his right side. Tori takes the back of uke's collar and pulls back…

4 …simultaneously striking him in the face with his right hand and knocking uke backwards (see detail).

5 Dropping to his left knee, tori controls the weapon-wielding arm by applying strong pressure it with his sword arm. At the same time tori applies pressure with his left handblade against uke's carotid (neck) artery. Do not apply too much pressure on the neck artery, unless uke is still very determined. The idea here is to encourage uke to let go of the weapon.

Step 4 detail
In the traditional irimi-nage technique you cut across uke's face/neck as you enter to throw him, giving him a chance to take ukemi or neutralize the attack. Because there is a weapon, it needs to be extracted from uke quickly. This simultaneous pull-back with the left hand and face strike with the other (open hand or fist can be used) disorients uke until he finds himself controlled.

Advanced Throws

As a student progresses, providing they develop a good understanding of ukemi, more advanced training is available. The pictures here show what is possible at an advanced level within aikido training. Looking at these as a beginner you would be forgiven for thinking that they appear daunting. The reality is, however, that once you have the ability to relax and harmonize with the movement, these throws become relatively easy.

Once again, there is no attitude of conflict within such training, and although the techniques are always practised with full commitment there is also an attitude of harmony between uke and tori. Uke attacks hard but then, as the technique is applied, uke waits for his balance to be taken and then becomes "the other half" of the technique. In this way tori and uke execute natural movements between themselves, tori performing the technique and uke effortlessly flipping over.

Ryo kube-shime koshi-nage

Above This is a ryote kube-shime koshi-nage, or two-handed choke-attack hip throw. Uke has extended his hands towards tori's neck to try to choke him. Just before uke's hands make contact tori grabs uke's wrists and begins to extend them over his head, bringing uke forward and unbalancing him. Tori then bends his knees, loads uke's body onto his hips and looks in the same direction as uke. Uke rides over tori's hips and flips forward into a natural ukemi. This is given impetus by a rapid reversing of the hips, as tori changes posture from right to left.

Ryote-dori kokyu-nage 1

Above This throw shows a stage before the ryote-dori kokyu-nage, or two-handed grab on two hands breath throw, which is shown on the opposite page. Here tori has just raised his upper body and is about to extend his arms upwards and outwards to complete the movement.

Ryote-dori kokyu-nage 2

Right This throw, called ryote-dori kokyu-nage or two-handed grab on two hands breath throw, involves uke attacking from the front and grabbing both of tori's wrists. Tori raises both hands simultaneously and drops his head and shoulders under uke's waist in front of his upper thigh. By harmonizing with uke's forward motion tori raises his upper body sharply and flips uke high into the air overhead. Tori also spreads his arms to add impetus to the throw and ensure that uke rides over his left or right shoulder.

Above This is another example of kokyu-nage or breath throw. Here uke has attempted to punch tori in the face with her right fist (jodan tsuki, or upper thrust). Tori has stepped in with his rear foot, lowering and turning his body inwards to avoid the attack and has come up from underneath with a large sweeping movement of both arms. This, combined with a strong hip turn flips uke over tori's leading leg.

Right This is a variation of irimi-nage called ganseki otoshi, or head-over-heels throw, and involves uke rolling over tori. As with all aikido techniques uke's safety is of paramount importance. So although this picture shows uke in a very vulnerable situation, the reality is that he is literally placed on his feet by tori and so is never in any real danger. This is an extremely exhilarating technique to practise as long as both uke and tori have complete confidence in one another.

Juji garami-nage

Right This technique is known as juji garami-nage, or crossed-arm twining throw. Uke has grabbed both of tori's wrists from behind (ushiro). Tori at first steps back with his right foot and then immediately back again and at the same time draws uke's arms over his head, capturing both of uke's wrists with a grip of his own. Then tori wraps uke's right arm over his left and exerts strong pressure against the joints. Tori enters and, with a hip turn, throws uke as shown. It is important to let go of uke's forward arm as depicted here. This is to enable uke to take ukemi properly and not be injured.

Ganseki otoshi

Learning More

Choosing a T'ai Chi Teacher, School and Style

This book is designed to kindle your interest in t'ai chi and the Taoist internal arts, and kick-start your practice. It provides you with usable methods to start learning t'ai chi principles and form, as well as serving as a reference for your continued development as you progress. However, the importance of finding a good teacher cannot be exaggerated. T'ai chi is a complex movement art, and it is possible to take wrong turns in your t'ai chi path without even realizing it. A competent teacher can show you the way and correct any mistakes, to help you make the most of the time and effort that you put into learning and practising t'ai chi. In addition, working with a teacher who has developed their own chi will have a direct effect on your energy, greatly accelerating your progress.

FINDING A TEACHER

Finding a good teacher is not particularly difficult if you know what to look for and where to look for it. The most obvious consideration is who is teaching t'ai chi in your area, within easy travel distance. Gather all the information you can on t'ai chi schools and teachers in your region. The internet is increasingly the best source of contacts for this, but you may also find flyers, brochures or posters locally,

and there may be tuition in your local health or sports centre. Separate out the schools and teachers that claim to teach one of the acknowledged major styles of t'ai chi. Good t'ai chi teachers generally emphasize their links with the major lineages, rather than creating their own "brand-name" of t'ai chi. Look for direct links with the major lineages of t'ai chi and well-known lineage masters of past and present. This makes it much more likely that your teacher will be in possession of genuine knowledge and skill, which they can then pass on to you.

CHOOSING A SCHOOL

Having found some likely candidates, take your time before committing to any school. Call ahead and visit several schools and watch both beginner's and intermediate classes. If a teacher refuses to let you watch a class before joining, this is not a good sign. Observe the atmosphere in the classes. Are the students enjoying themselves? Are they friendly and cooperative with one another, rather than competitive and overly serious? Is the teacher relaxed and easy-going yet also confident and commanding in their teaching style? What sort of feeling do you get from the teacher's energy? Is their energy relaxed yet full?

Talk to both the main teacher and some of the students. Do not be afraid to ask about the teaching style and methods. Ask about some of the principles and nei gung aspects of t'ai chi that are in this book. These concepts should be familiar to any good t'ai chi teacher. Ask the teacher who their main teacher is or was. Ask the students how long they have trained with that school and whether they have benefited and progressed.

Some schools are more martial in emphasis, some are more health and meditation oriented. The best are able

to offer both, with everything being done in a relaxed and non-aggressive manner.

Most good schools expect their students to show appropriate respect towards the teacher and the material being taught. However, a guru worship atmosphere is not appropriate.

The cost of classes should not be your major consideration – if you find a good school, you will certainly get value for money. Very cheap or free classes, or those in subsidized health clubs rarely yield the inner benefits of t'ai chi. Good teachers simply do not have to teach for free – they attract and retain paying students.

CHOOSING A STYLE

Which style of t'ai chi you choose will most likely depend on which teacher or school you choose. If you are lucky enough to have a choice of good schools of different styles, then try a short course in each style and make your decision based on which style instinctively feels right for you. Good t'ai chi is good t'ai chi in whatever style, so quality of teaching should come first; style is a relative second.

PROGRESSING

Once you have chosen a t'ai chi school, stick with it for at least six months. Learning t'ai chi can take a little perseverance, and initial frustrations may not be the fault of the school or teacher but simply part of the process. If after that time you are still convinced that a different school would suit you better, you may wish to change. As you progress, the school that you started with may cater for this, or you may find that you need to seek more advanced tuition elsewhere. Studying privately in one-to-one sessions with a good teacher is also an excellent adjunct to whatever group classes you are taking.

T'ai Chi Contacts and Further Reading

ANDREW POPOVIC ORIENTAL HEALING
Taoist Internal Arts
Chinese Medical Therapy
London, UK
Contact: Andrew Popovic
Web: www.orientalhealing.org
Email: info@orientalhealing.org
Tel: +44 (0)7939 663 082

B.K. FRANTZIS ENERGY ARTS
Fairfax, CA, USA
Web: www.energyarts.com
Email: admin@energyarts.com
Tel: +1 415 454 5243

JOHN DING INTERNATIONAL
ACADEMY OF T'AI CHI CHUAN
London, UK
Web: www.taichiwl.demon.co.uk
Email: JDIATCC@taichiwl.demon.co.uk
Tel: +44 (0)20 8502 9307

REAL TAOISM
Taoist Life Arts
Unit 9
170 Brick Lane
London E1 6RU
Tel: 020 7247 1399

T'AI CHI UNION FOR GREAT BRITAIN
Web: www.taichiunion.com
Email: secretary@taichiunion.com
Tel: +44 (0)141 810 3482

T'AI CHI FINDER
Web: www.taichifinder.co.uk

T'AI CHI MAGAZINE
International monthly publication
Wayfarer Publications
P.O. Box 39938
Los Angeles, CA 90039
USA
(800) 888-9119 toll-free
fax: 323-665-1627

WORLDWIDE T'AI CHI CHUAN
www.middx.org.uk/gordo/2tai_links.html
www.scheele.org/lee/tcclinks.html

WORLD T'AI CHI AND CHI GUNG DAY
www.worldtaichiday.com

FURTHER READING
Opening the Energy Gates of Your Body:
Gain Lifelong Vitality
Bruce Kumar Frantzis

Relaxing into Your Being: The Water
Method of Taoist Meditation Series, I
Bruce Kumar Frantzis

The Great Stillness: The Water Method of
Taoist Meditation Series, II
Bruce Kumar Frantzis

The Power of Internal Martial Arts:
Combat Secrets of Ba Gua, Tai Chi
and Hsing-I
Bruce Kumar Frantzis

Cheng Tzu's Thirteen Treatises on T'ai
Chi Ch'uan
Cheng Man-ch'ing

Tai Chi Touchstones: Yang Family Secret
Transmissions
Douglas Wyle

Tai Chi Chuan for Health and Self-
defense
T. T. Liang

Steal my Art: Memoirs of a 100 year-old
T'ai Chi Master
T. T. Liang, Stuart Alve Olson

Tao Te Ching: Lao-zu's Tao Te Ching
Lao-zi, Red Pine

Tao Te Ching: Definitive Edition
Lao Tzu, Jonathan Star

Hua Hu Ching: Later Teachings of
Lao Tzu
Hua-Ching Ni

The Taoist I Ching
Thomas Cleary

The Essential Chuang-Tzu
Sam Hamill, J. P. Seaton

The Way of Chuang Tzu
Thomas Merton

Styles of Aikido

There is only one traditional aikido and that is the art created by and disseminated by its founder, Morihei Ueshiba. This tradition is carried on today by the headquarters of the Aikikai Foundation (also called Hombu Dojo or Hombu) led by the founder's grandson, Moriteru Ueshiba, the aikido doshu, or "master of the way", and by the remaining uchideshi, who are teaching all over the world. Throughout its history aikido has seen many colourful characters, people who have contributed immensely to the art's diverse development. Minoru Mochizuki (1907–2003) was a student of judo's founder, Kano Jigoro, and was despatched by Kano to study with Morihei Ueshiba in 1930. In 1931, Mochizuki opened the Yoseikan dojo to establish a composite martial art combining elements of aikido, judo, kendo and, later, karate.

Another notable judoka was sent by Kano Jigoro to train with Morihei Ueshiba around the same time. Professor Kenji Tomiki (1900–79) had met the aikido founder in 1926 and was greatly

Above The late Yamaguchi Seigo 8th Dan Shihan, one of the most influential teachers from Hombu Dojo, teaching at a seminar in Oxford, England.

impressed by him. In 1940 Ueshiba awarded him Menkyo Kaiden, a certifying document that roughly equates to 8th Dan. He was the first aikido student to reach this level. He went on to amalgamate elements of his judo skills with aikido and created tomiki, or sport aikido. Competition is involved here with the use of rubber knives and a

points system that Kenji Tomiki believed would sharpen reflexes and make aikido more combat oriented. Gozo Shioda (1915–74) started aikido training in 1932. He established the yoshinkan style of aikido, characterized by short, sharp movements and the positive application of joint techniques. The world headquarters for yoshinkan aikido is in the same district of Tokyo as the Aikikai Foundation.

Koichi Tohei (b. 1920) is the only person to be officially awarded 10th Dan by the Hombu (1970). A year or so later he attempted to establish his teaching methods at Hombu, but was rejected, which ultimately led to his resignation from the Aikikai in 1974. He went on to establish the shin shin toitsu style, which places great emphasis on the development of ki. There are many great teachers of aikido who, although prior students of the founder, have gone on to create new branches of the art. Most follow the founder's way, though some do not – such is the nature of the art and the individual interpretation of its ideals.

Finding an Aikido Club

Above Chiba Sensei 8th Dan Shihan with Peter Brady, one of the authors, in Bridgenorth, England in 1987. Chiba Sensei was the official Aikikai Hombu delegate to Great Britain.

There is a lot of choice when looking for a suitable club. When looking for a dojo, make a shortlist of clubs in the your area that are officially recognized by a nationally accredited organization, and make sure that this organization is a member of the relevant aikido authority. Only then are you certain of the quality and service that you should expect. A club should insist that everyone is individually insured, as it is possible that your policy could be invalidated if the person you are training with is injured and has no cover. It is now a ruling in Great Britain that an instructor teaching students up to the age of 18 has to have a children's coaching award, too.

The organizations referred to opposite all represent Aikikai Hombu style traditional aikido, although some of them also act on behalf of other styles of aikido. Some countries have an umbrella body to regulate the member associations, whereas associations in other countries have full authority from that country's government to do whatever is necessary for the legitimate advancement of aikido. There are countless more clubs and groups of clubs outside any recognized authority in every country of the world. For peace of mind you are advised to look for a club that operates under the auspices of a recognized association or federation, for if you are injured or suffer some other misfortune you can look forward to their full support for a (in most cases) negligible fee.

AUSTRALIA
Shihan Seiichi Sugano, the Hombu representative to Australia established the Aikikai of Australia in 1964. They have authority from the federal government under the national coaching accreditation scheme to issue guidelines for the advancement of aikido for insurance, grading requirements and coaching qualifications.

CANADA
The Canadian Aikido Federation acts both as an insurance agent for the membership of an affiliated organization and also has a function as an umbrella body to other groups.

FRANCE
The Ministry of Youth and Sports in France recognizes the Union of Federations of Aikido of which the two Hombu recognized groups are the FFAAA headed by Christian Tissier Shihan and the FFAB lead by Nobuyoshi Tamura Shihan.

GERMANY
Aikido organizations in Germany include the Deutscher Judo Bund (DJB) with 1,500 aikidoka as members; the Deutscher Aikido Bund (DAB), the largest group with an enrolment of more than 4,500 practitioners; the German Aikikai with some 3,400 members; and the Freie Deutsche Aikido Vereinigung (FDAV), with about 300 members.

GREECE
Aikido organizations in Greece register through the Ministry of Culture and Sports and newly formed groups have to register with a lawyer.

Above Photograph taken in 1974 at the Philbeach Gardens Dojo in Earls Court, London. Back row from left: Peter Brady, Phillip Smith, Alwyn Joseph, David Jones, Graham Thomas, Marian Mucha, Terry Kenny; front row from left: Gordon Jones, Chiba Sensei, William Smith.

NEW ZEALAND
The New Zealand Aikikai is headed by Takase Shihan. This group is recognized by the government and has full authority to establish aikido guidelines.

SOUTH AFRICA
The South African Sports Confederation and Olympic Committee is the organization to which the Martial Arts Authority of South Africa is affiliated. Subordinate to that is the Aikido Federation of South Africa (AFSA), a Hombu recognized organization and a member of The International Aikido Federation.

SPAIN
Here, aikido is incorporated into a Judo federation called Diciplina Associada. This issues teaching certificates that are recognized by the government. However, because of the lack of a Hombu shihan in the organization many individuals affiliate to associations fronted by Tamura Sensei, Kitaura Sensei, Yamada Sensei and Endo Sensei.

UK
Aikido comes under the British Aikido Board (BAB), set up to oversee all styles of aikido and their development in terms of safety, behaviour and coaching. An instructor's qualification is ratified with the ascending categories of coach levels 1, 2 and 3 and coach tutor, rankings awarded only after rigorous testing. BAB. is working towards creating a system that will replace these and culminate in a National Vocational Qualification (NVQ) in aikido. It also acts as an insurance agent and looks after the implementation of any government or EU-driven policy changes.

USA
Hombu affiliated organizations in the USA register with the United States Aikido Federation (USAF), split into four regions: Eastern, Midwestern, Western and Latin American. Technical issues, grading requirements and the issuing of teaching licences are the responsibility of the Hombu shihan in charge of the respective region.

Aikido Contacts and Further Reading

THE AIKIKAI FOUNDATION

The headquarters of the Aikikai Foundation is the Aikikai-So-Hombu, Tokyo, Japan. The chairman is the founder's grandson, Moriteru Ueshiba, the world leader of traditional aikido with a mission to preserve the teachings of Ueshiba. Referred to as Hombu Dojo, the building is built on the same site as the original wooden structure Kobukan dojo created in 1932. People come from all over the world to train at the Hombu with the doshu and the professional shihan who teach there. The Foundation was commissioned in 1948 and now has more than 50 countries under its wing, all of which follow the rules and regulations laid down by the Foundation. All dojos affiliated to Hombu observe the same etiquette, and dan gradings issued worldwide are awarded. It is recognition by the Aikikai Foundation and the Ueshiba name that are magnets for many aikidokas (students) throughout the world.

Right Yamada Shihan, 8th Dan. Aikikai delegate to USA, Cardiff National Sports Centre, 1985, throwing Peter Brady with tenchi-nage, or heaven and earth throw.

THE INTERNATIONAL AIKIDO FEDERATION

As the popularity of aikido spread, there was a need for an official body to monitor and oversee this growth and to ensure that the national organizations that were officially recognized by the Aikikai Foundation could voice their opinions and needs on the international scene. In 1976 the International Aikido Federation (IAF) was created. The head of this organization is always the doshu, in his capacity as the world leader of aikido, and further consists of appointed delegates from each organization representing its respective country.

The IAF meets together in the form of a congress every four years at various locations around the world to discuss all matters relevant to aikido. There is usually a training course laid on to run concurrently to enable representatives from around the world to train together under the instruction of some of the world's top shihan. Decisions are made at these congress sessions by a process of democratic voting and results are ratified by a body known as the Superior Council, whose members are appointed to ensure that the traditional values of aikido, as taught by the founder, are adhered to. Another function of the congress is to elect officials to manage the IAF. These officials come under the auspices of another appointed body, the directing committee, which meets every two years to discuss items of less importance and are subordinate to the IAF congress. Currently, there are 43 aikido organizations worldwide that are members of the International Aikido Federation.

Left Peter Brady with Moriteru Ueshiba, grandson of the founder, Hombu Dojo, Tokyo, 2003.

THE AIKIKAI FOUNDATION

Aikido World Headquarters
17–18 Wakamatsu Cho, Shinjuku-ku, Tokyo, 162-0056 Japan
Tel: (+81) 3-3203-9236
aikido@aikikai.or.jp

THE INTERNATIONAL AIKIDO FEDERATION

Address as the Aikikai Foundation, above.
general.secretary@aikido-international.org
www.aikido-international.org

AUSTRALIA

MAKOTOKAN BUDO
Castle Hill, Sydney, NSW
Tel: +61 2 9639 7838

QUEENSLAND AIKIDO CENTRE

1/2 Sunlight Drive, Burleigh West
Gold Coast
Tel: +61 7 5559 5483;
www.qld.aikido.org.au

CANADA

CALGARY AIKIKAI
507 36 Ave SE, Calgary, Alberta T2G 1W5
Tel: +1 403 243 9880
www.calgaryaikikai.com

info@calgaryaikikai.com
JCCC AIKIKAI
c/o Japanese Canadian Cultural Centre
6 Garamond Court
Toronto, Ontario M3C 1Z5
Tel: +1 416 441 2345; www.jcccaikikai.ca

VANCOUVER WEST AIKIKAI
Kitsilano Community Centre
2690 Larch St., Vancouver, B.C. VDK
Tel: +1 604 222 2211
www.vancouverwestaikikai.com

FRANCE
FFAB
c/o Fédération Française d'Aïkido et de
Budo, Les Allées, 83149 Bras
Tel: +33 4 98 05 22 28
Anne Vovan at nfo@aikido-paris-idf.org

GERMANY
AIKIKAI OF GERMANY
Aikido-Schule Charlottenstrasse
Charlottenstrasse 26–28, Hamburg 20257
Tel: +49 40 4327 1913
info@aikido-schule-charlottenstrasse.de

GREECE
THE HELLENIC AIKIDO ASSOCIATION
FukiShinKan Dojo, 144 Athens GR112 51
Tel: +30 210 881 1768; aikidogr@acci.gr

S.C. ATRAPOS
Yudokan Kojo, 12 Vlaxernon Str.
551 33 Vizantio, Thessaloniki
Tel: +30 231 048 0089; aikido@atrapos.gr

NEW ZEALAND
AUCKLAND RIAI AIKIDO
Ponsonby Communty Centre, 20 Ponsonby
Terrace, Ponsonby
Tel: +64 9 444 0921;
auckland.info@aikido.org.nz

SOUTH AFRICA
AFSA, c/o Aikido Federation of South Africa;
P O Box 1182, Heidelburg 1438
Tel: +27 11 744 000
aikido@mweb.co.za

SPAIN
ASSOCIACION CULTURAL FEILEN AIKIDO
Dojo Central c/Liuva, 39 Bajos 08030, Sant
Andreu, Barcelona
Tel: +34 655 88 95 92;
aikifeilen@aikifeilen.com

UK
THE BRITISH AIKIDO BOARD (BAB)
General Secretary, 6 Halkingcroft, Langley,
Slough, Berkshire SL3 7AT;
john.burn@clara.co.uk

USA
AIKIDO SCHOOLS OF UESHIBA
29165 Singletary Road
Myakka City, FL 34251;
Tel: +1 941 322-1252

BERKELEY AIKIKAI
1812 San Pablo Avenue
Berkeley, CA 94702;
Tel: +1 510 549 1518

HIDEKI SHIOHIRA
2531 Titan Way, Castro Valley CA 94546
Tel: +1 510 481 1734
NEW YORK AIKIKAI
142 W. 18th Street, New York NY 10011
Tel: +1 212 242 6246;
secretary@nyaikikai.com

SAN DIEGO AIKIKAI
3844 Adams Avenue, San Diego
CA 92116
Tel: +1 619 280 7059
sdaikikai@aol.com

INTERNET SITES

www.aikidojournal.com
www.aikidofaq.com
www.aiki.com
www.aikiweb.com
www.aikido-world.com
www.britishaikikai.co.uk
www.ukaonline.co.uk

Above The late Saito Morihiro 9th Dan
Shihan, in Cambridge, England, 1989.

FURTHER READING
Aikido Basics
Phong Thong Dang

The Aiki News Encyclopedia
Stanley Pranin

The Essence of Aikido
John Stevens

Aikido and the New Warrior
Richard Strozzi Heckler

The Spirit of Aikido
Kisshomaru Ueshiba

Best Aikido: The Fundamentals
Ueshiba, Kisshomaru & Moriteru

Budo:Teachings of the Founder of Aikido
Morihei Ueshiba

The Aikido Master Course (Best Aikido 2)
Morihei Ueshiba

Aikido and the Dynamic Sphere
A Westbrook and O Ratti

The New Aikido Complete:
The Arts of Power and Movement
Yoshimitsu Yamada

Glossary of T'ai Chi terms

An	Push downwards	Kou	Tiger's mouth	Ting jin	Listening energy
Ba gua	Eight trigrams	Kung fu	Skill	Tsai	Pull down
Baihui	Crown of head	Kwa	Inguinal area at front of	Tsuan chuan	Drilling fist
Beng chuan	Crushing fist		pelvis	Tsuan jin	Drilling energy
Chan ssu jin	Silk-reeling energy	Lan	Merging	Tui na	Chinese massage
Chi	Energy	Laogung	Centre of the palm	Tui shou	Push hands
Chi gun	Energy work	Lieh	Split	Wei chi	Protective energy
Chien	Heaven	Lu	Roll back	Wei	External
Da lu	Moving step push hands	Ming men	Bright gate/gate of life	Wu chi	Ultimate emptiness
Fa jin	Issuing power	Moxa	Mugwort	Wushu	Fighting method
Fu	Yang organs	Nei gung	Internal work	Yongquan	Bubbling Well point,
Heng chuan	Crossing fist	Nei ji	Internal arts		hollow in ball of foot
Hsin	Heart-mind	Nien	Merging	Zang	Yin organs
Hsing-i	Mind-form fist	Pao chuan	Pounding fist	Zhan zhuang	Standing like a tree
Huiyin	Perineum	Pao twi	Cannon fist		
I	Intent	Pen	Ward off		
Jan	Yielding	Pi chuan	Splitting fist		
Ji	Press	San ti	Hsing-i standing posture		
Jiao	Lower organs	Shen	Spirit		
Jing	Essence	Sheng	Generating cycle		
Jou	Elbow stroke	Soong	Unbound		
Kao	Shoulder stroke	Suei	Magnetizing		
Ko	Controlling cycle	Tantien	Body's energy centre		

Glossary of Aikido Terms

Ai	Harmony	Bukiwaza	Weapons techniques	Hakama	Pleated skirt
Ai hanmi	Same or matched stance	Chikara no		Hanmi	Half stance (also kamae)
Aiki	Blended or matched ki	dashikata	The extension of power	Hanmi handachi	One standing, one sitting
Aiki jo	Staff or stick used in aikido	Chudan kamae	Middle stance	Hara	Stomach, abdomen
Aiki ken	Aikido swordsmanship	Dakishime	Hug	Henka waza	Variation technique
Aiki-nage	Aiki throw	Do	Way, path	Hidari	Left
Aiki otoshi	Aiki drop	Dogi	Practice suit (also gi,	Hito e mi	Stance (oblique hanmi)
Aiki taiso	Aiki exercises		keikogi)	Ho	Exercise, method
Ashi	Foot	Dojo	Training hall	Ikkyo	Arm pin
Ashi sabaki	Footwork	Doshu	Leader of the way	Irimi	Entering movement
Atemi	Strike or blow	Eri dori	Collar or lapel grab	Irimi-nage	Entering throw
Awase	Blending movement	Fuku shidoin	Assistant instructor	Jo	Short staff
Ayumi ashi	Walking	Futaridori	Attack by two opponents	Jodan	Upper position
Batto	Sword drawing	Futarigake	Attack by two opponents	Jodan no kamae	Upper stance with sword
Bo	Stick larger than a jo	Gedan	Lower	Jodo	Art of the jo
Bojutsu	Stick techniques	Gi	Practice suit (also keikogi,	Ju no keiko	Practise softly
Bokken	Wooden sword		dogi)	Ju no ri	Principle of gentleness
Bokuto	Wooden sword (bokken)	Gokkyo	Wrist pin	Jumbi taiso	Warm-up exercises
Budo	Martial way	Gyaku	Reverse, opposite	Jyugeuko	Free practice
Budoka	Martial artist	Gyaku hanmi	Reverse or opposite stance	Jyugi	Free attack and defence
Bujutsu	Martial technique	Haishin undo	After-practice back-	Jyuwaza	Free attack and defence
Bukidori	Against arms		bending exercise	Kaiten ashi	Forward-step pivot

Kaiten-nage	Rotary throw	Nikkyo	Control wrist by turning in
Kamae	Postures for combat	Nori	Attention stand
Kansetsu	Joint	Omote	Front
Kansetsu waza	Joint technique	Oyowaza	Applied techniques
Kata (1)	Form	Randori	Free-style practice
Kata (2)	Shoulder	Rei	Bow
Kata-dori	Shoulder grab	Renoji dachi	Stance "l"
Katame waza	Immobilization technique	Renshu	Practice, training
Katana	Long sword	Renzoku	Continuous
Katate	One hand	Ritsurei	Standing bow
Katate-dori	One-hand grab	Rokkyo	Elbow pin
Katatori	Shoulder grab (kata-dori)	Ryokata-dori	Two-shoulder grab
Keiko	Practice, training	Ryote-dori	Two-hand grab
Keikogi	Practice suit (also gi, dogi)	Ryu	Style, school
Kekka fusi	Sitting position	Sabaki	Movement
Ken dori	Against sword	Sankaku	Triangle
Ki	Spirit	Sankyo	Control wrist by twisting it
Kiai	Combative shout	Sannindori	Attack by three opponents
Kiritsu	Standing/stand	Seiza	Seated position
Kodachi	Short sword	Sensei	Teacher
Kogeki	Attack	Shidoin	Instructor
Koho tento	Falling backward	Shihan	Master instructor
Kokoro	Spirit, heart	Shiho-nage	Four-corner throw
Kokyu	Breath	Shikko	Samurai knee walking
Kokyu-ho	Breathing method	Shisei	Posture
Kokyu-nage	Breath throw	Shomen-uchi	Front-head strike
Kokyu no henka	Breath changes	Shumatsu dosa	After-practice back-
Kokyu-ryoku	Breath power (kokyu)		bending exercise
Kokyu tenkan ho	Breath turning	Sode	Sleeve
Koshi-nage	Hip throw	Sode-dori	Sleeve grab
Kote-gaeshi	Wrist out turn or twist	Sotai dosa	Paired exercise
Kote hineri	Wrist twist, sankyo	Suburi	Exercise for jo and bokken
Kote mawashi	Wrist in turn, nikkyo		
Kubi	Neck		
Kubi shime	Choke, strangle		
Kyu	Class, grade below		
	shodan		
Mawatte	Turn		
Ma-ai	Distance between		
	opponents		
Men	Head		
Menuchi	Head strike		
Metsuke	Eye-to-eye contact		
Migi	Right		
Mochi	Hold, grasp		
Morote-dori	Two-hand grab		
Mune-dori	Chest hold		
Nage	Throw		
Neko ashi dachi	Cat stance		

Sumi	Corner		
Sumi otoshi	Corner drop		
Suwariwaza	Seated techniques		
Tachi	Standing		
Tachidori	Sword taking		
Tachiwaza	Standing techniques		
Tai	Body		
Taijutsu	Body techniques		
	(unarmed)		
Tanden	Centre of stomach, or		
	gravity		
Tandoku dosa	Solo exercises		
Tandoku keiko	Practise by oneself		
Taninzudori	Attack by many		
	opponents		
Tanken	Knife		
Tanken dori	Knife-defence action		
Tanto	Knife		
Tanto dori	Knife-defence action		
Tatami	Straw practice mat		
Te Sabaki	Hand movement		
Tegatana	Hand blade		
Teiji dachi	Stance "t"		
Tekubi	Wrist		
Tekubi osae	Wrist pin, yonkyo		
Tenchi-nage	Heaven and earth throw		
Tenkan	Turn		
Tenkan ashi	Pivot		
Tsugi ashi	Following steps, shuffle		
	step		
Tsuki	Punch		
Uchi	Strike		
Uchideshi	Live-in student		
Ude	Arm		
Ude-hishigi	Arm smashing		
Ude-nobashi	Arm stretch		
Uke	One who receives		
Ukemi	The art of falling		
Ura	Back		
Ushiro	Rear, behind		
Waza	Technique		
Yame	Stop, finish or end		
Yoko	Side		
Yokomen	Side of the head		
Yokomen-uchi	Strike to side of the head		
Yonkyo	Inner arm nerve pinch		
Yudansha	Black-belt student		
Za ho	Sitting method		
Zarei	Formal sitting bow		

Biographies

TAE KWONDO

Ron Sergiew started training in tae kwon-do in 1972 and gained his black belt in 1976. He is currently 5th-*dan*.

Ron's competition career started in 1973 and spanned 16 years, during which he became British Champion on numerous occasions, and ultimately World and European Champion. Ron became a professional instructor in 1980, and since that time has produced many black belts. While teaching full time, he still managed to become involved in the founding of the Tae Kwon-Do Association of Great Britain, which is now the largest UK tae kwondo organization.

His responsibilities within that organization are: National Treasurer, Grading Examiner for coloured belt and black belt testings and North Midlands area representative.

WADO RYU

Eugene Alexander Codrington's competition career began in 1974 when he became the AKA Champion. He is currently 6th-*dan* and has achieved over 30 national and international titles on an individual and team basis, including five times British Champion, twice European All Styles individual and team champion and World Team Champion 1975. He founded his own karate organization in 1986, The Codrington European Karate-Do Development Organization. He is a national referee for the English karate governing body and head of the delegation for the national squad.

SHOTOKAN

Father Seamus Mulholland OFM is a 6th-*dan shihan*, shotokan karate; 6th-*dan* daisho-kenshi mu te katsu ryu takamura batto jutsu; and 3rd-*dan* katakori jo do. He is an exponent of tessan shon-to (Japanese fan) and a specialist in kata oyo (close-quarter combat).

AIKIDO

Peter Brady is currently a Shidoin (Hombu recognized Senior teacher) with the United Kingdom Aikikai. He also holds the position of Senior Coach and Children's Coach within the British Aikido Board. Peter is the chief instructor for five independently run clubs around the United Kingdom. As a result of Chiba Sensei's influence Peter has a strong interest in the weapon side of Aikido and also in the art of Sword drawing known as Iaido.

JU-JITSU

Kevin Pell Shihan, 6th-*dan*, has over 27 years' experience in martial arts. He is the founder of Ishin Ryu Ju-Jitsu Renmei, whose headquarters are in Hertfordshire.

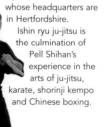

Ishin ryu ju-jitsu is the culmination of Pell Shihan's experience in the arts of ju-jitsu, karate, shorinji kempo and Chinese boxing.

JUDO

Neil Adams' (MBE) personal achievements are judo 7th-*dan*, World Judo Champion, 1981; Silver Medal, 1980 Moscow Olympic Games; Silver Medal, 1984 Los Angeles Olympic Games; seven times European Champion; 19 times British Champion (Junior and Senior); Olympic Judo Team Coach; 1996 Atlanta Olympic Games and British Schools Judo Association Coach, 1989–1997.

He is the author of several books, including: *A Life in Judo, Olympic Judo Throwing Techniques, Olympic Judo Preparation Training* and the *Judo Masterclass Series*.

WING CHUN

James Sinclair began martial arts training in 1972. He founded the UK Wing Chun Kung Fu Association in 1985 and graduated from the British School of Shiatsu-Do (London) in 1994. He is known as the teacher's teacher, due to the well-respected instructors he has produced.

Master James Sinclair has conducted seminars and demonstrations with many of the elite martial artists of the world, such as Dan Inosanto (JKD & Kali), Master Sken (Thai Boxing), Greg Wallace (6th-*dan* BASKA), Kevin Brewerton (World Semi-Contact Champion), Bob Fermor (Nunchaku and other weapons), Mike Billman (5th-*dan* shotokan karate), Terry Coughtrey (3rd-*dan* ju-jitsu) and Dave Oliver (tae kwondo 6th degree).

MOK-GAR

Paul J Boyer started his martial arts training in 1974. In 1976, he was introduced to Master Charles Chan, who taught traditional Shaolin mok-gar kuen kung fu.

He is highly experienced in weaponry and the internal tai chi wu style of t'ai chi chuan.

KICK BOXING

Elaine Adani began martial arts training in 1985 with lau gar kung fu. By 1988 she had achieved Green Sash status and had started to be interested in the sporting aspects of martial arts training. Since 1986 she has been to many tournaments throughout the UK and has held a world title as well as a British title. She has been successful in encouraging more women to take up the sport.

TAI CHI

Robert Poyton began training in traditional Yang Family tai chi chuan in the 1980s. He was the Chief Instructor of the San Chai T'ai Chi Academy. Robert has written for numerous publications and was Editor of *T'ai Chi International*, the UK's leading t'ai chi art magazine.

TAI CHI

Andrew Popovic has over 25 years' experience in Oriental martial arts and healing. He began training in Shotokan karate at the age of 15, and studied Japanese ju-jitsu before dedicating his practice entirely to the Chinese internal arts. Andrew continued his studies in the internal martial arts, chi gung and Taoist meditation under line-age master B.K. Frantzis, disciple of the late Taoist sage Liu Hung Chieh of Beijing, as well as under other renowned Taoist masters. Andrew is also a disciple of the great Tibetan Dzogchen master Chogyal Namkhai Norbu, and has studied with masters of the native American healing and spiritual traditions. Andrew has an honours degree in Traditional Chinese Medicine and treats patients with acupuncture, herbs and qigong therapy. He runs an international organization offering coaching in all aspects of the Taoist healing and self-development arts.

KENDO/IAIDO

Trevor Jones is a 6th-*dan* iaido, kendo 4th-*dan* and judo 1st-*dan*. He has been studying kendo and iaido for 20 years, including several years in Japan, and has represented Great Britain in European and World Championships for kendo. He currently teaches in London and is a former British Kendo Champion.

KENDO

Hiroshi Sugawara is 5th-*dan* kendo. He studied kendo in Miyagi Prefecture, Japan, for 20 years and in Hokkaido, Japan, for 10 years.

KENDO

Derek Raybold started in the art of kendo in 1976, forming the Birmingham Kendo Club in 1978. He is currently 4th-*dan* kendo and 2nd-*dan* aikido. He has been a member of the British Kendo Squad for five years and represented Great Britain in the 1985 World Kendo Championships in Paris.

IAIDO

Fay Goodman is internationally qualified to a very high level in many martial arts and is a leading exponent of shinto ryu (8th-*dan*) and iaido (7th-*dan*). In 1995 she was awarded the gold medal at the European Iaido championships, and today she is one of the highest-graded female martial art experts in the world. She is a coach with the British Kendo Association and of various other martial arts, including karate, aikido and ju-jitsu. She features regularly on television and radio and has completed a series on martial arts for television.

SHINTO RYU

Clive Preece has been involved with martial arts since 1968. He is the founder and Councillor of the European Martial Arts Academy, Chief Director of Junior Defence-Line, 8th-*dan* European Martial Arts Academy, 8th-*dan* shinto ryu, *dan*-graded judo, aikido, shukokai and shotokan.

Since 1985 he has been teaching self-defence and confidence building to children from ages 3½ to 16.

Index

Acknowledgements

Fay Goodman: I would like to say a special thank you to my family, friends, fellow practitioners and work colleagues who have supported me in the writing of this publication. The days and nights of burning the midnight oil, working over the festive season and New Year, was only achieved by the support and dedication of many people.

I have enjoyed writing this book, even though it was hard work. It is one of those projects I have wanted to write for many years. As they say, patience is a virtue, and when the time is right the door will open (a gentle opening would have been preferred to the force of a tornado!).

Andrew Popovic: I would like to thank my Taoist masters, especially my main teacher Lineage Master Bruce Kumar Frantzis. I would also like to thank Lineage Master John Ding. Thanks also to Chris Chappell for his insightful instruction and advice, and to my Tibetan Dzogchen masters, especially Namkhai Norbu Rinpoche. A special thanks to my family, friends and students.

Peter Brady: I would like to thank the aikido founder, the late Morihei Ueshiba. I would also like to thank T. K. Chiba Shihan and Nobuyoshi Tamura Shihan, Shihan W. J. Smith MBE and Yoshimitsu Yamada. There are many others who have helped with my aikido development to whom I am grateful. Thanks also to my fellow shidoin, to photographer Mike James and editor Emma Clegg. A particular mention to the students who assisted as models: Cliff Price, Cath Davies, Paul Jarvis, Eddie McCalla, Kelly Magna, Neil Mould, Bryn Ross, Richard Hughes, Kevin Beggan, Rivington Hermitt, Debbie Shadbolt and, last but by no means least, my children Charlotte, James and Jonathan.

The publisher would like to thank the following for the use of their pictures in the book (l=left, r=right, t=top, b=bottom, m=middle): Alamy: pp34t, p35b, p70, p230l; Peter Brady: p378, p379l, p379r, p390, p401b, p496t, p496b, p497, p498t, p498b, p499; Bridgeman Art Library: pp264, p266; Paul Clifton: pp102r, p150r, p152b, p183b; Corbis: pp55tr; p166l, p201b, p214r, p259, p260, p265, p268, p271, p272, p274, p275, p296, p364, p365; e.t. archive: pp71, p103; Mary Evans Picture Library: pp383tl, p383tr; Getty: pp16l, p17b, p30l, 31t; Hulton Getty: pp8, p32t, p35t, p102, p104l, p134, p216; Jesper Hoejdal: p383b; Herman Kempers: p391b; Daniel Kestenholz: p392tr; Simon Lailey: pp9b, p10b, p17, p30, p32 b, p34, p54, p55, p150, p151, p152–3, p166, p167, p168, p182t, p214, p233; Tammy Lee Anderson (Shinzen Dojo, Clovis, California, www.healing-wellness.com): p395b; Rex Features: p485; Michael Riehle: p391t; Tai Chi International: pp198, p200t; Fay Goodman: p230–2; Tony Stone: pp9t, p10t, p11, p31, p33, p71, p103, p135t, p183, p199; Werner Forman Archive: p215; Karen Wolek: p392tl.

Every effort has been made to find the copyright holders and acknowledge the pictures properly; however, we apologize if there are any unintentional omissions, which will be corrected in future editions.